WOMEN'S LEGAL LANDMARKS IN THE INTERWAR YEARS

Women's Legal Landmarks in the Interwar Years shines new light on 33 legal landmarks, many forgotten today, that affected women in England and Wales between 1918 and 1939.

It considers the work of feminist activists to bring about legal change which benefited – or aimed to benefit – women. Areas explored include property, inheritance, adoption, marriage, access to health care, criminal law, employment opportunities, pay, pensions and political representation. It also examines campaigns by key women's organisations, and assesses the impact of early women lawyers and politicians.

While some of the landmarks effected change during this period, others provided the foundation for measures in later decades. Together the landmarks demonstrate that far from being a relatively quiet period of British feminism, the interwar period played a key role in ongoing fights for recognition, representation and justice.

Women's Legal Landmarks in the Interwar Years

Not for Want of Trying

Edited by
Rosemary Auchmuty
Erika Rackley
and
Mari Takayanagi

• HART •
OXFORD • LONDON • NEW YORK • NEW DELHI • SYDNEY

HART PUBLISHING
Bloomsbury Publishing Plc
Kemp House, Chawley Park, Cumnor Hill, Oxford, OX2 9PH, UK
1385 Broadway, New York, NY 10018, USA
29 Earlsfort Terrace, Dublin 2, Ireland

HART PUBLISHING, the Hart/Stag logo, BLOOMSBURY and the Diana logo are trademarks of Bloomsbury Publishing Plc

First published in Great Britain 2024

A catalogue record for this book is available from the British Library.

Library of Congress Cataloging-in-Publication data

Names: Auchmuty, Rosemary, editor. | Rackley, Erika, editor. | Takayanagi, Mari, editor.

Title: Women's legal landmarks in the interwar years : not for want of trying / edited by Rosemary Auchmuty, Erika Rackley, and Mari Takayanagi.

Description: Oxford ; New York : Hart Publishing, 2024. | Includes bibliographical references and index. | Summary: "This book shines new light on 33 legal landmarks, many forgotten today, that affected women in England and Wales between 1918 and 1939. It considers the work of feminist activists to bring about legal change which benefited – or aimed to benefit – women. Areas explored include property, inheritance, adoption, marriage, access to health care, criminal law, employment opportunities, pay, pensions and political representation. It also examines campaigns by key women's organisations, and assesses the impact of early women lawyers and politicians. While some of the landmarks effected change during this period, others provided the foundation for measures in later decades. Together the landmarks demonstrate that far from being a relatively quiet period of British feminism, the interwar period played a key role in ongoing fights for recognition, representation and justice."—Provided by publisher.

Identifiers: LCCN 2024014601 (print) | LCCN 2024014602 (ebook) | ISBN 9781509969722 (hardback) | ISBN 9781509969760 (paperback) | ISBN 9781509969739 (Epub) | ISBN 9781509969746 (ebook)

Subjects: LCSH: Women—Legal status, laws, etc.—England—History. | Women—Legal status, laws, etc.—Wales—History. | Women's rights—England—History. | Women's rights—Wales—History. | Women lawyers—England—History. | Women lawyers—Wales—History. | Six Point Group (Great Britain) | Married Women's Association (Great Britain)

Classification: LCC KD734 .W667 2024 (print) | LCC KD734 (ebook) | DDC 342.4208/7809042—dc23/eng/20240402

LC record available at https://lccn.loc.gov/2024014601

LC ebook record available at https://lccn.loc.gov/2024014602

ISBN: HB: 978-1-50996-972-2
ePDF: 978-1-50996-974-6
ePub: 978-1-50996-973-9

Typeset by Compuscript Ltd, Shannon

ACKNOWLEDGEMENTS

This collection is a follow up to our earlier collection, *Women's Legal Landmarks: Celebrating the History of Women in Law in the UK and Ireland*. We're delighted that so many of contributors from that edition have agreed to be part of this collection. Rosemary and Erika are equally delighted to be welcoming new additions – not least a new editor: long-term collaborator and parliamentary expert, Mari Takayanagi.

As ever, it would not have been possible to organise a project on this scale without financial support. We are extremely grateful to the University of Reading and, in particular, James Devenney, Head of the Law School, for his financial support of our workshop at the Institute of Advanced Legal Studies (IALS). We are also grateful to Carl Stychin, who continues to provide a space for us at IALS without question and with minimal obligations (financial or otherwise), and to Daly Sarcos for her organisational support.

We also wanted to acknowledge the role Elizabeth Cruickshank played in relation to this collection, to our earlier collection and to the Women's Legal Landmarks Project. Sadly, Elizabeth died in September 2023. She was a pioneer in the field of women in law long before women's legal history became fashionable, and a constant source of inspiration and insight, both which she shared generously. She contributed two landmarks to our first collection, on Carrie Morrison and the Foundation of the Association of Women Solicitors, and we were delighted that she was able to attend, with her husband Don, our workshop at IALS earlier in 2023. We remember our conversations with great fondness and miss her warmth, interest and intellect.

We also continue to be grateful for the support and encouragement of Verity Stuart and Kate Whetter at Hart Publishing, in relation both to the *Women's Legal Landmarks* collections and to feminist legal history more generally. And we are enormously grateful for the close and careful eye of our copy editor for this edition, Catherine Minahan.

As ever, this collection is a true collaboration of expertise and insight. We are enormously grateful for the expertise and intellectual generosity of our contributors. We learned a huge amount as we were editing the collection, and we hope that others will too.

Rosemary Auchmuty, Erika Rackley and Mari Takayanagi
February 2024

CONTENTS

LIST OF CONTRIBUTORS

Rosemary Auchmuty is a Professor of Law at the University of Reading.

Joanne Beswick is a Senior Lecturer in the School of Justice, Security and Sustainability at Staffordshire University.

Judith Bourne is a Professor of Law and Head of School of the Law School at Roehampton University.

Frances Burton is an Emeritus Research Fellow at Buckingham University.

Joanne Conaghan is a Professor of Law at the University of Bristol.

Kelly-Ann Couzens is a Postdoctoral Research Fellow in the History Department at the University of Warwick and Honorary Research Fellow at the University of Western Australia.

Kay Crosby is a Senior Lecturer in the Law School at Newcastle University.

Madeleine Davies is an Associate Professor in the English Department at the University of Reading.

Caroline Derry is Professor of Feminism, Law and History at The Open University.

Brenda Hale is a member of the House of Lords, former President of the UK Supreme Court and an Honorary Professor of Law at University College London.

Lesley Hall is formerly Senior Archivist, now Research Fellow at the Wellcome Library, and Honorary Associate Professor in the Department of Science and Technology Studies, University College London.

Richard Hedlund is a Senior Lecturer in Law at the University of Lincoln.

Carol Howells is a Senior Lecturer in Law at The Open University.

Laura Lammasniemi is an Associate Professor in the Law School at the University of Warwick.

Anne Logan is an Emeritus Reader in Social Science at the University of Kent.

Anne Morris is an Honorary Senior Research Fellow at Liverpool Law School, University of Liverpool.

Caroline Morris is a Reader in Public Law at Queen Mary, University of London.

Aoife O'Donoghue is a Professor of Law at Queen's University Belfast.

Erika Rackley is a Professor in the Law School at the University of Kent.

Eduardo Reyes is commissioning and features editor at the Law Society Gazette.

Penelope Russell is a Lecturer in the Law School at the University of Sheffield.

Harriet Samuels is a Reader in Law at the University of Westminster.

Kanika Sharma is a Senior Lecturer in Law at SOAS, University of London.

Teresa Sutton is a Senior Lecturer in Law at the University of Sussex.

Mari Takayanagi is a Senior Archivist at the Parliamentary Archives.

Sharon Thompson is a Reader in Law in the School of Law and Politics at Cardiff University.

Jacqui Turner is an Associate Professor in the History Department at the University of Reading.

1

Women's Legal Landmarks in the Interwar Years

ROSEMARY AUCHMUTY, ERIKA RACKLEY
AND MARI TAKAYANAGI

As 1918 drew to a close, a new era opened for women in Britain. Not only had the Great War ended, but (some) women could now vote and stand for Parliament. Feminists confidently hoped that the presence of women in Parliament, together with the need for male MPs to take account of the female vote, would make it impossible for women's issues to be ignored any longer. With the enactment in 1919 of the Sex Disqualification (Removal) Act, women were able to become barristers, solicitors and magistrates, and they could sit on juries. Now, surely, the many legal disabilities and discriminations women suffered, and to which feminists had repeatedly drawn attention, would be tackled and removed.

And were they? The answer is equivocal. Some were tackled. Few were removed. New ones arrived in their place. And the promise of the first decade, which did indeed see a spate of woman-centred legislation, was not maintained into the 1930s.

The idea for this book, a supplement to our original volume, *Women's Legal Landmarks: Celebrating the History of Women and Law in the UK and Ireland*,[1] arose out of the discovery that the spread of landmarks in the earlier volume was so uneven. Covering more than a thousand years from 940 to 2018, that book was unsurprisingly dominated by landmarks dating from the past 50 years, partly because these were the ones most familiar to contemporary legal scholars, but also as a result of the impact of second-wave feminism. The interwar years, however, revealed 15 landmarks from 1918 to 1929, but *none* from the 1930s.[2] Why were there so many in the 1920s and so few in the following decade? What happened in the 1930s to stop that steady flow? Were there other landmarks we could uncover to challenge the assumption that no progress was achieved in that decade?

[1] Erika Rackley and Rosemary Auchmuty (eds), *Women's Legal Landmarks: Celebrating the History of Women and Law in the UK and Ireland* (Hart Publishing, 2019).

[2] *Edwards v Attorney-General of Canada*, though reported in 1930, was heard by the Privy Council in July 1929.

Our first collection was never meant to be comprehensive. Participants chose their own landmarks. However, such a striking difference between the two decades seemed to us to reflect something more than choice or chance. Hence this new volume, *Women's Legal Landmarks in the Interwar Years*, for which we have identified 24 new landmarks from 1918 to 1929, but also nine from the 1930s.

I. Feminism between the 'Waves'

For a long time, the interwar years were dismissed as a period of stasis for women in Britain, when feminism was in abeyance and little progress was achieved. As feminist historian Christine Bolt noted, '[t]he women's movements of England and America were once seen as being in unambiguous decline between the two world wars'.[3] The very fact that the 'first wave' of feminism is considered to have ended in 1918 and that the Women's Liberation Movement called itself the 'second wave' indicates that second-wave feminists genuinely believed that little had happened to advance women's cause in the intervening years. Writing in 1981, Olive Banks, sociologist and historian of feminism, called the years 1920–60 'years of intermission, when for the time at least, feminism seemed to have come to an end'.[4] 'It is as if the "woman question" was solved in 1918,' wrote women's historian Deirdre Beddoe in 1989,[5] before correcting this view.

Historians suggested a number of reasons for the gap. The young women who were beneficiaries of first-wave feminism now rejected it and just wanted to have fun ('the roaring twenties' was a common characterisation of the period). Slightly older women, who had lived through the war, wished to return to the 'normality' of domestic life. With the grant of the vote, women were viewed as 'equal' now, with no more need for 'rights'. Feminists were seen as an older and irrelevant generation, often as embittered spinsters in an era when finding your man was women's primary but for many inaccessible goal. The formerly unified women's movement split into two different strands, and this, together with the plethora of single-interest groups that sprang up, diluted the feminist impact. Other issues – economic depression and the peace movement – took women's energies.

There is some truth in all these observations. Feminist activist in this period, Ray Strachey, writing in 1936, acknowledged that '[m]odern young women know amazingly little of what life was like before the war, and show a strong hostility to the word "feminism," and all which they imagine it to connote'.[6] Older women did retreat to the home in increasing numbers. And there were disagreements among

[3] Christine Bolt, *Feminist Ferment: 'The Woman Question' in the USA and England, 1870–1940* (UCL Press, 1995) 95.

[4] Olive Banks, *Faces of Feminism* (Martin Robertson, 1981) 150.

[5] Deirdre Beddoe, *Back to Home and Duty: Women between the wars, 1918–1939* (Pandora, 1989) 132.

[6] Introduction to Ray Strachey (ed), *Our Freedom and its Results* (Hogarth Press, 1936) 10.

feminists over aims and tactics, as well as other issues to occupy them. But it did not mean that feminist activism ceased, as Dale Spender discovered when interviewing Mary Stott (who ran *The Guardian*'s women's page). She asked what Stott had done in the years when there was no women's movement. Stott responded indignantly, 'There's always been a women's movement this century!'[7] Spender's book of this title, published in the early 1980s, presented an early challenge to the myth of feminist inactivity in the interwar years. The reason we had believed this, she argued, was that no one had bothered to talk to surviving feminists, and that historical accounts of the period did not concern themselves with women's issues, let alone feminist activism. Feminist campaigns, their successes and failures, and the reasons for them, simply did not feature in the history-writing of the time.

In fact, the feminist struggles *had* continued, even if the gains were few; but, in fact, the gains were *greater* than we realised. Across the period just 37 women were elected as MPs, though there were never more than 16 at any one time, and most lasted for fewer than three years.[8] Yet women MPs introduced 29 bills in the years 1918–39.[9] Of these, eight were successfully enacted, including the Intoxicating Liquor (Sale to Persons under Eighteen) Bill, as well as the Registration of Nursing Homes Bill 1927, the Sentence of Death (Expectant Mothers) Bill 1931, the Hire Purchase Bill 1938 and the Adoption of Children (Regulation) Bill 1939.[10] Because the political parties expected their women representatives to speak in the debate on any issue that touched on women, in most years women MPs spoke more than the average male MP.[11] Indeed, women MPs often felt that they represented their sex as much as their constituency, and their mailbag reflected this.[12]

Feminist silence in the interwar years turned out not to be silence at all. 'The enduring legacy of the first wave of feminism is now acknowledged,' writes Christine Bolt, ' … and the interwar years emerge as a complex period of growth as well as disappointment for women campaigners.'[13] The almost total exclusion of women in the presentation of modern British history up to the 1970s led Spender to conclude that her history degree had been 'rigorously censored … I thought I was being taught the truth, and I was being fed political propaganda.'[14]

[7] Dale Spender, *There's Always Been a Women's Movement This Century* (Pandora, 1983) 125.

[8] Richard Kelly, 'Female Members of Parliament' House of Commons Library Research Briefing (2023). See also **'Parliament (Qualification of Women) Act 1918'**. To avoid excessive footnotes, all cross-references to other landmarks in this collection are in bold the first time they appear in another chapter.

[9] Josephine Kamm, *Rapiers and Battleaxes: The women's movement and its aftermath* (George Allen & Unwin, 1966) 225.

[10] Martin Pugh, *Women and the Women's Movement in Britain, 1914–1959* (Macmillan, 1992), 199. See also **'Intoxicating Liquor (Sale to Persons under Eighteen) Act 1923'**; **'Infanticide Act 1938'**; and **'Adoption of Children Act 1926'**.

[11] Brian Harrison, 'Women in a Men's House: The women MPs, 1919–1945' (1986) 29 *The Historical Journal* 623, 630–32.

[12] Beddoe, n 5, 141.

[13] Bolt, n 3.

[14] Dale Spender, n 7, 5.

This suppression of feminist activism was enabled, as her sister Lynne Spender pointed out, by the masculine control of the educational curriculum and publishing up to the 1970s and beyond, and men's ability to define what 'mattered' in history and in law:

> The history that women and men confront is men's history … Through the controls that gatekeeping has offered exclusively to men, male knowledge has been projected as universally true. The overall result is that women have been rendered invisible by the recorded data available in our culture, except in the roles that have been chosen for them by men and in relation to men.[15]

As an example, Jenny Keating notes that AJP Taylor's *English History 1914–1945*, published by Oxford University Press in 1965, makes no reference whatsoever to any legislation concerning women beyond the vote.[16]

So the first step for second-wave scholars was to put women back into the historical narrative from which they had long been excluded by virtue of the fact that only public events and public figures were deemed worth recording, and public life (and certainly law-making) was largely controlled by men.[17] The fact that interwar feminism had to be 'rediscovered' in the 1980s, wrote feminist historian Barbara Caine, showed just 'how tenuous a hold women have both on history and on popular traditions'.[18]

Yet even after historical revisions began to appear, and feminist campaigns were identified, the initial judgement of second-wave feminists was that interwar feminists failed to achieve very much (and mostly did not get what they campaigned for) because they were too cautious in their methods, too conciliatory and too reliant on male-dominated institutions to represent their interests. In short, *they did it wrong* (with the unspoken corollary that second-wave feminists were going to do it right).

While once again there is some truth in the description of feminist activity in the interwar years as often 'prudent',[19] this is an example of the classic tale of successive generations rejecting the style of earlier generations without fully realising the conditions in which their forerunners operated, or predicting their own fallibility. Once feminist historians started to look more closely, it became clear that the real problem was not the women themselves but the *men*. Men too wanted a return to normality (not all of them, of course, but the majority) and the normality they sought was the male domination of employment and public

[15] Lynne Spender, *Intruders on the Rights of Men* (Pandora, 1983) 11.

[16] Jenny Keating, *A Child For Keeps: The history of adoption in England, 1918–45* (Palgrave Macmillan, 2009) 87.

[17] For example, in addition to the sources in footnotes, Ruth Adam, *A Woman's Place 1910–1975* (Chatto & Windus, 1975); Joanna Alberti, *Beyond Suffrage: Feminists in War and Peace, 1914–28* (Macmillan, 1989); Sue Bruley, *Women in Britain Since 1900* (Macmillan, 1999); Pamela Horn, *Women in the 1920s* (Alan Sutton, 1995); Jane Lewis, *Women in England, 1870–1950* (Wheatsheaf, 1984).

[18] Barbara Caine, *English Feminism 1780–1980* (Oxford University Press, 1977) 173.

[19] As proposed by the title of Brian Harrison's book, *Prudent Revolutionaries: Portraits of British feminists between the wars* (Clarendon, 1987).

life, with women back in their 'proper place' in the home. And once they realised that the female vote did not radically change their electoral fortunes, the political parties, and most of the male MPs on whom the new women voters relied, became increasingly resistant to feminist claims. Though they conscientiously listened to 'the woman's point of view', as advanced by representatives of women's organisations as well as their own female party members, they rarely gave them what they asked for. Rhys Davies's motion to introduce pensions for all widows with children or mothers whose family breadwinner had become incapacitated was defeated in 1923 on grounds of cost,[20] as was equal pay for women.[21] The Labour Party refused in 1926 to adopt birth control as party policy for fear of alienating its Catholic voters.[22] In his study of *Women and the Women's Movement in Britain 1914–1959*, Martin Pugh portrays successive governments as actively finding 'ways in which to discriminate against married women'.[23] And it was not just married women. The need for returning servicemen to get jobs after the war, men's unemployment in the Depression, the Irish War of Independence and the threat of war in Europe, all presented more important priorities than measures to benefit women, whatever their status.

II. Feminist History and Feminist Legal History

Feminist legal historians have always had to challenge the representations of progress for women as inevitable and/or explicable in other ways. As feminist historian Cheryl Law pointed out in *Suffrage and Power: The Women's Movement, 1918–1928*:

> The activism of the 1920s has had to struggle to the surface to prove its existence in contention with several fictions. That all feminism ceased; that the vote was automatically conferred; that little feminism was left in the interwar years.[24]

Too often, legal changes that benefit women are presented as if they would have happened *irrespective* of feminist activism – equal franchise, for example, though the length of time it took to achieve suggests otherwise – or as happening for different reasons – take, for example, the Matrimonial Causes Act 1923, often said to have been enacted to tidy up inconsistencies in the application of the 1857 divorce law,[25] or the **Administration of Estates Act 1925**, typically portrayed as simply part of a wider design to streamline land law.

[20] **'Widows' Orphans' and Old Age Contributory Pensions Act 1925'**.
[21] **'*Report of the War Cabinet Committee on Women in Industry*, 1919'**.
[22] See further **'Ministry of Health Memorandum 153/MCW, 1930'**.
[23] Pugh, n 10, 93. See also **'*Short v Poole Corporation* (1926)'**.
[24] Cheryl Law, *Suffrage and Power: The Women's Movement, 1918–1928* (Tauris, 2000) 1.
[25] Rebecca Probert, 'The Controversy of Equality and the Matrimonial Causes Act 1923' (1999) 11 *Child & Family Law Quarterly* 33.

Certainly, where legal reform is concerned, there is often a mixture of different motivations: law-makers do not like gaps between the letter and the practice of the law, but then again, much legislation is allowed to linger on in disorder where there is no general appetite for change.[26] And yet, as feminists know from experience, suggestions of inevitability are all too easy, and certainly too convenient a method for ensuring the patriarchal control of knowledge. The representation of legal landmarks for women as being due to a reformed and benevolent legislature or judiciary anxious to do justice to women, often advanced expressly or by implication in traditional legal histories (on the odd occasion when they even mention legal reforms for women),[27] is a familiar trope deployed to ensure the erasure of decades of feminist endeavour. The effect has been to diminish the feminist contribution, even to non-existence. The Matrimonial Causes Act 1923, for example, was a measure that equality feminists favoured and one of the original six points of the **Six Point Group**. Parliament was very attentive to women's issues in the years immediately following their admission to the vote and to Parliament, so even if we cannot find any feminist energies directed at the position of women on an intestacy, for example, it is unquestionable that the land law reforms that included the Administration of Estates Act 1925 were indirectly influenced by feminist effort.

Former Labour MP and civil servant Mary Agnes Hamilton wrote in 1944 that 'It is wrong, and false to historic fact, to forget that two decades of which we now think so badly – and rightly, so far as international policies are concerned – were a period of steady and purposive advance at home.'[28] But even as we acknowledge feminist effort in legislative success during the interwar period, we must also recognise feminist failure. As labour historian Harold Smith cautions, presenting interwar legislation on women's issues as an unqualified feminist success gives the illusion of substantial reform, when sometimes it actually impeded change. What was most striking during this period, he contends, was 'the extent to which non-feminist forces guided the pressure for reform into channels which preserved women's traditional place in society'.[29] The landmarks in this volume bear out the truth of this assessment.

Twenty-first century women's historians have introduced a more subtle and considered approach to progress or advancement in studies of the interwar period. Krista Cowman has taken the long view of women and politics to replace 'heroic narrative' with 'a much less confident but more nuanced picture of multiple progressions and successes interspersed with periods of stagnation, defeat and

[26] This was certainly true of the land law reforms of 1925, which took decades to achieve thanks to the opposition of legal men.

[27] Erika Rackley and Rosemary Auchmuty, 'The Case for Feminist Legal History' (2020) 40 *Oxford Journal of Legal Studies* 878.

[28] Mary Agnes Hamilton, *Remembering My Good Friends* (Cape, 1944) 97.

[29] Harold L Smith, 'British Feminism in the 1920s' in Harold L Smith (ed), *British Feminism in the Twentieth Century* (Edward Elgar, 1990) 52.

even regression'.[30] Pat Thane and others have drawn attention to the impact and aftermath of suffrage, and Jacqui Turner and Daniel Grey made use of the centenary of **Nancy Astor**'s election to edit a collection considering issues of public women and gendered political culture.[31] Several of the interwar women MPs (including Eleanor Rathbone, Ellen Wilkinson and Edith Summerskill) have been the subject of useful new biographical study, although much more remains to be done in this area.[32] Helen McCarthy, Helen Glew and others have considered the women's movement in relation to professional and working women. Other fruitful areas of research that have emerged in recent years include the gendered role of spaces, material culture, emotion and passion in politics, and Parliamentary history.[33]

Feminist *history* is now an established discipline, with a large body of research and courses on most university degrees. *Legal* scholarship, however, is another story. However valued feminist research might be for funding or Research Excellence Framework (REF) purposes, much of law-teaching remains largely untouched by feminism. Students can still pass through an entire degree programme without ever needing to consider it. This is because the method used to deliver the core subjects in law too often conveniently focuses on the principles applicable in the present. Where their history is traced, it is usually without reference to the reasons why reform was needed or any agency in achieving it, apart from that of the (predominately male) lawmakers. English legal history has been largely presented as history of 'great men'. Sometimes literally: William Holdsworth's *Some Makers of English Law*, first published in 1938 and reprinted in 2009, credits almost 700 years of English legal history to the 'labour' of just 24 men. Legal history as a subject in its own right, typically a niche option on law degrees, is generally institution-heavy in its approach, with only those courses taught by dedicated feminists including women's issues in any depth. Of course, the absence of feminism and women from

[30] Krista Cowman, *Women in British Politics, c. 1689–1979* (Bloomsbury, 2010).

[31] Pat Thane, 'What difference did the vote make?' in Amanda Vickery (ed), *Women, privilege and power: British politics 1750 to the present* (Stanford University Press, 2001) 253; Julie Gottlieb and Richard Toye (eds), *The Aftermath of Suffrage: Women, Gender, and Politics in Britain, 1918–1945* (Routledge, 2013); Jacqui Turner and Daniel Grey (eds), 'Special collection: "An Unconventional MP": Nancy Astor, public women and gendered political culture' (2020) 6 *Open Library of Humanities* 2 at https://olh.openlibhums.org/issue/414/info/. All URLs were last visited on 20 December 2023 unless otherwise stated.

[32] Susan Pedersen, *Eleanor Rathbone and the politics of conscience* (Yale University Press, 2004); Paula Bartley, *Ellen Wilkinson: From Red Suffragist to Government Minister* (Pluto Press, 2014); Matt Perry, *'Red Ellen' Wilkinson: Her Ideas, Movements and World* (Manchester University Press, 2014); Laura Beers, *Red Ellen: The Life of Ellen Wilkinson, Socialist, Feminist, Internationalist* (Cambridge University Press, 2016); Mary Honeyball, *Edith Summerskill: The Life and Times of a Pioneering Feminist Labour MP* (Bloomsbury, 2022).

[33] Helen McCarthy, *Women of the World: The Rise of the Female Diplomat* (Bloomsbury, 2014); Helen Glew, *Gender, Rhetoric and Regulation: Women's Work in the Civil Service and the London County Council, 1900–55* (Manchester University Press, 2016); Nirmal Puwar, *Space Invaders: Race, Gender and Bodies Out of Place* (Berg, 2004); Sarah Richardson and Natalie Hanley Smith, 'Special Issue: Passion, Politics and Parliament' (2023) 42 *Parliamentary History* 1.

the law curriculum[34] and legal history is not universal. In recent years there has been a notable increase in scholarly books, and articles exploring feminist legal history, many by contributors to this volume, as well as an increase in the visibility of women's legal history more generally – through, for example, the work of the various feminist judgments projects and, more recently, the Selden's Sister collaboration, as well as our Women's Legal Landmarks Project.[35]

III. The Women's Legal Landmarks Project

The Women's Legal Landmarks Project started in 2014. A chance happening upon the blurb of a promised but yet-to-be written book on 'fifty legal landmarks for women', a conversation about the possibility of a large, collaborative project along the lines of the UK Feminist Judgments Project,[36] and a forthcoming anniversary – the centenary of women's formal entry into the legal profession, then just over five years away – and the Women's Legal Landmarks Project was underway. Our aim was to offer a scholarly intervention into the recovery of women's lost legal history by combining legal and historical expertise to identify and write about key legal landmarks that demonstrated women's agency and activism in the achievement of law reform and justice. Too often it seemed – to us at least – that historians with an interest in law, and legal scholars with an interest in history, talked past each other. The general ignorance about women's legal history was being exacerbated by the reluctance of legal scholars, even those keen to pursue feminist legal history, to turn to sources in disciplines other than their own, with the result that they were often unaware of the substantial body of feminist historical scholarship mentioned above that covered the very matters they wished to research. At the same time, we noted that many historians are vague on the law, how it works and how courts operate, leading to misunderstandings about the substance of a reform or the distinction between its enactment and its enforcement.[37]

[34] See, eg, Susan Atkin and Brenda Hoggett, *Women and the Law* (Basil Blackwell Ltd, 1984, repr IALS, 2018); and the survey of 'women and law' courses in the mid–late 1990s in Clare McGlynn, *The Woman Lawyer: Making the difference* (Butterworths, 1998). But it would be interesting to see how many of these modules are still running today.

[35] See further at https://womenslegallandmarks.com.

[36] The UK Feminist Judgments Project (FJP) ran from 2008 to 2010. Building on and developing the methodology of the Women's Court of Canada, participants sought to put feminist theory into practice by writing 'missing' feminist judgments to key cases in England and Wales (see further Rosemary Hunter, Clare McGlynn and Erika Rackley (eds), *Feminist Judgments: From Theory to Practice* (Hart Publishing, 2010)). To date there have been FJPs in Australia, New Zealand, Northern/Ireland, the US, India, Brazil and Scotland, as well as related projects on international law, medical law and ethics, wild law and children's rights.

[37] The **Guardianship of Infants Act 1925**, for example, as Brenda Hale points out in this volume, did *not* confer equal guardianship rights on fathers and mothers, as Pugh, n 10, 109 and others have averred. That did not come until just under 50 years later, by virtue of the **Guardianship Act 1973**.

The Women's Legal Landmarks project was framed to overcome these difficulties. Over the last 10 years, the project has brought together over 100 scholars from wide-ranging academic disciplines and backgrounds, including law, history, English literature, theology and criminology, as well as independent historians, archivists, civil servants, activists, lawyers and judges. Participants and contributors have included established scholars, postgraduate and early-career researchers, as well as those who have retired from their professional employment. Our earlier collection also included a number of our authors who were involved in some way in one or more of the landmarks. Most of our participants have met at least once in person at workshops, where we have been able to draw on our collective expertise and insights. This collaborative endeavour has continued across the two published collections at public-facing events, academic conferences and related research collaborations, and will, we hope, continue into the future in another collection focusing on the 1950s and 1960s.

IV. Landmarking the Interwar Years

The word 'landmark' is both a noun – a significant event, juncture or achievement marking an important stage or turning point in something – and a verb – declaring a building, an occasion, a piece of legislation a landmark. Throughout our project we have used 'landmark' in both senses. Our purpose – in line with the political and transformative purpose of feminist legal history more broadly – has been both to explore those statutes, cases, events or occasions that are already identified as key staging posts and to reveal – or declare – new ones.

Feminist legal history has both academic and political ambitions. So too has this collection. Through the recognition of hitherto overlooked or suppressed histories we seek once again to expose the continued marginalisation of women in law and public policy and, by providing a deeper understanding of the impact of law on the lived experience of women and the impact of women on law, to influence strategies for those currently seeking social justice. In so doing, we have adopted the same method and process as our earlier volume, with one exception. This time our requirement for inclusion was either that the landmark had some positive impact for women, however limited, fleeting or vexed, *or that it would had done so*, had it been successful. This arose out of the realisation that many much-desired feminist reforms had been blocked during the interwar years and were only achieved later, and accounts for the sub-title of this book: *Not for Want of Trying*. There may be fewer landmarks for women in the 1930s, but this is not because feminists had not campaigned for them. This has allowed us to include some 'steps along the way' that did not come to full fruition in the interwar period but were won later, such as Lady Rhondda's petition to admit hereditary women peers to the House of Lords (not achieved until 1963).[38] Even those that might be considered 'unsuccessful' – such as the failed implementation of the *Report of the War Cabinet Committee on Women in Industry* (1919) or *Short v Poole Corporation* (1926), which was lost on appeal – were (and in some cases continued to be) vital steps in securing later law reform.

We also continued with our landmarking of 'first' women, mindful of the contradictions involved in balancing heroine narratives with the recognition of ground-breaking achievement.[39] In our choice of landmark individual women we have sought to showcase a range of spheres of activity, as well as backgrounds and lifestyles, and to locate the women within relevant networks. Issues that are often dodged in 'heroine' accounts are noted: it is important for readers to know that women succeeded with greater or less ease because or in spite of their class, ethnicity, marital status or sexuality.

A call for expressions of interest, circulated through our own networks and those of the leading legal and historical societies, resulted in a working list of potential landmarks against which we identified others for which a specialist on that topic could be approached. Sometimes we were successful, sometimes not. Inevitably, there are other landmarks and 'first' women we could have included, such as the foundation in 1926 of the Open Door Council, which sought to remove all restrictions on women's employment, the Midwives Act 1936, which regulated the profession to increase women's safety in childbirth, the Hire Purchase Act 1938, which extended protection to women as consumers; or Margaret Wintringham, the first female Liberal MP, or Eleanor Rathborne, the first woman to sit as an independent MP. So while we make no claim to be comprehensive, we hope nevertheless that, when the 16 landmarks from the original volume (listed in section V) are added to the 33 here, we will have provided representative coverage of some well-known and less well-known legal developments that in some way advanced the position of women in the interwar years.

As with the original volume, the landmarks are set out according to a template that provides the context, details of the landmark (or life), what happened next and its significance. We asked authors to focus not simply on what was achieved, but also on what was *not* achieved, on the obstacles that were faced and the compromises that had to be made, and on the efforts that feminists had to make even to get the reform through, let alone to counter the inevitable backlash. To this end, and taken together, the landmarks appear not simply as individual events but rather, as Harriet Samuels notes in her landmark on *Short v Poole Corporation* (1926), as 'part of the process drawing attention to the inadequacy of the law, providing

[38] Life Peerages Act 1958, Peerage Act 1963. See Supuni Perera, 'Life Peerages Act 1958' in Rackley and Auchmuty (eds), n 1, 249.

[39] Rosemary Auchmuty and Erika Rackley, 'Feminist Legal Biography: A Model for All Legal Life Stories' (2020) 41(2) *The Journal of Legal History* 186, 205.

evidence of hardship and illustrating the urgent need for action', as novel and vital accounts of

> [w]omen resilient enough to stand up for themselves and others, in an intimidating court environment to demand equality, [who] deserve to be remembered by future generations as part of a feminist project that transformed women's lives.[40]

V. About the Interwar Landmarks

While just under half the landmarks are statutes, many of the landmarks included in this collection are not obviously 'legal'. We have also included, alongside accounts of 'first women' and cases, novels and textbooks, committee reports and (vitally for this period) accounts of the formation of women's organisations that played such an important role in the promotion of women's issues in these decades. Among the landmarks there is the expected mixture of the obvious and unmissable and the quirky and unexpected. Falling within the former category are examples both of those that Martin Pugh calls 'uncontroversial extensions of existing legislation' (such as the **Representation of the People (Equal Franchise) Act 1928**, which gave women the parliamentary vote on the same terms as men for the first time, and the **Matrimonial Causes Act 1937**, which equalised the grounds for divorce) and those he sees as representing women's role as wife and mother, 'undoubtedly the perspective through which most politicians preferred to see women'[41] (such as the Widows', Orphans' and Old Age Contributory Pensions Act 1925, which provided some women with a small amount of regular, definite income, or the Adoption of Children Act 1926, which enabled the legal adoption of children in England and Wales). Of the less obvious, the provision of women's lavatory accommodation at the Law Society's office in 1923 needs no justification to a readership still preoccupied with the subject of toilets for women.[42] Virginia Woolf's analysis of patriarchy – of how men's control of education, politics, work, culture *and* law worked to keep women poor and therefore powerless – in *A Room of One's Own*, while not directly about law, underpinned much feminist strategy, then and now.[43] In contrast, the first law textbooks on 'Women and Law' – *Women Under English Law* (1924), written by English solicitor Maud Crofts, which contained a supplementary chapter on 'Women Under Scots Law' by Scottish barrister Margaret Kidd, *Everyday Law for Women* (1932) by the prominent barrister Helena Normanton, and *The Rights and Duties of Englishwomen: a Study in Law and Public Opinion* (1934) by Manchester-based barrister Erna Reiss – while clearly more directly focused on

[40] '*Short v Poole Corporation* (1926)', section IV.
[41] Pugh, n 10, 114.
[42] **'Women's Lavatory Accommodation at the Law Society, 1923'.**
[43] **'*A Room of One's Own*, Virginia Woolf, 1929'.**

law as it related to women, are likely to be less familiar to today's readers than Woolf's text.[44]

There are just three landmark cases included in this collection. This is probably a reflection of the chosen law-reform strategies adopted by feminists and women's organisations during this period. The presence of women in Parliament and tried and tested male allies across the political divide, including Major Jack Hills MP (Liberal Unionist, later Conservative) and Arthur Henderson MP (Labour) in the House of Commons and Lord Buckmaster (Liberal) in the House of Lords, made legislative reform a more reliable option that the vagaries of the often hostile all-male judiciary. While *Short v Poole Corporation* (1926) involved the removal of the marriage bar for married teachers, and ***R v Bourne* (1939)** concerned women's access to abortion, ***Bradford Third Equitable Benefit Building Society v Borders* (1939)** was not a case directly about women. Yet, as our final landmark before the outbreak of the Second World War, it illustrates beautifully the twin aspects of women's role throughout the interwar years: their association with the home and domestic life, and their actual ability to transcend the restrictions that this imposed to act as independent agents in public life. And like the Law Society lavatories, the Borders' home has a defined physicality, allowing us actually to *see* their significance.[45]

Inevitably perhaps, given the prominence of debates concerning citizenship and suffrage during our period, several landmarks are connected with access to political representation: the vote,[46] the admission of women to Parliament,[47] the first women MPs and Cabinet Minister,[48] the first private member's bill from a woman that passed into law,[49] the petition to admit women to the House of Lords.[50] Others focus on women's participation in the legal profession and legal processes: in the Industrial Courts,[51] as jurors,[52] solicitors, barristers and legal academics.[53] Family law is represented by statutes on divorce, the guardianship and adoption of children and the age of marriage,[54] and criminal law by topics

[44] **'First Published Law Textbooks on "Women and Law" Written by Women Lawyers in Great Britain, 1924–34'**.

[45] Sadly, the original Industrial Court building in Old Palace Yard in Westminster was bombed during the Second World War.

[46] Representation of the People (Equal Franchise) Act 1928.

[47] Parliament (Qualification of Women) Act 1918.

[48] **'Constance Georgine Markievicz, First Woman Elected to Parliament, 1918'**; Nancy Astor, first woman to take her seat in the UK Parliament, 1919; **'Margaret Bondfield, First Woman Cabinet Minister, 1929'**.

[49] Intoxicating Liquor (Sale to Persons under Eighteen) Act 1923.

[50] **'Lady Rhondda's Petition for Women to Sit in House of Lords, 1922'**.

[51] **'Industrial Courts Act 1919'**.

[52] **'First Women Jurors, 1920'**.

[53] **'Ivy Williams, First Woman to Qualify as a Barrister, 1922'**; **'Monica Geikie Cobb, First Woman Barrister to Appear in Court, 1922'**; **'Agnes Twiston Hughes, First Welsh Woman to Practise as a Solicitor, 1923'**; **'Stella Thomas, First Black Woman to be Called to the Bar of England and Wales, 1933'**.

[54] 'Guardianship of Infants Act 1925'; Adoption of Children Act 1926; **Age of Marriage Act 1929**; Matrimonial Causes Act 1937.

including the age of consent, abortion and infanticide.[55] The world of work has three landmarks, only one of which is wholly positive for women, reflecting the increasing marginisation of women in employment.[56] Property law does better, with some substantial reforms in succession law.[57] There are important landmarks relating to women's access to reproductive autonomy, though these were clearly only 'steps on the way'.[58] There was legislation on widows' pensions, as well as clarification of married women's capacity to sue and be sued.[59] Changing ideas about sexuality are explored in the Criminal Law Amendment Act 1922 and the relationship between English law and Empire is demonstrated in the Age of Marriage Act 1929. Other of the landmarks are concerned with age – the age at which women could vote, the age of consent and of marriage, the age of criminal liability, even the age at which young people could drink alcohol.[60]

Two women's organisations are examined, out of the many we could have chosen:[61] the Six Point Group, with an equal-rights agenda, and **the Married Women's Association**, whose focus was women's roles as wives and mothers.

Notably, in contrast to more recent feminist landmarks, there are no landmarks directly relating to violence against women. This omission helps to explain why second-wave feminists in the 1970s were initially unaware that the subject had ever been addressed by feminists before.[62] What we do see, however, is an understanding that men's abuse of women and girls was a problem to be taken into account in associated legislation such as the Criminal Law Amendment Act 1922 and the Adoption Act 1926. Nor is there is a landmark relating to prostitution, though we know that women MPs did work on legal reform in this area.[63] Other issues – separate taxation for married women, for example – were certainly considered but not taken forward.[64]

Interwar feminists did not ignore women's international situation. Peace was a major and increasing preoccupation, and three of the landmarks here

[55] **'Criminal Law Amendment Act 1922'**; '*R v Bourne* (1938)'; Infanticide Act 1938.

[56] '*Report of the War Cabinet Committee on Women in Industry*, 1919'; 'Women's lavatory accommodation at the Law Society, 1923'; '*Short v Poole Corporation* (1926)'.

[57] 'Widows', Orphans' and Old Age Contributory Pensions Act 1925'; Administration of Estates Act 1925; **'Inheritance (Family Provision) Act 1938'**.

[58] '*R v Bourne* (1938)'; 'Ministry of Health Memorandum 153/MCW, 1930'.

[59] **Law Reform (Married Women and Tortfeasors) Act 1935**; Widows', Orphans' and Old Age Contributory Pensions Act 1925.

[60] Criminal Law Amendment Act 1922; Intoxicating Liquor (Sale to Persons under Eighteen) Act 1923; Representation of the People (Equal Franchise) Act 1928.

[61] For example the National Union of Societies for Equal Citizenship (NUSEC); National Council of Women; Women's Citizens Associations; Women's Institute; Townswomen's Guilds; the women's organisations of the major political parties; and many single-issue groups.

[62] Though of course it was a major concern of first-wave feminism.

[63] Paula Bartley, 'The mighty atom: Ellen Wilkinson and parliamentary politics, 1924–1947' (2014) 75 *Women's History Magazine* 6. Nancy Astor worked closely with the Association for Moral and Social Hygiene (AMSH) on this issue; Pat Thane, 'Nancy Astor, Women and Politics, 1919–1945' (2020) 6 *Open Library of Humanities* 2 at https://doi.org/10.16995/olh.542.

[64] Pugh, n 10, 116.

touch on Empire.[65] While acknowledging that the relationship and attitudes to women in the colonies were complicated and problematic, we can still recognise the courage of women MPs who drew attention to what they described as 'slavery under the British flag' (the subjugation of women and girls in India) and challenged British acceptance of what was comfortably considered a 'domestic custom'.[66]

Finally, it goes without saying that the landmarks in this collection are best read in conjunction with the 16 landmarks of the period in our original collection, which are:

- Representation of the People Act 1918
- Maternity and Child Welfare Act 1918
- Article 7 of the Covenant of the League of Nations 1919
- Sex Disqualification (Removal) Act 1919
- First Women Justices of the Peace, 1919
- First Woman to be Admitted to an Inn of Court, Helena Normanton, 1919
- Committee on the Employment of Women on Police Duties, 1920
- First Woman Law Agent, Madge Easton Anderson, 1920
- Foundation of the Association of Women Solicitors, 1921
- First Woman to Practise as a Barrister in Ireland and the (then) UK, Averil Deverell, 1922
- First Woman Solicitor in England and Wales, Carrie Morrison, 1922
- Matrimonial Causes Act 1923
- First Woman Member of the Faculty of Advocates, Margaret Kidd, 1923
- First Woman Professor of Law in Ireland, Frances Moran, 1925
- *DPP v Jonathan Cape and Leopold Hill* (1928)
- *Edwards v Attorney-General of Canada* (1929).

VI. Not for Want of Trying

Writing in 1984, Harold Smith, when answering the question 'What happened to the British women's movement after 1918?' suggested that 'by the end of the 1920s the feminist movement resembled an exhausted volcano'.[67] The landmarks in this

[65] 'Constance Georgine Markievicz, First Woman Elected to Parliament, 1918'; 'Age of Marriage Act 1929'; 'Stella Thomas, First Black Woman to be Called to the Bar of England and Wales, 1933'.

[66] Eleanor Rathbone, quoted in Mavis Curtis, *What the Suffragists Did Next: How the fight for women's rights went on* (Amberley, 2017) 149. Rathbone and the Duchess of Atholl also raised the issue of female genital mutilation in the House of Commons as early as 1929.

[67] Harold Smith, 'Sex vs Class: British Feminists and the Labour Movement, 1919–1929' (1984) 47(1) *The Historian* 19, 19.

volume, and from the interwar period in our previous collection, show that the implication that feminist activism in the 1920s 'erupted' in 1918 and throughout the 1920s, only to become inactive or dormant by the 1930s, is both misleading and inaccurate. It not only over-states the impact of feminism during the 1920s, and the lack of feminism from 1930s onwards, but it also fails to allow for any assessment of the quality of feminist activism and law reform across the period as a whole. As such, it risks equating any achievement, however minimal, with reaching the ultimate goal, of allowing quantity to overshadow quality.

In fact, as Caine observes, 'For feminists looking back on the 1920s, it is … the opposition to feminist aims and objectives which seems most noticeable.'[68] Though numerically higher than those in the later decade, many of the landmarks between 1918 and 1929 were disappointing, watered-down versions of what was asked for, designed to limit women's ability to challenge men's control of the public *and* private spheres. Take, for example, the Representation of the People Act 1918, which set the tone by restricting the parliamentary franchise to women householders aged 30 and over, while the same statute gave it to virtually all men aged 21 and over. Similarly, the Sex Disqualification (Removal) Act 1919, which had seemed to promise to remove the barriers to women's entry into the legal and other professions, was subsequently redefined as removing a disability, not creating a right – a sleight of hand, possible only because of the male monopoly on interpreting the law, which meant that women were unable to resist the marriage bars in teaching and the Civil Service.

As the decade progressed, the legislators went on as they had started. The Matrimonial Causes Act 1923 equalised grounds for divorce, removing the additional hurdle for women who could not sue solely on the basis of their husband's adultery, but ducked the opportunity to re-think the grounds for divorce, which would reframe the dissolution of a marriage in other than sexual terms. The Guardianship of Infants Act 1925 was intended to give parents equal rights in respect of their children, but it gave rights to mothers only in restricted situations. Pensions and unemployment benefits, only grudgingly offered to women in restricted circumstances in the first instance, were further limited in subsequent years.

Any progress that happened was met with, at best, obfuscation and, at worst, open hostility. Describing the winding back that occurred after Parliament agreed to equal pay in the Civil Service, Strachey wrote:

> Many were the disappointments which followed. Delays, obstructions, and circumlocutions were piled one upon another, and a great deal of really first-class energy and ability was devoted by the Treasury and other big departments to the task of evading the plain meaning of the decision of Parliament.[69]

[68] Caine, n 18, 182.

[69] Ray Strachey, *The Cause: A short history of the women's movement in Great Britain* (G Bell & Sons, 1928) 379.

In the professions, meanwhile, formal barriers preventing women from *entering* were replaced with subtler, more complex forms of discrimination, limiting their ability to achieve a successful and remunerative career.[70] Writing in 1978, lawyer Albie Sachs and historian Joan Hoff Wilson commented that

> [t]he professions, like clubs and elite schools, were not simply institutions from which women happened to be absent. Their maleness became part of their character, so that the admission of women was seen as not merely adding to their number or introducing some novelty, but as threatening the very identity of the institutions themselves … [Men] shifted their control away from the point of entry towards the routes of advancement. To say this is not to suggest that men conspire as a secret brotherhood to exclude women – though male condescension may well be nearly universal and male hostility fairly common – or even that individual male's bigotry is the dominant bar to female advancement. Institutions tend to have machinery for their self-perpetuation, and all professions are structurally organised so as to maintain male domination and female subordination.[71]

The legal profession was – and continues to be – no exception. So too Parliament.

Early women MPs were excluded from masculine spaces like the bars, smoking rooms or members' cloakrooms, being allocated instead only a small dressing-room with basic facilities, which all women MPs were expected to share, regardless of party, even as numbers grew. Ellen Wilkinson described how 'to reach the toilet-room provided for us meant a walk of nearly a quarter of a mile along three long corridors and up two flights of stairs'.[72] Inside the Chamber, Lady Astor acquired the reputation for being disruptive, regularly interrupting speeches and debates, but *Hansard* shows how often she was provoked. Speaking during the second reading of the Representation of the People (Equal Franchise) Bill in 1928, for example, Astor remarked:

> When I stood up and asked questions affecting women and children, social and moral questions, I used to be shouted at for five or 10 minutes at a time. That was when they thought that I was rather a freak, a voice crying in the wilderness.[73]

That said, Mary Agnes Hamilton, elected as a Labour MP in 1929, found the House of Commons a kinder place for women: 'there, if nowhere else, one was treated simply as a member,' she asserted.[74] The press, as always, focused on side-issues, such as what the women wore. In 1936, the choice of Florence Horsbrugh as the first woman MP to reply to the royal address prompted numerous newspaper

[70] See further 'Monica Geikie Cobb, First Woman Barrister to Appear in Court, 1922'.

[71] Abie Sachs and Joan Hoff Wilson, *Sexism and the Law: A Study of Male Beliefs and Judicial Bias in Britain and America* (Wiley-Blackwell, 1978) 170–71.

[72] Mari Takayanagi, 'The UK Parliament as a historical space for women' in Sophia Psarra, Uta Staiger and Claudia Sternberg (eds), *Parliament Buildings: The architecture of politics in Europe* (UCL Press, 2023).

[73] HC Deb 29 March 1928, vol 215, col 1452.

[74] Hamilton, n 28, 181.

articles to speculate on what she would wear. *Hansard* even officially noted she appeared 'in evening dress'.[75]

Overall, the early landmarks in this volume bear out what feminist historian Johanna Alberti has called 'the deeply engrained misogyny of the society' in which the feminists operated and 'the precarious nature of women's position within the political structures'.[76] Again and again we see the tactics men used to restrict and subordinate women and to maintain men's dominance and personal comfort. To the discovery of priorities more important than women's rights was added sustained pressure through custom and practice, reinforced by the media, to elevate the roles of wife and mother to the exclusion of all others for women, while heaping opprobrium on unmarried women. And where ideology failed to restrict girls' access to skilled training and higher education, quotas, low pay and the absence of childcare provision combined to keep women out of competition with men. For much of this period representation, for women, all too often meant being listened to but not heard, and certainly not acted upon.

But what of the 1930s? Without doubt, despite the hostility faced by many of the early women pioneers, by the end of the 1920s they had changed the legal landscape irrevocably. The landmarks bear out the characterisation of feminist historians of the years up to 1929 as largely progressive for British women, with a sweep of legislation clearly influenced by the presence of the first women voters and MPs. So what happened? What accounts for the scarcity of legal landmarks for women in the 1930s?

The answer lies not in a decline in feminist activism but, rather, in the increase in *reaction* against it. In short, the backlash that had been present in the 1920s began to have greater effect. This is amply borne out by the recognition that some of the landmark statutes in our original volume from the period immediately after the Second World War had, in fact, been aired repeatedly in Parliament in the 1930s but failed to pass. These included such significant measures as the Family Allowances Act 1945,[77] for which Eleanor Rathbone had long campaigned but which was not fully achieved until after her death, and the British Nationality Act 1948,[78] which allowed married women to keep their own nationality upon marriage instead of having to take their husband's. Many other post-war landmarks were products of decades-long activism (for example, the Married Women's Property Act 1964[79] and the Abortion Act 1967),[80] and others were repeatedly

[75] Krista Cowman, 'A Matter of Public Interest: Press Coverage of the Outfits of Women MPs 1918–1930' (2020) 6 *Open Library of Humanities* 2 at https://doi.org/10.16995/olh.583; HC Deb 3 November 1936, vol 317, col 14.

[76] Johanna Alberti, *Eleanor Rathbone* (Sage, 1996) 3.

[77] Lucy Vickers, 'Family Allowances Act 1945' in Rackley and Auchmuty (eds), n 1, 227.

[78] Helen Kay and Rose Pipes, 'British Nationality Act 1948' in Rackley and Auchmuty (eds), n 1, 233.

[79] This allowed married women to keep half the housekeeping money, which until then had belonged entirely to the husband (Sharon Thompson, 'Married Women's Property Act 1964' in Rackley and Auchmuty (eds), n 1, 263).

[80] Nicky Priaulx and Natalie I Jones, 'Abortion Act 1967' in Rackley and Auchmuty (eds), n 1, 275.

postponed because of powerful male opposition – for example, the appointment of any women to the higher judicial posts, which only happened in 1965.[81]

Yet what is also clear from the landmarks we uncovered for the 1930s is that most are surprisingly positive. Writing in the mid-1930s, Ray Strachey observed 'The purpose and nature of legislation are all profoundly different in balance and emphasis from those of pre-war years. Health, housing, pensions, education, maternal mortality and worker's conditions have leapt to the forefront of national affairs ….'[82] Though quieter than the previous decade – less 'volcanic' perhaps – the 1930s were not as disappointing as we have been led to believe.

The Ministry of Health Memorandum 153/MCW, published in 1930, brought birth-control advice to thousands of women, giving them the best chance to restrict their families and enjoy a more productive life in both the private and public spheres. *R v Bourne* decriminalised abortion in circumstances that took account of the mother's health, paving the way for future abortion law reform at a time when legislation would have been impossible. The Law Reform (Married Women and Tortfeasors) Act 1935 removed almost the last formal vestiges of coverture by giving married women the power to manage their own financial dealings, while the Matrimonial Causes Act 1937 finally widened the grounds for divorce. The Inheritance (Family Provision) Act 1938 challenged men's right to disinherit their wives and dependants, removing propertied men's long cherished right to control their wives financially even after death. The Infanticide Act 1938 recognised women's different experience in reducing the penalty for women who, suffering from post-natal depression, killed their babies. Though it did not go as far as feminists wished – it did not take into account a woman's depression caused by not by illness but by her impossible economic position – in the hands of a good Counsel, her defence could be reframed in statutory terms.

VII. 'New' and 'Old' Feminism and Feminist Collaboration

The importance of feminist networks, organisations and campaigns emerged as a strong theme throughout our earlier collection. The same is true of this one. Across the centuries, feminists have used a range of strategies to publicise, educate and influence law-makers and law reform.

During the interwar period, feminist campaigners continued to use private members' bills as a means to publicise a particular issue or cause. Though rarely successful in their original form, private members' bills brought women's issues to Parliament's attention and forced debate – often repeatedly, to the point where just occasionally they *were* adopted by governments and passed into law. And, of

[81] Judith Bourne and Frances Burton, 'First Woman High Court Judge in England and Wales, Elizabeth Lane, 1965' in Rackley and Auchmuty (eds), n 1, 271.

[82] Ray Strachey, (1936) 146 'Women in Parliament' *Fortnightly Review* 337, 342.

course, during this period women were – for the first time – occupying positions within political institutions and were able to do this directly. They did this with some considerable success – just over a quarter of the 29 bills introduced by women MPs during this period were successfully enacted. At other times, campaigners turned to test cases, as we see in *R v Bourne* and *Short v Poole Corporation*. Like private members' bills, the best result could change the law, but even failure publicised the issue and put in train a process of attrition that might lead eventually to the desired legal reform.

Both private members' bills and test cases illustrate the goal, shared by all feminist groups, to *educate the public* – voters as well as MPs – to appreciate the feminist agenda. In the words of Lady Rhondda, 'that fight of ours was only *ostensibly* concerned with changing the law'. Instead it was 'passionately, urgently' to 'change customs and influence ideas'.[83] 'Educating for citizenship' was ubiquitous and took many forms: it was for this purpose that Lady Rhondda set up her journal *Time and Tide* in 1920, but even the women's magazines that proliferated in the 1930s to address homemaking women regularly featured articles on legal and financial issues and careers for women, often written by feminist lawyers and professional women.

What we can also see from the interwar landmarks is that, despite a fracturing of the women's movement into two main strands and many single-interest groups in this period, feminists were still able to deliver important reforms for women, often working together. Both strands of feminism worked towards a generalised 'equality' of the sexes, albeit envisioning it in different ways – equal *and the same*, and equal *but different* – a departure from first-wave feminism, whose focus was rather on restraining the most egregious exercises of men's oppression. As Frances Hamilton points out, 'No nineteenth-century organization would have used the title "equal".'[84]

The 'old' feminists, many of whom (such as Lady Rhondda) had been suffragettes before the war, aimed for formal equality – equal *and the same* – in public and private life by removing all legal distinctions between men and women and all barriers to women's enjoyment of the citizenship rights that men enjoyed. From them came the campaigns for equal divorce, equal franchise and equal guardianship of children, and the opposition to protective legislation for women – or at least its equal extension to men.

For other interwar feminists, formal equality was not an end in itself but a necessary first step to reconsidering gender roles generally.

The 'new' feminists, amongst whom Eleanor Rathbone stood out, doubted the value of equality on men's terms when women's social position was still so very weak. For them, equality required a recognition of 'difference'. The first priority was to empower women in their current situation – that is, as wives and mothers,

[83] Viscountess Rhondda, *This Was My World* (Macmillan, 1933) 299–300.

[84] Frances Hamilton, 'Equality Arguments, Contemporary Feminist Voices and the Matrimonial Causes Act 1923' (2022) 43 *Journal of Legal History* 215.

dependent on their husbands, and rarely in a position to avail themselves of the equal *and the same* rights in employment promoted by the old feminists. They understood that keeping women dependent in the family was men's best means of maintaining their subservience, out of competition with men and actually in service to them. So their chief goal was to give housewives a measure of financial independence by means of such devices as family allowances, joint ownership and widows' pensions. The Married Women's Association, founded at the end of our period as a breakaway organisation from the Six Point Group, exemplified this approach. It was a strategy that was open to the criticism that reforms for home-makers risked confining women to that role and inhibiting their progress in other spheres: 'the tradition of woman as home-maker encumbers her intellectual and economic progress at every turn,' opined Winifred Holtby in 1934.[85] The increasing dominance of this approach, and its almost complete lack of concrete success, helps to explain why second-wave feminists wrote off interwar feminism as tactically misguided.[86]

However, in spite of their ideological differences, there was considerable overlap of support from old and new feminists for a wide range of reforms. New and old feminists backed the Criminal Law Amendment Act 1922, which increased the age of consent from 13 to 16, and also the Widows', Orphans' and Old Age Contributory Pensions Act 1925. The same names crop up in many different landmark accounts because the same women and the same organisations spoke to investigative committees and advised governments. This too was strategic. Feminists on both sides were not unaware of the importance of a show of unity in a political atmosphere so heavily weighted against them. In Parliament, the same people introduced and spoke in debates: in particular, Nancy Astor, Eleanor Rathbone and Ellen Wilkinson. Women MPs of all parties, and none, collaborated in pursuit of goals to benefit their sex, even in defiance of their own party: Astor (Conservative) and Wilkinson (Labour) enjoyed the warmest of relationships and 'worked closely together on a number of questions',[87] and Wilkinson was also friends with Liberal-turned-Conservative Lady Rhondda.[88] In later years, party loyalties caused divisions, especially in the Labour party, between women who espoused issues affecting their sex and those who toed the party line. Wilkinson, for example, argued passionately against the Labour Government's measure (proposed by a female Minister, Margaret Bondfield) to prevent married women from claiming benefits.[89] In 1936, Ellen Wilkinson was supported by every Tory woman MP except the Duchess of Atholl on equal pay for women.[90]

[85] Winifred Holtby, *Women* (John Lane The Bodley Head, 1934) 146.

[86] That said, just as a strand of first-wave feminism advocated 'wages for wives', a strand of second-wave feminism pursued a programme of 'wages for housework'.

[87] Bartley, n 63.

[88] Betty D Vernon, *Ellen Wilkinson* (Croom Helm, 1982) 115.

[89] The Unemployment Insurance Bill 1931, enacted as the Anomalies Act 1931.

[90] Pugh, n 10, 198.

So, in defiance of the recent vogue for locating individual women who 'succeeded against all odds' as if solely through their own determination and skill, what we see is that women's legal advances were all achieved through the efforts of women working *together*. Even the individual women named in this collection were part of a multi-stranded movement and succeeded thanks to the efforts of inter-connected networks of women (and men) campaigners. Behind almost all of the landmarks was a common desire to empower women financially. This motive underlay the equal-rights feminists' call for the removal of barriers to work as much as the new feminists' call for access to benefits, pensions and family allowances. For, as Holtby wrote in a conscious echo of Virginia Woolf, 'wealth means power, and women have been poor'.[91] The interwar feminists were desperate to change this – as we still are.

So where does this leave us? There is much to celebrate in this second volume of *Women's Legal Landmarks*, which expands our understanding of the mechanics of feminist activism as well as those of patriarchal resistance, not simply for the period under consideration – the interwar years – but also for today. History never exactly repeats itself, but there can be no doubt that the more we know about our past, the better armed we are to move forward.

[91] Holtby, n 85, 84.

2

Parliament (Qualification of Women) Act 1918

MARI TAKAYANAGI

The Parliament (Qualification of Women) Act 1918 enabled women to be elected to, sit in and vote in the UK House of Commons. Women were previously barred as a matter of common law rather than statute law. It followed the Representation of the People Act 1918, which had given some women over the age of 30 the parliamentary vote but not the right to stand. The Parliament (Qualification of Women) Act did not put any age restriction on standing, meaning that women could stand at the age of 21, the same as men. Women stood for the first time in the general election of December 1918.

I. Context

During the eighteenth century, some elite women participated in election campaigning and electoral politics on behalf of male relatives, and also exercised considerable influence as political hostesses.[1] However, they did not themselves try to stand for election because of long custom and tradition; there was no legislation that specifically barred women from standing as MPs. From 1711, MPs had to meet a property qualification to be eligible to stand (£600 a year from land for county MPs, and £300 a year for borough MPs), which would have been a potential barrier for many women, especially married women, whose property legally belonged to their husbands, and non-elite women.[2] Some women were able to play quasi-MP roles through family and society connections. For example, Martin Spychal has explored the role of Harriet Grote, wife of George Grote, MP for the City of London 1832–1841, as an accomplished political analyst and

[1] Elaine Chalus, *Elite Women in English Political Life c 1754–1790* (Clarendon Press, 2005).

[2] This law was amended in 1838 to include income, but not abolished until 1858. Even after that, MPs needed independent means, because salaries for MPs were not introduced until 1911.

radical tactician.[3] Such influence should not be underestimated; and yet it had its limits.[4]

In 1832, the Great Reform Act defined a voter as a male person, thus formally excluding women from the parliamentary franchise. The suffrage campaign that developed from the mid-nineteenth century focused on the right to vote rather than on the right to stand. One of the prominent early suffrage campaigners was Helen Taylor, who became the first woman to be selected as a prospective parliamentary candidate, by the Camberwell Radical Club in Camberwell North in 1885. Suffrage campaigners were divided in their response to Taylor's candidacy, some fearing it to be a social transgression that would invite ridicule and endanger the suffrage cause. The Presiding Officer refused to accept Taylor's nomination as valid, citing the Ballot Act 1872, which referred to candidates as 'his' and 'him'.[5]

As the suffrage campaign escalated in the early twentieth century, the prospect of women MPs was occasionally raised by anti-suffragists as an argument against women voting. For example, an anti-suffrage pamphlet tellingly titled *The Woman MP: a peril to women and the country* was published in 1909.[6] Hostile cartoonists lampooned the prospect of women sitting in the House of Commons, portraying the green benches filled with crying babies and fierce harridans. Male MPs also raised the terrifying prospect of having women alongside them, such as Rowland Hunt in 1913:

> If you once give votes to women they could undoubtedly sit in this House. You could not prevent it, and whether rightly or wrongly they could be War Ministers or anything else … We might have to address the Chair as 'Mrs Speaker, Ma'am,' for all we could tell … There are obvious disadvantages about having women in Parliament … How is a poor little man to get on with a couple of women wearing enormous hats in front of him?[7]

Lisa Berry-Waite has traced how women's emotions were used to discredit their political capabilities, including Helen Taylor's in 1885.[8] For this reason,

[3] Martin Spychal, *Victorian Commons*, blog series on Harriet Grote (2021–2022) at https://victoriancommons.wordpress.com/category/women/harriet-grote/.

[4] For more discussion, see Kathryn Gleadle, *Borderline Citizens: Women, Gender and Political Culture in Britain, 1815–1867* (Oxford University Press, 2009); Sarah Richardson, *The Political Worlds of Women: Gender and Politics in Nineteenth Century Britain* (Routledge, 2013).

[5] See Janet Smith, 'First Woman Prospective Parliamentary Candidate, Helen Taylor, 1885' in Erika Rackley and Rosemary Auchmuty (eds), *Women's Legal Landmarks: Celebrating the History of Women and Law in the UK and Ireland* (Hart Publishing, 2019) 77; Janet Smith, 'Crossing the Border of Citizenship: Helen Taylor, the Independent Radical Democrat Candidate for Camberwell North, 1885' (2020) 6(2) *Open Library of Humanities* 1.

[6] A C Gronno, 'The woman MP: a peril to women and the country' (Manchester Branch of the Women's National Anti-Suffrage League, 1909), Pamphlet, The Women's Library, LSE.

[7] HC Deb 5 May 1913, vol 52, cols 1788–89.

[8] Lisa Berry-Waite, '"A rancour and a passion would be introduced into politics": Perceptions of the Woman MP in Late 19th and Early 20th Century Britain' (2023) 42(1) *Parliamentary History Special Issue: Passion, Politics and Parliament* 148.

campaigners were keen to point out that the right to vote would not confer the right to stand. The veteran suffragist Emily Davies wrote to *The Times* in 1907 to point out that 'Many of the advocates of women's suffrage are decidedly opposed [to women MPs] … the question of women in Parliament is not practical politics.'[9] It seems likely that some suffrage campaigners may have privately supported women MPs, but not publicly; as Davies said, it was not practical politics.

Meanwhile in local government, women were successfully elected to many roles throughout the nineteenth century, including as Poor Law Guardians after 1834, to School Boards from 1870, and to urban and rural district councils from 1894. Following challenges to Lady Sandhurst and Jane Cobden's election to the London County Council in 1889,[10] campaigning by the Women's Local Government Society eventually ensured that women were allowed to stand for borough and county councils from 1907.[11] National politics was now the last challenge.

The Representation of the People Act, passed on 6 February 1918, gave the vote to women over the age of 30 who met minimum property qualifications, but it was silent on the right to stand for election.[12] As soon as the Act was passed, however, the Women's Freedom League (WFL) began discussing running or supporting women parliamentary candidates at its conference on 23–24 February. Political parties also began to explore the idea, with Violet Markham asked to stand by Liberals in Mansfield (formerly her brother's seat) as early as 28 February.[13]

Nina Boyle, a WFL member and one of the founders of the Women Police Volunteers during the war, put herself forward as a test case. She sought nomination for Keighley in a by-election in April 1918, prepared to fight any refusal in the courts. Her nomination was refused on a technicality; she presented two nomination papers, but one was signed by someone who was not an elector and the other by someone outside the constituency. The Deputy Returning Officer confirmed he would have accepted her nomination otherwise. Boyle claimed a moral triumph and did not try to stand again.[14]

The principle apparently having been established, Labour adopted Mary Macarthur as the prospective candidate for Stourbridge in May, making her

[9] *The Times* (4 February 1907). Davies, founder of Girton College, Cambridge, was a prominent campaigner for women in higher education.

[10] Sandhurst's election was overturned, and Cobden was barred from voting.

[11] Patricia Hollis, *Ladies Elect: Women in English Local Government, 1865–1914* (Clarendon Press, 1987).

[12] See Mari Takayanagi, 'Representation of the People Act 1918' in Rackley and Auchmuty (eds) (n 5) 113.

[13] Violet Markham, *Duty and citizenship: the correspondence and political papers of Violet Markham 1896–1953*, ed Helen Jones (Historians Press, 1994) 94. Previously an anti-suffragist, Markham later became one of two women to sit on the Industrial Court (see '**Industrial Courts Act 1919**').

[14] Cicely Hamilton, 'Nina Boyle' [1944], Pamphlet, The Women's Library, LSE.

the first woman to be officially selected by a political party.[15] Other women also began to be added to party lists of prospective candidates, and non-party feminist organisations planned how to support independent candidates. However, in the absence of explicit legislation, it remained the case that the decision to accept their nominations was potentially in the hands of hundreds of individual Returning Officers across the country at the next general election – a recipe for chaos.

Questions were asked and the Government sought legal advice. In June 1918, it was announced that the Labour Party would bring in a Bill to give women the right to stand, but the WFL reported on 2 August that Labour had decided this was not possible and only the Government could bring in such a bill.[16] On 8 August, the last day Parliament sat before adjourning for the summer, the legal advice was announced in the House of Commons by Andrew Bonar Law, Chancellor of the Exchequer: 'In the unanimous opinion of the Law Officers of England, Scotland, and Ireland a woman is not entitled to be a candidate for Parliament.' When prompted as to why, he said 'I have seen their decision, and, as usual, they were wise enough not to give their reasons'.[17]

Legislation was now clearly required. However, there was no opportunity for immediate action; Parliament promptly adjourned and did not return until 15 October. The War Cabinet's discussions on 14 October 1918 included the eligibility of women to sit in the House of Commons as the last item on its agenda for the day, but it was decided 'to leave the question to the decision of the House of Commons'.[18]

II. The Landmark

On 23 October 1918, the backbench Liberal MP Herbert Samuel introduced a resolution in the House of Commons, which read:

> That in the opinion of this House, it is desirable that a Bill be passed forthwith making women eligible as Members of Parliament.

Samuel reflected later in his memoirs that he regretted not having actively supported women's suffrage earlier, and remarked '[p]erhaps it was a feeling that I ought to make some amends that led me to take the initiative in Parliament in promoting legislation to make women eligible to the House of Commons'.[19] As well as the practical argument about Returning Officers, Samuel argued that this

[15] *The Times* (13 May 1918).
[16] *The Vote* (2 August 1918).
[17] HC Deb 8 August 1918, vol 109, cols 1534–35.
[18] TNA, CAB 23/8, 30.
[19] Herbert Louis Samuel, *Memoirs* (Cresset Press, 1945) 129–30.

was a logical consequence of the passage of the Representation of the People Act that women would make the House more representative and make a distinctive contribution to Parliament, and that they had proved themselves in local government roles.

There was still some die-hard opposition in the Commons, with MPs willing to argue that it was too soon after the Representation of the People Act, that militant suffragettes would be elected, and that the culture of the House of Commons, with its late sittings and packed benches, was not suitable for women. However, there were also prominent conversions, with well-known anti-suffrage MPs, including former Prime Minister Herbert Asquith, Charles Hobhouse and Arnold Ward (son of anti-suffrage leader Mrs Humphrey Ward) now speaking in support of women MPs.[20] Such MPs accepted it as the logical next step from suffrage; as Asquith said, 'You have the camel; you ought not to strain at the gnat.'[21]

Samuel's resolution was passed on a division overwhelmingly, with 274 votes to just 25. Parliamentary time was now very short, and the Government finally swung into action. Lord Robert Cecil, a Foreign Office Minister and long-time supporter of women in the legal profession, introduced a Bill that passed its second reading on 4 November 1918. The Act was very short, providing 'A woman shall not be disqualified by sex or marriage for being elected to or sitting or voting as a Member of the Commons House of Parliament.'[22]

Cecil's Bill deliberately did not introduce any restriction as to the age of women MPs, thus leading to the curious anomaly that women were allowed to stand at the same age as men – 21 – but could not vote until they were 30. There were attempts at committee stage to amend the Bill to change the age to 30, which did not pass. Cecil and Samuel argued there was no need; that men's being able to stand had never been linked to their ability to vote, and Samuel remarked that he himself had been a parliamentary candidate for some years before he was able to vote.[23] This is a useful reminder that before the Representation of the People Act 1918 was passed, approximately 40 per cent of men were unable to vote, as well as all women, and younger men in particular found it difficult to fulfil the registration requirements.[24]

The Bill passed swiftly through the Commons and Lords, and achieved Royal Assent on the last day of the parliamentary session, 21 November 1918 – just in time for the general election.

[20] Mari Takayanagi, '"One of the most revolutionary proposals that has ever been put before the House": the passage of the Parliament (Qualification of Women) Act 1918' in Lucy Bland and Richard Carr (eds), *Labour, British Radicalism and the First World War* (Manchester University Press, 2018) 56–72.

[21] HC Deb 23 October 1918, vol 110, col 839.

[22] Parliament (Qualification of Women) Act 1918, 8&9 Geo V ch 47, s 1.

[23] HC Deb 23 October 1918, vol 110, col 821.

[24] Neal Blewitt, 'The franchise in the United Kingdom, 1885–1918' (1965) 32(1) *Past and Present* 27; Duncan Tanner, *Political Change and the Labour Party 1900–1918* (Cambridge University Press, 1990).

III. What Happened Next

Although women formally had only 23 days to prepare for the election, a small number had already been selected by parties or been preparing individually for months. Sixteen nominations for women candidates were received by the 4 December deadline: four Labour, four Liberal, two Sinn Féin, one Women's Party (suffragette leader Christabel Pankhurst) and five independents. A seventeenth candidate, Alice Theresa Lucas (Conservative), was adopted later in a delayed poll after the death of her husband.[25]

At the general election on 14 December 1918, one woman was elected: **Constance Markievicz** in Dublin St Patricks, who did not take her seat. Of the rest, Pankhurst was the only woman with a 'coupon', the official letter of support from the Coalition Government, and came closest to success, achieving 47.8 per cent of the vote in Smethwick.[26] The next best performance was from Mary Macarthur, polling 32.7 per cent in Stourbridge. Her local popularity and name recognition may have been adversely affected after the Returning Officer insisted she stand under her married name of Mary Anderson.

A total of 29 women were elected in general elections and by-elections between 1918 and 1944. Numbers fluctuated, but the maximum in the House of Commons at any one time in this period was 16 (2.6 per cent of the total 615 MPs), for a few months in 1931.[27] Conservative **Nancy Astor** became the first woman MP to take her seat at Westminster, following a by-election in Plymouth Sutton in November 1919. The first Liberal woman MP was Margaret Wintringham, elected in a by-election in Louth, Lincolnshire, in 1921. The first three Labour women were elected in the general election of December 1923 – Dorothy Jewson, Susan Lawrence and **Margaret Bondfield**.

Before the passage of the **Equal Franchise Act 1928**, a number of women stood for election who were aged under 30 and therefore themselves too young to vote, meaning they could not cast a vote for themselves. Examples include Ursula Williams (Liberal), who stood in Consett, County Durham, in 1923 aged 27; Irene Ward (Conservative), who stood in Morpeth in 1924 aged 29; and Jennie Lee (Labour), elected in North Lanarkshire in 1929 before the Equal Franchise Act came into force, aged 24. Furthermore, at least one woman (Ellen Wilkinson)

[25] Mari Takayanagi, 'Lucas [née Stern], Alice Theresa (1853–1924), parliamentary candidate', *Oxford Dictionary of National Biography* (9 August 2018).

[26] Nicoletta F Gullace, 'Christabel Pankhurst and the Smethwick Election: right-wing feminism, the Great War and the ideology of consumption' (2014) 23(3) *Women's History Review* 330; June Purvis, 'The Women's Party of Great Britain (1917–1919): a forgotten episode in British women's political history' (2016) 25(4) *Women's History Review* 638.

[27] Nancy Astor, the Duchess of Atholl, Margaret Bondfield, Ellen Wilkinson, Susan Lawrence, the Countess of Iveagh, Jennie Lee, Ethel Bentham, Mary Agnes Hamilton, Megan Lloyd George, Cynthia Mosley, Marion Phillips, Edith Picton Turbervill, Eleanor Rathbone, Lucy Noel-Buxton and Leah Manning all sat between February and October 1931.

stood and was elected when she was over 30 but did not meet the minimum property qualification to vote.[28]

The numbers of women MPs continued to grow slowly after 1945 but remained small, as women found it difficult to be selected by the major political parties in winnable seats. A breakthrough took place at the 1997 general election, with 120 women (18 per cent of the total) elected; the result of the Labour party's adoption of all-women shortlists.[29]

After women were able to sit in the House of Commons, the attention of feminist campaigners moved to the right to sit in the House of Lords, with **Lady Rhondda's Petition in 1922,** and to increasing the numbers of women MPs. Specific campaigning groups encouraging women to stand and the adoption of female candidates include the 'Women for Westminster' group in the 1940s, Lesley Abdela's 'The 300 Group' in the 1980s and '50:50 Parliament' founded by Frances Scott in 2013.

IV. Significance

As of March 2023, there were 225 female MPs (31 per cent), the highest total in history. A total of 561 different women have been elected to the House of Commons; 55 per cent were first elected as Labour MPs and 31 per cent as Conservatives. Also as of March 2023, there were seven female Cabinet Ministers (30 per cent); the highest proportion of women in Cabinet was 36 per cent between 2006 and 2007. At the last general election in 2019, there were 1,123 female candidates, the highest number and proportion on record (33.8 per cent of all candidates).[30]

These figures show that although progress has been made, the UK is still some way away from having a 50:50 Parliament.[31] Feminist organisations argue that this matters, because Parliament should be representative of the UK population, that it should draw upon the widest possible pool of talent, and that diverse and inclusive bodies are more resilient and make better decisions.

In 2010, the Inter-Parliamentary Union introduced the concept of Gender Sensitive Parliaments (GSPs). These are founded on gender equality, where women and men have an equal right to participate without discrimination or

[28] HC Deb 29 March 1928, vol 215, col 1405.

[29] See Susan Atkins, 'Sex Discrimination (Election Candidates) Act 2002' in Rackley and Auchmuty (eds) (n 5) 511.

[30] House of Commons Library research briefing, *Women in politics and public life*, Standard Note 1250, March 2023, at https://researchbriefings.files.parliament.uk/documents/SN01250/SN01250.pdf.

[31] As of October 2023, Rwanda, Cuba, Nicaragua, Andorra, Mexico, New Zealand and the United Arab Emirates had 50% or more women in their lower House: see at https://data.ipu.org/women-ranking.

recrimination. Such Parliaments ought to be places that meet the requirements of both women and men in the way they are run and structured, and where women want to work; family-friendly environments, where sexist language or behaviour is not tolerated.[32] In 2016, Sarah Childs' report *The Good Parliament* made 43 recommendations as to how to make the House of Commons more gender-sensitive.[33] The House of Commons set up a Women and Equalities Select Committee in 2015, following cross-party demands by women MPs. It was initially temporary but became permanent in 2017.[34] In 2022, the Committee published a report that found that 18 of the 43 recommendations in *The Good Parliament* had been implemented, and which highlighted the need for further reform in various areas, including encouraging parties to select diverse candidates; addressing online abuse; support for MPs who are parents, carers, disabled or who have long-term health conditions; a gender- and diversity-sensitive working environment; and addressing bullying, harassment and sexual misconduct.[35]

Ultimately, however, the major political parties need to select more female candidates in winnable seats if the number of women MPs is to increase. Organisations such as the Fawcett Society and the Electoral Reform Society have pointed to the first-past-the-post electoral system as a barrier to this, as it effectively reserves seats to (usually male) incumbents. The UN Economic and Social Council has pointed to gender quota legislation as the main policy intervention that has improved women's participation in national and local decision-making.[36] While quotas remain voluntary, party organisations such as the Labour Women's Network and the Conservative party's Women2Win use other methods in encouraging female candidates, including mentoring, skills training and networking.

Further Reading

- Lisa Berry-Waite, '"A rancour and a passion would be introduced into politics": Perceptions of the Woman MP in Late 19th and Early 20th Century Britain' (2023) 42(1) *Parliamentary History Special Issue: Passion, Politics and Parliament* 148.

[32] Inter-Parliament Union 'Gender-sensitive parliaments' at www.ipu.org/impact/gender-equality/gender-sensitive-parliaments [accessed 13 September 2023].

[33] Sarah Childs, *The Good Parliament* (University of Bristol, 2016).

[34] Sarah Childs, 'Feminist Institutional Change: The Case of the UK Women and Equalities Committee' (2023) 76(3) *Parliamentary Affairs* 507.

[35] House of Commons Women and Equalities Committee, *Equality in the heart of democracy: A gender sensitive House of Commons*. Fifth Report of Session 2021–22, HC 131 (2022).

[36] House of Lords Library in Focus, 'Global gender equality in political life' (March 2021) at https://lordslibrary.parliament.uk/global-gender-equality-in-political-life/.

- Sarah Childs, *The Good Parliament* (University of Bristol, 2016).
- Mari Takayanagi, '"One of the most revolutionary proposals that has ever been put before the House": the passage of the Parliament (Qualification of Women) Act 1918' in Lucy Bland and Richard Carr (eds), *Labour, British Radicalism and the First World War* (Manchester University Press, 2018) 56.

3

Constance Georgine Markievicz, First Woman Elected to Parliament, 1918

AOIFE O'DONOGHUE

Constance Georgine Markievicz, often referred to as Countess Markievicz, was, in 1918, the first woman elected to the House of Commons. A feminist, socialist revolutionary and suffrage campaigner, she was also a leader of the Irish independence movement, politically, culturally and militarily, and a member of the first Irish Executive, as Minister for Labour, set up in Dublin during the War of Independence (1919–22). She was the second woman to hold a cabinet-level position in Europe.[1]

I. Life

Constance Markievicz was born in 1868 into the Anglo-Irish Gore-Booth family. Growing up in County Sligo on the west coast of Ireland, she and her younger sister, the suffragist and poet Eva Gore-Booth, were from an early age embedded in political, socialist and cultural debates, particularly as regards women's rights. In the 1890s she also moved to Paris and trained as an artist.[2] Here she met and married Casimir Markievicz, a Polish Count. They had one child together.

On moving to Dublin, she became engaged in the city's cultural revival, co-founding the United Arts Club. She also became involved with the Gaelic League, a body dedicated to preserving and promoting the Irish language. She then came into contact with other Irish revolutionary figures, and from 1908 became involved in Irish politics, joining and becoming a leading member of both Sinn Féin and Inghinidhe na hÉireann, a revolutionary women's movement founded by Maud Gonne. In this period, she was also involved with the suffrage movement, campaigning with her sister Eva Gore-Booth and Esther Roper to prevent Winston

[1] Yevgenia Bosch, the first, was appointed Minister of the Interior of Ukraine in 1918.

[2] Senia Paseta, 'Markievicz, Constance Georgine', *The Dictionary of Irish Biography* (Cambridge University Press, 2009).

Churchill's election at the Manchester North West by-election in 1908. In 1909, Markievicz founded Fianna Éireann, a nationalist boy scouting organisation. At its inaugural meeting, she was almost expelled, as some of those who joined her to establish the body felt that women should not be involved in physical-force activism. She rejected this view, arguing across her work that nationalism and feminism were equal, and that it was incumbent on women to get involved across all the nationalist organisations.[3] She was first arrested in 1911 for speaking in a protest at the visit of George V to Ireland.

In 1913, Markievicz joined the Irish Citizen Army, a volunteer force led by James Connolly that offered support to those affected by the 1913 Dublin Lock-out. As a member of the Irish Citizen Army, she took part in the 1916 Rising, fighting as second in command in St Stephen's Green. She was arrested and, like other leaders of the Rising, sentenced to death, but the sentence was commuted because she was a woman. She was transferred first to Holloway and then to Aylesbury Prison, and was released in 1917.

In 1918 she was arrested again for her part in anti-conscription activities, and it was during this imprisonment that she was elected to the constituency of Dublin St Patrick's, achieving nearly 66 per cent of the vote and becoming the only one of 17 women candidates across the UK and Ireland to be elected. Ironically, Sinn Féin, which was leading an open rebellion and running a parallel state, was concerned about the legality of running women candidates, though apparently far less concerned with the multitude of other highly illegal activities it was undertaking. The **Parliament (Qualification of Women) Act**, passed in November 1918, allowed women to stand, with Markievicz's potential disqualifications on grounds of nationality and conviction for treason overlooked. While Kathleen Clarke and Hannah Sheehy Skeffington were also offered seats by Sinn Féin, only Winifred Carney, who was also part of the Labour movement and active in the 1916 Rebellion, ran in Belfast, polling just over 4 per cent. The seats offered were almost impossible to win for any Sinn Féin candidate, but even more so for a woman.[4] Sinn Féin abstentionist policy, under which its MPs did not take their seats in Westminster as they did not recognise the authority of the British Parliament, meant that Constance Markievicz did not take her seat. Markievicz was in prison during the first meeting of the Dáil but was nonetheless named as Minister for Labour in the Cabinet, though only after persuasion that she had earned the same right as the men to be Minister.[5]

Markievicz left government in 1922 in opposition to the Anglo-Irish Treaty that ended the War of Independence, taking the anti-Treaty side during the Civil War, because she argued the Treaty failed both the republicanism and socialism of the 1916 Rising. In a speech to the Dáil she argued:

[3] Margaret Ward, *Unmanageable Revolutionaries: Women and Irish Nationalism* (Pluto, 1983).

[4] Maryann Giananella Valiulis, *The Making of Inequality: Women, Power and Gender Ideology* (Four Courts Press, 2019) 36–37.

[5] ibid 37.

> But looking as I do for the prosperity of the many, for the happiness and content of the workers … The Free State … to be set up to uphold English interests in Ireland, to uphold the capitalists' interests in Ireland, to block every ideal that the nation may wish to formulate; to block the teaching of Irish, to block the education of the poorer classes; to block, in fact, every bit of progress that every man and woman in Ireland today amongst working people desire to see put into force.[6]

She was returned to the Dáil in 1923 but did not take her seat and was arrested by Irish authorities in 1923, going on hunger strike before being released. She joined Fianna Fáil on its creation and was re-elected to the Dáil but died a short time after in 1927. By the time of her death, she had given away her entire wealth. She did not receive a state funeral. In his funeral oration, Eamon de Valera recast her as a philanthropist, and in the process, Maryann Giananella Valiulis notes, 'The complexity, the commitment, and vibrancy of her life, the multiplicity of her activities, were all denied. Constance Markievicz was flattened out, reduced, made to confirm to an imaginary non-threatening ideal.'[7]

II. Context

Markievicz was born into the Irish Protestant Ascendancy class. The Ascendancy comprised an elite group of Church of Ireland landowners, clergy and members of the professions, who monopolised political and legal power in Ireland from the seventeenth century to the early twentieth century.[8] The Gore-Booths were landowners, although recognised as sympathetic to their tenants. Growing up in relative luxury, Markievicz could well have followed a path of ease. Nonetheless, it is unsurprising that she followed a feminist, political, socialist and revolutionary path: many Irish women of her generation also took similar routes, seeking to create a different UK and, for those of a nationalist belief, an independent Ireland, where gender equality would be entrenched.[9] As is observable in Markievicz's activities, there was no sphere where women were absent in what would lead to the first break-up of the UK, just 100 years after the Acts of Union and, as part of that process, the election of the first woman to Westminster.

During the period of Markievicz's extensive political activities, women across Ireland were achieving several UK-wide legal firsts. Letitia Alice Walkington was

[6] Constance Markievicz, Dáil Debates 3 January 1922, vol T, no 103.

[7] Valiulis, n 4, 142.

[8] This was formalised in legislation, including An Act to restrain Foreign Education, 1695 7 Will 3 c 4; An Act for banishing all Papists exercising any Ecclesiastical Jurisdiction, and all Regulars of the Popish Clergy out of this Kingdom, 1697 9 Will 3 c 1; An Act for registering the Popish Clergy Citation, 1704, 2 Ann c 7; Disfranchising Act 1728 1 Geo 2 c 9; An Act for the Relief of His Majesty's Roman Catholic Subjects 10 Geo 4 c 7; Acts of Union 1801, 39 & 40 Geo 3 c 67.

[9] Karen Steele, 'Constance Markievicz's allegorical garden: Femininity, militancy, and the press, 1909–1915' (2000) 29 *Women's Studies: An Interdisciplinary Journal* 423, 424.

the UK's first female law graduate in 1888 from the Royal University of Ireland.[10] Frances Kyle and Averill Deverell were the first female barristers in 1921.[11] Georgina Frost was the first woman to hold public office in the UK in 1920.[12] Women were also making contributions to legal scholarship, including Sophie Bryant, who alongside other major contributions across education and science, wrote extensively about the Brehon Law and early Irish governance systems.[13] During the War of Independence, many women acted as judges within the parallel Dáil Courts.[14]

As a member of the non-militant National Union of Women's Suffrage Societies, alongside her sister Eva Gore-Booth and Eva's partner Esther Roper, Markievicz was also part of a generation of women across the UK placing themselves into the public sphere as active political agents, but who also saw themselves as part of a broader coalition of women across class and political perspectives, on both islands. From Markievicz's perspective, it was only amongst the suffrage campaigners that the spirit of ancient warrior women was alive and leading the resistance against attempts by men to civilise such spirit out of women.[15] She maintained close contact with her sister throughout her life, albeit they would come fundamentally to disagree about the use of physical force to achieve political ends. Markievicz would suggest to students in 1909 that each should 'pause before she joined a Suffrage Society or Franchise League that did not include in their programme the Freedom of their Nation'.[16]

Since the famine of the 1840s, political change had occurred quickly in Ireland. The Irish Land League led to the transfer of land ownership away from the Ascendancy and the politicisation of rural Ireland. The Home Rule crisis, which brought down several UK Governments and helped lead to the end of the House of Lords' veto over the Commons, further politicised rural and urban Ireland, including the stark divide between Unionist and Nationalist positions and the move towards physical-force nationalism and unionism.[17] The Home Rule crisis would also cause a split amongst feminists, between those who supported Home Rule and those who wanted complete independence, albeit this split lessened after

[10] Ivana Bacik, Cathryn Costello and Eileen Drew, *Gender InJustice: Feminising the Legal Professions?* (Trinity College Dublin, 2003) 53.

[11] Liz Goldthorpe, 'First Woman to Practise as a Barrister in Ireland and the (then) United Kingdom, Averil Deverell' in Erika Rackley and Rosemary Auchmuty (eds), *Women's Legal Landmarks: Celebrating the History of Women and Law in the UK and Ireland* (Hart Publishing, 2019) 175.

[12] *Frost v Rex* (1919) IR 84; Ronan Keane, 'Frost, Georgina [Georgie] (1879–1939)', *Oxford Dictionary of National Biography* (23 September 2004).

[13] Sophie Bryant, *Liberty, order [and] law under native Irish rule: a study in the book of the ancient laws of Ireland* (Harding, 1923).

[14] Dorothy Macardle, *The Irish Republic: A Documented Chronicle of the Anglo-Irish Conflict and the Partitioning of Ireland, with a Detailed Account of the Period 1916–1923* (Corgi Books, 1937).

[15] Steele, n 9, 423, 439.

[16] Constance Markievicz, 'Address to the Student's National Literary Society' 1909' in Sonja Tiernan (ed), *Irish Women's Speeches* (UCD Press, 2021) 32.

[17] Jeremy Smith, *Britain and Ireland: From Home Rule to Independence* (Taylor & Francis, 2014).

the 1916 Rising.[18] Poverty, both rural and urban, was rife, with Europe's second worst slums in Dublin. In that context, the rise of socialism in Ireland, particularly in urban Dublin, is unsurprising. The Dublin Lock-out of 1913, which involved about 20,000 workers and 300 employers, during which Markievicz joined the Irish Citizen Army and began organising with its Marxist founder James Connolly, further politicised the urban population. The Cultural and Gaelic Revival, of which Markievicz was also a figure, led the way in seeking to create and revitalise Irish culture.

The 1916 Irish Proclamation promised gender equality, and while written by James Connolly and Padraig Pearse, it was under the influence of women like Constance Markievicz. For many nationalist women, an independent Ireland was tied to ideas of gender equality.[19] That she was put directly into the first Dáil Cabinet as a Minister is testament to her place as a leader of Irish independence, but also of the steadfast belief of women of the period of their rightful place as active political agents in both forming and running a new state.

III. What Happened Next

Constance Markievicz changed the role of women in politics in both the UK and Ireland. Though her place in the pantheon is often downplayed, her accomplishments downgraded, or typical misogynist tropes used to make her more a joke than a substantive political actor, she remains a central figure of Irish feminism. The Ireland that Constance Markievicz and the other women of the period thought they were fighting for did not arrive in its entirety until nearly 100 years later. Nevertheless, many women continued to battle to return to the promises made to them in the 1916 Proclamation, despite vigorous attempts both after 1922 and under the 1937 Constitution to remove women from the public sphere. They continued to argue and fight, and they were successful. It is likely that had Constance Markievicz lived, she would have had a place in the Cabinet of Eamonn de Valera when he finally came to power in 1937. This would have less to do with de Valera's belief in women's right to be constituted power holders and more to do with the force of personality that Constance Markievicz had. It would have been impossible to exclude her.

Women were returned to the House of Commons in every election after Constance Markievicz, with **Nancy Astor** the next woman elected while **Margaret Bondfield** became the first woman to hold a cabinet position in the Labour Government in 1929. When Bernadette Devlin, another feminist socialist nationalist Irish woman, was elected to the House of Commons in 1969 as the then youngest woman elected, she declared it to be in the same tradition as Constance

[18] Beth McKillen, 'Irish Feminism and Nationalist Separatism, 1914–23' (1982) 17 *Éire-Ireland* 52.
[19] Valiulis, n 4, 16.

Markievicz.[20] Women MPs were also consistently returned to the House of Commons of the Northern Ireland Parliament during its existence between 1921 and 1972.

Women were also always returned to Dáil Eireann, with six women in the second Dáil in 1919, though not exceeding 10 until 1981. Women were always represented in Seanad Éireann too, the Oireachtas' upper house. However, it would not be until 1979, and Máire Geoghegan-Quinn, that a woman would once again be seen in an Irish Cabinet. This gap represents both the highpoint of women's political activity during the War of Independence and failure to fulfil the promises of the period. Women of that generation continued to protest and lead, inspiring new generations to break down the ultra-conservativism of the post-independence period.[21]

IV. Significance

Writing about Constance Markievicz is an important process of (re)knowing feminist history. She was an unruly, brash and pugnacious woman who proudly extolled her feminism, socialism and revolutionary zeal. She was an uncomfortable fit for both the establishment in the UK and Ireland, and, for different reasons, she did not fit the mould of the histories they wished to tell.

As with many other women, there has been a tendency to downplay or trivialise her accomplishments, her militancy, her socialism and her unwillingness to accept any compromise on women's role in society. De Valera's focus on her philanthropy, as opposed to her socialism and her role as a rebel, at her funeral, is just one example. Within Irish historical accounts her militancy, her voice and her passion were often mocked, and her accomplishments downgraded and attributed to the men around her, a common process of eradicating women from history.[22] Heroic status is attributed to men, whereas 'the political authority of women' is expunged.[23] Within UK historical accounts, her militant nationalism and her rejection of UK imperialism and constitutionalism made her an uncomfortable fit in any progressive account of history. She may be listed as a first, but the full extent of her political life is rarely extolled as positive or as a role model for other women.

But in this way, she was also a comfort for generations of women who were seeking to create the feminist world she and other women fought for and were

[20] Bernadette Devlin, 'I stand here as the youngest woman in Parliament, in the same tradition as the first woman ever to be elected to this Parliament, Constance Markievicz, who was elected on behalf of the Irish people' (HC Deb 22 April 1969, vol 782, col 281).

[21] Roy Foster, *Vivid Faces: The Revolutionary Generation 1890–1923* (Allen Lane, 2014) 315–17.

[22] Steele, n 9, 423, 242.

[23] Amy Benton, 'Woman Disarmed: The Militarization of Politics in Ireland 1913–1923' (1995) 50 *Feminist Review* 148, 155.

promised, and who also would be accused of similar shrillness, triviality and emotionality. Her existence, and in particular her election to Westminster, meant she could not be entirely written out of either state's history; rather, across the range of her activities, she remained an inspiration and touchstone.

Further Reading

- Lindie Naughton, *Markievicz: Prison Letters & Rebel Writings* (Merrion Press, 2018).
- Senia Paseta, 'Markievicz, Constance Georgine', *The Dictionary of Irish Biography* (Cambridge University Press, 2009).
- Margaret Ward, *Unmanageable Revolutionaries: Women and Irish Nationalism* (Pluto, 1983).

4

Nancy Astor, First Woman to Take Her Seat in the UK Parliament, 1919

JACQUI TURNER

On 1 December 1919, Nancy Astor became the first woman MP to take her seat in the House of Commons. Hers was the first female voice heard in the chamber as an MP; she was the first woman MP to ask a question, speak in a parliamentary debate and deliver a maiden speech, to sit on a parliamentary committee and to introduce a Private Member's Bill that resulted in the enactment of the **Intoxicating Liquor (Sale to Persons under Eighteen) Act 1923**. She was also instrumental in the passage of the **Representation of the People (Equal Franchise) Act 1928** that granted equal voting rights to women and men at the age of 21. However, her enduring significance was secured the moment she swore the oath.

I. Life

Writing in her autobiography, Astor (née Nancy Witcher Langhorne) stated that in 1897, 'I was born in Danville Virginia and had three brothers and four sisters, all of whom I adored.'[1] It was a secure and happy childhood, a typical American middle-class upbringing. She had a limited early education 'of a perfunctory kind,[2] and opportunities for more formal education were limited as her father 'did not believe in education for women'.[3] In 1897, she married Robert Gould Shaw II, and the following year their son Bobby was born. However, after several difficult years, fuelled by Shaw's alcoholism, they were divorced in 1903, leaving Nancy Astor with a long-standing aversion to alcohol. Nancy met Waldorf Astor on a transatlantic

[1] Nancy Astor, Draft of Autobiography (unfinished) 1951 (University of Reading [UoR], MS 1416/1/6/86).
[2] ibid.
[3] ibid.

voyage to England for the hunting season of 1905. They married in 1906, settling at Cliveden, Buckinghamshire.[4]

In 1910, Waldorf Astor was elected to Parliament as MP for Plymouth Sutton. If the experience of her first marriage to Shaw was the foundation of her loathing for alcohol, her work in Plymouth supporting her husband reinforced her conviction that the dire consequences of poverty and misery resulted from drink. It was also endorsed by her commitment to Christian Science and the belief in health through prayer; her faith had a profound impact on her personally, and thus on her political life.

When her husband was elevated to the House of Lords on the death of his father,[5] Nancy Astor was an unexpected replacement for him as the sitting Conservative and Unionist MP for Plymouth Sutton. For the party, she was an acceptable candidate because of her proximity to her husband and her popularity in the constituency. On 28 November 1919, she was elected by a landslide, securing more votes than the Liberal and Labour candidates combined. She subsequently won seven elections between 1919 and 1945 before retiring from Parliament. The longevity of Astor's tenure as an MP was a huge achievement that far outstripped many of her contemporaries. She was replaced by a woman MP, Lucy Middleton (Labour 1945–51).

Nancy Astor died at Grimsthorpe Castle, Lincolnshire on 2 May 1964.

II. Context

The 1920s heralded the end of more than 60 years of campaigning for the women's vote and the arrival of the first women MPs. The Representation of the People Act 1918 had delivered the vote to some women aged over 30 with certain property qualifications and virtually all men aged 21.[6] Hot on its heels came one of the shortest Acts in British political history, the **Parliament (Qualification of Women) Act 1918**, hurriedly passed and simply stating that 'A woman shall not be disqualified by sex or marriage for being elected to or sitting or voting as a Member of the Commons House of Parliament.'[7] Despite the age restriction on women's voting, there was no such restriction for women MPs, creating

[4] The couple went on to have five children: Bill (William), Nancy, Francis, Michael and Jakie (John). Bill, Michael and Jakie would follow her path into the House of Commons.

[5] Inheriting a peerage meant that Waldorf Astor automatically became a member of the House of Lords, making him ineligible also to sit in the House of Commons.

[6] Representation of the People Act 1918 (Parliamentary Archives, HL/PO/PU/1/1918/7&8G5c64). See also Mari Takayanagi, 'Representation of the People Act 1918' in Erika Rackley and Rosemary Auchmuty (eds), *Women's Legal Landmarks: Celebrating the History of Women and Law in the UK and Ireland* (Hart Publishing, 2019) 113.

[7] Parliament (Qualification of Women) Act 1918 (Parliamentary Archives, HL/PO/PU/1/1918/8& 9G5c47).

an interesting anomaly that women could be elected to Parliament but were themselves unable to vote.[8]

The general election of 14 December 1918 was the first in which some women could vote and all women could stand for election. With just six weeks to campaign, 17 women stood as candidates, including the former suffragette leader Christabel Pankhurst.[9] Of these women, four were Liberal, four Labour and one Conservative, plus two Sinn Féin and six independent female candidates. Just one woman was successful. **Constance Markievicz** was the first and only woman elected to the Westminster Parliament. She was in Holloway prison at the time, and as a member of Sinn Féin refused to take the oath, so did not take her seat. Almost a year later, Astor was elected as a Coalition Conservative at a carefully controlled by-election in Plymouth Sutton.

Suffrage campaigners were initially dismayed that the first woman MP was not a candidate from the women's movement. Astor's entry into politics had nothing to do with feminism or suffrage. In fact, of the 36 women who became MPs between the Wars, none had a suffragette pedigree, though some had been associated with the suffragist movement. Nonetheless, throughout the 1920s, Astor made efforts to work with other women, regardless of party affiliation, in particular on equal franchise in the 1920s, women police and access to the professions, education and nursery provision alongside her activity on the Woman Power Committee arguing for support and equal pay for working mothers during the Second World War. She could have avoided women's issues, as some among the first generation of women MPs did, but chose not to. Indeed, in her first contribution to Parliament, supporting an amendment from Major Jack Hills seeking to eliminate sex discrimination in the composition of the Governor's Legislative Councils, she noted that women's partial franchise in the UK had been granted 'only after enormous pressure from the ladies'.[10]

When reflecting on her career, Astor claimed that she had been 'as good a feminist as anyone'[11] and had a special responsibility to women and children, understanding their needs and ambitions in a way that men never could. She often expressed the view that women were more suited to public life, had 'moral courage' and were 'not so easily flattered'.[12] She had an active and vociferous commitment to achieving the equal franchise for women, acting as a conduit for suffrage organisations, and was instrumental in holding her party and Prime Minister Stanley Baldwin's Government to account for promises made regarding the equal franchise.

[8] This indeed happened with Jennie Lee, a Labour MP elected at by-election in North Lanarkshire in 1929 at the age of 24, before the **Representation of the People (Equal Franchise) Act 1928** came into force.

[9] Christabel Pankhurst was a candidate for the Women's Party (the post-war incarnation of the Women's Social and Political Union) in the new constituency of Smethwick. She was allocated a 'coupon' endorsed by the Lloyd George coalition, ensuring no coalition candidate stood against her.

[10] HC Deb 4 December 1919, vol 122, col 657.

[11] Nancy Astor Interview by Mary Stocks, *Woman's Hour*, BBC, 1956.

[12] Nancy Astor Interview (interviewer unknown), *Panorama*, BBC, 1959.

III. What Happened Next

As a Conservative MP, Astor was consistently overlooked by her party, and her political achievements have often since been overshadowed by the novelty of her sex and the circumstances of her election as the perceived 'proxy' or 'male-equivalent' of her husband.[13] In fact, while Astor had been active in supporting Waldorf Astor's political career, she did not have longstanding ambition to be a politician and openly declared that her 'husband put the idea in my head … and I should get out of it if he got rid of his peerage'.[14] However, despite some initial emphasis on continuity in her candidature, it was clear that she represented something new, even if the details of how that would unfold in practice were yet to be defined.

For Astor, on first entering Parliament she 'realized that I had ceased to be a person and had become a symbol'.[15] There was an expectation that her election would provide a blueprint for women to follow. Letters sent to Astor at the time of her election made it clear that she was 'no ordinary MP. You are a precedent'[16] and 'the ice of prejudice has been broken'.[17] Other local Conservative parties informed her '[w]e are today considering the question of adopting a woman as candidate … and your result will undoubtedly help us to overcome any prejudice on the part of the men'.[18] Likewise, women's groups recorded that there was a confidence that 'your success will give a great impetus to the nomination of other women candidates … and will encourage the electorate to vote for them'.[19] Such interpretations are in keeping with how Astor perceived herself. Speaking at the time, she stated that 'my hope is that I may pave the way for other women who aspire to enter the House of Commons'.[20]

Letters of congratulation following her by-election success and maiden speech suggest that those who saw her as a continuity candidate or proxy for the 'tried old firm of Astor and co'[21] were heavily outweighed by those urging her to be a champion for women and children, encouraging her to follow an independent philosophy that positioned her beyond party politics. In 1919, Millicent Fawcett, suffragist and leader of the National Union of Women's Suffrage Societies (NUWSS), credited Astor with reforming credentials – 'before she ever had the idea of entering Parliament, she took an active interest in improving the conditions

[13] Brian Harrison, *Prudent Revolutionaries: Portraits of British feminists between the Wars* (Clarendon, 1987) 79.

[14] Nancy Astor interview (interviewer unknown) BBC, 1945.

[15] Nancy Astor, *My Two Countries* (Heinemann, 1923) 3.

[16] Letter from Mrs Gould, NW3, 28 November 1919 (UoR MS 1416/1/1/1722).

[17] Letter from S Helen Wigg-Gilbert, 5 December 1919 (UoR MS 1416/1/1/1723).

[18] Letter from Deptford United Conservative and Unionist Association, 28 November 1919 (UoR MS 1416/1/1/1724).

[19] Letter from the Scottish Federation of Societies for Equal Citizenship, 11 December 1919 (UoR MS 1416/1/1/1724).

[20] Press cuttings, *Birmingham Post* (10 November 1919) (UoR MS 1416/1/6/31).

[21] Mabel Philipson, election address, 1923.

of working people'.[22] The hope and expectation that she would represent all women propelled her towards often underestimated causes, including social reform and temperance. This proved a natural space for Astor's reforming instinct, although her commitment to other issues, such as the equal franchise and the concerns of her naval constituency, should not be overlooked.

Whether she was forced into a female space by her party or chose it through her own commitment to the loyalty of the women of England who she believed supported her, Astor instinctively chose to champion the causes of women and children. With no political pedigree, she might never have been expected to find a place in the upper echelons of the Conservative party or gain high office anyway.[23] Nevertheless, as Clement Attlee noted, 'she made things hum'.[24] She supported legislation concerning women in the workplace and the safely of women out on the streets, she campaigned for nursery school provision, school nurses, and women's access to the Civil Service and judiciary alongside women police. By 1928, in the words of Ray Strachey, 'every bill had a women's side and the party Whips began eagerly to ask what the women thought'.[25] For Astor however, her position as a sex-candidate and the first female MP ultimately transcended any political allegiances.

Astor's parliamentary career was not without controversy, though she overcame many hurdles. She was strongly anti-Communist and initially supported appeasement, although her support for Churchill was unwavering by the outbreak of the Second World War. She was anti-Catholic and made anti-Semitic statements, although she called the accusation of anti-Semitism against her a 'terrible lie'.[26] She firmly believed that such criticisms were amplified in response to her sex.[27]

The second woman MP, Margaret Wintringham, a member of the Liberal Party, was elected at a by-election in 1921. Like Astor, she succeeded her husband, in her case after his death as sitting MP for Louth in Lincolnshire. Astor and Wintringham, who got on well and were mutually supportive, working together on many issues, both offer an ironic counterpoint to the pre-voting arguments of the anti-suffrage movement that women were adequately represented by their husbands. Candidates who were selected faced a 'political baptism of fire' and a maelstrom of press and public attention.[28] Public scrutiny of women's dress, deportment and conduct were often of far greater interest to the electorate and the press than their policies. All aspects of their lives were fair game.[29]

[22] 'An Historic Event – Mrs Henry Fawcett on the Advent of a Woman MP' *Daily Graphic* (29 November 1919) (UoR, MS 1416/1/7/33).

[23] Astor, n 11.

[24] Clement Attlee, *The Observer* (2 May 1964) 23.

[25] Ray Strachey, *The Cause: A Short History of the Women's Movements in Great Britain* (Kennikat, 1969) 367. Ray Strachey become Astor's parliamentary secretary in 1931.

[26] *Jewish Telegraph Agency* (24 March 1938).

[27] Lady Astor: propaganda against her, 1942–1943 (UoR MS 1416/1/1/1573).

[28] Cheryl Law, *Suffrage and Power: The Women's Movement 1918–1928* (Bloomsbury, 1997) 150.

[29] ibid.

By 1923, the election of Astor, Wintringham and Mabel Philipson (Conservative)[30] was having a profound effect on the Labour party. Women had been able to join the party on equal terms to men since its inception, and in 1918 the Labour general election manifesto announced 'The Labour party *is* the woman's party'.[31] However, Labour had not succeeded in establishing a woman in Parliament and was pushed into reconsidering its approach to provide women with safe seats with strong grass roots, avoiding marginal constituencies. Eight more female MPs, including the first Labour women MPs, **Margaret Bondfield**, Susan Lawrence and Dorothy Jewson, were elected in 1923. But the number of women candidates remained tiny throughout the interwar period. In interwar elections, the number of women MPs peaked at 15 at the 1931 general election,[32] supporting Edith Summerskill MP's recollection that 'Parliament, with its conventions and protocol, seemed a little like a boys' school which had decided to take a few girls'.[33]

IV. Significance

Nancy Astor's election to the British Parliament, becoming the first woman to take her seat, changed British democracy forever. For the first time, a woman was able to be heard in the chamber of the House of Commons, directly influencing the parliamentary debate and the writing of the laws of her own country. She won seven elections between 1919 and 1945 before retiring from Parliament. Her subsequent electoral successes and longevity as an MP ran counter to the narrative that women MPs were merely a novelty.

Astor's appeal as 'a threefold representative: as woman, wife, mother', and her ability to embody ordinary 'feminine virtues' associated with mothers and caregivers, made her seem the 'right woman'.[34] Thus, the hope that she would represent all women meant that her election came with a weight of expectation that had no parallel for any male MP.

Astor remained a conviction politician motivated more by her mailbag than her party's political principles. She had a determination to prove that women were as physically capable as men of being full participants in the rigours of political life. Her political character was instinctive, and her personal inclinations

[30] Mabel Philipson (Conservative) was also elected to her husband's seat, Berwick-upon-Tweed, at a by-election on 13 May 1922. He had been unseated on petition for electoral irregularities by his agent.

[31] Labour Party General Election Manifesto 1918.

[32] The number of women elected fell to nine in 1935. It rose once more to 24 in 1945, where it remained, more or less, until the 1980s (Richard Cracknell, 'The history and geography of women MPs since 1918 in numbers' *House of Commons Library*, 18 November 2013).

[33] Edith Summerskill, *A Woman's World: Memoirs* (Heinemann, 1967), quoted in 'Women MPs 1931–1945' (2020) at https://ukvote100.org/2020/08/31/women-mps-1931-1945/ [accessed 27 October 2023].

[34] Press cuttings, n 20.

increasingly focused on solving women's social and political oppression. This ultimately placed her feminism above her Conservatism and inevitably hampered her relationship with the party, squeezing her out of broader, traditional right-of-centre politics. To some extent it also helps us to better understand what has been judged the decline of her later parliamentary career.[35] Astor was an unconventional MP and charted a path through previously unnavigated parliamentary politics and the gendered culture of the early twentieth century in which she operated.

Further Reading

- Nancy Astor, *My Two Countries* (Heinemann, 1923).
- Daniel Grey and Jacqui Turner (eds), 'An Unconventional MP: Nancy Astor, Public Women and Gendered Political Culture' (2020) 6(2) *Open Library of Humanities Journal* at https://olh.openlibhums.org/issue/414/info/.
- Christopher Sykes, *The Life of Lady Astor* (Academy, 1972).

[35] Letters from Waldorf to Nancy Astor, UoR MS 1416/1/3. Astor stood down under pressure from her husband and family who, along with the ageing local Plymouth Conservative party, did not feel they had another election left in them. She believed that the electorate in Plymouth would have voted for her again, and this difference of opinion caused a personal estrangement.

5

Report of the War Cabinet Committee on Women in Industry, 1919

ANNE MORRIS

In September 1918, the War Cabinet set up a Committee on Women in Industry, 'To investigate and report on the relation which should be maintained between the wages of women and men having regard to the interests of both as well as to the value of their work.' Its recommendations were to 'have in view the necessity of output during the war and the progress and well-being of industry in the future'.[1] Known as the 'Atkin Committee', after its chair, Sir James Atkin,[2] the Committee was established in the aftermath of a strike in 1918 by women transport workers, who had been denied the pay rises given to their male colleagues. Though the women had been awarded a back-dated pay rise, it was agreed that the issue of women's wages should be subject to a special inquiry, since it involved a question of general principle of national importance. Despite the failure of the Committee directly to influence law and policy after the war, its reports illuminate the harsh working conditions of women and the extent to which assumptions about women's roles in the home and the labour market militated against sex equality. The wealth of evidence gathered in the Report also showed, however, that women were more than capable of successfully filling jobs previously the preserve of men, and in that sense it is a vital contribution to the struggle for equality and an important part of the campaign for equal pay that continues to this day.

I. Context

Women have always been wage earners. Even before the outbreak of war in 1914, over two million women were employed in industry (alongside 1.6 million in domestic service).[3] In the textile and clothing industries, women outnumbered men.

[1] *Report of the War Cabinet Committee on Women in Industry* (Cmd 135, 1919) (hereinafter 'Report').
[2] Later Lord Atkin of *Donoghue v Stevenson* [1932] AC 562 fame.
[3] Report, n 1, 14.

These numbers disguise, however, two important constants. First, within any industry – even where women predominated – work was gendered: there were 'women's jobs' and 'men's jobs'. Second, men's jobs were more highly paid. It is estimated that before 1914, a typical female employee received around one-half of the wages of a man in manual and non-manual jobs.[4] Of course, the pay differential between men and women existed before industrialisation, but it became more acute as trades were mechanised and skilled jobs were commandeered by men. One reason for this persistent under-valuing of women's work was the widely held belief that women belonged in the home, supported by a breadwinner husband bringing home a 'family wage'. Single women, it was argued, did not need such a family wage, nor did married women as their earnings were secondary or supplemental to those of their husbands. Women who aspired to higher-paid jobs typically found themselves blocked by a combination of employer prejudice and trade union hostility: employers did not consider women to be reliable or productive workers, while the unions feared they would drive down male wages. Where unions did argue for equal pay, it was to exclude women, as employers would not hire them at the higher rates.[5]

There had been campaigns, including industrial action, to improve women's pay prior to 1915.[6] In 1888, Clementina Black, a feminist and delegate from the Women's Trade Union League, successfully presented to the Trades Union Congress a motion that in trades where women and men did the same work, they should receive the same wages. However, this had had little impact, not least because men and women were rarely employed in the same jobs. Even where men and women did the same or similar jobs, demands for equal pay were resisted. In the Civil Service, for example, the Association of Post Office Women Clerks, and its successor the Federation of Women Civil Servants, had unsuccessfully campaigned for equal pay from the turn of the century.[7]

Even among feminists and social reformers, there was disagreement about the wisdom of pursuing equal pay either because of fears that women would be priced out of the labour market, or because it was argued that the focus should instead be on women's access to better-paid jobs.[8] In fact, for the majority of working women, the more pressing problem was *low*, rather than *equal*, pay. The suffragist Mary Macarthur was prominent in the struggle to improve pay and conditions in the

[4] ibid ch II. See also Martin Pugh, *Women and the Women's Movement in Britain 1914–1999* (2nd edn, Macmillan, 2000) 27.

[5] Pugh, n 4, 36.

[6] See Sarah Boston, *Women Workers and the Trade Unions* (Lawrence and Wishart, 1987) ch 3. For a general overview, see Mary Davis, 'An Historical Introduction to the Campaign for Equal Pay' at www.unionhistory.info/equalpay/roadtoequality.php [accessed 1 December 2022].

[7] See Helen Glew, *Gender, Rhetoric and Regulation: Women's Work in the Civil Service and the London County Council 1900–55* (Manchester University Press, 2016) ch 3.

[8] Compare, for example, Beatrice Webb, 'Personal Rights and the Woman's Movement: Equal Remuneration for Men and Women' *New Statesman* (1 August 1914) 525 with Millicent Fawcett, 'Mr Sidney Webb's Article on Women's Wages' (1892) 2(5) *The Economic Journal* 173.

so-called 'sweated trades', leading ultimately to the Trade Boards Act 1909, which laid down minimum wage rates in specified industries.[9] By 1914. the Trade Boards covered about 400,000 workers, 80 per cent of whom were women. However, while minimum rates were an improvement, they did not mean equal rates, and women's rates remained lower than men's.

While many women lost their jobs at the outbreak of the First World War in 1914, particularly in the textile and clothing industries, and in domestic service as the middle classes reduced their spending, it was not long before women were needed to fill the jobs vacated by men volunteering for the armed services. By 1915, there had been a marked increase in the numbers of women employed in manufacturing and industrial processes, including those linked to the war such as munitions, as well as in transport and clerical occupations. Because women were routinely paid less than men, the prospect of women moving into 'men's' jobs was opposed by trade unions. The impasse led to the Government's assuming control over munitions and allied industries in order to guarantee wartime production. It entered into a series of agreements with the unions, starting in March 1915, one aim of which was to protect male rates of pay in occupations where men were temporarily replaced by women.[10] The extent to which this entitled women to the men's rates was contested from the outset. Complaints from women that the agreements had not been honoured were investigated by the Atkin Committee.[11] The Majority Report found that the agreements had not been breached – a conclusion with which Webb, in her Minority Report, vehemently disagreed. Whatever the precise meaning of the agreements, it was clear that employers had found ways to avoid paying men's rates – for example, by sub-dividing jobs into constituent parts or introducing new processes – so that women employed to replace the men were not in fact employed to do work *ordinarily done by men* and therefore did not qualify for the men's rates.[12] This 'dilution' resulted in women's being paid significantly less than the men they replaced.

The patriotic fervour surrounding war work, together with legislation outlawing strikes,[13] partially quelled unrest for much of the war – though there continued to be pockets of industrial action, often prompted by the practice of awarding wage increases only to men. And when the transport strike in 1918 threatened to spread, the Government was sufficiently concerned to set up the Atkin Committee.

[9] Mary Macarthur was instrumental in the creation of the National Federation of Women Workers, a general union open to women. She was joined in her campaigns relating to the 'sweated trades' by, among others, Violet Markham, one of the first women appointed to the **Industrial Court**.

[10] Report, n 1, ch IV.

[11] ibid pt III.

[12] Mary MacArthur, 'The Lesson of the Bus Girls Strike: Why women must have equal pay' at www.unionhistory.info/britainatwork/emuweb/objects/nofdigi/tuc/imagedisplay.php?irn=1123.

[13] Munitions of War Act 1915.

II. The Landmark

The significance attached to the question of women's pay was reflected in the eminence of the Committee members: Sir Lynden Macassey, later an assessor on the Permanent International Court of Justice; Sir William Mackenzie, later the First President of the **Industrial Court**; Sir Matthew Nathan, Secretary to the Ministry of Pensions; Miss Janet Campbell, the first full-time woman medical officer at the Board of Education and later a Senior Medical Officer in the new Ministry of Health; and Mrs Beatrice Webb, social reformer and active member of the Fabian Society.[14] The Committee produced two reports, one reflecting the views of the majority (together with a note by William Mackenzie outlining two points of disagreement) and a Minority Report by Beatrice Webb. A separate Memorandum was written by Janet Campbell, drawing on her enquiry into the health of women in industry, and formed part of the majority recommendations.

A. The Majority Report

Having considered the voluminous evidence gathered by the Committee, the Majority Report made 27 recommendations relating to the wages and employment conditions of women. Some of these were remarkably positive, including improved working conditions (reduced hours and provision of facilities such as canteens), the provision of technical training for women and the abolition of separate examinations for women clerks in the Civil Service.[15] On the fundamental issue of whether there should be a general principle of equal pay, however, the majority view was coloured by prevailing notions of men's and women's roles. Central to the majority's recommendations was the issue of the value of the worker to the employer. With few exceptions, employers had complained that women were less efficient than men and more expensive to employ. Some of the 'inefficiencies' clearly arose from women's inexperience and lack of training, as well as ongoing and onerous domestic responsibilities that led to absences. Of course, the 'evidence' of such inefficiencies was far from scientific. Nevertheless it provided the basis for the Committee's principal recommendation that women doing the same or similar work as men should receive 'equal pay for equal work' in proportion to efficient output.[16] It was accepted that it would indeed be possible to introduce a 'rate for the job', allowing for men and women to be paid equally, but this was rejected since employers would refuse to employ women at men's rates.[17] Moreover, the principle of equal pay adopted by the majority applied only to occupations in which both

[14] Beatrice Webb also served on the Royal Commission on the Poor Laws and Relief of Distress (Cd 4499, 1909).

[15] Report, n 1, recommendations 16, 17 and 14.

[16] ibid recommendation 1.

[17] ibid 213.

men and women were employed: in women-only or men-only jobs it could not apply, since '[t]here is no way of making a comparison between the efforts and sacrifices of a coalminer and a nursemaid'.[18]

In relation to the future wages of women, the Majority Report was slightly proactive. Recognising that before the war most women were being paid less than a living wage, and that many remained outside the remit of the minimum rates laid down by Trade Boards, it feared (correctly) that women's wages would fall after the war – and that this would have repercussions for men. It therefore recommended there should be a minimum wage for women such as was sufficient for the needs of a single woman over 18.[19] This was, of course, less than that needed by a man of the same age, on the basis that

> the fact that the average young man does look forward to supporting a family, and works with this in view, while the average girl looks forward to marriage and to being supported while rearing a family, is a real factor.[20]

Unable to ignore the fact that some women did have dependants, it was recommended that the Government should consider the introduction of pensions for widows and deserted wives, along the lines of pensions payable to war widows.[21] The majority did not, however, agree with the suggestion that there should be governmental support for the 'endowment of motherhood'.[22]

B. The Minority Report

Webb's Minority Report was also published as a Fabian Society pamphlet.[23] She dissented not only from the majority's conclusions but also from the very basis of the Committee's investigation, believing that it should have considered more generally whether wage differentials between men and women could be justified:

> To concentrate the whole attention … upon the employment of women … is to assume, perhaps inadvertently, that industry is normally a function of the male, and that women, like non-adults, are only to be permitted to work for wages at special hours, for special rates of wages, under special supervision and subject to special restrictions by the Legislature. I cannot accept this assumption.[24]

[18] It was hoped that wages in women-only occupations would increase if women's wages rose elsewhere (ibid 210). This apparently insurmountable difficulty has now been addressed by the Equality Act 2010, s 65 of which allows for claims of equal value.

[19] Report, n 1, recommendation 19. William Mackenzie dissented on this point, preferring rates to be set by individual trades.

[20] ibid 202.

[21] Once again, Mackenzie disagreed, believing this fell outside the scope of the Committee's remit. See further **'Widows', Orphans' and Old Age Contributory Pensions Act 1925'**.

[22] Report, n 1, 202.

[23] Her report continues to be widely praised. See Dave Lyddon, 'Beatrice Webb and Equal Pay: Foreword to the Wages of Men and Women: Should They be Equal?' (2011) 31/32 *Historical Studies in Industrial Relations* 181.

[24] Minority Report, pt 1.

Webb concluded that the notion of 'equal pay for equal work' was so ambiguous and easily avoided as not to constitute any principle at all. Rather, she advocated occupational or standard rates that could be applied equally to men and women, for, as far as she was concerned, 'for the production of commodities and services, women no more constitute a class than do persons of a particular creed or race'.[25] She further recommended that there should be a 'national minimum', encompassing wages and other working conditions, in which there should be no sex inequality. Wages should be based on a subsistence wage identical for men and women. In addition, however, she called for urgent consideration of 'public provision for maternity and childhood'[26] – a proposal that would have built on measures such as the Old Age Pensions Act 1908 and the National Insurance Act 1911.

III. What Happened Next

The timing of the Report in April 1919 could hardly have been less propitious for those hoping for improvements in women's pay and conditions. With peace declared, there was no need for the Government to attend to its recommendations or to placate restive women workers who had been so crucial – and so lauded – in the war effort. The focus shifted to the demobilisation of soldiers and their speedy re-employment. Employers, including the Government, began dismissing women in large numbers, encouraged by the trade unions, using the Restoration of Pre-War Practices Act 1919, which codified the temporary nature of the agreement that had allowed women to take men's jobs.[27] The economic climate of the 1920s and 1930s enabled the Government to claim that it was not fiscally sensible to introduce equal pay (a line frequently repeated over the next decades). Reforms that potentially benefited women, such as the **Representation of the People Act 1918** and the Sex Disqualification (Removal) Act 1919, made little difference to the young working-class women who made up so much of the wartime labour market. Women with the requisite qualifications could aspire to the professions previously closed to them, but the 1919 Act did not encompass equal pay nor did it outlaw the marriage bar, which allowed the dismissal of women from jobs such as teaching once they married.[28]

Although the 1920s and 1930s saw a resurgence in the insistence that a women's rightful place was in the home, the pursuit of equality for working women did not disappear.[29] With the departure of many women from wartime industries, focus

[25] ibid, Summary of conclusions.
[26] ibid.
[27] Boston, n 6, 139.
[28] See further **'*Short v Poole Corporation* (1926)'**.
[29] The **Six Point Group**, for example, had equal pay for teachers as the fifth of its first six points. Political and literary review magazine *Time and Tide*, founded by Lady Rhondda in 1920, continued to report on meetings for equal pay, including, for example, for women municipal bath and lavatory attendants (*Time and Tide* (23 November 1928)).

shifted to professions such as the Civil Service and teaching. The issue of equal pay surfaced several times in Parliament, although the Government always managed to deflect it. Labour MP and long-term supporter of women's rights and equality, Jack Hills, had a motion passed in favour of equal pay as early as 1920.[30] In 1936, Labour MP Ellen Wilkinson successfully proposed a motion in favour of equal pay in the Civil Service.[31] Though this was supported in the House of Commons, the Government swiftly made it a question of confidence in order to ensure its defeat.[32]

With the outbreak of the Second World War, women faced many of the problems that their predecessors had experienced, including that of pay significantly lower than that of the men they replaced. But they had learned from history, and equal pay achieved new prominence with the establishment of the Equal Pay Campaign Committee chaired by Conservative MP Mavis Tate.[33] The Government appointed a Royal Commission on Equal Pay (largely to avoid dealing with it), which concluded that certain groups (including teachers and civil servants) should get equal pay.[34] Teachers did not receive equal pay until 1961, but following a cross-party campaign led by four women MPs – Patricia Ford (Ulster Unionist), Irene Ward (Conservative) and Edith Summerskill and Barbara Castle (Labour) – who presented a petition to Parliament demanding equal pay signed by 80,000 signatories in March 1954, a scheme for female civil servants was adopted in 1955, to be introduced over several years.[35] It was not until 1970, driven by industrial unrest and the UK's imminent membership of the European Economic Community, that the Equal Pay Act 1970 enshrined (at least to some extent) a legally enforceable right to equal pay for equal work.[36]

IV. Significance

Some landmarks signal the end of a journey, others mark progress along the way. The *Report of the Committee on Women in Industry* did not revolutionise the working conditions of women. But the Majority Report's acknowledgement of the inadequacy and injustice of women's wages (albeit coloured by prevailing

[30] HC Deb 19 May 1920, vol 129, cols 1539–80.

[31] HC Deb 1 April 1936, vol 310, col 2017; HC Deb 6 April 1936, vol 310, cols 2444–79.

[32] Harold L Smith, 'British Feminism and the Equal Pay Issue in the 1930s' (1996) 5:1 *Women's History Review* 97. A similar tactic was used in 1944 to defeat an amendment proposed by Thelma Cazalet Keir giving equal pay to teachers (HC Deb 28 March 1944, vol 398, cols 1355–96; HC Deb 30 March 1944, vol 398, cols 1578–1656).

[33] Harold L Smith, 'The Problem of "Equal Pay for Equal Work" in Great Britain during World War II' (1981) 53(1) *Journal of Modern History* 652.

[34] *Report of the Royal Commission on Equal Pay 1945–1946* (Cmd 6937, 1946).

[35] For the campaign that preceded this, see https://ukvote100.org/2017/11/09/women-demand-equal-pay/.

[36] See now Equality Act 2010.

prejudices) drew attention to deep-seated discrimination faced by women, while Webb's masterful Minority Report and cogent arguments as to the unjustifiability of paying women less on grounds of their sex, and its forensic examination of the evidence, continue to have lasting influence. Webb's assertion that women would benefit from sex-blind wage rates was far more apt for the areas in which women workers proliferated in the post-war period, including teaching, the Civil Service, local government and clerical work, and foreshadowed modern understandings of sex equality.

As the gender pay gap between male and female earnings persists,[37] so does the determination of women to achieve parity of pay. From highly paid public figures[38] to under-valued shopworkers,[39] women continue the struggles of the women who came before them.

Further Reading

- Gail Braybon, *Women Workers in the First World War* (first pub 1981, Routledge 2013).
- Barbara Drake, *Women in Trade Unions* (first pub 1921, Virago 1984).
- Deborah Thom, *Nice Girls and Rude Girls: Women Workers in World War 1* (IB Taurus & Co Ltd 2000).

[37] Office for National Statistics, 'Gender pay gap in the UK: 2022' (26 October 2022).

[38] 'Carrie Gracie calls watchdog's report on BBC equal pay a "whitewash"' *BBC News* (12 November 2020).

[39] *Sainsbury's Supermarkets Ltd v Clark and others* [2023] EWCA Civ 386.

6

Industrial Courts Act 1919

ERIKA RACKLEY

The Industrial Courts Act 1919 established a permanent Industrial Court to provide voluntary arbitration in trade disputes. Section 1 provided that the Court should consist of independent persons, persons representing employers, persons representing workmen and 'in addition one or more women'.[1] Thus, at a time when women were unable to formally practise law,[2] before they were able to sit as magistrates, let alone be paid judges in the civil and criminal courts,[3] the Industrial Courts Act contained a statutory quota recognising women's capacity as 'persons of experience, of known impartiality; judicially-minded and capable of estimating evidence and reaching a reasonable decision according to the revealed facts of the case'.[4]

I. Context

While legislative and industry efforts to ensure the peaceful resolution of trade disputes can be dated back to an Elizabethan statute of 1562,[5] the idea really took hold after the Industrial Revolution. Boards of arbitration were established for individual trades, including the pottery and carpet-weaving industries, the Macclesfield silk trade, the Cheshire salt trade and the Birmingham wire trade.[6] Each board operated along similar lines. Issues were first discussed between the employers and workers involved, they being best placed to resolve the dispute.

[1] Repeated in s 2 in relation to the make-up of panels and s 3 in relation to appointment of assessors.

[2] See further Mari Takayanagi, 'Sex Disqualification (Removal) Act 1919' in Erika Rackley and Rosemary Auchmuty (eds), *Women's Legal Landmarks: Celebrating the History of Women and Law in the UK and Ireland* (Hart Publishing 2019) 133.

[3] Anne Logan, 'In Search of Equal Citizenship: the campaign for women magistrates in England and Wales, 1910–1939' (2007) 16(4) *Women's History Review* 501.

[4] JR Clynes MP, Labour MP for Platting, HC Deb 6 November 1919, vol 120, col 1724.

[5] The Statute of Artificers 1562 (5 Eliz Cap 4).

[6] William Mackenzie, 'The British Industrial Court' (1921) 3(1) *International Labour Review* 41, 41–42.

If this failed, the matter was passed to a referee or an arbitrator. By the end of the First World War, with the exception of measures introduced by wartime legislation, the settlement of industrial disputes fell within the remit of the Conciliation Act 1896, and responsibility for their peaceful resolution lay with the Board of Trade, a Government department.

In October 1916, the Committee on Relations between Employers and Employed (known as the 'Whitley Committee' after its Chairman, JH Whitley, later Speaker of the House of Commons) was tasked with making 'suggestions for securing a permanent improvement in the relations between employers and workmen'.[7] It reported in January 1918, recommending that there be a Standing Arbitration Council to which parties could refer any dispute.[8] It continued:

> Such tribunal should include in its membership persons who have practical experience and knowledge of industry, and who are acquainted with the respective standpoints of employers and workpeople.[9]

The following year, on 6 November 1919, Sir Robert Horne, Minster for Labour, introduced the Industrial Courts Bill for its second reading in the House of Commons. Its aim was to provide continuity of decision-making, building on the success of the earlier bodies, particularly the Committee of Production, through a standing 'body of people who are able to take a comprehensive view of the labour question and, in particular … the wages question'.[10]

II. The Landmark

Despite a flourishing women's trade union movement[11] and there having been women members of the predecessors to the Industrial Court,[12] there was no specific mention of women members in the original Bill. One reason may have been that women's presence on such arbitration boards had become so integral to the operation of the earlier bodies that their inclusion did not need specific mention. Or maybe, as was argued during the course of the debates by the Solicitor General, Sir Ernest Pollock, the soon-to-be enacted Sex Discrimination (Removal) Act 1919 would render any such provision superfluous.[13] Certainly there is nothing

[7] Committee of Production, Terms of References, quoted in Harold Morris, 'The Industrial Court and Its Working' *Economica* (March 1928) 16, 16.

[8] Committee on Relations between Employers and Employed (1916–1919), *Report on Conciliation and Arbitration* (31 January 1918), quoted in Morris, n 7, 17.

[9] ibid.

[10] Sir Robert Horne, HC Deb 10 November 1919, vol 121, col 128.

[11] See, eg, the minutes of the Manchester and Salford Women's Trades Union Council at www.mswtuc.co.uk.

[12] Lucy Deane Streatfeild, one of first women factory inspectors, and who later went on to be one of the first women magistrates, had sat on both the Committee of Production and Interim Court.

[13] HC Deb 10 November 1919, vol 121, col 149.

in the parliamentary debates to suggest that the Court would not, when appropriate, positively welcome women's 'knowledge and experience' in its deliberations.[14] But neither was there anything to determine when this would be, or to secure their equal footing around the table when they did so.

And so, on 10 November 1919, Alexander Shaw MP,[15] a member of the Scottish Liberal Party, introduced an amendment in Committee requiring the presence of one or more women 'in every proper case'.[16] Drawing on what were likely to have been familiar arguments for equal representation,[17] he argued that women's presence on the Court was a matter of trust and fairness. By tying it directly to women's citizenship and the recent extension of the franchise, he explained,

> the thousands of working women in the country [would not] feel … that they have been fairly treated by the Government for which they voted at the General Election … I seriously doubt whether, if you set up a tribunal without the element of experience which women can give, women will really trust the tribunal.[18]

Crucially, it would also ensure the quality of the Court's decision-making:[19]

> My own experience for some fourteen months as chairman of an Arbitration Tribunal with women as colleagues was that the experience of women in dealing with these women's cases was quite invaluable. I cannot imagine any Arbitration Tribunals dealing efficiently with cases in which women are concerned without the experience and guidance of women who have made a special study of these matters.[20]

Members from both sides of the house agreed. Major John (Jack) Hills MP, Liberal Unionist MP for Durham City and a great supporter of feminist causes, warned of 'disastrous' consequences if women were 'shut out the body' that controlled and regulated their wages.[21] Labour MP William Graham went further, advocating for the inclusion of women members on *all* cases on the basis that 'there is no

[14] See, eg, Horne, HC Deb 10 November 1919, vol 121, col 138.

[15] Alexander Shaw was the son of Lord (Thomas) Shaw, a Lord Appeal in Ordinary. At the time the Industrial Courts Act was being debated, Lord Shaw was rendering 'valuable assistance' in the formation of the League of Nations, Art 7 of the Covenant of which stated that its Secretariat would be open to both women and men (Aoife O'Donoghue, 'Article 7 of the Covenant of the League of Nations,1919' in Rackley and Auchmuty (eds), n 2, 125).

[16] Alexander Shaw MP, HC Deb 10 November 1919, vol 121, col 137.

[17] See, eg, the Women's Freedom League, which was openly sceptical about the fairness of the legal system, arguing that without women solicitors, barristers and magistrates, 'it is exceedingly difficult to have any confidence in the administration of British justice' *The Vote* (5 September 1919) quoted in Logan, n 3, 505).

[18] Shaw, HC Deb 10 November 1919, vol 121, col 141.

[19] See further Erika Rackley, 'A Short History of Judicial Diversity' (2023) 76(1) *Current Legal Problems* 265.

[20] Shaw, HC Deb 10 November 1919, vol 121, col 137.

[21] Major John Hills MP, HC Deb 10 November 1919, vol 121, col 138. Hills, a former solicitor and related by marriage to Virginia Woolf and Vanessa Bell, played a pivotal role in campaigns for women to enter the legal professions, introducing legislation to this effect on several occasions (Rosemary Auchmuty, 'Whatever happened to Miss Bebb? *Bebb v Law Society* and women's legal history' (2012) 31 *Legal Studies* 199).

industrial dispute affecting men in which women are not directly or indirectly interested also'.[22]

When the Minister for Labour said he would only commit women's inclusion as 'ad hoc' assessors, the size of the Court being too small to guarantee their inclusion,[23] Shaw pushed for a vote. The amendment failed (Ayes, 75; Noes, 119).[24] However just 8 days later, the Minister had changed his mind, introducing an amendment ensuring one or more women on the Court 'with the prestige of full membership'.[25] It was agreed to without debate. Women's participation on an equal footing (albeit not in numbers) with their male colleagues was embedded in the constitution of the Court.

Two days later, on 20 November 1919, the Industrial Courts Act 1919 received Royal Assent.

III. What Happened Next

Writing in 1921, Sir William Mackenzie, the first President of the Court, suggested that 'the aim in constituting the Court was to create a body, which it was hoped would inspire general confidence in respect of its ability, knowledge, and representation of different points of view'.[26] It largely succeeded in this aim. Over the years the Court developed a wide substantive remit relating to basic wages, bonuses, overtime, night work, Sunday work, hours of labour and leave across a range of industries, including engineering and shipbuilding (which provided the largest number of cases in the Court's early years), the public utilities and other manufacturing industries.[27] During its first decade, it heard an average of 175 cases a year,[28] and by 1928 it had become the principal arbitration panel in England and Wales.[29]

The Court consisted of 13 members. Of these, four, including the President, were designated 'independent persons', with the others representing either 'employers' or 'workmen'. There were also two women members: Miss Violet Markham and Miss Cécile Matheson. Both were well-known. Cécile Matheson was Warden of the Birmingham Women's Settlement and a prominent member of the National Union of Women Workers, the International Council of Women and

[22] William Graham MP, HC Deb 10 November 1919, vol 121, cols 141–42.

[23] Horne, HC Deb 10 November 1919, vol 121, cols 137–38, 139.

[24] HC Deb 10 November 1919, vol 121, cols 142–43.

[25] Horne, HC Deb 18 November 1919, vol 121, col 460. It is not clear how this happened – it may be that Horne felt out-manoeuvred by Shaw. When introducing his amendment, Horne remarked on his disappointment with Shaw's decision to push the matter to a vote the previous week. Shaw's response was conciliatory: none of those involved in the earlier debate, Shaw assured him, had 'ever had a shadow of doubt of his own personal sympathy' or support for women's cause (ibid).

[26] Mackenzie, n 6, 46.

[27] Ducksoo Chang, *British Methods of Industrial Peace: A Study of Democracy in relation to Labour Disputes* (Columbia University Press 1936; repr AMS Press 1968) 152.

[28] ibid.

[29] Morris, n 7, 20–22.

the National Union of Women's Suffrage Societies.[30] Violet Markham had worked alongside Lucy Deane Streatfeild on campaigns to reform the so-called 'sweated industries', and had acted as Deputy and later Director of the Women's Section of the short-lived National Service Department, set up by Neville Chamberlain in 1916 – where she most likely oversaw the appointment as Commissioner for the West Midland division of Miss Bebb.[31] She was also an imperialist,[32] though her *Oxford Dictionary of National Biography* entry suggests that her views 'evolved' under the influence of Canadian politician Mackenzie King.[33]

Almost immediately the composition of the Court was challenged, not by the men who had opposed the appointment of women members but by the National Federation of Women Workers (NFWW), who believed that different women should have been appointed.[34] As it stood, the Act made no mention of whether the women members of the Court were intended to represent the employers or workers, or were expected to be independent. In March 1920, just four months after the Industrial Courts Act was passed, Charles Sitch MP (who had voted in favour of Shaw's amendment), in a written question to the Minister of Labour, referred to ongoing 'remonstrations' by the NFWW that there was no representative of organised women on the Court.[35] It is not clear whether the NFWW was lobbying to replace the current members or to include an *additional* woman to represent organised women. Nor is there any record of its success. In the account of the early years of the Court by Mackenzie (now Lord Amulree), published almost a decade later, Markham and Matheson are the only women listed as the original members of the Court.[36] In fact, it appears that Markham and Matheson were not often called on to hear a case. In the first year of the Court's operation, Markham did not sit at all (most likely because she was overseas with her husband) and Matheson sat in just 5 per cent of cases, despite just over a quarter involving discussion of women's wages and/or working conditions.

In 1971, the Court was re-named the Industrial Arbitration Board under section 124 of the unpopular Industrial Relations Act 1971. It retained much of

[30] Georgina Brewis, 'Matheson, (Marie) Cécile', *Oxford Dictionary of National Biography* (9 August 2018).

[31] Helen Jones, 'Markham, Violet Rosa', *Oxford Dictionary of National Biography* (24 September 2004). Miss Bebb was one of four women chosen to bring a case against the Law Society, seeking to allow women to join the legal profession in 1914 (see further Auchmuty, n 21).

[32] Eliza Riedi, 'Options for an Imperialist Woman: The Case of Violet Markham, 1899–1914' (2000) 31(1) *Albion: A Quarterly Journal Concerned with British Studies* 59.

[33] Jones, n 31.

[34] See further correspondence between Gertrude Tuckwell (Chairman of the Women's Trade Union League), Susan Lawrence (secretary of the Working Women's Legal Advice Bureau), Violet Markham, the National Federation of Women Workers and Sir Robert Horne in the weeks after the Act was passed (Women's Library archives, MARKHAM 26/41).

[35] Once again, Horne dismissed their concerns with the familiar assurance that the Court might rely on ad hoc assessors where necessary (HC Deb 11 March 1920, vol 126, col 1562).

[36] Lord Amulree, *Industrial Arbitration in Great Britain* (Oxford University Press, 1929). The sleeve cover of Markham's autobiography, published in 1953, states that she served on the Industrial Court until 1946, though curiously there is no mention of her time on the Court in the text itself. Violet Markham, *Return Passage: The Autobiography of Violet Markham CH* (Oxford University Press, 1953).

its previous constitution and remit, save for one exception: there was no *requirement* for women members. In fact, an amendment along the exact lines of Shaw's in 1919, initially proposed by Lord Diamond and supported by Lord Janner, had been withdrawn by Lord Diamond during an earlier debate.[37] Far from underpinning the Industrial Court's institutional integrity and quality, and the ability of the Court to do the best job possible, the requirement was recast 'unnecessary'[38] and 'insulting'.[39] As the Lord Chancellor, Lord Hailsham, noted:

> [T]he presence of a woman, or women, on this Court would be of the greatest possible value, but we must try to get away from the old conception of the statutory woman. In the old days, when there was a certain prejudice in these matters, and just after women's rights in 1919, we got into the frame of mind that there must be a statutory woman on every bench. The implication was that women could not get there on their merits. I hope that that is now a thing of the past and that we may expect, in any appointments there are, whether it be to a committee of inquiry or a bench of magistrates or a court, that it will be recognised that women are playing a full part … in our national life, and do not need special preference in order to get on committees.[40]

In the event, the absence of a statutory requirement in the 1971 Act made little difference to the composition of the re-named Industrial Arbitration Board. In 1975, the *Sunday Times* reported that there were three women among the lay members of the Board.[41] Shaw's amendment back in November 1919 had done its job. In contrast to the ongoing exclusion of women from the legal profession and judiciary,[42] women's presence was embedded in the operation of the Industrial Arbitration Board, and as such insulated their inclusion from the vagaries of politics and shifts in personnel.

The Industrial Courts Act 1919 was finally repealed in July 1992 by schedule 1 to the Trade Union and Labour Relations (Consolidation) Act 1992.

IV. Significance

In many ways the Industrial Courts Act was part of a broader picture and movement of its time. Women had been playing important philanthropic – and often

[37] HL Deb 27 May 1971, vol 319, cols 1299–1312.

[38] Baroness Emmet (who had herself been a 'statutory woman'), HL Deb 27 May 1971, vol 319, col 1309.

[39] Lord Conesford, HL Deb 27 May 1971, vol 319, cols 1307–08.

[40] ibid col 1304.

[41] 'More equal than others?' *Sunday Times* (4 May 1975).

[42] In 1971, over 50 years since women were able to formally join the legal profession, they made up 6.2% of practising barristers and just 1% of QCs. Less than one-third of chambers in London and just over one-quarter of chambers elsewhere had two or more women. Women were outnumbered in the senior judiciary by 83:1. In 1972, just four women sat on the High Court and circuit benches combined. Overall, men made up just over 98% of the judiciary (Equal Opportunities Commission, *Women in the Legal Services* (EOC, 1978) 14, 16, 23).

quasi-legal or judicial – roles in public and civic life as local government councillors, factory inspectors and Poor Law guardians for some time. Inside the Chamber, many MPs involved in the debates would have been familiar with (though, of course, not necessarily supportive of) arguments for women's political representation and equal citizenship or, like Alexander Shaw, Jack Hills and Robert Horne, were lawyers and/or involved in national and international campaigns for women's representation in the legal profession. Others would have worked alongside 'statutory women' on government committees or Royal Commissions and the like. Described by Anne Logan as a 'shadowy but essential political role', the genesis of the 'statutory woman' is found in the aftermath of suffrage.[43] In the words of Lady Stocks, herself a veteran of many government committees:

> Thanks to a changed climate of opinion with regard to women in public life which followed the First World War, it became a regular ministerial practice for every government committee or Royal Commission to contain at least one woman … But though the country as a whole teemed with able and public-spirited women, those who sojourned in the 'corridors of power' did not know who or where they were, and took little trouble to find out … As a result, the few they *did* know about were used over and over again. They became a kind of stage army appearing on one government assignment after another. At a later stage somebody – I forget who – described them very aptly as 'statutory women'.[44]

The Industrial Court was also, however, ahead of its time. At a time when women's presence at the Bar continued to be resisted, when women's assumed bias was seen as an impediment to their appointment as judges, the Industrial Courts Act – in contrast to the enabling provisions of the Sex Disqualification (Removal) Act 1919 – positively *required* women's presence on the most senior industrial tribunal of its time. Today, as gender quotas continue to be rejected by those in the position to effect change, the Act demonstrates what we already know: quotas work.[45] In 1919, the statutory requirement for representation contained in section 1 of the Industrial Courts Act ensured the appointment of two women to the Court. It would take just shy of 100 years for two women to sit on the UK Supreme Court. And just five years after that for it to slip away.[46]

[43] Anne Logan, 'Political Life in the Shadows: the post suffrage political career of S Margery Fry (1874–1958)' (2014) 23(3) *Women's History Review* 365, 366–67.

[44] Mary Stocks, *My Commonplace Book* (Peter Davies, 1970) 165, quoted in Logan, n 43, 367. Without doubt, Violet Markham fulfilled the 'statutory woman' brief (see correspondence between Markham and Horne around the time of the passing of the Act: Women's Library archives, MARKHAM 26/41).

[45] See further Rackley, n 19, 289–94.

[46] Lady Hale was appointed to the Appellate Committee of the House of Lords in 2004. She became the first woman Justice of the Supreme Court when it was established in 2009. She was the only woman Justice until Lady Black joined the Court in October 2017. Lady Arden was appointed the following year. Hale and Black retired in 2020 and 2021 respectively. Following Lady Arden's retirement in January 2022, Lady Rose was again the only woman on the UK Supreme Court until Lady Simler's appointment in October 2023.

Further Reading

- William Mackenzie, 'The British Industrial Court' (1921) 3(1) *International Labour Review* 41.
- Harold Morris, 'The Industrial Court and Its Working' *Economica* (March 1928) 16.
- Erika Rackley, 'A Short History of Judicial Diversity' (2023) 76(1) *Current Legal Problems* 265.

7

First Women Jurors, 1920

KAY CROSBY

On 29 July 1920, *The Times* reported that 'Women jurors were empaneled for the first time at the Bristol Quarter Sessions yesterday.' A jury of six women and six men had 'adjudicated on six cases'. Prosecuting counsel used the

> unfamiliar phrase 'Ladies and gentlemen of the jury'. As far as he knew it had not been used before in the annals of the jurisdiction of this country. He congratulated women on at last taking their proper place in the jurisdiction of the country, and also congratulated the cause of justice that they had done so.[1]

Women had now served on a jury in England for the first time since their categorical exclusion from the jury box had been brought to a close by the passage of the Sex Disqualification (Removal) Act 1919, seven months earlier.[2] The rules left the men selecting juries a great deal of discretion regarding the qualified people who would actually serve; and it is significant that the jury that was empaneled on this occasion comprised six women and six men. There was a symbolic equality here, but it was an equality that did not survive in the jury system for very long.

I. Context

In fact, this was not the first time women had appeared on a jury. Only the previous December, 12 women had been assembled at the Manchester Assizes to sit as a 'jury of matrons' to determine whether a woman, sentenced to death for the murder of her illegitimate 2-year-old child, should have her execution postponed due to pregnancy.[3] Nor was it the first time that women had been summoned (as

[1] 'Women Jurors: mothers excused from serving to-day' *The Times* (29 July 1920) 9.

[2] See Mari Takayanagi, 'Sex Disqualification (Removal) Act 1919' in Erika Rackley and Rosemary Auchmuty (eds), *Women's Legal Landmarks: Celebrating the History of Women and Law in the UK and Ireland* (Hart Publishing, 2019) 133.

[3] 'Bolton Murderess Respited' *Manchester Evening News* (8 December 1919) 5. This was a fact that did not go unnoticed in the popular press. In the months between the passage of the 1919 Act and the empaneling of the Bristol jurors, various publications sought to utilise a single instance from 1847 of

opposed to empaneled) as trial jurors after the passage of the Act, which appears to have taken place in Essex two months earlier.[4] These women, unlike those at Bristol a few months later, never actually made it on to a jury, having been systematically challenged out of what would have been the first ever mixed jury by their male defendant. In fact, the Women's Freedom League's publication *The Vote* pointed to women jurors appearing in multiple instances during the fifteenth century, using this to argue that the Bristol jurors in 1920 had significance not as an innovation but rather as a 'restoration of women's ancient right'.[5] Furthermore, the fact that women had been 'serving this country as magistrates, borough councillors, guardians, inspectors, aldermen, and mayors' – tasks that 'require much more experience and judgment than is possessed by the average juror' – demonstrated the suitability of women for jury service.[6] In an argument that can also been seen in the discussion of the industrial courts elsewhere in this volume, women were now seen not only to be cognitively capable of being jurors, but also to bring with them specialist knowledge and experience.[7] *The Vote* also thought that women should be used first on trials involving women and children.

In England and Wales, a person was qualified for jury service if they were registered as the occupier of land to a sufficient value (a requirement that, as feminist groups pointed out, was far more likely to exclude a woman than a man),[8] though in Bristol, as in nine other towns across England and Wales, this requirement did not apply until the end of 1920.[9] From 1882, electoral registration was also required, although this appears to have been routinely ignored in practice until at least 1922.[10] A person was also entitled to an exemption on various medical or occupational grounds,[11] and when women were summoned they were specifically advised that they could seek an exemption on unspecified feminine medical grounds.[12]

Despite this final point, the law on women jurors after 1919 was unusually inclusive, in the sense that it tended towards a greater participation of women by

the matrons' having got it wrong, to undermine women's claim to have a sound capacity for judgement. See, eg, 'Jury of Matrons' *The Globe* (29 December 1919) 12; 'The Jury of Matrons' *Sheffield Daily Independent* (31 December 1919) 4.

[4] 'Women on the Jury: Man prisoner's objection at Colchester' *Cambridge Daily News* (28 April 1920) 3.

[5] DM Northcroft, '"Ladies and Gentlemen of the Jury!" Restoration of women's ancient right' *The Vote* (6 August 1920) 149.

[6] ibid.

[7] **'Industrial Courts Act 1919'**.

[8] Anne Logan, '"Building a new and better order"? Women and jury service in England and Wales, c 1920–70' (2013) 22 *Women's History Review* 701.

[9] Kay Crosby, 'Restricting the Juror Franchise in 1920s England and Wales' (2019) 37 *Law and History Review* 163, 181–89.

[10] ibid 198–206.

[11] On the juror summoning rules generally, see Kay Crosby, 'Creating the Citizen Juror in Interwar England and Wales' (2023) 44 *Journal of Legal History* 32, 33.

[12] Rules of the Supreme Court (Women Jurors) 1920.

not formally making their service optional.[13] Anyone was in practice able to be excused from jury service on medical grounds, and women were only unusual here in having this fact pointed to in specifically gendered terms. But while the rules were nominally more inclusive than elsewhere, there was no real way of ensuring that qualified women would actually serve. This was because the formal rules only specified who must be excluded from jury service, and said little about which qualified jurors should be called upon. This left it open for the people selecting jurors to effectively choose what kinds of people would be called upon to serve in their areas.

There was, however, one exception, and it concerned the overall representativeness of an area's jury pool in terms of the numbers of men and women. Shortly before the first women were summoned to the Bristol quarter sessions, central government had instructed local officials that the proportion of women to men summoned should reflect the proportions of qualified men and women in the local area. Furthermore, they were to ensure that they summoned at least 14 women, in order to accommodate a trial judge who (somewhat implausibly) decided to order a jury made up entirely of women.[14] None of this said anything at all about the kinds of women who should be selected from the pool of available women. It only said that there should be some women of some sort.

II. The Landmark

As it happened, the Bristol officials did a good job of following these new rules at their quarter sessions in July 1920. In the summer of 1925, 18 per cent of the city's 8,522 qualified jurors were women;[15] and in July 1920, 17 out of 60 summoned jurors (or 28 per cent) were women.[16] Ten of these women had their status listed either as 'Mrs' or, in one case, as 'Mrs/Widow', making it impossible for us to learn very much about their social status. But of the remaining seven, four were skilled craftspeople, working as either a milliner or a hatter, and three were retailers, listed as either a draper or a tobacconist. A newspaper article pasted into the court records specifies that 'They were mostly ladies in business in the City, with one or two Labour representatives'.[17] Louisa Senington, who was listed simply as

[13] See Andrew L-T Choo and Jill Hunter, 'Gender Discrimination and Juries in the 20th Century: Judging Women Judging Men' (2018) 22 *International Journal of Evidence and Proof* 192, 198; Sonia Walker, 'Battle-Axes and Sticky Beaks: Women and Jury Service in Western Australia 1898–1957' (2004) 11 *Murdoch University Electronic Journal of Law* [17]; and Neil Cameron, Susan Potter and Warren Young, 'The New Zealand Jury' (1999) 62 *Law and Contemporary Problems* 103, 105.

[14] Rules of the Supreme Court (Women Jurors) 1920. But see Gwen Seaborne, 'Judging the Feelings of Women' *Bracton's Sister Blog* (18 October 2018).

[15] Kay Crosby, 'Keeping Women off the Jury in 1920s England and Wales' (2017) 37 *Legal Studies* 695, 706–07.

[16] Jury Book, 1905–23 (Bristol Archives: JQS/J/2), data compiled from across the jurors' book.

[17] Newspaper clipping in City of Bristol Quarter Sessions Record Book, 1910–1930 (Bristol Archives: JQS/D/61) 160.

'Mrs', became the city's second woman to be sworn in as a magistrate the following April,[18] and two years later her husband became the city's Lord Mayor.[19] As the city's officials had explained to an official inquiry into the jury system a few years earlier, when they were looking for men to populate their jury lists, they sought out 'tradesmen in a good way of business' for their ordinary trial juries and 'leading business men' for their special juries.[20] This is mirrored in the city's first group of women jurors. Those summoned to serve at its quarter sessions all appear to be of reasonably high social status.

Five juries were assembled at the Bristol quarter sessions.[21] Three of these juries were evenly split between women and men, while one featured only one woman and one featured none. The first of these juries featuring women – the jury that is strictly speaking the focus of this landmark – heard two larceny trials. One defendant was found guilty of the larceny charge, while the other was found guilty only of receiving. This was fairly routine work for the quarter sessions at this time. While we do not know how long either of these trials lasted, the city's quarter sessions book records four trials that day. So these six women would not have been seated for very long compared to what a juror might expect today.

III. What Happened Next

The most immediate thing that happened next was that several of these women spoke to a local newspaper about their experiences. Much of the reporting on women jurors over the next few years involved inviting women to denounce their position by reflecting on how emotionally difficult a particular trial had been for them.[22] Such questions were not asked of the men on these juries; and this line of questioning would subsequently feed into a narrative suggesting that women were unsuitable for jury service, that they were inevitably replaced by men and so there was little point summoning them in the first place.

The newspaper report records the views of five of the 15 women to have sat on a jury across the five juries at the midsummer sessions. Two of the women regarded

[18] Register of oaths upon appointment as magistrate, 1902–1931 (Bristol Archives: JMag/Adm/6/3) 78.

[19] When Mr Senington became Lord Mayor, Mrs Senington was described by one newspaper as 'the well known JP who frequently sits on the magisterial Bench at Bristol Police Court': 'Bristol's Labour Lord Mayor' *Western Daily Press* (Bristol, 6 October 1923) 10. Another said she was 'well known in social work': 'Labour Lord Mayor of Bristol' *Somerset Guardian and Radstock Observer* (Radstock, 12 October 1923) 5. When the King and Queen visited Bristol in 1925, the Seningtons were among 16 Bristolians formally presented by the Lord Mayor: 'Bristol's Welcome to King and Queen' *Western Daily Press* (Bristol, 10 June 1925) 4.

[20] Lord Mersey (Chair), *Report of the Departmental Committee Appointed to Inquire into and Report upon the Law and Practice with Regard to the Constitution, Qualifications, Selection, Summoning, &c of Juries*, vol 2 (Cd 6818, 1913) 182.

[21] City of Bristol Quarter Sessions Record Book, n 16, 157–64.

[22] Crosby, n 15, 712–13.

jury work as men's business. More common amongst these five women, however, was the view of the only one who was quoted at length, apparently verbatim:

> I did not want to serve, and tried all I could to get out of it. Now, however, I am very glad to have had the experience. I find it very interesting. I had never been in such a place as a law court in my life before. I found no difficulty, however, in following the procedure. As the result of my experience I am satisfied that ladies serving on juries will be very useful, especially in cases in which women are concerned, because women understand women and their temptations and downfalls better than men. I found no embarrassment in the atmosphere of the court – it was much nicer than I expected. The judge and barristers seemed to do all they could to get at the real facts of the case, and give the prisoner every chance. I think women summoned for jury service should be women of experience, but I do not think women should be called in particularly repulsive cases. In ordinary trials, however, there is no objection at all. I am glad to have served, and I would not have missed the experience for anything. Many women may fear the ordeal as I did, but after they have experienced it they will be glad as I am to have shared in the duties.[23]

But while these women were afforded a voice with which to explain their experiences and their perspectives, jury service remained something that was only open to a relatively small group, in part owing to the property qualifications mentioned in section I. These qualifications, it was thought, stopped women from serving as jurors because many married couples occupied property that was listed only in the husband's name. Abolish the property qualifications, the argument went, and more women will be qualified, inevitably leading to more women serving. This would lead to more women having the kind of active citizenship experience that these Bristol women had.

There is a problem with this argument, however. As of the summer of 1925, Bristol had 197,052 registered voters, of whom 1,503 women and 6,758 men were qualified for jury service.[24] Abolishing the property qualifications would have added a little under 190,000 extra people to the pool of qualified jurors, and substantially equalised the gender balance of the juror pool. But there were already 1,500 qualified women, and in 1925 a total of 357 people were summoned as trial jurors to the city's assizes and quarter sessions. A random selection from the city's juror pool would have yielded 100 women and 257 men, and yet only 70 women were actually summoned. Even putting aside the property qualifications, local officials already could have chosen to summon more women. Indeed, at the city's assizes, which heard the most serious criminal offences, this free hand – the high degree of agency handed over to the people doing the selecting – meant that no women were called upon until February 1921, when no more than two women made it onto a single jury.[25]

[23] Newspaper clipping in City of Bristol Quarter Sessions Record Book, n 17, 160.
[24] Crosby, n 15, 706–07.
[25] Crown Minute Book: Western Circuit 1920–1922 (The National Archives: ASSI 21/85) unpaginated.

Indeed, at Leicester, which had a similar gender balance in the jury pool to the one found at Bristol, the minimum of 14 women per session was met every single time juries were summoned to the city's quarter sessions between 1921 and 1939. At Bristol's quarter sessions, this feat was achieved only five times. And while Bristol never had a majority of women on any of its interwar juror panels, at least 50 per cent of the jurors summoned to the Leicester sessions were women on 29 separate occasions. Bristol had the first seated women jurors, but across the following two decades, the city had far fewer women jurors than could be seen in some places. The level of choice that was open to summoning officials can also be seen at the sessions at Burton, for example, where 50 per cent of all summoned jurors were women, but only up until 1924, when the numbers of women being summoned collapsed.[26] And at the provincial assizes and at the Old Bailey, the prevalence of trials deemed unsuitable for women either to hear or to discuss with their male peers led to a regular exclusion of women.[27]

At least in England, the *rules* had not got worse regarding the inclusion of women on the jury. An attempt in 1921 to make jury service become optional for women (as was the case in Ireland from 1927) had failed.[28] But at the same time, the formal rules did not get much better. In the early 1930s, the National Council of Women attempted on two separate occasions to broaden qualification rules to include the wife of any qualified man, to ban lawyers challenging jurors for no other reason than that they were women, to stop judges ordering single-sex juries (invariably this meant ordering juries of men), and to replace the rules permitting women to excuse themselves for reasons of specifically feminine medical unfitness with a more general rule exempting anyone for whom jury service would create hardship 'on account of physical unfitness or household considerations'. Viscount Sankey defeated these proposals by promising his government would give them serious consideration, but then did nothing about them.[29] The gendered nature of the jury qualification rules would remain fundamentally unchanged until the 1970s.[30]

IV. Significance

Ultimately, this event – of women sitting in judgment as trial jurors for what may have been the first time in the history of English law – is notable as a first, and

[26] Crosby, n 9, 39.

[27] Shamena Anwar, Patrick Bayer and Randi Hjalmarsson, 'A Jury of Her Peers: The Impact of the First Female Jurors on Criminal Convictions' (2019) 129 *The Economic Journal* 603; Crosby, n 15.

[28] Anne Logan, *Feminism and Criminal Justice: a historical perspective* (Palgrave, 2008) 89.

[29] Crosby, n 9, 56–57.

[30] Anne Logan, 'Section 25 of the Criminal Justice Act 1972' in Erika Rackley and Rosemary Auchmuty (eds) *Women's Legal Landmarks: Celebrating the History of Women and Law in the UK and Ireland* (Hart Publishing, 2019) 309.

as a moment within a series of broader and longer processes. Women were now citizens, and as citizens they had a right to take their place as jurors beyond the specifically gendered context of the jury of matrons. Alternatively, the trial jury was no longer a gendered space, and so now any kind of citizen was entitled to join, provided they were not covered by a set of specific exclusions.

But citizenship is not simply a question of your legal rights. It is also a question of your ability to participate in society. And while English law was unusual in extending the jury franchise to women without immediately qualifying it – 'You know you don't *really* have to do this, don't you?' – there was still a live question regarding how real this new aspect of women's citizenship was actually going to be.

Feminist campaigners at the time focused on the legal rules that, on paper, continued to limit women's access to the jury box: the fact that judges could order a jury of men, that lawyers could tell a woman to leave the box without needing to give a reason, that the property qualifications made it much less likely that even a middle-class woman would qualify to serve compared to her male peers. These were things that, to contemporary activists, clearly had to be challenged.

But as historians, we have something contemporary activists did not have: we have access to court records that can show us just how important the spaces in between the rules were in continuing to keep many women off the jury well after 1919. We can see how, even once women started to enter the jury box, their continued presence ultimately came down to the vision of society that the men who were selecting the juries wanted to see.

Further Reading

- Andrew L-T Choo and Jill Hunter, 'Gender Discrimination and Juries in the 20th Century: Judging Women Judging Men' (2018) 22 *International Journal of Evidence and Proof* 192.
- Kay Crosby, 'Creating the Citizen Juror in Interwar England and Wales' (2023) 44 *Journal of Legal History* 32.
- Anne Logan, '"Building a new and better order"? Women and jury service in England and Wales, c 1920–70' (2013) 22 *Women's History Review* 701.

8

Formation of the Six Point Group, 1921

SHARON THOMPSON

The Six Point Group (SPG) was established in 1921 as a non-political pressure group that was the first post-suffrage group of its kind to, in one member's words, work towards establishing 'equality between men and women in status, in opportunities, in rewards, in rights, and in responsibilities'.[1] As its name suggests, the SPG worked on six points at a time, and it influenced – both directly and indirectly – the law on women's citizenship, income tax, compensation for injury in air raids[2] and the right to work, while igniting campaigns for equal pay. It was a hub for equal rights feminists campaigning on a broad range of issues, with numerous other pressure groups arising from it, including the **Married Women's Association**.[3] Thus, the SPG can be regarded as one of the leading lights of feminist activism in the interwar period and into the mid-twentieth century.

I. Context

When the SPG was formed in 1921, two important landmarks had been achieved: the Representation of the People Act 1918 enfranchised women over 30 who met a property qualification, and the Sex Disqualification (Removal) Act 1919 enabled women to enter professions such as law and accountancy for the first time.[4] Yet as SPG founder Lady Rhondda – who historian Deirdre Beddoe has suggested was 'Britain's leading feminist' between the wars[5] – put it, these reforms were 'a far cry'

[1] Hazel Huskins-Hallinan, 'Foreword' in Hazel Huskins-Hallinan (ed), *In Her Own Right* (Harrap, 1968) i.

[2] For further detail, see Sharon Thompson, *Quiet Revolutionaries* (Hart Publishing, 2022) 19–20, 38.

[3] Other groups arising from the SPG include the Income Tax Reform Council and Women for Westminster.

[4] See further Mari Takayanagi, 'Representation of the People Act 1918' and 'Sex Disqualification (Removal) Act 1919' in Erika Rackley and Rosemary Auchmuty (eds), *Women's Legal Landmarks: Celebrating the History of Women and Law in the UK and Ireland* (Hart Publishing, 2019) 113 and 133.

[5] Deirdre Beddoe, 'Thomas [*married name* Mackworth], Margaret Haig, *suo jure* Viscountess Rhondda (1883–1958)', *Oxford Dictionary of National Biography* (23 September 2004).

from 'the end of the road'.[6] Rather, Lady Rhondda saw women as having achieved 'a half-way position, and that is never a position which makes for stability'.[7] The success of the 1918 and 1919 Acts may even have seemed pyrrhic to Lady Rhondda and other feminists.[8] The legislation had squashed more radical reforms, such as wider franchise and better rights for married women, that had garnered support in the Women's Emancipation Bill.[9] Moreover, the 1919 Act failed to address the employer's ability to dismiss women, particularly in relation to the marriage bar, and did not contain enforcement mechanisms.[10] Women had therefore been denied both equal opportunity and equal pay.[11] For Lady Rhondda, these reforms were tantamount to a 'leaky saucepan',[12] and it was now up to the next generation of feminists to continue the fight for women's equality, with the SPG as their platform.

But the ideological differences among this next generation of post-suffrage feminist groups were becoming more marked. Such differences are frequently described as being a clash between 'old equal rights' and 'new' feminism.[13] The 'old' strategy was associated with breaking down barriers; reforming laws that said women could not vote like men, that women could not be solicitors or be awarded university degrees like men. 'New' feminism contended that, when women were treated the same as men in law, the work that women typically did – housework and care work – continued to be undervalued and unrecognised, because men did not do this work. New feminism drew attention to this, arguing that women's roles were different yet were of equal value. Feminist campaigner and MP Eleanor Rathbone was a figurehead of this ideology, and in 1919 she succeeded Millicent Fawcett as the president of the National Union of Societies for Equal Citizenship (NUSEC), formerly the National Union of Women's Suffrage Societies. For many women of the 'old guard' who had campaigned for the vote (including Fawcett herself), equality was of primary importance and, to them, the new feminist ideas propagated by Rathbone and NUSEC overshadowed issues such as equal pay and women's right to work.[14] It was amidst these tensions that the SPG was formed by Lady Rhondda and her colleagues of the militant suffragette movement, who considered themselves to be firmly within the 'old' equal rights tradition of feminism.

[6] Angela John, *Turning the Tide: The Life of Lady Rhondda* (Parthian, 2013) 367.

[7] ibid.

[8] Judith Bourne, 'Great expectations and hard times: The advent of the Sex Disqualification (Removal) Act 1919 and women's entry to the legal profession' (2022) 32 *Women's History Review* 793.

[9] Mari Takayanagi, 'Sacred year or broken reed? The Sex Disqualification (Removal) Act 1919' (2020) 29(4) *Women's History Review* 563, 565.

[10] ibid 564.

[11] Barbara Caine, *English Feminism 1780–1980* (Oxford University Press, 1997) 193. See further **'*Report of the War Cabinet Committee on Women in Industry* 1919'**.

[12] John, n 6, 371 citing *Daily Sketch* (16 October 1922).

[13] For more on this see Caine, n 11, 187–97.

[14] Dorothy Stetson, *A Woman's Issue: The Politics of Family Law Reform in England* (Oxford University Press, 1982) 113.

II. The Landmark

With women making up one-third of the electorate following the 1918 reform[15] Lady Rhondda felt strongly that it was women's responsibility to harness this new electoral power to push for reforms that benefitted their sex.[16] Formally inaugurated on 17 February 1921,[17] the group set out to pursue six specific points:

1. Satisfactory legislation as to child assault.
2. Satisfactory legislation for the widowed mother.
3. Satisfactory legislation for the unmarried mother and her child.
4. Equal rights of guardianship for married parents.
5. Equal pay for teachers.
6. Equal opportunities for men and women in the Civil Service.

If reform was achieved in one of these targeted areas then another issue would take its place. These six points were published in Lady Rhondda's *Time and Tide*, the leading feminist journal of its day, to which SPG members regularly contributed.

The group's focus on strict equality differentiated the SPG from other feminist associations at the time. The 'new feminists' within NUSEC were concerned about the status and welfare of wives and mothers,[18] prioritising issues such as proper information on birth control. But as Barbara Caine put it, for the SPG, 'improvements in family life, while desirable, remained questions of social reform rather than of feminism'.[19] These new feminist ideas were challenged repeatedly by SPG members in *Time and Tide*.[20] Lady Rhondda led the attack. As a former suffragette and strict adherent to 'old feminism', she argued that only when formal equality was won would it be possible for feminists to address broader social attitudes, then with the law on their side.[21]

By the mid-1920s, the SPG was concentrating increasingly on legal and economic equality.[22] The specific issues to first appear on the SPG charter were replaced with equality in six general areas: political, occupational, moral, social, economic and legal. Though 'legal' equality had its own strand, all six areas required reforming the law. Political issues included equal franchise – finally achieved in 1928[23] – as well as the right for women to take up peerages in the House of Lords; a right Lady Rhondda had been denied when she inherited her

[15] John, n 6, 369.
[16] Erika Rackley and Rosemary Auchmuty, 'Centenary of the Six Point Group', *Law Society Gazette* (21 June 2021).
[17] John, n 6, 369.
[18] Caine, n 11, 187.
[19] ibid 185.
[20] ibid 188.
[21] Rackley and Auchmuty, n 16.
[22] Caine, n 11, 187.
[23] **'Representation of the People (Equal Franchise) Act 1928'**.

father's title.[24] Occupational inequalities of concern to the SPG included women's exclusion from employment in industries such as the building trade as a result of trade union restrictions,[25] for, as the group stated, '[t]he denial to any woman of the right freely to choose her own occupation is a denial of her fundamental rights as a citizen'.[26] Moral equality saw the SPG demand reform to the Vagrancy Act 1824 and other associated legislation, which the group argued discriminated against women 'under the pretext of morality', for a woman charged as being 'a common prostitute' was denied a fair trial as a result of the prejudicial language used to describe her.[27] An example of the social equality sought by the SPG was the removal of the marriage bar, which prevented married women from being employed in several professions,[28] including teaching, the Civil Service and local government. Issues such as equal pay were at the forefront of the SPG's efforts to achieve economic equality. And finally, through the ambition of legal equality, the SPG aimed to have *all* sex distinction removed from legislation, noting that 'curiously enough', one instance where this *had* been removed from statute was the **Law Reform (Married Women and Tortfeasors) Act 1935**, which members pithily observed 'pressed hardly on men'.[29]

The SPG's aims were not confined to Britain.[30] From 1930 until the outbreak of the Second World War, the group sent a delegation to Geneva to urge the International Labour Organisation (ILO) to 'raise the status of women citizens' and push the issue of equal pay. During the Spanish Civil War, the SPG helped Spanish women to reach the French frontier so that they could give evidence to the ILO. With such a broad range of both specific and expansive aims, the degree to which these ambitions were realised is not a straightforward assessment. But for the SPG, the status of women was an international question that needed to be pressed beyond Britain's borders.[31]

III. What Happened Next

As is so often the case with feminist activism, the results of the SPG's campaigns were mixed. Several of the original six points were tackled soon after the group's formation. The **Criminal Law Amendment Act 1922** raised the age of consent

[24] **'Lady Rhondda's Petition for Women to Sit in House of Lords, 1922'**.
[25] Caine, n 11, 193.
[26] Dorothy Evans and Claire Madden, *Dorothy Evans and the Six Point Group* (Six Point Group, 1945) 11.
[27] ibid 8.
[28] **'*Short v Poole Corporation* (1926)'**.
[29] The sex distinction removed by this Act was to make a wife liable for her own debts, when previously this was the legal responsibility of her husband.
[30] Evans and Madden, n 26, 7.
[31] Carol Miller, 'Geneva – the key to equality": inter-war feminists and the league of nations' (1994) 3(2) *Women's History Review* 219.

from 13 to 16, and provided that perpetrators of indecent assault would no longer be able to argue in their defence that they had reasonable cause to believe the child was 16. Then the **Guardianship of Infants Act 1925** gave equal guardianship rights to separated fathers and mothers. These reforms followed pressure from the SPG through pamphleteering, pressure on MPs to back earlier iterations of these reforms[32] and public addresses, including in Hyde Park, where SPG members Vera Brittain and Winifred Holtby canvassed support for what became the 1922 Act.[33] Points two and three of the original six points were addressed in part by the **Widows' Orphans' and Old Age Contributory Pensions Act 1925** and the Bastardy Act 1923 respectively, the latter of which made some improvements to provision for children of unmarried parents but was viewed by the SPG as 'inadequate' for failing to put the child first and for seeing illegitimacy as a women's issue.[34] Thus, even these relatively piecemeal successes were partial and did not achieve what the SPG had sought. The SPG had argued that the age of consent should be 18, not 16, and that equal guardianship should be a right for parents within intact marriage too. And while the new feminists of NUSEC supported the equal guardianship reform, the SPG did not, with Lady Rhondda declaring:

> If I ask for roast beef and am provided by one cook with roast beef, horse radish and Yorkshire pudding and by a second with horse radish and Yorkshire pudding but no beef – I feel justified in feeling I have something different.[35]

Equal guardianship for *all* mothers was not possible until 1973.[36] The successes of the SPG were therefore almost always characterised by compromise, falling short of the equality envisaged by the SPG charter.

Other SPG ambitions took much longer to realise. Equal pay for teachers and civil servants was not introduced until the mid-1950s. Crucially, however, the SPG's work provided the framework for the post-war equal pay campaign, for, as Caine observed, the group's demands for women in teaching, the Civil Service and other professions to be paid as their male counterparts were 'had been a powerful rallying cry' for the movement as a whole.[37] Tracing the successes of the SPG is therefore complicated; while its impact may not have been immediately apparent, its influence was nevertheless significant.

Over time, the leadership of the SPG evolved, and so too did the group's ideology. By the 1930s, SPG chair Dorothy Evans had become increasingly convinced that equality outside the home was inextricably linked to equality inside it, and the focus of the group turned to the structural inequalities faced by married women,

[32] For instance, the Criminal Law Amendment Act 1922 followed an earlier unsuccessful Private Member's Bill of the same name in February 1921.
[33] John, n 6, 370.
[34] ibid 373.
[35] ibid 378.
[36] Married mothers continued to have unequal guardianship rights until the Guardianship Act 1973.
[37] Caine, n 11, 231.

which at that time made up a large proportion of the population.[38] This led to the establishment of a group dedicated to equality in marriage, which became the Married Women's Association in 1938. Like SPG founder Lady Rhondda, Evans had been a militant suffragette. She was also lesbian and personally opposed to marriage. Yet while she recognised the need to pursue equality in terms of treating men and women the same, campaigning for issues such as married women's right to earn outside the home,[39] Evans saw the need to redress structural inequalities too, such as the devaluing of women's work inside the home. In other words, Evans complicated the boundaries of 'old' and 'new' feminism, for as Blackford explained, she was one of the few feminists 'able to bridge the generation gap between older women like herself, who had been involved in the suffrage struggle, and younger women who had come into politics during the 1930s and 1940s'.[40] Other SPG members said Evans 'carried the hallmark of true genius; we shall not look upon her like again'.[41] According to SPG member Sybil Morrison, who was also Dorothy Evans' long-term partner, Evans '*was* the Six Point Group'.[42] And so it would be a mistake to assume the views of the SPG were always coterminous with those of its founder Lady Rhondda.

When the history of the SPG is assessed under Evans' leadership, it appears that although the SPG was clearly aligned with old feminism when formed, this identity was less clear-cut as time went on.[43] Indeed, the group's membership comprised a plurality of feminisms, and they campaigned alongside new feminists with some success.

One example of this was the campaign to reform the nationality of married women. Under the British Nationality and Status of Aliens Act 1914, a married woman's nationality was to be determined by her husband, and so she lost her British citizenship if she married a foreigner. The issue was of considerable concern to many feminists of the interwar era, for it could leave a married woman stateless, jobless and without a parliamentary vote. According to Baldwin, it 'provided an important bridge between organizations',[44] with NUSEC, the National Council of Women and the Women's Cooperative Guild, as well as the SPG, all campaigning for reform. Reform was eventually introduced under the British Nationality

[38] In the late 1930s–early 1940s, the proportion of married women was the highest on record: ONS (2022) *Marriages in England and Wales: 2019*.

[39] Helen McCarthy, *Double Lives: A History of Working Motherhood* (Bloomsbury, 2020) 150.

[40] Catherine Blackford, 'Wives and Citizens and Watchdogs of Equality: Post-War British Feminists' in Jim Fyrth (ed), *Labour's Promised Land: Culture and Society in Labour Britain 1945–51* (Lawrence & Wishart, 1995) 61.

[41] Evans, n 26, 17.

[42] Brian Harrison interview with Sybil Morrison, 3 April 1975 (LSE, The Women's Library 8SUF/B/038).

[43] Caitríona Beaumont, 'Citizens not feminists: the boundary negotiated between citizenship and feminism by mainstream women's organisations in England, 1928–39' (2000) 9 *Women's History Review* 411, 413.

[44] M Page Baldwin, 'Subject to Empire: Married Women and the British Nationality and Status of Aliens Act' (2001) 40(4) *Journal of British Studies* 522, 532.

Act 1948, providing that marriage would have no effect on British women's nationality. Yet, as Baldwin has noted, 'the campaign to equalize nationality laws is not included in the list of interwar feminist victories',[45] even though its influence extended far beyond the assistance to the women concerned, but also dealt a further blow to women's loss of rights and status through marriage generally.

The SPG continued its work until 1983, when its then president, Hazel Huskins-Hallinan, died.[46] In contrast to the hive of activity of the Women's Liberation Movement throughout the 1970s, the SPG reported dwindling membership and little direction on which issues it should pursue.[47] The group had 'hung on' with little income since the 1930s for a remarkably long time, but it had become isolated 'from the mass of women for whom [it] wished to speak' and '[was] eventually overtaken by a new generation of feminists'.[48]

IV. Significance

Though the SPG has not been excluded from accounts of feminism in the twentieth century, its importance as a *legal* landmark has largely been overlooked. Because the Sex Discrimination Act was passed in 1975, it is easy to associate demands for equal occupational opportunities with the Women's Liberation Movement, even though this had been one of the core objectives of the SPG from the interwar period until its fragmentation. However, the SPG is significant because it is representative of continuity rather than change within the women's movement,[49] as well as the indirect ways in which law is influenced by feminist activism.

The breadth of campaigns pursued by the SPG underscored the fact that post-suffrage, there were many different inequalities affecting women's emancipation rather than one single issue to dominate women's activities in those interwar years.[50] From this perspective, it is perhaps easy to dismiss the SPG as a small and relatively insignificant organisation concentrated in and around London.[51] Sybil Morrison recalled that the SPG 'really was a committee more than anything else … I doubt if there would ever have been more than a few hundred members'.[52] And with its membership dominated by educated middle-class women, it has been criticised for appealing mainly to professional rather than working-class women.[53]

[45] ibid 555.

[46] When Huskins-Hallinan became too unwell to run the SPG it went into abeyance, but the group was never rejuvenated following her death: Caine, n 11, 240.

[47] ibid 239–40.

[48] Martin Pugh, *Women and the Women's Movement in Britain Since 1914* (3rd edn, Palgrave, 2015) 201.

[49] Beaumont, n 43.

[50] Pugh, n 48, 37.

[51] ibid 38.

[52] Brian Harrison interview with Sybil Morrison, n 42.

[53] Rackley and Auchmuty, n 16.

Nevertheless, it is clear that the SPG sought to represent all women. In 1968, 50 years after women achieved partial suffrage, the SPG published an edited collection focused on women's role in society, which in part highlighted how much the law continued to let women down.[54] Its blurb states that the SPG 'aims to provoke controversy'. It is striking that it was so controversial for members simply to ask for legal reform recognising that '[f]ar from being merely a mother and household drudge, a woman is a person *in her own right*'.[55] Their work not only aimed to show how far short most women fell from these ideals,[56] but also paved the way for change. Understanding this broader ambition produces valuable insight into the aims and strategies of feminist activism during the interwar period. The law was only ever seen as a tool for change; and reforming legislation was not the ultimate goal. For as Lady Rhondda wrote in 1933, 'that fight of ours was only *ostensibly* concerned with changing the law'.[57] Instead, it was to 'passionately, urgently, change customs and … influence ideas',[58] an influence more difficult, but nonetheless of vital importance for historians to record.

Further Reading

- Dorothy Evans and Claire Madden, *Dorothy Evans and the Six Point Group* (Six Point Group, 1945).
- Angela John, *Turning the Tide: The Life of Lady Rhondda* (Parthian, 2013).
- Hilda Kean, 'Searching for the past in present defeat: the construction of historical and political identity in British feminism in the 1920s and 1930s' (1994) 3(1) *Women's History Review* 57.

[54] Hallinan, n 1.
[55] ibid (original emphasis).
[56] ibid.
[57] Viscountess Rhondda, *This Was My World* (Macmillan, 1933) 299–300 (emphasis added).
[58] ibid.

9

Ivy Williams, First Woman to Qualify as a Barrister, 1922

CAROLINE MORRIS

On the evening of 10 May 1922, Dr Ivy Williams became the first woman to be called to the Bar of England and Wales. Women would no longer be simply subjects of law and passive and silent before the courts; as a result of this change, they would be able to join barristers' chambers, appear in court, become senior practitioners and, eventually, take judicial office. But although as a young woman Williams had wished to join her solicitor father and barrister brother as a lawyer, at the time of her call she chose not to practise. In 1920 she was appointed a tutor in jurisprudence at Oxford, and she pursued that career until her retirement, as England's first woman legal academic.

I. Life

Ivy Williams was born in 1877 in the small Devonshire town of Newton Abbot. Her family hailed from Oxford, and it was there they returned in 1880. Williams spent the rest of her life in Oxford, where she was home-schooled and then attended the University of Oxford as a member of the Society of Home Students (now St Anne's College)[1] from 1896 to 1902. She was only the third woman to study law at Oxford, after Cornelia Sorabji and Alice Adams. She passed the exams for the BA in Jurisprudence in 1900 and those for the BCL (Bachelor of Civil Law) in 1902. Even as she was studying at Oxford, she studied at the same time for an LLB and then an LLD (Doctor of Laws) at the University of London, graduating with these degrees in 1901 and 1903. In 1920, when Oxford permitted women to graduate, she received her BA, MA and BCL at the first ceremony for women graduates.

[1] The Society of Home Students was an association for women who chose not to live in at a women's college. See RF Butler and MH Pritchard (eds), *Saint Anne's College: A History*, vols I and II (private publication, 1930).

After finishing her studies, Williams declared that she had 'been educated expressly for the legal profession'.[2] But her attempt to be admitted to an Inn of Court was unsuccessful and, after the deaths of her brother and her father in quick succession, she turned away from public life to care for her mother and manage the considerable family finances. During the First World War she served as the Treasurer of the Cowley War Savings Association, as well as working as a Russian translator and Italian tutor. Between May 1918 and February 1919, she worked as a law clerk at the Oxford law offices of Thomas Mallam.

In 1920, Williams joined the Society of Home Students as a Tutor in Jurisprudence, continuing in that role until her retirement in 1945. During that time she taught all of the women studying law at Oxford. Of her teaching, it was said:

> Those of us who were tutored by Ivy Williams soon came to realize that, though she worked hard, she let us go our own ways with splendid objectivity, and that beneath a shy and remote exterior she concealed a personality that was both kind and courageous, though her aloofness made it difficult for the immature to know her at all intimately. It was not until many years later that those who had kept in touch with her learnt to delight freely in the range of her keen intelligence and to admire the magnificent courage with which she faced blindness, ill-health and old age.[3]

In 1923, she was the first woman to be awarded a non-honorary DCL (Doctor of Civil Law) by Oxford in recognition of her academic work in private international law.

In the meantime, in 1922, Williams was called to the Bar, six months ahead of the other women in her cohort. This was thanks to a provision in the regulations that enabled her to be excused from two terms of the dinners required as part of the qualifying process because she had taken first class in her law examinations. She represented the British Government in 1930 at the League of Nations Conference for the Codification of International Law, speaking on the position of married women's nationality. From 1932 to 1939 she was a member of the Aliens Deportation Advisory Committee, advising the Government whether proposed deportations on the grounds of the 'public good' should be carried out.

Williams neither married nor had children but shared her home with women companions, including the Oxford geography tutor Nora MacMunn (the second woman to be appointed to an academic post in Oxford) and a retired former missionary. She died in Oxford in 1966.

II. Context

Women were not allowed to practise as lawyers in the nineteenth century. From mid-century, feminists campaigned for entry. A petition was organised

[2] 'Our Lady Lawyer' *Dundee Evening Post* (1 April 1904) 8.
[3] S Penley and EO Dodgson, 'Dr Ivy Williams: An Appreciation' (1966) *The Ship* 38.

by Maria Grey, who had opened a stationers' office to train female legal clerks in 1860, asking the Law Society to open its professional examinations to women. In 1873, Eliza Orme undertook an unofficial pupillage with a sympathetic barrister and then opened her own legal office with women friends who 'devilled' (drafted legal documents) for Counsel. The University of London admitted women to its LLB classes in 1878, and Eliza Orme became the first woman to graduate there with a law degree in 1888. Cambridge admitted its first woman law student in 1879 and Oxford in 1889.[4]

But the possession of a law degree did not qualify a person to become a lawyer. For that, they needed to be accepted into the Law Society examinations (to become a solicitor) or called to the Bar (to become a barrister). Both professional bodies were strongly opposed to women's entry. In 1901, Margaret Hall's application to the Society of Law Agents of Scotland to take their qualifying exams was refused, just as in December 1903 Bertha Cave unsuccessfully applied to the Benchers of Gray's Inn to admit her as a student of law. In January 1904, Ivy Williams herself and Christabel Pankhurst applied to the Inns of Court for admission and were both rebuffed. In 1913, Gwyneth Bebb unsuccessfully challenged the refusal of the Law Society to allow women to enrol for their qualifying examinations.[5]

Williams' call to the Bar was made possible by the enactment of the Sex Disqualification (Removal) Act 1919. That Act removed the bar to women's entry to the legal profession and required the Inns of Court to admit women as members and allow them to begin the course of study that would result in their call to the Bar or admission to the roll of solicitors.[6]

III. What Happened Next

As 'first woman to be called to the Bar', Ivy Williams represents something of a paradox. Since she never practised, her status as a barrister was mostly symbolic, as it began and ended on her night of call. She was not the first to be admitted to an Inn after the passing of the 1919 Act (this was Helena Normanton);[7] she was not the first to complete her Bar examinations (this was Olive Clapham); and she was not the first woman in the UK to qualify as a lawyer after the Act (that honour goes to Frances Kyle and April Deverell, who were called to the Irish Bar

[4] Rosemary Auchmuty, 'Early women law students at Cambridge and Oxford' (2008) 29 *Journal of Legal History* 63.

[5] Rosemary Auchmuty, 'Whatever happened to Miss Bebb? *Bebb v the Law Society* and women's legal history' (2011) 31 *Legal Studies* 199.

[6] See further Mari Takayanagi 'Sex Disqualification (Removal) Act 1919' in Erika Rackley and Rosemary Auchmuty (eds), *Women's Legal Landmarks: Celebrating the History of Women and Law in the UK and Ireland* (Hart Publishing, 2019) 133.

[7] Judith Bourne, 'First Woman to be Admitted to an Inn of Court, Helena Normanton, 1919' in Rackley and Auchmuty (eds), n 6, 147.

in November 1921).[8] So it fell to the other 11 women in her cohort, who were called in November 1922, and their successors to demonstrate that women could be competent lawyers on the same basis as men, unconfined as to subject matter. They faced considerable opposition and sexist discrimination, and it was not until 1949 that the first women King's Counsel, Helena Normanton and Rose Heilbron, were appointed.

What did not happen, either immediately or for some decades, was a large influx of women into either branch of the legal profession. In the 1920s and 1930s, the annual number of new women barristers and solicitors only just reached double figures. It was not until the 1970s that the percentage of women solicitors picked up. Women now comprise 51 per cent of all solicitors. The Bar has doubled in size between 1990 and 2020, but women still make up only 38 per cent of barristers. Moreover, attrition and lack of progress continue to bedevil the attainment of true equality: women comprise 62 per cent of all new solicitors, but only 35 per cent are partners;[9] 50 per cent of all pupil barristers, but 18 per cent of KCs.[10] These inequalities are reflected in women's financial position in the profession. As of October 2022, the pay gap between men and women at the Bar was currently 34 per cent, slightly improved from the pre-pandemic figure of 39 per cent.[11] Women solicitors fare better, but the median pay gap between men and women as at June 2022 was 25 per cent.[12]

A similar situation faced women legal academics. During Williams' 25-year tenure as Tutor in Jurisprudence at Oxford, only one other woman taught in an English law school: Edith Hesling, assistant lecturer at Victoria College, Manchester, from the mid-1930s. It was not until 1949 that Sylvia Tolson became assistant lecturer at Kings College, London, followed by Olive Stone at the LSE in 1952;[13] and it is only recently that women's participation in legal education has achieved near equality with men's. And even though Trinity College Dublin appointed its first woman law professor in 1925, Frances Moran,[14] in the UK the first woman law professor was not appointed until 1970, when Dr Claire Palley became Professor of Law at Queen's University Belfast, moving to the University of Kent in 1973.[15]

[8] Liz Goldthorpe, 'First Woman to Practise as a Barrister in Ireland and the (then) United Kingdom, Averil Deverell, 1921' in Rackley and Auchmuty (eds), n 6, 175.

[9] Solicitors Regulation Authority, 'How diverse is the solicitors' profession?' (27 June 2023).

[10] The Bar Council, 'Key trends shaping recruitment and retention at the Bar' (31 October 2022).

[11] Zara Nanu and Dana Denis-Smith, *Closing the Gender pay gap in the legal profession* (Gapsquare, June 2022) 3.

[12] ibid.

[13] Rosemary Auchmuty and Jennifer Temkin, 'The road to Olive Stone' in Ulrike Schultz et al (eds), *Gender and Careers in the Legal Academy* (Hart Publishing, 2021) 446.

[14] Emma Hutchinson, 'First Woman Professor of Law in Ireland, Frances Moran, 1925' in Rackley and Auchmuty (eds), n 6, 199.

[15] Fiona Cownie, 'First Woman Professor of Law in the UK, Claire Palley, 1970' in Rackley and Auchmuty (eds), n 6, 297.

IV. Significance

In becoming the first woman called to the Bar of England and Wales, Ivy Williams opened the door to a new area of professional working life for women. By 1922, women were already doctors, teachers, factory inspectors, academics, accountants, dentists and MPs. After Ivy Williams' call, the 'woman barrister' was no longer an abstract prospect but a personalised reality. Williams' appearance in the barrister's gown and wig made national and international news. Women were no longer limited to being imagined as barristers; now, they *were* barristers. Conscious of her historic achievement, it was reported, she 'spoke of the women who would follow and who would practise at the Bar, and she asked that every help and encouragement would be given them in the difficulties they would face'.[16]

Thanks largely to feminist efforts to insert women into legal history, prompted by the centenary of women's admission to the legal profession, Williams' role in the transformation of the profession has been commemorated in traditional ways: a blue plaque marks Williams' childhood home in Oxford, and the centenary of her call was observed by special Judicial Office events, a commemorative lecture at the Inner Temple and an exhibition at the UK Supreme Court.[17] Lady Hallett, the first woman to chair the Bar Council and the fifth woman to be appointed a Court of Appeal judge, named Ivy Williams as her inspiration in law.[18] But there are also some less traditional examples of her impact. Williams' 'unwavering drive and dedication' has inspired the naming of a scented candle, as well as a multi-academy educational trust in Devon (the Ivy Education Trust)[19] and the specialist women's legal outfitters, Ivy & Normanton, a business that is now possible due to the number of women barristers.[20]

Further Reading

- Caroline Morris, 'Dr Ivy Williams: inside yet outside' (2020) 29(4) *Women's History Review* 583.
- Mary Jane Mossman, *The First Women Lawyers: A Comparative Study of Gender, Law and the Legal Profession* (Bloomsbury Press, 2006).
- Bridget Wheeler, *Ivy Williams* (Woodbridge Publishers, 2022).

[16] 'First Englishwoman barrister' *The Guardian* (11 May 1922).
[17] 'Celebrate 100 years of women at the Bar at the Supreme Court' (23 September 2022).
[18] Heather Hallett, 'My legal hero: Dr Ivy Williams' *The Guardian* (10 February 2011).
[19] Ivy Education Trust at https://ivyeducationtrust.co.uk [accessed 15 May 2023].
[20] As the website notes, 'The profession has changed since Ivy and Helena first joined, but the shirts and collars they wore have remained much the same' (Ivy and Normanton, 'About Us' at https://ivyandnormanton.com [accessed 22 November 2022]).

10

Lady Rhondda's Petition for Women to Sit in House of Lords, 1922

MARI TAKAYANAGI

Viscountess Rhondda, a hereditary woman peer in her own right, was the first woman to petition to take her seat in the House of Lords. No woman had attempted this previously because of long-established custom and lack of precedent. Although her petition was ultimately refused by the Committee for Privileges in 1922, it was a legal landmark in establishing that legislation was required for women to enter the Upper House of Parliament and an essential stepping-stone in the process that eventually led to women's entering the House of Lords as life peers in 1958, hereditary peers in 1963 and bishops in 2015.

I. Context

The origins of the House of Lords can be traced back to the Anglo-Saxon Witan or 'wise men', councils of ecclesiastical leaders and noblemen consulted by the monarch. Such assemblies might have occasionally included abbesses and royal women. Bede writes extensively of Hilda, Abbess of Whitby, who presided over a synod in 664, where 'the kings, both father and son [King Oswy and his son Alchfrid], came thither' along with bishops and priests.[1] Evidence is otherwise scanty, however, with sources typically coming from antiquaries writing many centuries later.[2]

[1] *Bede's Ecclesiastical History of England, A Revised Translation with Introduction, Life, and Notes by AM Sellar* (George Bell and Sons, 1907) ch 25.

[2] For example, 'In Wighfred's great Council at Beconsceld, AD 694, the Abbesses sat and deliberated; and five of them signed decrees of that council along with the King, Bishops, and Nobles'. Thornagh Gurdon, *The History of the High Court of Parliament* (1731), citing Sir Henry Spelman, *Concilia, decreta, leges, constitutiones, in re ecclesiarum orbis Britannici* (1639). Gurdon also describes abbesses being summoned to Parliament by Henry III and Edward I, and noblewomen represented by proxies under Edward III. Such notable occasions were clearly the exception rather than the rule.

By the fourteenth century, the House of Lords had emerged as a distinct body made up of the Lords Spiritual and Lords Temporal. The Lords Spiritual consisted of bishops, abbots and priors, until the dissolution of the monasteries in the fifteenth century removed the abbots and priors, and therefore also any future claims from abbesses and prioresses. As women could not become priests in the Church of England, let alone rise to the position of bishop, they could not become Lords Spiritual. Women began to campaign actively to become priests in the early twentieth century, led by Maud Royden and the Church League for Women's Suffrage.

The Lords Temporal consisted of five ranks of peers: duke, marquess, earl, viscount and baron. Virtually all these titles were hereditary by male primogeniture, passed to oldest sons and then nearest male relatives, and went into abeyance if no male heir could be found. However, there were a few routes by which women could inherit a peerage.[3] Women could succeed to a barony by writ (which applied to some early English baronies) and to a Scottish peerage,[4] as both these methods usually specified descent to 'heirs general' rather than heirs male. Women could succeed by special remainder, a device by which a man with no sons could allow a daughter or other relative to succeed him and avoid the peerage's becoming immediately extinct on his death. In this case women were seen as 'accidental conduit pipes established in the hope of making permanent male succession',[5] rather than the device's conferring peerage rights upon them. Finally, women were occasionally created life peers by monarchs (notoriously, the mistresses of some kings).[6]

However, parliamentary historians agree that none of these women peers ever sat in the House of Lords by custom and precedent. Simon Payling says of medieval parliaments, 'if a female member of the Lords was at least conceptually possible … such membership did not lie within the realm of practical politics'.[7] Andrew Thrush similarly commented of the early modern period that '[a]lthough no law barred women … the only formal role accorded to women in the parliamentary sphere was ceremonial', noting that when Mary Beaumont was created Countess of Buckingham in 1618, the question of whether this gave her the right to sit in the Lords was dismissed as '"silly"'.[8]

[3] Helpfully outlined in Duncan Sutherland, 'Peeresses, Parliament and prejudice: the admission of women to the House of Lords, 1918–1963' (2000) 20(1) *Parliaments, Estates and Representation* 215.

[4] The Acts of Union 1707 and 1801 allowed a representative selection of 16 Scottish and 28 Irish peers to sit in the House of Lords; no woman was ever selected as such a representative. Irish peers left the Lords at the creation of the Irish Free State in 1922; all Scottish peers were allowed to sit in the Lords by the Peerage Act 1963.

[5] Earl of Birkenhead, HL Deb 24 June 1926, vol 64, col 596.

[6] Charles II, James II, George I and George II all awarded life peerages to distinguished ladies.

[7] Simon Payling, 'Women and Parliament in the Fifteenth Century' *History of Parliament* (16 January 2018) at https://thehistoryofparliament.wordpress.com/2018/01/16/women-and-parliament-in-the-fifteenth-century/.

[8] Andrew Thrush, 'Women in early modern parliamentary politics' *History of Parliament* (3 April 2020) at https://thehistoryofparliament.wordpress.com/2020/04/03/women-in-early-modern-parliamentary-politics/.

Despite this exclusion, many aristocratic women exercised considerable public and behind-the-scenes political influence, as queens, political hostesses, and during election campaigns. Wives of peers can occasionally be seen to directly exercise power, such as Eleanor, Countess of Sussex, who refused her consent to a vote when her husband was too ill to attend Parliament in person in 1641.[9] The House of Lords was a popular social location for elite women, particularly during the State Opening of Parliament, where so many women were known to pack the benches that peers complained they had nowhere to sit.[10] Women also attended the Lords as politically engaged observers, sitting in a roped-off area in the public gallery. When they were temporarily banned in 1739, a group of indignant ladies, led by the Duchesses of Queensberry and Ancaster, battled their way in past doorkeepers to hear a debate on the conduct of the Spanish Government, Mary Pendarves recording that 'we bore the buffets of a stinking crowd from half an hour after ten till five in the afternoon without moving an inch from our places'.[11]

From the mid-nineteenth century, the women's suffrage movement was active, including a small number of aristocratic women such as Lady Frances Balfour and the Countess of Selborne. Their names and titles were welcomed by suffrage societies as bringing legitimacy to the cause, as well as for their influence on their menfolk. A few were even militant suffragettes, such as Princess Sophia Duleep Singh (Queen Victoria's goddaughter and daughter of Maharaja Duleep Singh) and Constance Lytton (daughter of the Earl of Lytton), who were members of the Women's Social and Political Union. Authorities were reluctant to punish elite women: Singh was never arrested and Lytton was arrested but released by authorities when they discovered her identity. Lytton consequently disguised herself as a working-class woman, and as such was imprisoned and forcibly fed, permanently damaging her health. In the Coronation Procession of 1911, suffrage campaigners dressed as Abbess Hilda and attendant nuns as part of a historical pageant, intended to illustrate political power held by women in times past.

In February 1918, the Representation of the People Act gave the vote to the first women.[12] This was followed by the **Parliament (Qualification of Women) Act 1918** in November, which allowed women to sit in the House of Commons. The title of the Bill had been drafted to potentially include the Lords, and there were attempts during its passage to amend it to include the Lords, but these failed. The early women MPs included a number of titled women, including (Countess) **Constance Markievicz** and (Viscountess) **Nancy Astor**, but these were titles gained through marriage rather than being conferred on the holders in their own right.

[9] ibid.

[10] Elaine Chalus, *Elite Women in English Political Life c 1754–1790* (Oxford University Press, 2005).

[11] Lady Llanover (ed), *The Autobiography and Correspondence of Mary Granville, Mrs Delany*, 3 vols (Richard Bentley, 1861) ii, 44–45. Mary Pendarves to Ann Granville, 1 March 1739.

[12] Mari Takayanagi, 'Representation of the People Act 1918' in Erika Rackley and Rosemary Auchmuty (eds), *Women's Legal Landmarks: Celebrating the History of Women and Law in the UK and Ireland* (Hart Publishing, 2019) 113.

Now women could sit in the Commons, campaigners turned attention to the House of Lords. In 1919, the Women's Emancipation Bill was introduced by the Labour party, which would have allowed hereditary women peers to sit in the Lords. It was replaced by the Government's Sex Disqualification (Removal) Bill, which initially included a clause allowing women with special remainders to sit in the Lords, but this was deleted in the Lords before the Bill was passed.[13]

II. The Landmark

The test case that came forward was that of Viscountess Rhondda (1883–1958).[14] Born Margaret Haig Thomas, she was the daughter of David Alfred ('DA') Thomas, a Welsh Liberal MP and industrialist, and Sybil Margaret Thomas, née Haig. Margaret married Sir Humphrey Mackworth in 1908; they divorced in 1922. A feminist from an early age, thanks to the influence of her mother, Margaret was a militant suffragette in her youth. She was secretary of the Newport branch of the Women's Social and Political Union, and was jailed for setting fire to a post box in 1913. She went on to become one of the leading feminists of the interwar period, founder of the **Six Point Group** and *Time and Tide* magazine.

She was also a successful businesswoman in an era when there were few. As her father's confidential secretary, she was returning from a business trip on the *Lusitania* in 1916 when it was bombed, and spent hours in the freezing water before being rescued. She reflected later that the experience gave her self-confidence, as 'I had found that when the moment came I could control my fear'.[15] She inherited her father's business interests after his death, and became the first female president of the Institute of Directors in 1926.

Her father, DA Thomas, was made first Baron Rhondda and then Viscount Rhondda by David Lloyd George, in recognition of his services in the First World War. As he had no legitimate sons, he stipulated that the peerage should pass to his daughter by special remainder. He died in July 1918 and Margaret became Viscountess Rhondda in her own right. Had she been male, she would have inherited her father's seat in the House of Lords. By the terms of the instrument, as a woman she could have passed the right on to her children, but she had no children.

Lady Rhondda petitioned the Crown to take her seat in the Lords in 1920, and her petition was passed to the House of Lords Committee for Privileges in 1921. She based her claim on the Sex Disqualification (Removal) Act 1919, section 1 of which stated that 'A person shall not be disqualified by sex or marriage from the

[13] Mari Takayanagi, 'Sex Disqualification (Removal) Act 1919' in Rackley and Auchmuty (eds), n 12, 133.

[14] For a full biography of Lady Rhondda, see Angela V John, *Turning the Tide: The Life of Lady Rhondda* (Parthian, 2013).

[15] Lady Rhondda, *This Was My World* (Macmillan, 1933) 259.

exercise of any public function ...'.[16] Led by Attorney-General Sir Gordon Hewart, a suffrage sympathiser who declared himself 'very much in agreement' with Rhondda, the Committee initially found in her favour.[17] Rhondda was cautious, however, writing privately on 16 March 1922, 'I am not in the House of Lords yet, in spite of the Committee of Privileges, and I am afraid the Lord Chancellor is going to move against me'.[18]

She was quite right: the Lord Chancellor (FE Smith, Lord Birkenhead), a staunch anti-feminist, reconvened the Committee and packed it with his own supporters. Unfortunately for Rhondda, by this time Gordon Hewart had been made Lord Chief Justice, and the new Attorney-General, Sir Ernest Pollack, was not a sympathiser. After some stormy proceedings, the Committee reversed its decision and found against her in May 1922.[19] Their argument was that the 1919 Act removed disabilities but did not create new rights; admission of women to the Lords was a new right requiring specific legislation. Millicent Fawcett wrote to *The Times*, 'This situation seems to plain people simply scandalous.'[20]

III. What Happened Next

The way forward was now clear; legislation was required. Various Bills enabling hereditary women peers to sit in the House of Lords were drafted by Rhondda's lawyer and introduced by Viscount Astor, husband of Nancy Astor, as Private Members' Bills in the 1920s. None proceeded. After numerous defeats, Viscount Astor concluded in 1931 that women could not be admitted except as part of wider Lords reform, and the parliamentary battle paused.[21] Lady Rhondda moved on to other feminist campaigns, although she never gave up on the issue, reflecting in her memoirs in 1933, 'It would, after all, if one could get there, be a useful enough platform for all sorts of purposes, quite apart from the value of breaking down that particular barrier.'[22]

After the Second World War, the issue was revived, and Rhondda was one of five hereditary women peers who signed a petition organised by Edward Iwi and presented to the House of Lords on 2 March 1948.[23] Iwi was a solicitor and constitutional expert; his wife Esther was a magistrate and lawyer, called to the Bar by Gray's Inn in 1956.[24] Iwi also organised a wider public petition on the subject,

[16] Parliamentary Archives (HL/PO/DC/CP/4/153).
[17] John, n 14, 445.
[18] Parliamentary Archives (STR/19/4/8d). Correspondence between Viscountess Rhondda and John St Loe Strachey, editor of *The Spectator*, 1922.
[19] Sutherland, n 3.
[20] *The Times* (14 June 1922).
[21] Sutherland, n 3.
[22] Rhondda, n 15, 298.
[23] Parliamentary Archives (HL/PO/JO/10/10/1391 no 878).
[24] *The Palgrave Dictionary of Anglo-Jewish History* (Palgrave Macmillan, 2011) 462.

which collected 50,000 signatures but was never presented, because in 1949 the House of Lords finally declared itself in favour of admitting women peers, with a motion passed 45 votes to 27. No legislation followed, however, as the Labour Government was not keen to extend the hereditary principle, and the question was caught up in wider questions of Lords reform at that time, which led to the Parliament Act 1949.

When legislation came, it was to enable the creation of life peers rather to admit women as such. The Life Peerages Act 1958 allowed the first women to sit, with section 1(3) removing any doubt by including the specific provision, 'A life peerage may be conferred … on a woman.'[25] Four women life peers were created in 1958: Baroness Swanborough, Baroness Wootton of Abinger, Baroness Elliot of Harwood and Baroness Ravensdale of Kedleston.[26] However, the position of hereditary peers such as Lady Rhondda was unchanged. Indeed, Baroness Ravensdale was also a hereditary peer in her own right but unable to sit as such. Lady Rhondda lived to see the passage of the Life Peerages Act but not its implementation; she died in July 1958, aged 75.

The principle of admitting hereditary women peers was finally agreed by a division in the Lords on 21 January 1959, narrowly carried by 59 votes to 51, but like life peerages, it was not proceeded with until other Lords reform issues required action a few years later. The Peerage Act 1963 was passed primarily to allow hereditary peerages to be renounced, following a high-profile campaign by Tony Benn MP (previously the 2nd Viscount Stansgate). The Joint Committee that considered the matter took the opportunity to deal with other peerage issues, including allowing hereditary women peers to sit. By now this was not controversial, and had indeed become an embarrassment, preventing the UK from signing up to the UN Convention on the Political Rights of Women. After the passage of the Peerage Act on 31 July 1963, female hereditary peers in their own right became eligible to sit in the Lords. The first to take her seat was Baroness Strange of Knokin later that year, and a total of 25 sat between 1963 and 1999.

In 1999, the House of Lords Act removed the right of all but 92 hereditary peers to sit and vote in the Lords. These 92 consist of two held by virtue of hereditary office (the Earl Marshall and Lord Great Chamberlain) and 90 elected by their fellow peers, the number maintained as necessary following death or resignation by by-elections. Five women were among the 90 first elected; as of 2023, no further women had been elected.

[25] Supuni Perera, 'Life Peerages Act 1958' in Rackley and Auchmuty (eds), n 12, 249; Mari Takayanagi, 'A changing house: the Life Peerages Act 1958' (2008) 27(3) *Parliamentary History* 380.

[26] Barbara Wootton (Baroness Wootton) was appointed for her expertise on sociology, criminology and penal reform. Stella Isaacs (Baroness Swanborough, also known as Lady Reading from her marriage) was the founder of the Women's Voluntary Service. Katharine Elliot (Baroness Elliot) had extensive experience working in prison reform, childcare, consumer and international affairs. Irene Curzon (Baroness Ravensdale) was recognised for her voluntary work with young people.

In 2011, the Perth Agreement set out a wish by 16 Commonwealth nations to amend the line of succession to the British Crown, including by ending male primogeniture. The Succession to the Crown Act 2013 duly replaced male primogeniture with absolute primogeniture for those in line of succession to the British throne born after 28 October 2011 (the date of the Perth Agreement), meaning the oldest child now succeeds regardless of sex.[27] However, this Act only affected the Royal family and not the wider peerage. The Daughters' Rights Campaign was founded by Charlotte Carew Pole in 2016 to advocate for daughters to have the same inheritance rights as sons, including inheriting peerages, baronetages and seats in the House of Lords. To date, the Government has refused on the grounds that this is apparently too complicated.[28]

Separately, the Appellate Jurisdiction Act 1876 had allowed the creation of a specific kind of life peer to exercise the judicial functions of the House of Lords. In 2004, Brenda Hale became the first female Lord of Appeal in Ordinary, arguably a long-delayed effect of the Sex Disqualification (Removal) Act 1919, which had allowed women to become lawyers and, ultimately, judges. No other women were appointed Law Lords before the establishment of the Supreme Court in 2009 removed the judicial function from the House of Lords.[29]

Also separately, women continued to press to become priests in the Church of England, which would eventually allow them to become Lords Spiritual. Following renewed campaigning by the Movement for the Ordination of Women from 1979, the Church of England Synod finally agreed to have women priests in 1992, the measure passing in 1993.[30] The first women priest to be ordained was Angela Berners-Wilson, one of 32 women ordained in alphabetical order in 1994. A generation of further campaigning later, by which time a third of clergy were women, the Church of England agreed to appoint women as bishops in 2014.[31] Twenty-one bishops are appointed to the House of Lords by virtue of seniority, with five more sitting *ex officio*, meaning it would have potentially taken many years for women bishops to arrive in the Lords. However, the Lords Spiritual (Women) Act 2015 was passed soon afterwards to speed up the process by positive discrimination. This Act stipulated that for the next 10 years, whenever a vacancy arose among the Lords Spiritual, the position had to be filled by a woman if there was one who was eligible.[32] As a result, Rachel Treweek, Bishop of Gloucester from 2015, became the

[27] Succession to the Crown Act 2013, c 20.

[28] See https://daughtersrights.co.uk/. See also **'Administration of Estates Act 1925'**.

[29] Constitutional Reform Act 2005, c 4. The 12 Lords of Appeal in Ordinary in 2009 were disqualified from sitting or voting in the Lords until they retired as Supreme Court Justices, after which they could return as full members of the Lords. Hale retired from the Supreme Court in 2020, at which point she resumed full membership of the Lords. Supreme Court Justices appointed since 2009 do not sit in the Lords.

[30] Priests (Ordination of Women) Measure 1993 (No 2).

[31] See further Miranda Threlfall-Holmes, 'Bishops and Priests (Consecration and Ordination of Women) Measure 2014 and Canon C2 "Of the Consecration of Bishops", 2014' in Rackley and Auchmuty (eds), n 12, 611.

[32] Lords Spiritual (Women) Act 2015, c 18.

first woman bishop to sit in the House of Lords when a vacancy arose in October 2016. As of 2023, five women bishops have sat by this route, with another, Sarah Mullally, sitting *ex officio* as Bishop of London from 2018.

IV. Significance

Lady Rhondda's petition demanded that as a female hereditary peer, she should have the same right to sit in the House of Lords as a male hereditary peer. This did not happen for more than 40 years, by which time Rhondda herself had died. Even then, it was a niche issue, giving rights to a tiny number of women. The underlying inequality of male primogeniture succession to hereditary peerages was not affected, nor did Rhondda campaign for it to be. The impact on the Lords is even smaller today, since the number of hereditary peers was reduced in 1999. As of 2023 there are no female hereditary peers in the Lords, all having since died or retired since 1999, the last being the Countess of Mar who retired in 2020.[33]

However, there was broader significance in terms of gender equality. As Rhondda said in 1922:

> The refusal to admit women to the House of Lords has just slightly lowered the status of all women so that it is just a little more unlikely that any professional or working woman will get a fair chance ungoverned by the accident of her sex.[34]

As the second chamber of the UK Parliament, the House of Lords plays a key role in scrutinising legislation and holding the Government to account. It was a glaring constitutional inequality that women did not sit in the Lords, and Lady Rhondda's petition was the key legal landmark in the battle for women's admission. It established that legislation was required to allow women to sit in the Lords, laying out the route for future campaigning. As such, its effects live on with the presence of women in the Lords today. Since 1958, more than 1,500 life peerages have been created, including for more than 320 women, approximately 21 per cent. As of 2023, there are 662 life peers in the House of Lords, of whom 220 – one-third – are women; and of the 26 Lords Spiritual, five are women. Studies of the impact of women on the Lords over time have found that despite their small numbers, women have made a 'considerable mark' upon the work of the Lords in various ways, including as office-holders, in attendance and contribution to debates.[35]

[33] House of Lords Library Briefing, 'Women, hereditary peerages and gender inequality in the line of succession' (3 October 1922).

[34] *Time and Tide* (9 June 1922). Quoted in Sutherland, n 3.

[35] Gavin Drewry and Jenny Brock, *The Impact of Women on the House of Lords* (Centre for the Study of Public Policy, University of Strathclyde, 1983); Duncan Sutherland, 'Ladies in a Lords' House: Women in the House of Lords Since 1958' in Bruce Kinzer, Molly Baer Kramer and Richard Trainor (eds), *Reform and Its Complexities in Modern Britain: Essays Inspired by Sir Brian Harrison* (Oxford University Press, 2022) 203.

As Duncan Sutherland has recently concluded, their admission 'extended a lifeline to an assembly whose short-sighted conservatism toward its own reform had undermined its long-term effectiveness … While strengthening parliament, women peers have also empowered women.'[36]

Further Reading

- Angela V John, *Turning the Tide: The Life of Lady Rhondda* (Parthian, 2013).
- Duncan Sutherland, 'Peeresses, Parliament and prejudice: the admission of women to the House of Lords, 1918–1963' (2000) 20(1) *Parliaments, Estates and Representation* 215.
- Mari Takayanagi, 'A changing house: the Life Peerages Act 1958' (2008) 27(3) *Parliamentary History* 380.

[36] Sutherland, n 35.

11

Monica Geikie Cobb, First Woman Barrister to Appear in Court, 1922

CAROLINE DERRY

On 1 December 1922, Monica Mary Geikie Cobb became the first woman barrister in England and Wales to appear in court. She had qualified as a barrister on 22 November that year, one of the first small cohort of women to do so intending to pursue a legal career. Their success followed a long battle for admission into the legal professions, against resistance by the professional bodies. It became possible only after the Sex Disqualification Removal Act 1919 became law, opening the legal professions, magistracy and juries to women.

When Cobb won her case at the Birmingham Assizes just nine days after qualification, that success did not only represent a milestone in women's entry to the legal professions and a personal triumph. It also, thanks to press interest in the occasion, played a vital part in shaping public perceptions of women barristers, confirming that they were capable professionals. Cobb's court appearance was thus one significant step in a much longer process that continues today.

I. Life

Cobb was born in 1891, the third child of the Rev Dr Geikie Cobb. He was an active supporter of the women's movement, favouring women's ordination and supporting the Order of Women Freemasons; he was later to speak at Emmeline Pankhurst's funeral. It is unsurprising, then, that Cobb was able to pursue higher education. After graduating from University College London (UCL) with a BA in Philosophy in 1914, she returned four years later to take her LLB, which she completed in 1921.[1]

Cobb had worked during the First World War, and then through her LLB and Bar examinations, as Joint Secretary of the Professional Classes War Relief

[1] Caroline Derry, 'Cobb, Monica Mary Geikie (1891–1946)', *Oxford Dictionary of National Biography* (8 November 2018).

Council. She received an MBE for her work.[2] Among the many bodies represented on the Council, which aimed to relieve distress among the professional classes through practical assistance, were the Barristers' Benevolent Association, General Council of the Bar, National Union of Women's Suffrage Societies and National Union of Women Workers, suggesting possibilities for useful connections for her future career.[3]

She was called to the Bar by Middle Temple in November 1922: an event that marked her qualification as a barrister.[4] Her subsequent appearance for the prosecution at Birmingham Assizes was widely reported in the press. Articles recorded how she successfully prosecuted bricklayer Thomas Fallow for bigamy, but they showed more interest in the novelty of the woman barrister. However, despite this initial success, establishing a legal practice was not easy. Cobb found a pupillage with Theobald Mathew, whose other pupils would include the future Lord Diplock, Lord Hailsham and Clement Attlee, but she seems to have struggled to find work. She registered for a PhD at UCL in 1925, which suggests that she was contemplating leaving the Bar for academia, but did not continue her degree after being appointed deputy chairman of London's Court of Referees in 1926.[5] This appointment, with its fee of 2½ guineas a sitting for hearing cases under the Unemployment Insurance Act 1920, seems to have enabled Cobb to remain at the Bar. Although details of women's legal practice are scant, it seems that Cobb became the most successful of her cohort, specialising in commercial cases.

II. Context

Women had been struggling to enter the ranks of lawmakers – lawyers and politicians – for over half a century by the time Cobb was called to the Bar. The fight for the vote is relatively well known.[6] The legal profession proved no less resistant: women had been studying law at university since the 1870s but could not enter the professions.[7] The four Inns of Court (Inner Temple, Middle Temple, Lincoln's Inn and Gray's Inn), which controlled admission to the Bar, and the Law Society, which fulfilled a similar role for solicitors, adamantly refused to admit women. The first requests, in the 1870s, were rebuffed by Lincoln's Inn and the Law Society. Eliza Orme sidestepped these restrictions and opened her own office in 1875, doing legal paperwork for male lawyers.[8] Cornelia Sorabji was the first woman to study

[2] *Third Supplement to the London Gazette* (30 March 1920) 3822.

[3] Professional Classes War Relief Council, *Professional Classes War Relief Council* (1914).

[4] 'Calls to the Bar' *Solicitor's Journal and Weekly Reporter* 67 (25 November 1922) 115.

[5] The Court of Referees reviewed disputed decisions about unemployment benefit claims.

[6] See **'Representation of the People (Equal Franchise) Act 1928'**.

[7] Rosemary Auchmuty, 'Early Women Law Students at Cambridge and Oxford' (2008) 29 *Journal of Legal History* 63.

[8] Mary Jane Mossman, *The First Women Lawyers: A Comparative Study of Gender, Law and the Legal Professions* (Hart Publishing, 2006).

law at Oxford University, taking her postgraduate Bachelor of Civil Law examinations in 1892, but could not be called to the Bar and was only able to practise in the Indian courts after being given special status to do so.[9] Bertha Cave's appeal against rejection of her application to join Gray's Inn in 1903 was heard and refused by a panel of judges in the House of Lords.[10] Noted suffragette Christabel Pankhurst responded to her rejection by Lincoln's Inn by co-founding the Committee for the Admission of Women to the Legal Profession in 1904. Another clergyman's daughter, Gwyneth Bebb, lost her case against the Law Society in 1913.[11]

While some women won the vote in 1918, the legal professions remained closed. Among the women challenging their exclusion was Helena Normanton, a suffragette with longstanding ambitions to become a barrister. She applied to join Middle Temple and was refused; while her petition against this decision awaited a hearing, the Sex Disqualification (Removal) Act 1919 received the Royal Assent on 23 December. Thanks to her relationship with the Middle Temple, the treasurer's office opened specially to admit her.[12] Other women, including Cobb, followed at the first opportunity, in the New Year. The legislation applied throughout the United Kingdom, and indeed lawyers qualified earlier in Scotland and Ireland: in 1920, Madge Easton Anderson was admitted as a law agent (solicitor) in Scotland, while Frances Kyle and Averil Deverell were called to the Irish Bar in 1921.[13] In England and Wales, the first woman solicitor, Carrie Morrison, was admitted in December 1922.[14] **Ivy Williams** had already become the first woman barrister in May 1922 but never practised. It is not known why Cobb was the first of the 10 women called in November to be briefed, but the explanation may lie in her father's connections with solicitors who supported the women's movement.

III. What Happened Next

Cobb's court appearance was a landmark not just because it was the first by a woman. It also set the tone for women's entry into the courtroom – and that

[9] Mary Jane Mossman, 'Cornelia Sorabji (1866–1954): A Pioneer Woman Lawyer in Britain and India' (2019) 29 *Women's History Review* 737.

[10] Judith Bourne, 'Cave [Married Name Altof], Bertha (1881–1951), Campaigner', *Oxford Dictionary of National Biography* (8 November 2018).

[11] *Bebb v The Law Society* [1914] 1 Ch 286; Rosemary Auchmuty, 'Whatever Happened to Miss Bebb? *Bebb v The Law Society* and Women's Legal History' (2010) 31 *Legal Studies* 199; and see generally Mossman, n 8; Patrick Polden, 'Portia's Progress: Women at the Bar in England, 1919–1939' (2005) 12 *International Journal of the Legal Profession* 293.

[12] Judith Bourne, 'First Woman to Be Admitted to an Inn of Court, Helena Normanton, 1919' in Erika Rackley and Rosemary Auchmuty (eds), *Women's Legal Landmarks: Celebrating the History of Women and Law in the UK and Ireland* (Hart Publishing, 2019) 147.

[13] Liz Goldthorpe, 'First Woman to Practise as a Barrister in Ireland and the (Then) United Kingdom, Averil Deverell, 1921' in Rackley and Auchmuty (eds), n 12, 175.

[14] Elizabeth Cruickshank, 'First Woman Solicitor in England and Wales, Carrie Morrison, 1922' in Rackley and Auchmuty (eds), n 12, 183.

mattered, because their appearances would remain a matter of lively press interest for some years. National papers reported women's first appearances in murder trials, in the higher courts and so on, but local papers were equally interested in the first women to appear in their local magistrates' courts.

The press attention was unhelpful to these women as they sought to establish a practice, since clients rarely welcomed the media spotlight and the Inns frowned upon any hint of self-publicising by barristers. Common themes, already apparent in the reports of Cobb's courtroom debut, did little to challenge sexist stereotypes. The focus in many news stories upon women's appearance was patronising: Cobb was depicted as 'trim and neat, in her perfectly fitting silver horse-hair wig and black gown'.[15] They frequently pretended a condescending surprise that women could contain their supposed natural loquaciousness, finding it necessary to point out that Cobb 'was the soul of brevity'. In retrospect, however, it is apparent that the critical element of the press appraisal was its conclusion that Cobb 'confined her remarks to essential points in the charge, every one of which she drove home with clarity and force'.[16] She thus challenged stereotypes of women as lacking the intellectual focus and precision needed for law. Key criticisms of women barristers were therefore countered at the outset, helping to pave the way for her own and others' careers. Like many barristers of the period, Cobb moved away from criminal cases as she gained in experience. She became a specialist in commercial law, and thus also challenged the assumption that women would make their careers in more 'feminine' fields of law.

That is not, of course, to say that women barristers' struggles were over. Having achieved the landmark of qualification, they faced a continuing and uphill battle for work. Barristers are self-employed, so their workload and income depend upon their being briefed in individual cases. Establishing themselves was not easy for most barristers, but particularly difficult for women who faced sexism from clients, solicitors and the chambers clerks who allocated work, as well as the threat of press scrutiny. In 1937, Cobb's peer Ethel Bright Ashford expressed her doubts that 'many women … were making a large, or even a subsistence living out of their practices'.[17] Unsurprisingly, some of the first women to qualify soon left the profession. Others remained at the Bar but did not make a living there, relying upon private means or other work such as journalism.

The number of practising women barristers remained tiny until late in the twentieth century. Today it is significantly higher but barriers remain, particularly at the higher levels of the profession. Fewer than a third of barristers with over 15 years' experience, and fewer than a third of judges, are women. They make up only 17 per cent of King's Counsel (senior barristers recognised for their advocacy and experience).[18] At the time of writing, there are three times as many men called

[15] 'Women Lawyers' *Aberdeen Press and Journal* (4 December 1922) 3.

[16] ibid.

[17] Portia 'House and Home', *Hull Daily Mail* (22 December 1927) 10.

[18] Ministry of Justice, 'Diversity of the Judiciary: Legal Professions, New Appointments and Current Post-Holders' (Ministry of Justice, 2020) 11–18.

David as there are women among the 12 Supreme Court Justices: in fact, there is just one woman, Lady Rose.[19]

IV. Significance

In a common law system such as that of England and Wales, the law is shaped by the cases that are appealed and the ways in which counsel argue them and judges decide them. Women's exclusion from the Bar thus cut them off from this aspect of law-making as thoroughly as their inability to vote or stand for Parliament excluded them from the legislative process. There were also more immediate implications: a woman appearing in court (whether as a party or a witness) would find herself in masculine territory. The lawyers, court staff, judges and jurors would all be men. They would listen to, cross-examine her on, and make judgments about the most intimate areas of her life without relevant lived experience or attention to women's subjectivities. The courtroom could therefore be a hostile space for individual women, while the law it ultimately developed took little account of their perspectives.[20]

That did not change overnight once Cobb stepped into Birmingham Assize Court, but her appearance did mark the start of a crucial shift. Far too slowly, but inexorably, women have risen through the ranks of the legal profession. We had to wait until after the interwar period for the first women King's Counsel (Rose Heilbron and Helena Normanton, 1949)[21] and first woman High Court judge (Elizabeth Lane, 1965),[22] while the first Black woman High Court judge, Dame Linda Dobbs, was appointed only in 2004[23] – the same year Brenda Hale made history as the first woman Law Lord (and later, Justice of the Supreme Court).[24] Women's presence in the judiciary, however slowly it has been attained, matters. Its importance is manifest not only in feminist judgment projects that reimagine key legal rulings, but also in the actual feminist judgments of women such as Lady Hale.

The law has not been magically transformed by the admission of women into its professions. Feminists remain rightly cautious about its seductive promises, which are often diluted or distorted in practice. Nonetheless, key advances have

[19] In October 2023 it was announced that the King had approved the appointment of Lady Justice Simler.

[20] See, eg, Helena Kennedy, *Eve Was Framed: Women and British Justice* (Vintage, 1993); Helena Kennedy, *Eve Was Shamed: How British Justice Is Fialing Women* (Chatto and Windus, 2018); Ngaire Naffine, *Criminal Law and the Man Problem* (Hart Publishing, 2019).

[21] Laura Lammasniemi, 'First Woman to Hold Regular Judicial Office in England and Wales, Rose Heilbron, 1964' in Rackley and Auchmuty (eds), n 12, 257.

[22] Judith Bourne and Frances Burton, 'First Woman High Court Judge in England and Wales, Elizabeth Lane, 1965' in Rackley and Auchmuty (eds), n 12, 271.

[23] 'High Court Gets First Black Judge' *BBC News*, 2 September 2004.

[24] Erika Rackley, 'First Woman President of the UK Supreme Court, Brenda Hale, 2017' in Rackley and Auchmuty (eds), n 12, 645.

been made – and they have been achieved largely because women do now have an increasingly powerful voice in the legal system. The process is by no means complete (nor is progress steady or certain), but that does not diminish the importance of its beginning: when Monica Geikie Cobb stepped into a court and, under the scrutiny of the press and the profession, demonstrated that women could hold their own in the hitherto masculine domain of the courtroom.

Further Reading

- Rosemary Auchmuty, 'Whatever Happened to Miss Bebb? *Bebb v The Law Society* and Women's Legal History' (2010) 31 *Legal Studies* 199.
- Caroline Derry, 'Cobb, Monica Mary Geikie (1891–1946)', *Oxford Dictionary of National Biography* (8 November 2018).
- Rose Pearson and Albie Sachs, 'Barristers and Gentlemen: A Critical Look at Sexism in the Legal Profession' (1980) 43 *Modern Law Review* 400.

12

Criminal Law Amendment Act 1922

CAROLINE DERRY

The Criminal Law Amendment Act 1922 extended legal protections for children throughout the United Kingdom in relation to sexual activity, addressing significant gaps in the 1885 Act of the same name. The earlier Act had raised the age at which girls could consent to sexual intercourse from 13 to 16 years old but imposed a six-month time limit for bringing prosecutions for the relevant offence, unlawful sexual intercourse.[1] This was now raised to nine months: an important amendment as many cases were only discovered when a pregnancy could no longer be concealed. The defence of reasonable belief that a girl was over 16 was also now limited to men under 23 years old. And perhaps most significantly, the age of consent to indecent assault was increased from 13 to 16, for both girls and boys.

The 1922 Act therefore brought greater consistency to sexual age of consent law, in ways that began to challenge the patriarchal Victorian model of sexuality. Less obviously, it is also significant for what it did not do: a Bill the previous year had failed, thanks to a controversial proposal to criminalise sexual activity ('gross indecency') between women. The 1922 Act's lack of reference to gross indecency between females saw the end of these efforts at criminalisation.

I. Context

Historically, the age of consent had been linked to the age for marriage.[2] Extramarital sexual activity between a man and a woman was in any event viewed as illegitimate (albeit not an offence in the secular courts). Between men, it was wholly illegal. Sex between women was silenced and suppressed, although it was not the

[1] Originally three months. See further Lois Bibbings, 'Section 5(1) of the Criminal Law Amendment Act 1885' in Erika Rackley and Rosemary Auchmuty (eds), *Women's Legal Landmarks: Celebrating the History of Women and Law in the UK and Ireland* (Hart Publishing, 2019) 83.

[2] Laura Lammasniemi, '"Precocious Girls": Age of Consent, Class and Family in Late Nineteenth-Century England' (2020) 38 *Law and History Review* 241, 248.

subject of a specific offence. By the late nineteenth century, these longstanding attitudes had cohered into a particular, highly patriarchal model of sexuality in which penile penetration was the only 'real' sex, and it involved a dominant, active and desiring man who penetrated a submissive, passive and essentially desireless woman. The same model was transposed on to sex between men, which became an abhorrent subversion of the natural gender order; it rendered sex between women unthinkable.[3] While alternative models might be found elsewhere (not least, in the women's movement and the new field of sexology),[4] this one had significant cultural and medical force and prevailed in law.

The later nineteenth century had seen growing concern about the sexual exploitation of children and the law's inability to prevent or punish it. A broad coalition of campaigners for effective legislation included people with very different perspectives.[5] In particular, leading feminist organisations sought to challenge the sexual double standard that punished women but not men for extramarital sex. Chief amongst these was the organisation that would later become the Association for Moral and Social Hygiene (AMSH), headed by Josephine Butler. She led opposition to the Contagious Diseases Acts, which had sought to control prostitution in military towns through compulsory inspection and treatment of women believed to be prostitutes while leaving men's behaviour unchallenged.[6] Passed in the 1860s, they would be repeated in 1886. The AMSH continued to favour the abolition of legislation regulating prostitution thereafter, and would be the main organisation to campaign for this in the interwar years.[7]

By contrast, 'social purity' campaigners, including the Salvation Army and other evangelical Christian bodies, opposed 'immorality' in all its forms and were happy to see girls and women punished in order to suppress it. They also welcomed provisions in the 1885 Act that increased regulation of soliciting and brothel-keeping. That enthusiasm for regulation was shared by groups advocating the newer 'social hygiene' approach, which focused upon the need to prevent the transmission of infection and generally secure the reproductive health of the nation. However, the division between the abolitionist and pro-regulation parts of the movement was not clear-cut, and indeed many campaigners worked with and across groups on both 'sides'.[8]

[3] Caroline Derry, *Lesbianism and the Criminal Law: Three Centuries of Regulation in England and Wales* (Palgrave Macmillan, 2020) ch 3.

[4] See, for example, Lucy Bland, *Banishing the Beast: English Feminism and Sexual Morality 1885–1914* (Penguin, 1995); Lesley A Hall, 'Hauling Down the Double Standard' (2001) 16 *Gender and History* 36; Sheila Jeffreys, *The Spinster and Her Enemies: Feminism and Sexuality 1880–1930* (Spinifex, 1985).

[5] Deborah Gorham, 'The "Maiden Tribute of Modern Babylon" Re-Examined: Child Prostitution and the Idea of Childhood in Late-Victorian England' (1978) 21 *Victorian Studies* 353, 364.

[6] Judith R Walkowitz, 'Butler [Née Grey], Josephine Elizabeth (1828–1906), Social Reformer and Women's Activist', *Oxford Dictionary of National Biography* (23 September 2004).

[7] Julia Laite, 'The Association for Moral and Social Hygiene: Abolitionism and Prostitution Law in Britain (1915–1959)' (2008) 17 *Women's History Review* 207, 207–08.

[8] Gorham, n 5, 354–65.

Despite its internal differences, this coalition had successfully campaigned for the Criminal Law Amendment Act 1885, which created the offence of unlawful sexual intercourse with a girl under 16. While parliamentary opponents were unable to stop the Bill, they significantly moderated its effects by including a time limit for bringing prosecutions and a defence of reasonable belief that the girl was over 16, which made successful prosecutions difficult in practice. A last-minute amendment had also introduced an offence of gross indecency between males, which explicitly criminalised all sexual contact between men. Such conduct had already been prosecuted using other offences, such as attempted buggery,[9] but the provision (known as the 'Labouchère amendment' after the radical MP, Henry Du Pré Labouchère, who introduced it) gave fresh encouragement to such prosecutions.

The 1885 legislation therefore met only part of the coalition's aims, and the practical effects of its apparent protections for girls were severely limited. (Parliament proved more willing to strengthen laws regulating prostitution, which it did in the Criminal Law Amendment Act 1912.) Campaigners continued to seek age-of-consent reform, and after the First World War a similarly broad coalition of over 50 organisations, led by the feminist and abolitionist AMSH, maintained the pressure for reform. The AMSH, under the leadership of Alison Neilans, was committed to opposing state regulation of women's sexuality, particularly the regulation of prostitution. The Association accepted that legal protections for girls were appropriate, but it was concerned – as many of its allies were not – to ensure that girls were not punished for perceived immoral behaviour. Neilans was therefore often in the difficult position of having to address her allies' willingness or enthusiasm for regulation as well as her opponents' more obvious aversion to reform.[10]

II. The Landmark

The Criminal Law Amendment Act 1922 did not meet all the campaigners' demands, but it did achieve their main aims. Sixteen was now the age of consent for both sexual intercourse and indecent assault. Girls were thus given more comprehensive legal protection, while the application of the same age to boys for indecent assault was a small chip in the façade of the sexual double standard. On a practical level, amendments made the law more readily enforceable. The extension of the time limit for prosecuting unlawful sexual intercourse meant that cases that became known only when a pregnancy became obvious could now be prosecuted. A more restricted reasonable belief defence would also facilitate successful prosecutions.

[9] Charles Upchurch, *Before Wilde: Sex between Men in Britain's Age of Reform* (University of California Press, 2009).

[10] Caroline Derry, 'Lesbianism and Feminist Legislation in 1921: The Age of Consent and "Gross Indecency between Women"' (2018) 86 *History Workshop Journal* 245, 251–54.

Anomalies remained: unlawful sexual intercourse could only be committed against a girl, so sex between a woman and boy had to be prosecuted as indecent assault. All sexual conduct between males remained criminal. The extension of the time limit for unlawful sexual intercourse prosecutions was still inadequate and would later be extended to a year by the Criminal Law Amendment Act 1928. The defence to unlawful sexual intercourse of a reasonable belief that the complainant was over 16 was confined to a 'young man's defence' rather than abolished. Interestingly, neither the defence nor the time limit was applied to indecent assault.

Those partial successes are indicators of the compromises that had to be made in order to get the legislation through Parliament. For the AMSH and its leader Neilans, the dangers came from their own allies as well as parliamentary opponents. In particular, other organisations were willing to accept (or even welcomed) repressive measures to which the AMSH was completely opposed. The National Vigilance Association, formed to monitor the implementation of the 1885 Act, took an overtly moralistic approach and defined its purpose as 'the repression of criminal vice'.[11] Many feminist organisations supported the Bill, although their main work and expertise was elsewhere, and Neilans was aware of the risk that they would accept measures amounting to 'neo-regulation' without understanding their implications. For example, when a similar Bill had come before Parliament in 1917, the AMSH had opposed amendments allowing the detention of sexually 'misbehaving' girls under 18 but other campaigners had not.[12]

Given these internal tensions, Neilans' leadership achieved remarkable success not only in getting the 1922 Act passed but also in ensuring that it did not contain more repressive measures. When a similar Bill had been introduced by the Bishop of London in 1921, the AMSH had proved willing to lose the Bill rather than see an amendment passed that would have criminalised gross indecency between women.[13] That Bill, a consolidation of three similar Bills introduced in 1920, had been allowed only very limited parliamentary time by the Liberal/Conservative Coalition Government: it could only pass if it remained agreed (and therefore did not need to move back and forth between the House of Commons and House of Lords). This meant that a 'spoiling amendment' that made the Bill controversial would prevent its becoming law. Such an amendment had therefore been introduced in the House of Commons by Conservative MPs Frederick Macquisten, Howard Gritten and Sir Ernest Wild; the subject matter they chose was criminalisation of gross indecency between women.

[11] Quoted in Alan Hunt, *Governing Morals: a Social History of Moral Regulation* (Cambridge University Press, 1999) 161.

[12] Derry, n 10, 252.

[13] ibid.

This was an effective choice for several reasons. First, it could be presented as a matter of sex equality, since it mirrored the 1885 Act's Labouchère amendment. Second, the proposers may have known or suspected that some of the leading reformers, including Neilans, were lesbians themselves. Third, while parliamentarians agreed that sex between women was a very bad thing, the consensus on how to address it was showing signs of stress. The longstanding policy of regulating sex between (respectable, higher-class, white, Christian) women by silencing its existence was seemingly under threat. The rise of sexology had brought discussion of the topic to a wider audience (albeit primarily elite men, including doctors and lawyers), as had a notorious trial a few years earlier. Celebrated dancer Maud Allen had been accused by right-wing MP Noel Pemberton-Billing of belonging to the 'cult of the clitoris' – that is, being a lesbian – and thus, according to his conspiracy theory, being one of thousands of male and female homosexuals compromised by German agents. She had lost her libel trial, whose subject matter remained obscure in the press but was an open secret among lawyers and parliamentarians.[14]

The MPs proposing the spoiling amendment presented lesbianism as a present and growing danger. Its opponents insisted that silencing remained effective while criminalisation would make it public knowledge that 'there was this offence; that there was such a horror'.[15] The amendment passed in the House of Commons, where about a third of MPs voted. Some members of the House of Lords would have been willing to accept the amendment rather than lose the Bill, but timely lobbying by Neilans ensured that this did not in fact happen. Prompted by her representations, the Lords rejected the amendment. No longer agreed, the Bill failed for lack of time.[16]

Faced with popular anger at the Bill's failure, and with a general election approaching, the Government made sufficient parliamentary time available the following year and reintroduced the measure as a government Bill. Thanks to Neilans' organising, opposition to a gross indecency amendment had become the coalition's policy. Among activists, there was even discussion of the need to decriminalise male homosexuality: Neilans addressed this explicitly in an editorial for the AMSH journal, *The Shield*.[17] In the event, the coalition did not have to assert its opposition to criminalisation. The Bill's opponents did not give up and attempted to reintroduce an amendment criminalising gross indecency between women, but this time it was ruled out of order. The 1922 Act became law without any such provision.

[14] Lucy Bland, *Modern Women on Trial: Sexual Transgression in the Age of the Flapper* (Manchester University Press, 2013) ch 1.

[15] The Earl of Desart, HL Deb 15 August 1921, vol 46, cols 572–73.

[16] Derry, n 10, 259–60.

[17] Alison Neilans, 'Editorial' *The Shield* (November–December 1921) 203–04.

III. What Happened Next

Having achieved its main aims, the uneasy alliance that had promoted the 1922 Act faded away. The AMSH's law reform activity centred upon attempting to get solicitation laws criminalising 'common prostitutes' repealed. It was remarkably successful in gaining the support of other feminist organisations, and was even instrumental in the establishment of a departmental Committee on Street Offences in 1928, whose findings partly supported the AMSH position. However, despite its efforts, it did not succeed in obtaining a full Royal Commission or in the ultimate goal of repeal.[18]

Women's organisations had long engaged in other forms of legal work, including observing court cases and supporting complainants. They were therefore well aware that changes to age-of-consent law were one small part of the picture, and their continuing work on sexual exploitation of women and girls largely focused on areas such as prosecutorial practice and sentencing. They also led resistance to both sex trafficking and state regulation of prostitution, nationally and internationally. The AMSH continued to do so within a framework of opposition to state regulation of women – and, as editorials in its journal made clear, of opposition to the criminalisation of both male and female homosexuality.[19] They thus pre-empted the legal developments of the later twentieth century, which moved the criminal law away from regulation of private morality.

It would be some decades before there were major changes to the legal regime of which the 1922 Act formed part. Following the 1956 Wolfenden Report,[20] the public debate shifted to a clash between moralism and liberalism in sexual regulation. The latter approach made a significant advance when sexual activity between men was partially decriminalised by the Sexual Offences Act 1967. However, the same report prompted greater criminalisation of soliciting by women, which would have been anathema to Neilans and her colleagues.

The provisions of the 1922 Act in relation to the age of consent for girls remained largely unchanged until their replacement by the gender-neutral provisions of the Sexual Offences Act 2003. The Sexual Offences Act 1956 consolidated them but did little to change them. The law remained sharply gendered. Sexual intercourse with a boy under 16 remained outside the statutory regime, to be dealt with as indecent assault instead. Indecent assault was also charged in cases where unlawful sexual intercourse could not be charged within the narrow time limit, a very real issue given the difficulties of disclosing child sexual abuse. All sexual activity between males remained a criminal offence until partial decriminalisation in 1967, but the liberalising legislation imposed a significantly higher age of consent of 21.[21]

[18] Laite, n 7, 218.

[19] Derry, n 3, 156–57.

[20] Committee on Homosexual Offences and Prostitution, *Report of the Committee on Homosexual Offences and Prostitution* (Cmnd 247, 1957).

[21] Sexual Offences Act 1967.

Lesbianism remained legally silenced, despite the growing influence of sexology and its theories of 'female inversion'. The most prominent British sexologist, Havelock Ellis, painted a picture of masculine 'true inverts' whose innate sexuality not only influenced them physically and psychologically but also attracted feminine 'pseudo-inverts' who would otherwise turn to men. That model proved culturally influential and coloured perceptions of lesbianism for many decades. It was aired in court in the obscenity proceedings against Radclyffe Hall's novel *The Well of Loneliness* (a plea for tolerance of the female invert) in 1928, but met with a moralist response from judge Sir Chartres Byron.[22] While the trial of 'Colonel' Barker the following year drew more closely upon sexological discourse, that proved to be a temporary aberration. Silencing remained the dominant legal response to sex between women, and sexology would make significant inroads into legal and popular discourse only in the 1950s. Meanwhile, Parliament would not explicitly discuss lesbianism again until the debates on section 28 of the Local Government Act 1988, which prohibited the 'promotion of homosexuality' by local authorities.[23]

IV. Significance

The 1922 Act increased protection for girls under 16 from sexual assault, abuse and exploitation. The process leading to its passing also ensured that sex between women never became explicitly criminalised. In all these ways, the Act shaped the criminal law on sexual offences for decades to come. Indeed, its effects are still felt today: the age of consent remains at 16, for example. It is thanks to the efforts of feminist campaigners that the Act was passed at all; that it did not criminalise sex between women; and that it did not extend repressive, quasi-criminal regulation of young women's sexual behaviour.

However, the provisions of the 1922 Act were imperfect, and their implementation by the criminal justice system exacerbated their shortcomings. The structure of sexual offences remained profoundly gendered in ways that drew upon the sexual double standard. The corollary of its underlying assumption that men were dominant sexual actors was that women and girls were expected to act as sexual gatekeepers. As the less desiring partners, it was up to them to resist male advances; and when they failed to do so to the limits of their physical powers, the fault was understood to be theirs. Thus the apparently universal protections for girls under 16 proved inaccessible to those who were not virgins: whatever the letter of the law, police officers and courts understood such girls to be outside their protection.

[22] Caroline Derry, 'DPP v Jonathan Cape and Leopold Hill (1928)' in Rackley and Auchmuty (eds), n 1, 271.

[23] Derry, n 3, chs 5 and 6.

Those shortcomings have persisted to the present day. Rape myths continue to exert a powerful influence over the criminal justice system – and despite the name, they also affect prosecutions for other sexual offences. Meanwhile, the age of consent has become a settled aspect of the criminal law. The specific age of 16, which was largely a matter of pragmatism, has taken on something of a moral as well as legal force. Proposals to lower it have met with little support and often outright condemnation. There has been no movement for a higher general age of consent – something many of the 1922 campaigners favoured – although it has been raised to 18 where the older party is in a position of trust. Feminists continue to find themselves attempting to educate lawmakers and the criminal justice system on wider issues of exploitation and abuse, which the age of consent can play only a limited role in addressing. They have had some success with greater legal recognition of grooming and coercive control, but rates of prosecution and conviction for age-of-consent offences remain very low.

Sex between women has never fully escaped the silencing imposed upon it by lawmakers. Despite the brief moments of visibility mentioned here, it has generally attracted little consideration in its own right. Rather, since the Wolfenden Report of 1957, whose recommendations led to partial decriminalisation of male homosexuality, sex between women has been understood as a parallel but lesser version of sex between men. Women were characterised in that report as less troublesome and less sexual beings than their male counterparts, and those assumptions remain powerful today. Thus legal reforms aimed at removing discrimination from the law, culminating in the Sexual Offences Act 2003, have paid little attention to their specific needs and perspectives. The ways in which relationships between women can nonetheless be criminalised have attracted little attention, even where they resulted in substantial sentences. There has been greater recent consideration of the law on 'deceptive consent' in this context, but the battle to ensure that women's subjectivities are considered remains ongoing.

Further Reading

- Lucy Bland, *Banishing the Beast: English Feminism and Sexual Morality 1885–1914* (Penguin, 1995).
- Caroline Derry, 'Lesbianism and Feminist Legislation in 1921: The Age of Consent and "Gross Indecency between Women"' (2018) 86 *History Workshop Journal* 245.
- Julia Laite, 'The Association for Moral and Social Hygiene: Abolitionism and Prostitution Law in Britain (1915–1959)' (2008) 17(2) *Women's History Review* 207.

13

Intoxicating Liquor (Sale to Persons under Eighteen) Act 1923

MARI TAKAYANAGI

The Intoxicating Liquor (Sale to Persons under Eighteen) Act 1923 introduced the principle that people should be aged 18 to drink alcohol in bars and pubs. Before this, a person had to be 14 years old to buy and drink beer, or 16 years old to buy spirits. It was introduced by **Nancy Astor** MP, a great advocate of temperance and of measures to protect children and young people. Called 'Lady Astor's Bill' during its parliamentary passage, it was the first Private Member's Bill from a female MP to be passed and become law. The principle established by this legal landmark lives on to this day.

I. Context

Temperance, the promotion of moderation or abstinence from alcohol, was a prominent social reform movement from the early nineteenth century and throughout the Victorian era, particularly among some religious organisations. An early female temperance advocate from the 1830s was Irish philanthropist Anne Jane Carlile, whose work with Elizabeth Fry on prison reform convinced her that alcohol was the cause of many social problems. She was particularly concerned with women and children, and in 1847 she co-founded the Band of Hope, which aimed to teach children the importance and principles of sobriety and teetotalism.[1]

The British Women's Temperance Association (BWTA) was formed in 1873, influenced by the US Women's Christian Temperance Union (WCTU). Many of its members also campaigned on other feminist causes, including married women's property, the Contagious Diseases Acts and suffrage. Its early presidents included writer and philanthropist Clara Lucas Balfour and Liberal suffragist

[1] Richard Froggatt, 'Ann Jane Carlile (1775–1864): Temperance campaigner', *The Dictionary of Ulster Biography* at www.newulsterbiography.co.uk/index.php/home/viewPerson/2098.

Margaret Bright Lucas.[2] Its president from 1890 to 1903, Lady Henry Somerset, was a close friend of Frances Willard, leader of the WCTU. Somerset wanted the BWTA to pursue a broader reform movement of women's emancipation than temperance, including peace, labour reform and suffrage.[3] In 1893, following a change in policy to support suffrage, the BWTA became the National BWTA (NBWTA) and a breakaway group was formed, the Women's Total Abstinence Union (WTAU), which focused exclusively on temperance.[4] The NBWTA president from 1903 was Rosalind Howard, Countess of Carlisle, who held the position until her death in 1921. Somerset and Howard were also successively presidents of the World's WCTU (Somerset from 1898 to 1906, Howard from 1906 to 1921).[5]

Temperance campaigners sought to influence culture and attitudes about the evils of drink, and also lobbied for legal measures to restrict supply and consumption. The first measure to restrict sale of alcohol to children came in London in 1839, when the Metropolitan Police Act 1839 prohibited the sale of 'any Sort of distilled excisable Liquor to any Boy or Girl apparently under the Age of Sixteen Years, to be drunk upon the Premises'. The Licensing Act 1872 extended this outside London, and the Intoxicating Liquor (Sale to Children) Act 1886 banned the sale of all alcohol to any person under the age of 13 years.[6]

However, these Acts only applied to consumption on the premises. In 1897, while President of the BWTA, Lady Somerset gave evidence to the Royal Commission on Liquor Licensing Laws. In relation to children, she talked about children being induced to enter pubs with sweets and oranges; children clubbing together to pool coins until they had enough to buy a bottle of port between them; and a girl of 13 who simply went into a pub, bought alcohol, and then sat and drank it on the doorstep. Asked at how early an age she had seen children coming out of public houses, she answered, 'At five, six, seven, and eight, at any time at which they could possibly hold a jug and walk … It is a very common thing to see children with sweets in one hand and the jug of beer in the other.'[7] It was feared that children were buying alcohol ostensibly for their parents and then drinking it on their way home, or that

[2] Margaret Barrow, 'Teetotal feminists: temperance leadership and the campaign for women's suffrage' in Claire Eustance, Joan Ryan and Laura Ugolini (eds), *Suffrage Reader: Charting Directions in British Suffrage History* (Leicester University Press, 2000) 69.

[3] Ian Tyrrell, 'Somerset [née Somers-Cocks], Lady Isabella Caroline [Lady Henry Somerset]', *Oxford Dictionary of National Biography* (23 September 2004, rev 2012). In 1895, Somerset set up Duxhurst 'Colony for Women Inebriates', for the treatment and care of women alcoholics, in Reigate, Surrey. It closed soon after her death.

[4] Gemma Louise Outen, 'The Women's Total Abstinence Union and periodical Wings, 1892–1910: A Study of Gender and Politics' (PhD thesis, Edge Hill University, 2017).

[5] David M Fahey, 'Howard [née Stanley], Rosalind Frances, countess of Carlisle', *Oxford Dictionary of National Biography* (23 September 2004, rev 2006).

[6] Metropolitan Police Act 1839, 2 & 3 Vic c 47; Licensing Act 1872, 35 & 36 Vic c 94; Intoxicating Liquors (Sale to Children) Act 1886, 49 & 50 Vic c 56.

[7] *Third Report of the Royal Commission on liquor licensing laws* (Cmnd 8694, 1898). Evidence of Lady Henry Somerset, 25 May 1897, 164–84.

publicans were topping up the jugs with extra for the children. As a result of this, the 'Child Messenger Act' banned sale of alcohol to children under 14 years old, except in pint measures and corked.[8]

Following the election of a Liberal Government in 1906 committed to a programme of social reform, among many child welfare measures, the Children Act 1908 banned children under the age of 5 from being given alcohol except for medicinal purposes.[9] It also banned children under 14 from bars, and although this measure was initially not widely enforced, the advent of the First World War led to increased concern about drunkenness in society, and Act was used to regulate the presence of children inside and immediately outside pubs.[10] In 1915, the Central Control Board (Liquor Traffic) was established, whose members included Waldorf Astor, husband of Nancy. The Board introduced measures that included reducing the alcoholic strength of liquors and hours of sale, raising prices, introducing food and non-alcoholic refreshments in licenced premises, and prohibiting incentives to drink such as 'treating' (buying rounds). Another wartime measure was the 'Carlisle Experiment', state management of public houses and breweries in the naval town of Carlisle. The Board was abolished in 1921, but many of its measures continued for many years, and the Carlisle Experiment carried on until the 1970s.

Nancy Astor was elected MP for Plymouth Sutton in 1919. She had a strong, unwavering personal commitment to temperance, influenced by family upbringing, religious views and personal experience (her first husband was an alcoholic), as well as being part of her feminism and concern for children and young people.[11] In 1927, she was asked by Conservative Central Office to send a message of support to Lady Iveagh, who was standing at a by-election in Southend. Astor replied 'Of course it will be excellent to have another woman in the House, and I am delighted about it. But I don't quite see how, holding the views I do about temperance, I can come out and support her.'[12] Thus showing, on this occasion at least, that temperance was more important to her than party affiliation or solidarity between women MPs.

It was therefore appropriate that on 24 February 1920, Astor made her maiden speech in the House of Commons on Liquor Traffic (Restrictions), opposing attempts by some MPs to relax wartime alcohol restrictions. Also in 1920, the Temperance (Scotland) Act 1913 came into force, introducing the 'local option' in Scotland, which empowered a local area to take a vote on the sale of intoxicating liquor in that area. Astor supported extending the local option to the rest of the UK, but was unable to gain wider parliamentary support for a Private Member's Bill.

[8] Intoxicating Liquor (Sale to Children) Act 1901, 1 Ed VII, c 27.

[9] Children Act 1908, 8 Ed VII c 67.

[10] Stella Moss, '"A Grave Question": The Children Act and Public House Regulation, c 1908–1939' (2009) 3(2) *Crimes and Misdemeanours: Deviance and the Law in Historical Perspective* 98.

[11] Mari Takayanagi, 'Astor the Fairy Godmother: The Intoxicating Liquor Act 1923' (2020) 6(2) *Open Library of Humanities*.

[12] University of Reading [UoR], MS1416/1/626.

Meanwhile, some temperance organisations moved their focus to protecting children. In 1921, the Teachers National Petition Committee organised a petition asking for the prohibition of the serving of intoxicating liquors to under-18s, for the sake of the moral and physical welfare of young people. Waldorf Astor played a large role in gathering signatures. It was signed by 115,867 teachers from public, secondary and elementary schools.[13]

Over in the USA, the Eighteenth Amendment banned the sale, production and transport of alcoholic beverages between 1920 and 1933. Prohibition was a tiny movement in the UK by comparison, but November 1922 saw the election of Edwin Scrymgeour, leader of the Scottish Prohibitionist Party, in Dundee, ousting Winston Churchill. Scrymgeour's uncompromising attitude was that the local option was 'the supreme heresy', and anyone not for prohibition was regarded as being decidedly against it.[14] Nancy Astor, in contrast, hoped that the time for prohibition would come, but regarded it as not practical politics.[15]

II. The Landmark

In 1923, Astor won third place in the ballot for Private Members' Bills, meaning she had guaranteed parliamentary time to introduce a bill of her choice and ensure at least a second reading. With cross-party support, her Bill was introduced into the House of Commons on 16 February 1923, to 'Amend the law relating to the sale of intoxicating liquor to persons between fourteen and eighteen years of age'.

At its second reading on 9 March, Astor credited the Teachers' Petition as her inspiration, and explained that the Bill had the support of 'all organised women', medical authorities and church leaders. Her passion and knowledge of the subject were crucial to her success during parliamentary debates, and she drew on her personal experience as a mother:

> When I look into the eyes of a child and see the hope and the purity there, I do not know what it is, but there is something about the eyes of a child that gives me courage to stand up against the worst opposition that any woman has ever had to face.[16]

Opposition was led by Conservative MPs, with arguments including practical difficulties, claims that drinking as children had never done them any harm and hints that prohibition would be next. However, the Government chose to allow a free vote, and the Bill passed two divisions, with clear victories of 335 to 70

[13] UoR, MS1416/2/6.

[14] William M Walker, 'The Scottish Prohibition Party and the Millennium' (1973) 18(3) *International Review of Social History* 353.

[15] Takayanagi, n 11.

[16] HC Deb 9 March 1923, vol 161, cols 920–21.

and 338 to 56. Some historians regard Waldorf Astor as the 'mastermind' behind the Bill. He did play an important role in research, analysis and drafting the Bill, as well as getting it through the House of Lords, but this should not detract from Nancy Astor as the person who had to get it through the Commons against considerable opposition backed by the drink trade, making the case and crafting the arguments.[17]

The Bill then had a tumultuous time in Standing Committee, where two important amendments were made that materially altered the Bill from Astor's original intentions.[18] The first of these was the introduction of the word 'knowingly', so that the Act as passed declared that a licence holder should not 'knowingly' sell intoxicating liquor to persons under 18. The argument was that it was unjust to convict people who did not know they were committing an offence. However the Bill's promoters argued it gave landlords an 'out'. The 'knowingly' amendment passed on division, with 24 votes to 16.[19]

The second amendment made an exception to the 'age 18' rule by allowing 'beer, porter, cider or perry' to be supplied to 16- and 17-year-olds with meals. The argument was that stronger liquors, such as spirits and wine, were bad for young people, but not weaker liquors, such as beer and cider, which were harmless and natural. Astor and her supporters rightly saw these clearly as wrecking proposals, 'designed to emasculate and destroy the bill'.[20] Ultimately, it was only possible to get the Bill through the committee with this amendment, with Astor concluding that something was better than nothing.

Temperance organisations continued to support the Bill and encouraged their members to write to their MPs. The Bill returned to the Commons, where it survived first an attempt to talk it out and then another chaotic and rowdy sitting through report stage and third reading on 13 July, with attempted wrecking amendments. Maud Scott from the WTAU wrote how Members tried almost every means in their power to block the Bill: 'no words can adequately convey … the tense anxiety of those two hours'.[21] Opponents included not only those opposed to liquor limitations, but also Edwin Scrymgeour, who called the Bill 'this ridiculous piece of humbug'.[22] This assisted Astor by helpfully positioning her Bill at the moderate end of the temperance spectrum.

The Bill then passed the House of Lords, led by Waldorf Astor, without a division or any further amendment. It achieved Royal Assent and became an Act on 31 July 1923.

[17] Takayanagi, n 11.

[18] ibid.

[19] Another legislative example where lack of knowledge of age was used to temper the effect of the law is the **Criminal Law Amendment Act 1922**, with the 'young man's defence' of 'a reasonable belief' that the complainant was aged over 16.

[20] HC Deb, Standing Committee C, 27 March 1923, cols 840–68.

[21] *Wings* (August 1923) 149.

[22] HC Deb 13 July 1923, vol 166, col 1776.

III. What Happened Next

The principle established by Astor's Bill remains to this day. However the implementation of the Bill was immediately found to be limited. Astor's correspondence includes a case in Blackpool in June 1924, when a landlord served a girl of 17; it was found the offence was committed 'unknowingly', and on that account the case was dismissed.[23] Such cases are likely to have deterred many further attempts at prosecution.

The trend in consumption of intoxicating liquor fell, but it had been falling even before Astor's Bill. Alcohol consumption fell from over 11 litres per head per annum in 1899 to less than 4 litres during the First World War, a trend not reversed until after the Second World War.[24] The period 1920–1960 saw an overall downward trend in beer consumption and convictions for drunkenness. It cost more to drink less, and other leisure pursuits and goods attracted spending. New housing also inspired new public houses, which were family-friendly and served food, and even had toilets.[25]

The fear that Astor's Bill would be a stepping-stone to prohibition was not borne out. Edwin Scrymgeour twice attempted to introduce bills that would have banned the manufacture, importation or sale of alcohol as a beverage. The first of these was during the passage of Astor's Bill in 1923; the second was in 1931. On both occasions his Bills were overwhelmingly voted down at second reading. Scrymgeour lost his seat in the 1931 general election to the Conservative Florence Horsbrugh, and the Scottish Prohibition Party disbanded in 1935.

The NBTWA and the WTAU re-united in 1926 to become the National British Women's Total Abstinence Union (NBWTAU). Temperance organisations declined in membership and influence over the years after Astor's Bill, but church leaders, social workers and the medical profession continued to show active interest in the subject. The 'drink problem' came to be framed in broader health and social terms, with a focus on deeper social causes of alcoholism, such as housing, education and working conditions, rather than drink as an evil in itself.[26]

IV. Significance

Astor's Bill is a legal landmark as it introduced into law the principle that people had to be aged 18 to drink. Yet compromises were made. The amendments to add the word 'knowingly' and to allow younger people to have some types of alcohol

[23] UoR, MS1416/1/1/194.

[24] Laura Fenton, 'Practices of learning, earning and intimacy in women's drinking biographies' (PhD thesis, University of Manchester, 2018).

[25] Paul Jennings, *The Local: A History of the English Pub* (Tempus, 2007).

[26] John Greenaway, *Drink and British Politics since 1830: A Study in Policy Making* (Palgrave Macmillan, 2003).

with food reflect the enormous difficulties Astor faced in getting the Bill through the House of Commons, and demonstrate the continuing strength of the drink trade and of drinking culture in the UK after the First World War.

Despite this, the successful passage of a Private Member's Bill was a considerable success for Astor as a backbench MP. It is fitting that her great personal legislative achievement was about temperance, given her lifelong commitment to it as a cause. She also continuously supported measures for the welfare of children throughout her parliamentary career, and the Intoxicating Liquor Bill is consistent with her many other campaigns for the protection of children against poverty and abuse, support for unmarried mothers and their children, widows' and orphans' pensions, and publicly funded nursery schools.[27]

More broadly, Astor's Bill was a great success for temperance campaigners after 1918, and shows the UK temperance movement, including women's organisations such as the WTAU, enjoying legislative success well beyond its Victorian heyday, into the interwar period and beyond.[28] Astor might be pleased to know that although temperance is no longer a major movement today, it is rather a broader sentiment in society, with general agreement that alcohol should be regulated by the state, and that individual consumption should be managed and at times avoided.[29] With regard to children, Laura Fenton's work has shown that although alcohol is not much associated with childhood, apart from at Christmas, a moral holiday where a taste of a drink is about joining celebrations, in adolescence, alcohol use is associated with chasing independence and experimentation.[30]

Further Reading

- Lady Astor, 'The English Law Relating to the Sale of Intoxicating Liquors' (1923) 109 *The Annals of the American Academy of Political and Social Science* 265.
- Paul Jennings, *The Local: A History of the English Pub* (Tempus, 2007).
- Mari Takayanagi, 'Astor the Fairy Godmother: The Intoxicating Liquor Act 1923' (2020) 6(2) *Open Library of Humanities.*

[27] Pat Thane, 'Nancy Astor, Women and Politics, 1919–1945' (2020) 6(2) *Open Library of Humanities.* See also **Widows', Orphans' and Old Age Contributory Pensions Act 1925**.

[28] Today, the White Ribbon Association, successor to the BWTA, is a charity dedicated to raising awareness of the harmful effects of drugs, alcohol, tobacco, gambling and more.

[29] Virginia Berridge, *Demons: our changing attitudes to alcohol, tobacco, & drugs* (Oxford University Press, 2013).

[30] Fenton, n 24.

14

Women's Lavatory Accommodation at the Law Society, 1923

EDUARDO REYES

On 28 March 1919, the Law Society Council responded to the certainty of legislation requiring the bar to be lifted on women entering the legal professions[1] with a Special Meeting to consider a motion that ended the Society's previous opposition. For supporters of equality, there was a celebratory atmosphere. Few had spoken against the motion and the vote – 50 in favour and 33 against – was a convincing victory. Council member Samuel Garrett, a London solicitor, former Law Society President, and brother of suffragist leader Millicent Garrett Fawcett, caught the mood of the winning side: 'Minorities,' he said, 'had a way of becoming majorities in these progressive times.'[2]

However, it took the Society four further years to agree building works to provide women students and solicitors with cloakroom and lavatory facilities. It was not until 16 February 1923 that the Council adopted a recommendation by the House Committee to provide 'cloak-room and lavatory accommodation' for women.[3] Nevertheless, decades before women solicitors achieved numerical equality, this measure of equality was built into the permanent physical architecture of the solicitor profession at its own Hall[4] – the location not just for ceremony, but also for teaching, study, examination and professional encounters.

[1] The Sex Disqualification (Removal) Act 1919.

[2] *Solicitors Journal* (5 April 1919) 415.

[3] 'Lavatory' and 'w.c.' (water closet) are used interchangeably in records from the interwar period, and sometimes tautologically. More modern references given here state 'toilet'. Though identical in meaning, each is used in context here. In similar vein, quoted passages use the original punctuation, grammar, indentation and italics found in the original documents.

[4] The solicitor profession's building at 113 Chancery Lane was consistently and interchangeably referred to as its 'Hall' until well into the 1960s, before gradually falling out of use. As 'Hall' has a professional as well as a physical significance, and was in use in the interwar period, I have used it here.

I. Context

A change in Law Society policy and Royal Assent for the Sex Disqualification (Removal) Act 1919 were seismic in that they removed two absolute bars to women's entry to the profession. But access rights turned out to be narrowly defined. The Act's bar on sex-based disqualification had limitations as enabling legislation.[5] It was not read as referring to women's access to the legal profession's messes, clubs and societies, lavatories, canteens or bars. That lack of automatic access presented early women law students and lawyers with barriers to full participation in the profession. Buildings and clubs were made open to women only one space and society at a time. The piecemeal process of securing equal access and facilities continued into the 1970s.[6]

As a result, women's access and the provision of facilities for them were in some instances considered and denied. The *Solicitors Journal* (which like the *Law Society Gazette* also covered professionally noteworthy events and news at the Bar) reported on 30 January 1923 that the Bar Mess at the Old Bailey

> held a general meeting to consider the application of a woman for membership. There was no wish to exclude the lady in question, who is personally the most popular with her male colleagues of the new lady barristers; but unforeseen difficulties, arising from the nature of the Mess premises, had shown themselves in the way of admitting women to the Mess. It was therefore decided not at present to admit women.[7]

It was the same in the regional Circuit and Sessions Messes. 'Now that a number of women have been called to the Bar the various Circuit and Sessions Messes are faced with the problem of their admission to these closed Bars,' the *Solicitors Journal* reflected at the end of 1922. 'There are privacies of mess life which render it inconvenient to mix the sexes,' in light of which,

> [v]arious circuits and sessions are adopting slightly different plans, but the general scheme seems to be the admission of women with full rights of membership, but without the right to attend mess … In this way women receive all the usual benefits as regards notice of sittings, postal arrangements, attendance in court, court briefs, admission to the poor persons' defence list, and the like; while the seclusion of the masculine mess is preserved.

After all, the article concluded, 'Women … can form a mess of their own and adopt a Bar hotel of their own in each circuit town … On the whole, the proposed compromise … seems fair and liberal.'[8]

[5] Mari Takayanagi, 'Sex Disqualification (Removal) Act 1919' in Erika Rackley and Rosemary Auchmuty (eds), *Women's Legal Landmarks: Celebrating the History of Women and Law in the UK and Ireland* (Hart Publishing, 2018) 136.

[6] Women acquired full equality in the Law Society's dining facilities in 1975 when the 'Ladies' Annex' closed (see section IV).

[7] *Solicitors Journal* (20 February 1923) 290.

[8] *Solicitors Journal* (23 December 1922) 179.

So, the presence of women in spaces that had been traditionally all-male was certainly a talking point, even if the talk vastly overstated their numbers. The *Solicitors Journal* remarked upon the impact of Bar students and married residents on the atmosphere of such spaces: 'There was a time within the memory of men now living when the presence of a woman in the Temple, other than a laundress or the wife of a porter, would have been regarded as little short of sacrilege … now they overrun it.'[9] Was the presence of the handful of women now in the Temple too many for some? Far from overrunning the heart of barrister London, women were excluded from some of its key societies.[10]

II. The Landmark

But what had been happening at the Law Society? There were at least interim measures in place within the building. The House Committee related, 'As regards the lavatory accommodation, the women students have made use of the room attached to the President's suite of rooms on the third floor, West side.'[11] Yet women students, and their male supporters, were becoming impatient for more – they wanted adequate, permanent facilities. Things came to a head in late 1922. On 23 December, members were informed 'A Special General Meeting of the members of the Society will be held in the Hall of the Society, on Friday, the 26 January, at 2 o'clock.'[12] The meeting had just two topics tabled, and was held at the behest not of the Council but of ordinary members of the Society.

The first was a question and motion put by London solicitor Mr Percy Chambers. Chambers asked whether the Council intended to provide women with 'suitable separate cloak-room and lavatory accommodation notwithstanding they have hitherto refused to grant such accommodation to the women students'. And he proposed a motion stating the 'imperative' of providing the accommodation 'without further delay … and that the Council be required … to take immediate steps'. To his surprise, the Law Society President Arthur Copson Peake replied in the affirmative. He said the Council 'intend to provide them with suitable cloak-room and lavatory accommodation'. He added 'this matter had been receiving the consideration of a committee of the council for several weeks. Plans had been now passed which would entail a considerable amount of expense.' He meant that the House Committee had already been tasked with considering 'Women members and students. Additional cloak-room and lavatory accommodation', and would report to the Council within weeks.[13]

[9] *Solicitors Journal* (1 September 1923) 844.

[10] At Bar debating club The Hardwicke Society, even a rule change was insufficient – opponents of women's membership had to be prevailed upon not to black-ball women applicants. *Solicitors Journal* (6 September 1924) 917–18.

[11] The Law Society, *Reports 1919–23*, 251–52.

[12] *Solicitors Journal* (23 December 1922) 197.

[13] The Law Society, n 11, 251–52.

Wrongfooted, Chambers withdrew his motion, but his explanation makes clear his links to students who had been pushing for permanent cloakroom and lavatory facilities for women. Those students included his daughter, Katharine Elizabeth Chambers, a founder member of the 1919 Club (forerunner of the Association of Women Solicitors),[14] and Carrie Morrison, another 1919 Club member.[15]

> In justification to himself, he must state that the matter had been before the council not only for the last three weeks but for the last three or four years; because the students' committee had during the past three years made recommendations that the question should be attended to.[16]

In addition to his direct family link to the students and the 1919 Club, Chambers must have worked with 20 or more fellow solicitors to meet the threshold needed for the Special Meeting to be called (20 was also the quorum required for the meeting to proceed on the day).[17]

Chambers, to pick up on common links among many supporters of equality in the profession, was a London solicitor. At the 1919 Special Meeting, the Law Society's London members had dominated the speeches in favour of a change in policy. Lieutenant Wood, who eye-catchingly attended in his khaki uniform, had spoken for the change. Another was Edward Bell, who had appeared as a witness in the High Court in the 1913 case brought by Gwyneth Bebb and others against the Law Society, stating that he would offer Bebb articles if her case succeeded.[18] Bell was part of a London legal network of solicitors and barristers involved in events like the *Bebb* case.[19] Bell had been deeply impressed with Mrs Pankhurst, whom he met at a will signing 'at the home of one of her supporters'. In his memoirs, published in 1939, he recalled her 'beautiful voice, which animated an almost fanatical enthusiasm, controlled by a stateswoman's mind'. He evidently came to know Pankhurst and her daughters through further meetings. Law graduate Christabel, he said, 'possessed a visionary disposition'. And of Sylvia, he wrote 'she is a wonderful leader and a clear voluminous writer – a striking little personality who, with her vivid intensity, can influence a large audience even to political aggression'.[20] As well as his involvement in the *Bebb*

[14] *Hutchinson's Woman's Who's Who 1934–35* (Hutchinson & Co, 1935) 109. Katharine Chambers was articled to her father's firm, qualifying in 1925. She was still at the firm in 1935, as was another woman solicitor, Clara Maudle Aldred, qualified in 1930 (ibid 30). See further Elizabeth Cruickshank, 'Foundation of the Association of Women Solicitors, 1921' in Erika Rackley and Rosemary Auchmuty (eds), *Women's Legal Landmarks: Celebrating the History of Women and Law in the UK and Ireland* (Hart Publishing, 2019) 167.

[15] *Hutchinson's*, n 14, 353.

[16] *Solicitors Journal* (3 February 1923) 279–80.

[17] *Handbook of the Law Society* (1924) 59. There is no surviving handbook for 1922/23, but the rules for a special meeting are identical in the 1905 edition of the *Handbook*.

[18] *Bebb v The Law Society* [1914] 1 Ch 286.

[19] Judith Bourne, 'Gwyneth Bebb: the past explaining the present' *Law Society Gazette* (20 September 2022).

[20] Edward A Bell, *These Meddlesome Attorneys* (Martin Secker, 1939) 50–51.

litigation, he promoted the admission of women in the pre-Great War Law Society's meetings.[21] He continued to press the Council on the admission and equality of women after 1919.[22]

London Council member Sir Walter Trowers seconded the 1919 motion that changed the Society's policy to one of support for the admission of women. Other London supporters were Law Society vice-president Mr WA Sharpe (who succeeded Pinsent as president), Mr Braby and Mr Charles Mackintosh. London had long been a centre for the organisation of suffragist and suffragette campaigning. In addition to Bell's acquaintance with the Pankhursts, the Women's Social and Political Union (WSPU) had links to the London legal community through figures like Emmeline Pethick-Lawrence's husband Frederick, an independently wealthy barrister and a major financial backer of the WSPU until he was sidelined in 1913. So too the office of Law Society president. Trowers, like Garrett, was both a London Council member and a former president (1913). As president in March 1919, Richard Pinsent used his position in the chair to signal his support. Sharpe succeeded Pinsent as president. JJ Dumville Botterall (president from July 1921) was also a supporter.[23]

But why was Chambers taken by surprise by the House Committee's work? It is speculation, but if the provision of women's cloakroom and lavatory facilities had not been a priority, the prospect of the passing of a critical motion at a Special Meeting, called not by the Council but at the behest of a well-organised and respected group, may have spurred the Law Society's senior officers, including its president, Peake, to act. The resolution of a Special Meeting was not binding on the Law Society until adopted by the Council, but the Council was bound to adopt or bring the matter to the next General Meeting of the Law Society.[24] If the matter became drawn out, it had the potential to embarrass the Law Society through the sort of publicity that had attached to other episodes involving women solicitors.

Certainly the House Committee and the Society's architect were working at speed. We know this because the works described by Peake at the Special Meeting were quite different from those recommended by the House Committee and adopted by the Council a few weeks later, on 16 February. And the House Committee's report noted the admission of 'one woman' solicitor, meaning it was still working on its report after 23 December 1922 – therefore after a date had been scheduled for the Special Meeting.

[21] Bell's memoirs state (ibid 256) 'I remember nearly 30 years ago venturing to idealize the Society's masculinity by suggesting that women should be admitted to the ranks of the profession. I was heartened by the support of a distinguished member of the Council whose memory I hold in reverential regard. Nevertheless, a preponderating majority of the Council and members present shuddered in avoidance and shelved tendencious subversion by resolving forwith to pass to the next business.'

[22] *Solicitors Journal* (15 July 1922) 654.

[23] ibid.

[24] *Handbook*, n 17, 63.

Of the women's use of the president's third-floor lavatory, the Committee said:

> This lavatory accommodation has always been regarded as a temporary measure, and the House Committee, in view of the election of a woman member, considered it essential that the general question of permanent women's lavatory accommodation should be taken into consideration.

The full set of works proposed by the Committee and approved by the Council was for the creation of four lavatories, each with an attached room 'for the exclusive use of women'. The first set, for 'women members', would displace the members' cloakroom, moving it to the right-hand side of the Chancery Lane entrance; a prestigious location, opening onto the same main entrance hall as the Law Society's 'Reading Room'. The second set, for women students, would convert a ground-floor room used by the president. A third set on the second floor, also for women students, would displace 'the existing coal store', with a new coal store being constructed 'on the outside roof of the same floor'. And finally there was a fourth set, 'for the accommodation of women attending the Society's examinations'. The Architect estimated 'an outlay of between £1,000 and £1,200'.[25]

Why did the House Committee recommend changes on this scale? The decision had the knock-on effect of depriving the president of some accommodation, and in the context of the 'Building and Repairs' budget, the expenditure was significant. Perhaps this was a case of professional status, and a sense of hierarchical propriety, trumping other considerations. Perhaps a solicitor could not be expected to share facilities with students and examination candidates. In any event, this is a somewhat different picture from the traditional account in which a lavatory was created in a coal hole.[26]

III. What Happened Next

Were all the works carried out? It seems so. At the Law Society's AGM on 25 July 1924, its grandly titled 'Chancellor of the Exchequer' Mr Hickley (who had succeeded Trowers) observed that '[t]he item "buildings and repairs" showed a heavy increase, but this was due to the adaptation of the Society's buildings to the use of lady solicitors'. While he had superintended the increase, he marked the moment by reaching for patronising levity:

> Whether or no the fair sex would eventually take possession of the building and leave mere males to find accommodation elsewhere remained to be proved; but at the moment there did not seem any probability of such an event taking place during his term of office.[27]

[25] Around £48,000–£58,000 at today's values, according to the Bank of England 'Inflation Calculator'.
[26] Recounted orally as anecdote.
[27] *Solicitors Journal* (2 August 1924) 854.

The accounts for 1923, and the comparator of adjacent years, point to the carrying out of substantial building works under 'Buildings and Repairs'.[28]

The surviving fabric of the building, 113 Chancery Lane, provides further evidence of at least some of the works carried out. The new cloakroom that displaced a consulting room remains the members' cloakroom.[29] A small room accessible at its corner of what was the members' cloakroom before 1923 is surely a candidate for the location of the 'lavatory basin and w.c.'. On the second floor there is a store room built on a roof nearby, above the Reading Room – surely the 'new' coal store for the second floor. The modern layout and fabric of the building makes it difficult to provide further physical evidence from the superficial survey possible.[30]

IV. Significance

'Everybody's got a bathroom story, haven't they,' UK Supreme Court Justice Lady Hale said in conversation with US Supreme Court Justice Ruth Bader Ginsberg in 2008.[31] Bader Ginsberg recalled the creation, shortly after her arrival at the US Supreme Court in 1993, 'done at speed', of a 'women's bathroom' by the Justices' robing room that was 'in space equal in size to the men's … the court staff at least had a view of how things will be'. (Such spatial courtesy had not been extended to the Court's first woman, Justice Sandra Day O'Connor.) In the UK, the Privy Council, appeal court for Crown dependencies and several Commonwealth countries, acquired a women's toilet shortly after the arrival of Hale as its first woman judge in 1999.[32]

Why does the presence and position of lavatory facilities matter? First, as the history shows, such facilities could be used as the basis for direct discrimination – their absence an open justification for excluding women from appointments in the profession or participation in its associations. Second, where only 'temporary arrangements' were made for women, as at the Law Society from 1919 to 1923, this was both signal and evidence of an unequal status. Conversely, permanent, adequate, convenient arrangements signal equality and professional respect.

Third, the manner in which facilities for women, and membership of clubs and societies, were made available allows us to infer important points about women's entry into the legal profession after 1919. They continued to face both inconvenience and resistance to their presence. Each accommodation, and the membership of each society or professional social space, was a stand-alone victory, and long into

[28] *Annual Report of the Council of the Law Society* (1923) 46; (1924) 52.

[29] The likely location of the women's 'room' is by coincidence the newly named Carrie Morrison Room, a business lounge directly opposite the current cloakroom.

[30] Site visit by the author on 15 December 2022, when all relevant areas were accessible.

[31] 'The British and United States Legal Systems', Georgetown University Law Centre, 24 January 2008.

[32] Hale joined the Court of Appeal at the same time, the Court's second woman judge.

the post-war period these rarely set a precedent that was automatically followed in other spaces. As with the Law Society's change of policy towards the admission of women in 1919, facilities and rule changes might respond to, or coincide with, legislation on equality.

These last two points are further evidenced by a postscript to the Law Society's original provision of lavatory facilities to women members. By the 1960s, a growing number of women solicitors and female guests were running up against arcane etiquette relating to Chancery Lane's dining and social facilities. A woman solicitor could bring a male guest to lunch, but not a non-lawyer woman guest; neither could a male lawyer bring a non-lawyer woman guest. The solution reached by the Council was not to change the rules but to create the Ladies' Annexe, where male or female solicitors could bring their women guests to drink and dine.[33] Equal rights in the Society's facilities were achieved in 1975, likely as a response to the Sex Discrimination Act 1975, just as the Council had anticipated the 1919 Act by changing its policy on admission.

As for inequality in lavatory provision itself, this had also persisted in the wider legal profession. Hilary Heilbron KC, daughter of the first senior woman judge Rose Heilbron KC, was called to the Bar in 1971. She recalls toilet facilities (the lack thereof) being used as a reason to exclude women from chambers on the eve of the 1975 Act.[34]

Thus, in 1923, by replacing the makeshift arrangement of women's access to the Law Society president's third-floor lavatory and creating spaces for women, the Society had built a degree of equality into the permanent physical architecture of the solicitor profession at its Hall. In this regard, the Law Society was ahead of other legal sector organisations, in some cases by more than half a century. Moreover, though it had taken four years to achieve, once the House Committee was tasked with recommending facilities, its hand apparently forced by Chambers – father of a 1919 Club founding member – its recommendations were of a scale that anticipated future demand.[35]

[33] Eduardo Reyes, 'A great many she bears' *Law Society Gazette* (9 December 2019).

[34] Hilary Heilbron, 'Women at the Bar: an historical perspective', *Counsel Magazine* (31 May 2013).

[35] *Hutchinson's*, n 14, 395, has entries for 80 women solicitors. *The Woman's Who's Who* (Shaw Publishing Co Ltd, 1934) 11, records 314 women in its 'Occupational statistics' under 'Legal', though it does not specify what categories of job are counted.

15

Agnes Twiston Hughes, First Welsh Woman to Practise as a Solicitor, 1923

CAROL HOWELLS

Agnes Twiston Hughes was the first Welsh woman to qualify as solicitor in Wales, to hold a practising certificate and to run a legal practice. Her quiet contribution to the opening up of the profession was made in her local area and in her local community, where she knew she had the ability and opportunity to make a difference. In the words of Janet Corke, her first articled clerk:

> She could make you tremble in your boots … dressed in a well-cut suit … cigarette in one hand, a glass in the other, tall and confident, ready to take on the world – a remarkable feminist in the best sense of the word.[1]

I. Life

Born in late 1895, Agnes Twiston Hughes was the youngest daughter of John William and Elizabeth Harriet Hughes. Together with her sister, she attended the Welsh School in Ashford, Kent, originally a British Charity School intended to educate the children of Welsh parents: it had its own chapel. She later moved to Bangor County School for Girls, which, situated 15 miles from Conwy in North Wales, was much nearer home.

In 1918, she gained a second-class Bachelor of Science (Economics) degree from the London School of Economics, which, founded in 1895 and focused on the social sciences, had a reputation for gender equality that would have made it a more congenial place to study than most other universities at the time. The following year women were admitted to the legal profession for the first time. In 1923, Hughes took her Law Society examinations, coming top of her year.[2]

[1] Elizabeth Cruickshank, 'Agnes Twiston Hughes: like father, like daughter' *Law Society Gazette* (17 May 2023).

[2] It would be another 25 years before another woman matched her achievement.

She was awarded the Sheffield Prize (for which she received £35), the John Mackrell Prize (for which she received £13)[3] and the Clement's Inn prize.[4]

Having joined her father's firm – JW Hughes & Co – which was located in a former pub building in the centre of Conwy, she worked her way up from articled clerk to, after her father's death in 1949, senior partner. She retired in 1961.

Hughes did not marry. But then, as Elizabeth Cruickshank points out, 'neither did almost 40 per cent of the women who qualified as solicitors in the first decade' after the passing of Sex Disqualification (Removal) Act 1919.[5] She died 1981 in Coed Celyn, the house where she was born. JW Hughes & Co continues to operate in Conwy today.

II. Context

At the beginning of the twentieth century, North Wales was undergoing a period of upheaval, with significant political activism and public debates around social justice, together with a literary and religious revival. Land reform, equality for labourers and tenant farmers, the disestablishment of the Church of England in Wales, voting rights and devolution for Wales were widely discussed and hotly debated.

Conwy was and is a busy market town situated in North Wales. Since 1848, a railway station had connected the town with the Holyhead and Chester line. However, despite the arrival of the railways, canals and early tourism, much of North Wales remained isolated. Conwy retained many of its medieval buildings, was circled by ancient walls and dominated by its castle. Sunday was strictly observed as a non-working day, set aside for worship at church or chapel.

At the time of the 1921 census, 39 per cent of the Welsh population spoke Welsh. However, in North Wales, away from the industrialised valleys of South Wales, Welsh was more widely understood than English, despite a requirement to learn English as a second language. But it could not be used for official purposes.[6]

Wales in the late nineteenth and early twentieth centuries had seen the acknowledged emergence of women into public life. In art, literature, politics, education and professional life, the work and influence of women was being recognised. From Sarah Jane Rees (Master Mariner, headteacher and poet), through leaders of the fight for equality, such as Lady Rhondda,[7] Winifred Coombe Tennant and

[3] *The Times* (31 March 1923) 10.

[4] A prize awarded to her father some 20 years earlier in 1903.

[5] Elizabeth Cruickshank, 'Agnes Twiston Hughes', 30 November 2016 at https://first100years.org.uk/agnes-twiston-hughes/ [accessed 12 December 2023].

[6] Henry VIII had banned the use of Welsh following the Laws of Wales Acts 1535 and 1542. The use of the Welsh language was a topic of debate. See, for example, the infamous 1847 *Reports of the Commissioners of Inquiry into the State of Education in Wales*, which caused uproar in Wales, known in Wales as the Blue Books.

[7] **'Lady Rhondda's petition for women to sit in House of Lords, 1922'.**

Charlotte White Price, to MPs such as Edith Picton-Turbervill[8] and university professors such as Millicent Mackenzie, Welsh society was being changed by pioneering women.[9] Their stories were shared through written and spoken traditions, and would have been well known throughout Wales.

III. What Happened Next

Hughes' legal work was similar to that carried out by many small practices of the time. Reference to the firm can be found in court and probate records. Whilst undertaking general practice providing advice on wills, contracts, conveyancing and family matters, and appearing before local magistrates' courts, Hughes seems to have gained a reputation for adoption work.[10] She was regarded as a formidable legal opponent with a passion for her work and supporting others.[11]

Despite running a busy legal practice, Agnes Twiston Hughes stood for election as a local independent councillor for Conwy.[12] Here she found a new forum for her passions and views. She was the sole dissenting voice when Conwy Council sought to demolish Thomas Telford's 138–year-old suspension bridge through a Private Member's Bill. Working with others, she succeeded in protecting what is now a world heritage site.[13] Her strong convictions and direct approach were not always well received in the Conwy Council chamber.[14] Like many other women in senior positions, she gained a reputation as an 'old battle-axe', reducing at least one male councillor to tears.[15] It appears Hughes paid little heed to this. In 1954, she became the first female Mayor of Conwy, and in this role she continued to demonstrate her strong convictions and beliefs: for example, she insisted on changing the venue of the annual civic service from the Anglican parish church of St Mary & All Saints[16] to the Welsh Methodist Tabernacle chapel.[17]

[8] Edith Picton-Turbervill introduced the Sentence of Death (Expectant Mothers) Bill, which went on to become law, ensuring that no pregnant woman should be executed.

[9] Martha Hughes Cannon, the first woman senator in the USA, had spent her early life in North Wales.

[10] It is said that several individuals in whose adoptions she had been involved as a solicitor returned to Conwy looking for her, believing she was their mother. Informal adoption was common in Wales until the Adoption of Children Act 1926 created a formalised process. See further **'Adoption of Children Act 1926'**.

[11] Including the daughters of her mother's first cousin when they were orphaned.

[12] John William Hughes had been an Alderman.

[13] 'Trust "to take over Conway bridge"' *The Guardian* (27 March 1965) 3.

[14] Cruickshank, n 1.

[15] ibid.

[16] The Church has been the parish church of Conwy since 1284. The Church in Wales was formed in 1920 following disestablishment from the Church of England. It was against a backdrop of heated religious debates around disestablishment and nonconformity that Agnes had been brought up.

[17] 'Viva: Leader of the pack' *Daily Post* (13 July 2004). The Chapel was where Agnes Twiston Hughes and her family had worshipped.

Hughes had a demonstrable commitment to civic duty, community and service, evidenced by the many voluntary positions she held and causes she supported: for example, as county organiser of the Women's Voluntary Service for Civil Defence in Caernarfon during the Second World War. She was a member of the Solicitors' Benevolent Association and of her local Law Society. She was also lady captain of her local golf club; a photograph of her in her Mayoral robes still hangs in the clubhouse.

As a lawyer and councillor, she would have been aware of the debates surrounding use of the Welsh language and the place of Wales within the legal system of England and Wales. The language of her 'official' life was English,[18] but for many of her clients and for many in her constituency English was a second language, and some would have had no understanding of English.

Agnes Twiston Hughes would have been unusual as a woman solicitor working in North Wales in the 1920s and 1930s. Though women solicitors tended to fare better than their female colleagues at the Bar,[19] Patrick Polden suggests that there were 'hardly any' women working on the Welsh circuit until the 1940s.[20] Nevertheless, by the time she retired in 1961, the proportion of women in the solicitor's profession had grown to around 2.7 per cent. Today women make up 57 per cent of lawyers in Wales (compared to 53 per cent in England and 48 per cent of the workforce in Wales).[21]

IV. Significance

Agnes Twiston Hughes was an unassuming trailblazer who went on to have a long and successful career in legal practice. Although she was undoubtedly supported by her father, to whom she was very close, following his death she continued to run and develop the practice in her own right, demonstrating that it was possible for women to lead a successful local firm. In her turn she developed it, taking on articled clerks and training some of the future generations of female lawyers. Her own success is evidenced by the significant amount left in her will, some £302,988.

[18] The Welsh Courts Act 1942 enabled witnesses to use Welsh if they would be disadvantaged by using English.

[19] Elizabeth Cruickshank, 'First Woman Solicitor in England and Wales, Carrie Morrison' in Erika Rackley and Rosemary Auchmuty (eds), *Women's Legal Landmarks: Celebrating the History of Women and Law in the UK and Ireland* (Hart Publishing, 2019) 183. See also Elizabeth Cruickshank, 'Follow the Money' in *First Women Lawyers in Great Britain and the Empire Record: Volume 1* (St Mary's University, 2016) 44.

[20] Fellow Welshwoman, Enid Rosser Locket, for example, joined the south-eastern circuit (Patrick Polden 'Portia's progress: women at the Bar in England, 1919–1939' (2005) 12(3) *International Journal of the Legal Profession* 293, 324).

[21] Solicitors Regulation Authority, 'How diverse is the solicitors' profession?' (updated 11 December 2023) at www.sra.org.uk/sra/research-publications/gender-pay-gap-report-2023/.

Described as 'formidable', inevitably perhaps, by some of her male colleagues,[22] she was regarded as someone who provided good advice and support for those she trained and those with whom she worked.[23] This was done quietly and generously. As one former articled clerk remarked:

> The day I qualified I went to see her sitting behind her desk in six cardigans, because the office was unheated. She smoked like a chimney. And she said to me, 'Well done, Janet. I have only one thing to say to you, never assume anything my dear and good luck'.[24]

Tucked away in a small county town practice in Conwy, her work enabled her to make a difference where it mattered to her, to the lives of her clients, to those she worked with and trained, and to her local community. Within her local and Chapel communities she provided inspiration and evidence that a woman could have a career, be involved in local politics, but also have a social life, whilst always remaining part of a family and community.

Further Reading

- Deirdre Beddoe, *Out of the Shadows: A History of Women in Twentieth-century Wales* (University of Wales Press, 2001).
- Angela V John, *Our Mothers' Land: Chapters in Welsh Women's History, 1830–1939* (University of Wales Press, 2011).
- Angela V John, *Rocking the Boat – Welsh Women Who Championed Equality 1840–1990* (Parthian Books, 2019).

[22] Cruickshank, n 1.
[23] Including others in local practice, such as solicitor Dorothy Metcalfe, who considered Agnes 'very helpful' (ibid).
[24] ibid.

16

First Published Law Textbooks on 'Women and Law' Written by Women Lawyers in Great Britain, 1924–34

ANNE LOGAN

In the 15 years following the admission of women to the legal professions in England, Wales and Scotland under the Sex Disqualification (Removal) Act 1919, three important textbooks focusing on the law as it related to women were published in Great Britain. All three were written by recently qualified women lawyers, all of whom were among the first women in Great Britain to become solicitors or barristers. The three texts (in order of publication) were *Women under English Law* (1925) by Maud Crofts, a solicitor, which contained a supplementary chapter, 'Women Under Scots Law' by Scottish barrister Margaret Kidd; *Everyday Law for Women* (1932) by the prominent barrister Helena Normanton; and *Rights and Duties of Englishwomen: a Study in Law and Public Opinion* (1934) by Manchester-based barrister Erna Reiss. These therefore were the first published law textbooks to be written *by* qualified women lawyers *about* laws relating to women in Great Britain.

I. Context

According to its catalogue, the British Library holds publications concerning the law in relation to women dating back at least to the early eighteenth century. The best-known treatise on the subject forms part of William Blackstone's *Commentaries on the Laws of England* (1768), particularly the chapter on 'Husband and Wife', which outlined the common law regarding marriage, including the principle of 'coverture' under which the husband and wife were as one person in law.[1] Blackstone

[1] For a discussion of William Blackstone's *Commentaries* and other early works concerning women's legal position, see Joanne Conaghan, 'A Brief Summary of the Most important Laws Concerning Women, Barbara Leigh Smith Bodichon, 1854' in Erika Rackley and Rosemary Auchmuty (eds), *Women's Legal Landmarks: Celebrating the History of Women and Law in the UK and Ireland* (Hart Publishing, 2019) 55.

provided the basis for another landmark text on women's legal position, Barbara Leigh Smith Bodichon's *A Brief Summary of the Most important Laws Concerning Women*, published in 1854. As Joanne Conaghan argues, Bodichon's pamphlet brought 'the issue of the legal status of women to the fore' and 'ignited feminist activism', although nearly 30 years passed before there was significant reform, in the shape of the Married Women's Property Act 1882.[2] This statute was followed in 1883–84 by a flurry of publications explicating arrangements under the new law, and in the 1890s, as the rights of women became an ever-greater socio-political issue, leading textbook publishers such as Sweet & Maxwell, Stevens & Sons and G Routledge & Sons began to release books dedicated to the topic of the legal status of women and/or historical surveys of the changing position of women under the law.[3] Hardly any of these texts were written by women, who at this stage were unable to obtain professional legal qualifications, although it was possible for women to study law at some universities.

A perusal of the British Library catalogue therefore suggests a strong relationship between the appearance of publications on the topic of women's legal position and the activities of feminist reformers, as well as the legislative landmarks that their agitations procured. The upsurge of women's suffrage agitation in the early twentieth century produced a more intensive, forensic examination of women under the law, extending beyond the issues of marriage and property to women's (lack of) political and civic rights, employment opportunities and position in relation to the criminal law. Much legal commentary about women written by women was to be found in the pages of women's suffrage journals, particularly *Common Cause*, published by the National Union of Women's Suffrage Societies (NUWSS), and *The Vote*, the paper of the Women's Freedom League (WFL). Factual commentary on women's unequal position under the law appeared in these journals, together with calls for women to be involved in the machinery of the law not only as legal professionals but also as magistrates and jurors.[4] While the fight for the parliamentary vote appeared to dominate suffrage campaigning discourse before 1918, it was regarded by many in the movement as merely a means to an end, with the ultimate goal of a rebalancing of relations between the sexes though a lengthy and detailed legal reform agenda. As Mari Takayanagi explains, the opening of the parliamentary suffrage to some women in 1918 was swiftly followed by the Sex Disqualification (Removal) Act 1919, which opened professions, juries and the magistracy to women, and which itself was followed by many statutes that altered the legal position of women in myriad ways.[5]

[2] ibid 60.

[3] For example, Arthus Rackham Cleveland, *Woman Under the English Law* (Hurst and Blackett Ltd, 1896); Ernest J Schuster, *The Wife in Ancient and Modern Times* (Williams & Norgate, 1911); Edward Abbott Parry, *The Law and the Woman* (C Arthur Pearson, 1916).

[4] Anne Logan, *Feminism and Criminal Justice: a Historical Perspective* (Palgrave, 2008) 12. The WFL also published in 1908 a pamphlet entitled *Women Under the Law*, by WG Earengey, husband of Florence Earengey, a WFL activist who later became a barrister.

[5] Mari Takayanagi, 'Sex Disqualification (Removal) Act 1919' in Rackley and Auchmuty (eds), n 1, 133, 137.

The sheer number of legislative changes in the years 1918–25 alone strongly suggested the need for new textbooks to provide updated commentary on women's legal position, and the entry of women into the legal professions supplied relevantly qualified authors. But a readership was also required. The networks sustained by former suffrage societies and other women's organisations, including not only the National Council of Women (NCW) but also new organisations such as the Women's Institutes, provided that readership. As the National Union of Societies for Equal Citizenship (NUSEC, the renamed NUWSS) and WFL revitalised their memberships with the new, post-suffrage feminist agenda of piecemeal legal reform, they continued to publicise their progress in their periodicals. Notably, in 1923 the NUSEC journal, now called *Woman's Leader*, started a regular, legal feature entitled 'The Law at Work', co-edited by two of the new women magistrates, Margery Fry and Clara Rackham, and Maud Crofts herself.[6] Aimed primarily at their increasing band of public-spirited readers who were undertaking new civic duties such as the magistracy (or perhaps running birth-control clinics or educating women as citizens), the column was a reliable source of information on legal and criminal justice topics of interest to its readers.

It is important to note that two of the three textbooks discussed here demonstrate their authors' close connections to the NCW and NUWSS/NUSEC, organisations that led the field in the promotion of English feminist legal reform between the two World Wars. Crofts' volume was first published by the NCW in 1925 'with the assistance of the Stansfeld Trust': its author was a member of the NCW executive.[7] The Foreword was supplied by Dame Millicent Fawcett, the NUWSS's most famous figurehead. Reiss's book contained a Foreword by Eleanor Rathbone MP (Fawcett's successor as NUWSS/NUSEC president) and was dedicated 'to the Honourable Mrs Cawley and my friends of the National Council of Women'. Cawley was president of the Manchester NCW branch, and Reiss herself was actively involved on the branch executive. However, Normanton's work is simply 'dedicated with great respect to the women magistrates of England', and the Preface and Introduction were all her own work. Normanton had a history of active involvement in women's organisations, but her connections to the feminist movement were not made explicit in her publication.

II. The Landmark

The three books display contrasting styles and approaches to the subject matter. However, with the exception of Kidd's chapter on Scotland, appended to Crofts' book, they all concentrate on the law of England and Wales (although the latter

[6] Logan, n 4, 23.

[7] James Stansfeld, a Radical Liberal politician, was a committed opponent of the Contagious Diseases Acts. The Trust established after his death financially supported various women's causes.

is not mentioned specifically). Two of the books contain the word 'English' in the title; Normanton's does not.

Like the 'Law at Work' column, *Women under English Law* appears to be directed at the educated, engaged female reader: an active member of a women's organisation undoubtedly, perhaps also a magistrate or local councillor, certainly a voluntary worker. In her Preface, Crofts is emphatic that her imagined reader has no legal training but is 'interested in questions concerning the legal status of women under English Law and in the far-reaching changes' of the 'last fifty years'.[8] Crofts places women at the centre of her book's structure, examining the law as it affected them first as citizens, then as wives, mothers and workers. The penultimate chapter (preceding Kidd's) deals with criminal law, including aspects relevant to women as victims and offenders. The book is short – only 101 pages including a chapter on Scotland and the Index – and provides an up-to-date snapshot of women's legal position amid a period of rapid change. Legislation passed in 1925, the year of publication, is featured and discussed, for example the **Administration of Estates Act 1925**, which took effect after the book's publication.

In contrast, Normanton foregrounds the law rather than women, an approach evident in her chosen chapter headings. It is hard to ascertain Normanton's imagined reader: the book is called *Everyday Law for Women*, but which women? Perhaps a clue can be found in the extensive sections on employment law, regarding domestic servants, and in the chapter on 'Travelling', which reprints the entire 1931 'Highway Code' with the permission of the then Minister of Transport.[9] It is likely, therefore, that the reader is envisioned as a wealthy, middle-class, car-driving, servant-employing, probably married lady: the sort of woman who might seek the advice of a prominent woman barrister such as Normanton. Notably, Normanton gives attention to the role of women as employers, whereas Crofts does not. The book runs to 415 pages and contains 15 chapters, beginning with 'Lawyers and their Clients' and ending with 'Crime', taking in citizenship, marriage, trusts, wills, contracts, torts, contract, commercial law and much more on the way. Only pensions, industrial law and national insurance were left out, because 'they would occupy a bulk too enormous for adequate explanation in this unassuming work'.[10] Compared with Crofts' work, this is an idiosyncratic journey, less succinct in its summary of women's legal position and more meandering within its subject matter.

Of the three texts, Reiss's work is the most academic publication, replete with copious footnotes referencing statutes, case law, legal commentaries, historical sources and much more. The intended audience, therefore, may be presumed to be a legal academic one, supplemented by university-educated women in general.[11]

[8] Maud Crofts, *Women under English Law* (National Council of Women, 1925) v.

[9] Helena Normanton, *Everyday Law for Women* (Ivor Nicholson and Watson, 1932) 293–301.

[10] ibid xi.

[11] In her Foreword, Rathbone advocates that not only English women should read it, but also 'women of other countries, especially perhaps those of India'. Erna Reiss, *Rights and Duties of Englishwomen: a Study in Law and Public Opinion* (Sherratt and Hughes, 1934) ix.

Published by Sherratt and Hughes of Manchester, a bookshop and publishing house that had formerly served as Manchester University's official publisher, *Rights and Duties* appears to be a revision of Reiss's doctoral thesis of the same name, submitted for examination in 1924,[12] the same year in which the author was called to the Bar. So although it appeared 10 years after the Crofts volume, it is likely that the bulk of the Reiss's research and writing took place in a similar timeframe to Crofts'. In her Preface, Reiss thanked the academics who supervised her thesis, Professor RA Eastwood of Manchester University and Professor JL Brierly (who moved to All Souls, Oxford, after a brief period teaching at Manchester), both distinguished legal scholars. The latter was also a recognised friend of the women's movement in Oxford, where he served on the governing bodies of two women's colleges.[13]

As her book's subheading indicates, Reiss's organising thesis was to place the changing legal position of women within a historical context of 'public opinion', altered social mores and even social history in general. Yet her book also contains details of post-1925 legislative developments, and even gives examples of recent, failed attempts to improve women's legal position, such as a 1931 proposal by NUSEC (introduced to Parliament by Eleanor Rathbone) to amend the law regarding wills and family maintenance, and a 1933 Bill promoted by the NCW to reform the representation of women on juries.[14] Like Crofts, Reiss placed women in the foreground of her study, which, after an introductory chapter setting the scene in 1837, is structured around women as wives, mothers and property owners, before examining their position with regard to contracts, the criminal law, public rights and duties, and, finally, their right to education and work. At 269 pages, *Rights and Duties* is a substantial and comprehensive volume, which, like the other two books discussed here, provides a 'snapshot' of women's legal position in the interwar period, but with a lot more social historical context than either Crofts' or Normanton's book.

III. What Happened Next

Taken together, the publication of three books about women's legal position by writers who were among the first women to obtain entry to the legal professions represents a significant landmark in retrospect. However, the initial response to these ground-breaking texts appears to have been muted. Of the three, only Crofts' volume received a second edition, published by Butterworth's, the London-based legal publisher, in 1928. Despite their very different approaches to the subject matter, the three books were essentially competing for the same, small (but not negligible) readership: educated, socially conscious women with a strong interest in the law and civil society.

[12] University of Manchester Library Special Collections, JFW/1/24.

[13] Humphrey Waldock, 'Brierly, James Leslie (1881–1955)' *Oxford Dictionary of National Biography* (23 September 2004).

[14] Reiss, n 11, 145, 212.

Judith Bourne explains that despite some positive reviews for *Everyday Law for Women* (including in *The Times*, which thought that much of the law covered in the volume applied also to men), Normanton became quickly dissatisfied with her publisher's efforts at promotion. Bourne concludes politely that it was 'not a best seller', despite Normanton's receiving a substantial advance of £120 from the publisher. Normanton continued her career as a barrister, from which she derived most of her earnings (becoming one of the first women to be made King's Counsel in 1948). However, according to Bourne, she also tried to make money from her 'prolific' writing and contributed articles to myriad publications, as well as producing two volumes for the 'Famous Trials' series.[15]

Crofts likewise carried on her career, in her case as a partner in her family's firm of solicitors, where she specialised in family law. Her involvement in feminist legal campaigns continued at least until 1933, when she joined an NCW deputation in support of the proposed jury reforms.[16] From 1928 she gave talks 'to wives' on the BBC regarding 'law and the home', which would have been an opportunity to become better known.[17] Importantly, she established a dynasty of women solicitors, with both a daughter and granddaughter following her into the profession.[18]

Reiss continued her association with the NCW and other feminist organisations in the north of England, where she also made broadcasts for the BBC, including a series on famous northern women. The fact that her book was published in Manchester probably reduced its impact, but it received several reviews in the national as well as regional press, with the *Leicester Evening Mail* praising it as 'a remarkably detailed survey of the gradual emancipation of women' and an 'invaluable document'.[19] Reiss later served on the Manchester Court of Referees and chaired the National Insurance tribunal for Stockport, Crewe, Nantwich and Sale, for which she was awarded the Order of the British Empire in 1961.[20] She also had further publications to her name, contributing a chapter on changes in the law to the Hogarth Press's volume of feminist commentary, *Our Freedom and its Results* in 1936 and co-authoring *The Logic of Liberty* in 1966.[21]

IV. Significance

Despite their generally positive reviews, the three books appear to have made little impact in the longer term. Presumably they remained on bookshelves and in

[15] Judith Bourne, *Helena Normanton and the Opening of the Bar to Women* (Waterside Press, 2016) 220–22.

[16] *The Vote* (4 August 1933) 2.

[17] *Illustrated London News* (1 December 1928) 54.

[18] *The Times* (6 January 1998) 33.

[19] *Leicester Evening Mail* (25 October 1934).

[20] Queen's Birthday Honours, 1961.

[21] Eleanor Rathbone et al, *Our Freedom and Its Results By Five Women* (Hogarth Press, 1936); George Elliott Dodds and Erna Reiss, *The Logic of Liberty* (Unservile State Group, 1966).

library stacks, but they were largely neglected for several decades and are still little-known.[22] As the laws relating to women continued to change, the texts became increasingly outdated, although the historical analysis in Reiss's work would have aged less quickly than other aspects of the books.

Between the 1930s and the late 1970s, the number of women solicitors and barristers rose very slowly, and before the expansion of universities in the 1960s, numbers of women students and academics were similarly restricted, including in law faculties. Therefore, it was not until 1984 that the next work to take a general, critical look at women and the law, the ground-breaking text *Women and the Law* by Susan Atkins and Brenda Hoggett, was published. In the authors' words, this publication 'helped to legitimise this area of study and was followed by a growth in courses within UK law faculties on gender and the law'.[23] Fittingly, one of the co-authors (Hoggett) was based at Manchester University, where Reiss had decades earlier studied for her PhD. Like Reiss's work, *Women and the Law* took a historical approach, but while the three earlier works were implicitly optimistic that women's legal position had improved and would continue to advance, Atkins and Hoggett argued that the 'formal equality' had not brought 'substantive equality, especially where family roles followed traditional stereotypes'.[24]

Perhaps it was this implicit optimism of Crofts', Normanton's and Reiss's work and their apparent acceptance of the familial status quo that limited the long-term impact of their works. Yet the three volumes retain significance as books that capture a significant, landmark moment in feminist legal history, when a lot had been achieved, more was changing even as they wrote, but much still remained to be done.

Further Reading

- Maud Crofts, *Women under English Law* (National Council of Women, 1925).
- Helena Normanton, *Everyday Law for Women* (Ivor Nicholson and Watson, 1932).
- Erna Reiss, *Rights and Duties of Englishwomen: a Study in Law and Public Opinion* (Sherratt and Hughes, 1934).

[22] The author's copy of *Rights and Duties* was purchased when it was withdrawn from Kent County Library in 2007.

[23] Susan Atkins and Brenda Hoggett, *Women and the Law* (Blackwell, 1984), discussed in Brenda Hale and Susan Atkins, '*Women and the Law*, Susan Atkins and Brenda Hoggett' in Rackley and Auchmuty (eds), n 1, 375.

[24] Hale and Atkins, n 23, 378.

17

Guardianship of Infants Act 1925

BRENDA HALE

The Guardianship of Infants Act 1925 was a significant step, both in the long march of married women towards equal rights over their children and in the recognition of the importance of the welfare of children when making decisions about their care and upbringing.

I. Context

At common law, the husband was the sole guardian of his wife's children (who were assumed to be his unless it was proved beyond reasonable doubt that they were not). He could decide how the children were to be brought up, with whom they should live, and appoint a guardian to make these decisions after he died.

The Court of Chancery did on very rare occasions decline to enforce the father's common law rights, most notably in *Shelley v Westbrooke* (1821).[1] The poet Percy Bysshe Shelley deserted his first wife Harriet Westbrook and their children and went off with Mary Wollstonecraft Godwin, author of *Frankenstein*, but when Harriet committed suicide he demanded the children back. This was refused on the grounds that he was an immoral atheist and proposed to bring the children up that way.

But refusing to enforce the father's rights was very different from giving the mother any rights, as Caroline Norton, granddaughter of the playwright Richard Brinsley Sheridan, and a great beauty, society hostess and author, found out the hard way. She married George Norton, an unsuccessful lawyer, who from time to time subjected her to serious violence. He was also jealous of her social success and political connections. When she left him in 1836, he brought an action for 'criminal conversation' (adultery) against the then Prime Minister, Lord Melbourne. This failed, but it ruined his wife's reputation and her friendship with Melbourne. George Norton also took their three children away from her and sent them to live

[1] *Shelley v Westbrooke* (1821) 1 Jac 266, 37 ER 850.

with his sister, who looked after them so badly that one of them died, but there was nothing Caroline Norton could do to get them back. She wrote vividly about her wrongs and campaigned for a change in the law, eventually persuading Serjeant Talfourd to promote the Custody of Infants Act 1839.

The 1839 Act empowered the Lord Chancellor or Master of the Rolls to give the mother custody of infants up to the age of 7 and access to them up to the age of majority, then 21, provided that she had not been found (in an action for criminal conversation or by an ecclesiastical court) to have committed adultery. It said nothing about the principles to be applied, so it is probable that fathers would be deprived of their rights only if they had misbehaved.

The Matrimonial Causes Act 1857 removed divorce from Parliament, and other matrimonial suits from the ecclesiastical courts, to the new Court for Divorce and Matrimonial Causes. This could grant decrees of judicial separation to either husband or wife on the grounds of adultery, cruelty or two years' desertion.[2] It could grant a husband a divorce on the ground of his wife's adultery, but a wife could only divorce her husband on the ground of adultery coupled with some other offence, such as sodomy or bestiality.[3] When decreeing judicial separation, nullity or divorce, the Court could 'make such provision … as it may deem just and proper with respect to the custody, maintenance and education' of the children of the marriage.[4] Matrimonial behaviour or misbehaviour would loom large in what was deemed 'just'.

The 1839 Act was replaced by the Custody of Infants Act 1873. This empowered the Court of Chancery to give the mother custody of or access to infants up to the age of 16, and to give the father access if the mother had custody. It did not repeat the adultery proviso. It also validated a father's agreement in a deed of separation to give up custody to the mother; but this was not to be enforced if it would not be for the benefit of the child or children. This is the first time the interests of the children get a mention.

However, we can still assume that the Court would be reluctant to interfere with the rights of the father. This was, after all, the age of the notorious case of *Re Agar-Ellis, Agar-Ellis v Lascelles*. A Protestant father had agreed, when marrying a Roman Catholic wife, that their children would be brought up as Catholics. But he soon changed his mind. Nevertheless, the mother 'so indoctrinated' their three daughters in Catholicism that at the ages of 9, 11 and 12 they refused to go to a Protestant church. The father promptly made them wards of court and obtained an injunction prohibiting the mother from taking them to confession or to Roman Catholic places of worship without his consent.[5] He then took the children away from their mother and placed them with others, allowing the mother to visit them

[2] s 16. See further Penelope Russell, 'Matrimonial Causes Act 1857' in Erika Rackley and Rosemary Auchmuty (eds), *Women's Legal Landmarks: Celebrating the History of Women and Law in the UK and Ireland* (Hart Publishing, 2019) 63.

[3] s 27.

[4] s 35.

[5] *Re Agar-Ellis, Agar-Ellis v Lascelles (No 1)* (1878) 10 Ch D 49.

only once a month, and supervised all correspondence between them. When their second daughter reached 16, she asked to be allowed the free exercise of her religion and to live with her mother. The father agreed to the former but not the latter. Mother and daughter then asked that the daughter spend a summer holiday with her mother and for free access and communication, which the father strongly opposed. The Court refused to interfere with the father's right 'to control the person, education and conduct of his children until they are 21 years of age'.[6] As Brett MR declared:

> The law does not interfere because of the great trust and faith it has in the natural affection of the father to perform his duties, and therefore gives him corresponding rights … The rights of the father are sacred rights because his duties are sacred duties.[7]

The Court would only interfere if the father had forfeited his rights by gross immorality or (perhaps) cruelty or abandoning the child to other people. Cotton LJ explained the principle

> that when, by birth, a child is subject to a father, it is for the general interest of families, and for the general interest of children, and really for the interest of the particular infant, that the Court should not, except in very extreme cases, interfere with the discretion of the father, but leave to him the responsibility of exercising that power which nature has given him by the birth of the child.[8]

Bowen LJ explained that the 'benefit of the infant'

> is not the benefit to the infant as conceived by the Court, but it must be the benefit to infant having regard to the natural law which points out that the father knows far better as a rule what is good for his children than a Court of Justice can.[9]

These notions, that one person must be in charge and the courts really cannot decide what is best for children, were to loom large in the discussions which led to the 1925 Act.

However, section 5 of the Guardianship of Infants Act 1886 gave the court power to order custody to the mother and access to either parent up to the age of majority as it saw fit, 'having regard to the welfare of the infant, to the conduct of the parents, and to the wishes as well of the mother as of the father'. This was clearly a move away from the predominant rights of the father. The mother was also to become guardian after the death of the father, either alone or jointly with any guardian appointed by the father; and she could appoint a guardian after they had both died; or nominate a person to serve jointly with the father after she had died, which the court could confirm but only if the father was 'unfit' to serve alone. Perhaps more important still, 'the court' was no longer limited to the High Court but included the local county courts, making the jurisdiction much more accessible, at least to the middle classes.

[6] *Re Agar-Ellis, Agar-Ellis v Lascelles (No 2)* (1883) 24 Ch D 317.
[7] ibid 328 and 329.
[8] ibid 334.
[9] ibid 337–38.

II. The Landmark

The movement for women's equality saw notable successes as the First World War drew to a close. Some women became eligible to vote;[10] all women became eligible to stand for Parliament;[11] and all women became eligible to train for professions, including the legal profession, and to take public office, including the magistracy and judiciary.[12] In 1919, the National Union of Women's Suffrage Societies changed its name to the National Union of Societies for Equal Citizenship (NUSEC). It was committed to achieving 'real equality of liberties status and opportunities between men and women'. Equal rights of guardianship were at the forefront of NUSEC's programme. Equal guardianship for married women was also one of points of the **Six Point Group**, founded in 1921 by Lady Rhondda, herself a notable feminist campaigner.

The politicians, no doubt conscious that some women now had the vote, also appeared sympathetic. In the election held soon after the armistice in 1918, the leaders of the Coalition Government – David Lloyd George (Liberal) and Andrew Bonar Law (Conservative) gave an election pledge 'to remove all existing inequalities in law between men and women'. The Coalition was returned with a massive majority. It looked as if the time for mothers' equality had come.

A Bill giving married mothers equal rights with fathers was introduced in the House of Commons in 1920 and 1921 by Sir James Greig (Liberal), and given a second reading on both occasions.[13] Bills were introduced in both Houses in 1922 and a Joint Committee of both Houses was set up to examine them. Then the Coalition Government fell in October 1922 and Bonar Law took over as Conservative Prime Minister. Lord Cave, who was to play an important part in the 1925 Act, took over from Lord Birkenhead as Lord Chancellor.[14] Bills were again introduced in 1923; a Joint Committee of both Houses, chaired by Lord Askwith (a lawyer specialising in trade disputes) was again set up to examine them, but his draft report was never finalised. The election in December 1923 produced a hung Parliament. The Conservative Government was defeated in the debate on the King's Speech. Ramsay MacDonald was invited to form the first (minority) Labour Government. A further Bill giving married mothers equal rights was introduced by Margaret Wintringham (Liberal, only the third woman to be elected and the second to take her seat).

[10] **Representation of the People Act 1918**, s 4 enfranchised mainly middle-class women aged 30 or over.

[11] **Parliament (Qualification of Women) Act 1918**.

[12] Sex Disqualification (Removal) Act 1919.

[13] For an historian's account of the debates leading to the passage of the Guardianship of Infants Act, see Mari Takayanagi, 'Equality in law? The passage of the Equal Guardianship Act 1925' in 'Parliament and Women c 1900–1945' (PhD thesis, King's College London, 2012) ch 3 at https://kclpure.kcl.ac.uk/portal/en/studentTheses/parliament-and-women-c1900–1945 [accessed 27 October 2023]. However, the Act was not called the Equal Guardianship Act and that is not what the 1925 Act provided.

[14] There being a 'dearth of talent' because many had stayed loyal to the Coalition, at least according to RF Heuston, *The Lives of the Lord Chancellors* (Clarendon Press, 1964).

But there were powerful voices raised against equal rights. Some were prepared to say that they did not believe in equality. Lord Benbow of Southam argued that women were 'not equal, they never will be equal, and you cannot make them equal'.[15] Others voiced more practical doubts, which found echoes for much of the twentieth century. Lord Askwith himself was concerned that dividing parental authority would be bad for children: 'What is at stake … is the well-being of the child itself [*sic*], and any duality of control must militate against that.'[16] Sir Chartres Biron, the Chief Magistrate, told the 1922 Joint Committee that interfering with the father's natural primacy would 'sacrifice entirely the peace of the home and the interests of the children'.[17] In his experience, the women who appeared in his court were not bothered about equal guardianship. If they had equal rights there would have to be a way of resolving disputes, and the intrusion of the courts into family life would bring discord.[18] Some thought that such disputes were inherently non-justiciable. Sir Claude Schuster, the legendary Permanent Secretary in the Lord Chancellor's Office, told the 1922 Joint Committee that courts are about rights, but 'there are no rights here. It is a question of discretion. To take a ridiculous instance, a dispute whether a child is to go to one school, or to another school – how on earth is a court to deal with that?'[19] Sir Claude also argued that it was 'essential from an administrative point of view' that a household should be treated as a single unit and there should be one person within it entitled to take decisions.

In June 1923, these officials asked parliamentary counsel to draft clauses to reflect their views. During the course of 1924 there were negotiations between the officials who were opposed to equal rights and Mrs Wintringham and her supporters. The Government introduced the compromise Bill in May 1924 and it went through all its stages in the Lords. The Labour Government fell in October 1924 before the Bill could pass. But the Conservative manifesto pledged to ensure equal rights for women in the guardianship of children. The Conservatives won the election with a large majority. The King's Speech committed them to introduce legislation. However, it was the 1924 compromise which they introduced.

The Guardianship of Infants Act 1925 did not give married mothers equal rights and authority over their children. But it did provide that parents had equal rights to go to court about matters relating to the child's custody and upbringing. The welfare of the child was to be the court's 'first and paramount' consideration, and the court was not to take into account whether from any other point of view the claim of the father was superior to the claim of the mother or vice versa.

[15] HL Deb 29 July 1924, vol 58, col 368.

[16] *Proceedings of the Joint Committee on the Guardianship of Infants Bill [HL], Minutes of Evidence and Appendix*. HL 95 & HL 163 (1924).

[17] Minutes of Evidence, 19 July 1922, 2, 8.

[18] Echoed by Lord Evershed MR in his Foreword to *A Century of Family Law 1857–1957*, eds RH Graveson and FR Crane (Sweet & Maxwell, 1957).

[19] Minutes of Evidence, 25 July 1922, 28. I recall having no difficulty in resolving a dispute about whether a rugby-mad boy should go to Gordonstoun or Ampleforth by deciding that he should go to Sedbergh.

The mother could get an order while the parents were still living together, although it would not be enforceable until they separated. The mother also had an equal right to appoint a guardian to act after her death.

Perhaps most important of all, jurisdiction to make these orders was extended to magistrates' courts, so for the first time working-class women could claim the right to look after their own children.

III. What Happened Next

Married mothers still only got rights if the father died or a court gave her some. That is why it was standard practice to make custody and access orders in divorce and separation proceedings. It is also why the practice of splitting custody from care and control grew up – to accommodate the perceived need for the father to retain some authority over his children even though they were being looked after by their mother.

Some family law experts continued to believe that the mother's lack of rights and authority did not matter while the parents were still living together. But it mattered very much for such things as getting a passport, consenting to medical treatment, going on school trips, and all the myriad decisions which have to be made about children while they are growing up. Third parties, such as schools and healthcare professionals, needed to know where they stood. It took until the Guardianship Act 1973 for married mothers at long last to achieve 'equal rights and authority' over their children's upbringing without a court order or their husband's death. This has not led to the sort of problems Sir Claude Schuster feared. There are no known cases of the courts' having to resolve disputes between parents who are still living together.

But courts and lawyers are creatures of habit, and it remained standard practice to include custody, care and control and access orders in divorce and separation cases, even though this was no longer necessary. This is why the Children Act 1989 expressly states that the court is not to make an order unless doing so would be better for the child than making no order at all.[20]

There was another relic of the 1925 compromise which took time to sort out. The Bill put forward by the women's groups had made the child's welfare the 'sole' consideration in deciding questions about care and upbringing. But Lord Chancellor Cave successfully proposed amending this to 'first and paramount'. He believed that such things as the conduct and wishes of the parents should be independently relevant. However, in 1969, the House of Lords declared that the child's welfare was not only the first because it was of first importance but it was paramount because it 'ruled on or determined the course to be followed'.[21] Hence

[20] Children Act 1989, s 1(5).

[21] *J v C* [1970] AC 668, Lord MacDermott at 711.

the Law Commission's draft of the Bill that became the Children Act 1989 said that the child's welfare was to be the court's 'only concern'.[22] But the Act says that it is 'paramount'. Fortunately, the Supreme Court has since held that this means that all other considerations are relevant only insofar as they pertain to the welfare of the child.[23]

IV. Significance

The 1925 Act was a fudge. The women's groups may have been placated by the preamble, which stated that Parliament had 'sought to establish equality between the sexes, and it is expedient that this principle should obtain with respect to the guardianship of infants and the rights and responsibilities conferred thereby', but the Act did no such thing. Even so, it was a huge milestone in mothers' rights, giving them the right to go to court and equality when they got there. A case like *Agar-Ellis* could no longer happen.

Further Reading

- Steven M Cretney, '"What will the women want next?": the struggle for power within the family 1925–1975' (1996) 112 *Law Quarterly Review* 110.
- Margaret Forster, 'Caroline Norton 1808–1977' in *Significant Sisters – The Grassroots of Active Feminism 1839–1939* (Penguin, 1984) ch 1.

[22] *Report on Guardianship and Custody*, Law Com No 172, 1988, Draft Children Bill, cl 1(2).
[23] *Re B (A Child) (Residence: Second Appeal)* [2009] UKSC 5, [2009] 1 WLR 2496.

18

Widows', Orphans' and Old Age Contributory Pensions Act 1925

TERESA SUTTON

The Widows', Orphans' and Old Age Contributory Pensions Act 1925 allowed some women to reduce the impact of poverty and the vagaries of the Poor Law on their lives by promising a small amount of regular, definite income.[1] From 4 January 1926, qualifying newly widowed women received a pension of 10 shillings per week, with additional allowances for children under the age of 14 (or 16 if still at school). This continued unless they remarried or cohabited.[2] Women who were already widows at time of the legislation were eligible only if they had a child under 14, and their payments ceased when the youngest child was 14 and a half.

I. Context

At the start of the twentieth century, the only assistance for the aged poor was from friendly societies or trade unions, their own family and community, or the inadequate and stigmatising Poor Law. More than one-third of people over the age of 65 from a working-class background received poor relief at some point in 1908.[3] Women of all ages were more likely to experience poverty for many reasons, including supporting young children alone, living longer in ill health, having more limited options for work, being victims of violence, receiving lower pay, and having less savings and fewer opportunities to join friendly society and union schemes for sickness and old age.[4] Widowhood was particularly difficult.

[1] The Act also introduced non-means tested old-age pensions for persons over 70 and contributory pensions for those over 65. All the pensions were to be funded by new compulsory insurance contributions, payable alongside National Health Insurance payments by those in qualifying employment.

[2] For discussion of 'unmarried wives' see Rebecca Probert, *The Changing Regulation of Cohabitation: From Fornicators to Family, 1600–2010* (Cambridge University Press, 2012) 208.

[3] George Boyer, *The Winding Road to the Welfare State: Economic Security and Social Welfare Policy in Britain* (Princeton University Press, 2018) 143.

[4] Pat Thane, 'Women and the Poor Law in Victorian and Edwardian England' (1978) 6 *History Workshop* 29, 33.

In 1907, socialist reformer Sidney Webb described the 'young widow of the laborer' with small children as the 'most difficult of poor law problems' and estimated that widowhood accounted for 30 per cent of 'all pauperism'.[5] The Old Age Pensions Act 1908 provided a basic maximum weekly means-tested pension of 5 shillings a week from the age of 70. This compared to an average weekly wage for a male manual worker of 27 shillings and was not intended to be enough to live on. Between 1908 and 1911, David Lloyd George, then Chancellor of the Exchequer, did consider pensions for widows and orphans, but no provision was made for them within the first schemes for social insurance for sickness and unemployment under the National Insurance Act 1911, parts I and II as it was deemed too expensive.[6]

Eleanor Rathbone's *Report on the Condition of Widows under the Poor Law in Liverpool*, written when she was an independent member of Liverpool City Council and presented to the Liverpool Women's Industrial Council in 1913, underscored the depth of the issue.[7] The Report examined outdoor relief in Liverpool (as opposed to workhouse provision) in the light of the Poor Law Commission Reports of 1909. Seventy-seven widows receiving poor relief were visited at home, and their families, employment, budgets and housing detailed. It was found that 56 of the families had an income less than 'Rowntree's minimum' – that is 'incomes which are insufficient even if perfectly administered, to provide them with necessaries for the maintenance of purely physical efficiency' – something Rathbone described as 'really appalling'.[8] Rathbone pointed out that whilst there had been legislation removing the 'stigma of pauperism' from unemployment, old age and sickness, '[f]or the widowed mother alone, the Poor Law is apparently still thought good enough'.[9] Rathbone attributed this to the fact that '[a]ll widows are women, and none of them therefore are Parliamentary voters'.[10]

The Government had begun paying pensions to those who had been financially dependent upon men who died on active service during the First World War.[11] The exclusion of civilian widows with children was taken up by feminist and women's organisations following the partial extension of the franchise in 1918. A resolution was passed at the National Union of Societies for Equal Citizenship (NUSEC)'s[12] General Council Meeting in 1919, putting pensions for widows with dependent

[5] Sidney Webb, *Pauperism and Old Age Pensions* (Fabian Society, 1907) 12.

[6] Pat Thane, 'The Making of National Insurance, 1911' (2011) 19 *Journal of Poverty and Social Justice* 211, 214.

[7] Eleanor Rathbone, *Report on the Condition of Widows Under the Poor Law in Liverpool* (Liverpool, 1913).

[8] ibid 14, 16. Rowntree's minimum is reference to Seebohm Rowntree, *Poverty: A Study of Town Life* (Macmillan, 1902).

[9] Rathbone, n 7, 31.

[10] ibid 32.

[11] Naval and Military War Pensions &c Act 1915.

[12] NUSEC's objective was to obtain all reforms needed 'to secure a real equity of liberties, status and opportunities between men and women' (*NUSEC Annual Report 1918*, 3).

children and those incapacitated by age or infirmity from earning a living on the programme of the Union. Pensions were sought 'as of right', not subject to inspections or withdrawal outside of a tribunal, and to be administered separately from the Poor Law. The NUSEC Parliamentary Report for 1919 records the 'important' and 'hopeful' work of preparing a Bill for pensions for widows, including lobbying MPs, 'unofficial' conversations with the Government and attempting to raise the public profile of NUSEC's campaign.[13]

A Bill was introduced by William Tyson Wilson (Labour MP for Westhoughton) in February 1920 but did not progress.[14] Although MPs from different political parties continued to press the Government for the reform in the House of Commons, the Minister of Health, Dr Christopher Addison, maintained that 'the cost of the scheme made it impracticable at the present time'.[15] NUSEC continued to educate the public on the need for reform throughout the early 1920s – including commissioning a film, to be written by the popular author Annie S Swan, starring actress Dorothea Baird and Lady Cynthia Mosely[16] – but at this point NUSEC accepted that it was economically unrealistic to press for a Bill before Parliament.[17]

In a programme of issues set out by Lady Rhondda in *Time and Tide*, which later formed the agenda of the **Six Point Group**, the position of widowed mothers with young children was listed as the second point of reform for 'women as mothers'. It also 'coincided with the better protection of children', an issue on which Lady Rhondda argued women tended to have 'especially strong and definitely thought-out views'.[18]

II. The Landmark

In March 1923, Rhys Davies (Labour MP for Westhoughton) introduced a motion seeking to ensure that provision of

> pensions adequate for the proper upbringing and maintenance of children should be paid to all widows with children or mothers whose family breadwinner has become incapacitated, such pensions to be provided by the State and administered by a committee of the municipal or county council wholly unconnected with the Poor Law.[19]

[13] *NUSEC Annual Report 1919*, 31, 32.
[14] HC Deb 13 February 1920, vol 125, col 388; *Annual Report of NUSEC 1920*, 9.
[15] HC Deb 26 October 1920, vol 133, col 1568, in answer to a question from John Swan (Labour MP for Barnard Castle). See also, for example, question from Alfred Reaper (Conservative MP for Islington East) (HC Deb 9 August 1920, vol 133, col 21). Provision was made for police widows in the Police Pensions Act 1921.
[16] *NUSEC Annual Report 1921*, 14.
[17] *NUSEC Annual Reports 1918 to 1922.*
[18] *Time and Tide* 1.28 (19 November 1920) 560, accessible via Women's Print Media in Interwar Britain at https://interwarfeminism.omeka.net/items/show/38 [accessed 29 January 2023].
[19] HC Deb 6 March 1923, vol 161, col 378.

It was defeated because of cost.[20] Both **Lady Astor** (Conservative MP for Plymouth South) and Margaret Wintringham (Liberal MP for Louth) spoke in support,[21] Lady Astor observing that there was no more 'pitiable case, or anybody who suffers more' than a widow with young children.[22] She declared that if 'women had anything to do with running the country' they would have seen long before then that the country could not afford to allow the current position to continue given the impact on the surviving children.[23]

Later in 1923, NUSEC called for all interested societies to start a new campaign for a cheaper scheme limited to widows with children, which it hoped would be uncontroversial. The rate of payment was to be the same as for war widows, and administration was to be through the Ministry of Health and local pensions authorities, independent of poor relief, with a 'substantial proportion' of members of the pensions authorities to be women. In February 1924, Charles Dukes (Labour MP for Warrington) and Walter Baker (Labour MP for Bristol East) used their maiden speeches to propose and second a successful private motion in support of 'Mothers' Pensions'.[24] Charles Dukes argued that there was 'no difference between the dependants of the man who loses his life in the service of the community, either in a mine or a workshop, and the man who by accident of circumstances may have to sacrifice his life as a result of war services'.[25] Margaret Wintringham also spoke in favour, stressing the amount of cross-party support for the motion, expressing regret at the length of time taken to progress the issue, and highlighting the better provision in America, Canada, Australia, New Zealand and Denmark.[26] The Labour Chancellor, Philip Snowden, expressed support for the resolution and committed to introducing legislation on the matter, but the Government fell before there was the opportunity to do so.

In the subsequent election, all three major political parties referred to the need for pensions for widows with children in their manifestos. The King's Speech at the opening of the new Parliament in December 1924 signalled the path to come – pensions for widows, but not in the form of the NUSEC Bill. The Speech referred to the possibility of including pensions for widowed mothers within the existing systems of social insurance provision.[27]

[20] The wording of the motion was the same as that used in 1924 (see n 24 below) (HC Deb 6 March 1923, vol 161, cols 378–429); *NUSEC Annual Report 1923–1924*, 11. The motion was defeated on division by 64 votes.

[21] In 1921 Margaret Wintringham became the third woman to be elected to the House of Commons and the first woman Liberal MP. She became a friend of Lady Astor. She also supported the **Equal Guardianship Act 1925**, was on the Executive Committee of the NUSEC and connected to the National Union of Women Workers, the Townswomen's Guilds and Women's Institutes.

[22] HC Deb 6 March 1923, vol 161, col 393.

[23] ibid, col 391.

[24] It was resolved '[t]hat, in the opinion of this House, pensions adequate for the proper upbringing and maintenance of children should be paid to all widows with children, or mothers whose family breadwinner has become incapacitated, such pensions to be provided by the State and administered by a committee of the municipal or county council wholly unconnected with the Poor Law' (HC Deb 20 February 1924, vol 169, col 1925).

[25] ibid col 1885.

[26] ibid col 1910.

[27] HL Deb 9 December 1924, vol 60, col 9.

Neville Chamberlain, Minister of Health in Baldwin's new Conservative Government, had been taken with the idea of 'all-in' insurance that would amalgamate provision for unemployment and health insurance schemes and open the door to contributory pensions. A report of an inter-departmental committee, the Anderson Committee, recommended contributory pensions for those aged 65 to 70. Chamberlain prepared a new Bill working with the encouragement of the Treasury, for whom the legislation was politically advantageous and at a low cost. In her study of *Old Age in English History*, Pat Thane observed that '[y]et again, pensions legislation was driven above all by government determination to minimise costs'.[28] The ensuing Widows', Orphans' and Old Age Contributory Pensions Bill combined new contributory pensions for all widows (with and without dependent children), orphans and those aged 65 to 70.

In June 1925, NUSEC published a lengthy memorandum on the Bill by Eleanor Rathbone, who by this time had published *The Disinherited Family*, arguing for family allowances.[29] Rathbone criticised the size of the allowances for children as falling short of that needed for maintenance, and suggested limiting the proposed pensions for widows without dependent children to release funds to raise them. There was debate in Parliament over the cost of the scheme to industry, the contributions payable and the amount of the pensions.[30]

Acknowledging that a non-contributory scheme was unobtainable at that time, NUSEC chose to accept the structure of the Government's scheme and pushed for amendments to improve the position of women who might benefit from it.[31] One of its 'champions' (in the words of NUSEC) was Ellen Wilkinson (Labour MP for Middlesborough East), who received much support in the House for drawing their attention to the anomaly in the Bill that left a woman who had paid compulsory insurance through her own employment ineligible for benefits if she married an uninsured man.[32] Some of NUSEC's successful interventions were the extension of allowances for children at school up to the age of 16, reductions in contributions required from older men and women, and allowing an uninsured man to make voluntary contributions if he married an insured woman; but basic payments remained small.[33] The Act received Royal Assent on 7 August 1925.

[28] Pat Thane, *Old Age in English History. Past Experiences, Present Issues* (Oxford University Press, 2000) 319–27, 325.

[29] Eleanor Rathbone, *Widows', Orphans', and Old Age Contributory Pensions Bill, Memorandum* (NUSEC, 1925); Lucy Vickers, 'Family Allowances Act 1945' in Erika Rackley and Rosemary Auchmuty (eds), *Women's Legal Landmarks: Celebrating the History of Women and Law in the UK and Ireland* (Hart Publishing, 2019) 227.

[30] HC Deb 30 June 1925, vol 185, cols 2253–91, 2292–2490.

[31] *NUSEC Annual Report 1925–1926*, 9.

[32] HC Deb 30 June 1925, vol 185, col 2270. Ellen Wilkinson was the only woman Labour MP elected in 1924 and one of only four women in that Parliament. She was elected at a time when she was ineligible to vote herself, as she did not meet the required property qualification. Ellen Wilkinson had connections to the National Union of Women's Suffrage Societies and the Women's International League for Peace and Freedom.

[33] *NUSEC Annual Report 1925–1926*, 10.

III. What Happened Next

Thane estimates that the Act as a whole brought 15,090,000 people within pensions insurance in January 1926.[34] The *NUSEC Annual Report 1924–26* recorded a 'real legislative harvest' in 1925 and described the Act as 'a whale among the minnows', coming as a 'great surprise to the whole country', including the NUSEC Committee. The view was taken that, whilst all the legislation passed might fall 'short' of the 'measures of perfection' sought, that should not lead to any under-estimation of value.[35]

The provisions the Act made for widows were regarded as a success. NUSEC was aware, however, of how inadequate the payments were and the fact that many widows were excluded from the scheme either because their husbands had not been insured through employment or because the threshold of contributions had not been met. These widows could only rely on the earlier 1908 non-contributory pensions scheme.

While pensions for widows with dependent children had been a common cause for many feminists, some were against the new life-long provision of pensions for younger widows on the basis that they assumed dependence. As a result, some feminists focused on reforms that would provide further financial security for women, such as family allowances, not won until 1945.[36] Others concentrated on equality reforms. The Open Door Council, for example, attracted former members of NUSEC who had campaigned on the issue of widows' pensions. Established in May 1926 by Lady Rhondda from the **Six Point Group**, Elizabeth Abbott from NUSEC, Miss Clegg from the London Society for Women's Service, Emmeline Pethick Lawrence from the Women's Freedom League, and Virginia Crawford from St Joan's Social and Political Alliance, it sought equal rights and opportunities and protections for women.

The 1925 scheme proved difficult to administer. New legislation was needed in 1929, 1931, 1936 and 1937. Nevertheless, the Government estimated that by 1929 about 229,000 widows of insured men who died after January 1926 were receiving pensions.[37] The 1929 Act extended pensions to another 500,000 'Pre-Act' widows aged 55 or over who had been excluded as they had been bereaved before the benefit was introduced. Between 1926 and 1929, 133,000 widows had been awarded a pension for children, and the 1929 Act extended that pension to all children under the age of 16. Wives married to men over 70 were now allowed a pension at 65, and requirements for proof of national insurance contributions in final years of employment were relaxed. These changes were together estimated to add another 44,000 claims.

[34] Thane, n 28, 326.
[35] *NUSEC Annual Report 1925–1926*, 1.
[36] Vickers, n 29.
[37] HL Deb 26 November 1929, vol 75, col 651.

Since qualification for the 1925 widows', orphans and old-age pensions turned on compulsory contribution, paid via employment, it excluded independent workers such as shopkeepers, accountants, plumbers, carpenters, journalists, domestic workers and dressmakers. The 1937 Act allowed these people to make voluntary contributions and therefore benefit.[38]

The debate over what – if any – support should be provided to widows without dependent children or unable to work through old age or ill health continued throughout the twentieth century. Legislation pushed the age for entitlement for pensions higher and then brought it lower, before the Welfare Reform and Pensions Act 1999 abolished widows' benefits for women whose husbands died after 9 April 2001 and replaced them with short-term bereavement payments for both widows and widowers.[39] Those already receiving widows' pensions retained them. This was unsuccessfully challenged as gender discrimination at the European Court of Human Rights by widowers bereaved before 2001 who were excluded from the ongoing pensions.[40] In a judgment that reached right back to 1925, the Court stated that

> [a]t its origin … and until its abolition in respect of women whose spouses died after 9 April 2001, WP [Widow's Pension] was intended to correct 'factual inequalities' between older widows, as a group, and the rest of the population … [and this] was reasonably and objectively justified …[41]

The Court had observed that the original legislation was introduced in 'recognition of the fact that older widows, as a group, faced financial hardship and inequality because of the married woman's traditional role of caring for husband and family in the home rather than earning money in the workplace'.[42]

In the longer run, of course, no old-age pensions system has yet provided equality for women. Writing in 2006, Thane observed that the issue of poverty amongst older women has been 'evaded by successive governments', and a system with a 'state pension too low to live on' and reliance on occupational and private pensions is difficult for women who are often low-paid and 'irregularly employed'.[43] There is no official figure for a gender pension gap in the UK, but it was estimated at 37.9 per cent in 2019–20.[44] Auto-enrolment is improving private pension provision, but equality will not be achieved in the context of the continuing gender pay gap and patterns of employment for women who are

[38] Widows', Orphans' and Old Age Contributory Pensions (Voluntary Contributors) Act 1937.

[39] For reform, see the National Insurance Act 1946, the Family Allowances and National Insurance Act 1956, the National Insurance Act 1970, the Social Security Act 1986 Social Security Contributions and Benefits Act 1992, the Welfare Reform and Pensions Act 1999 and the Pensions Act 2014.

[40] *Runkee and another v United Kingdom* [2007] ECHR 42949/98.

[41] ibid [40].

[42] ibid [37].

[43] Pat Thane, 'The "Scandal" of Women's Pensions in Britain: How Did It Come About?' in Hugh Pemberton, Pat Thane and Noel Whiteside (eds), *Britain's Pensions Crisis, History and Policy* (Oxford University Press, 2006) 89.

[44] Rajiv Prabhakar, *The Gender Pensions Gap* (House of Commons Library, 2022); Prospect, *Achieving Gender Equality on Pensions. Prospect's 2021 report on the gender pension gap* (2021).

more frequently affected by caring responsibilities for younger and older generations. Coupled with statistics that show on average women live longer than men, this means that a significant number of older women, including widows, will continue to face poverty.[45]

IV. Significance

The key significance of the legislation in 1925 was the provision of some limited financial provision for women outside of the stigmatising, inadequate and inconsistent Poor Law. The campaigning feminist groups of the 1920s never achieved the 'as of right' pensions restricted to widows with dependent children or widows unable to work through old age or incapacity that they envisaged. However, at the time, the existence of provision within the wider scheme of the 1925 Act was an achievement to be celebrated. The contributory provision in that legislation through national insurance – for very small widows', orphans' and old-age pensions – has been the bedrock of pension provision ever since. From 2017, Bereavement Support Payments providing a lump sum and supplementary payments for 18 months, uplifted where there is parental responsibility for a child, are still based on national insurance contributions or equivalent.[46]

Further Reading

- Eleanor Rathbone, *Report on the Condition of Widows under the Poor Law in Liverpool* (Liverpool, 1913).
- Pat Thane, *Old Age in English History, Past Experiences, Present Issues* (Oxford University Press, 2000).
- Pat Thane, 'The "Scandal" of Women's Pensions in Britain: How Did It Come About?' in Hugh Pemberton, Pat Thane and Noel Whiteside (eds), *Britain's Pensions Crisis, History and Policy* (Oxford University Press, 2006) 89.

[45] Pat Thane, 'The Old Age Pensions Act, 1908' (2008) 60 *Journal of Liberal History* 5, 12.

[46] Most recently, the Bereavement Benefits (Remedial) Order 2023 (SI 2023/134) extended Bereavement Support Payments to bereaved cohabitants with dependent children as a result of *Re McLaughlin's Application for Judicial Review (Northern Ireland)* [2018] UKSC 48 and *Jackson and Others v Secretary of State for Work and Pensions* [2020] EWHC 183.

19

Administration of Estates Act 1925

ROSEMARY AUCHMUTY

The Administration of Estates Act 1925 reformed the intestacy rules to allow women to benefit on the same terms as men. The distinction between the treatment of land (which had formerly gone to the heir-at-law) and personal property was removed, and primogeniture and the old sex-specific allocations were abolished.

I. Context

The Administration of Estates Act 1925 was part of a comprehensive overhaul of English land law that had been in contemplation since the late nineteenth century and came to fruition in 1925 with the enactment of seven major statutes that essentially codified the law. The aim of the reforms was to do away with the arcane forms of property interest and processes of land transfer derived from an earlier era and to standardise the rules across the whole body of law. The main impetus was the increase in transactions in land that gathered speed after the First World War, when the landscape of home ownership changed dramatically. Before the First World War, only a small proportion of the population owned land, and it was viewed (except by the aristocratic owners of the great houses) not as a home but as an investment and source of rental income. After the war, the Government's plan to extend home ownership down the social classes transformed this understanding and not only provided a powerful lever for modernising the law by facilitating land transfer, but also rendered obsolete the mediaeval forms of land ownership that had become irrelevant to most owners of the future.

Among the new principles that underpinned the 1925 legislation was that of sex equality. The Married Women's Property Acts (MWPA) 1870–93,[1] no less than the very recent advances in women's civil rights – their admission to the vote[2] and the

[1] Andy Hayward, 'Married Women's Property Act 1882' in Erika Rackley and Rosemary Auchmuty (eds), *Women's Legal Landmarks: Celebrating the History of Women and Law in the UK and Ireland* (Hart Publishing, 2019) 71.

[2] Mari Takayanagi, 'Representation of the People Act 1918' in Rackley and Auchmuty (eds), n 1, 113.

professions[3] – made their assimilation in other areas of law, even property, an unobjectionable next step. The result was that, like the Sex Disqualification (Removal) Act 1919, the Law of Property Act (LPA) 1925 removed all differential treatment based on sex or marriage from its provisions. For instance, in reducing the number of legal estates to two (freehold and leasehold), the LPA 1925 did away with the 'tenancy by entireties', a form of land ownership in which a married couple were treated as having a single share in co-owned property rather than two.[4]

A further impetus for the Administration of Estates Act was the legislators' desire to remove the distinction between the way that land and personal property were treated on intestacy. This led to absurd results with some estates, as one of the architects of the 1922 Act, Arthur Underhill, pointed out, particularly because of the different treatment of males and females. While 'Lord Cave [the Lord Chancellor] and Lord Phillimore [a Liberal peer from a legal family] both seemed to think that "the existing rules which have been in operation for many generations" ought not to be disturbed', his view was that 'now women have votes and seats in Parliament, the existing rules were not likely to escape drastic alteration'.[5] An American commentator, Herbert A Smith, concurred: 'to adopt for land the existing rules as to personal property would mean a discrimination between the sexes which the influence of women in Parliament would soon eradicate'.[6] Indirectly, therefore, feminist successes (or the expectation of greater feminist impact on policy in future) influenced the reforms, even though there is no evidence that women ever campaigned for them.

When Maud Crofts (who, as Maud Ingram, had been one of Gwyneth Bebb's associates in the campaign to gain admission to the legal profession,[7] and who had subsequently qualified as a solicitor) published her *Women under English Law* in 1925,[8] she was obliged to describe both the intestacy rules in existence at the time of writing and those that replaced them on 1 January 1926 in the new Act.[9] The old rules were complicated and had evolved from mediaeval times. Land (real property) was treated differently from personal property, which then included leaseholds – even those of 999 years. The land passed under primogeniture – that is, to the eldest son, if there was one. Males were preferred because, AD Hargreaves explained, land ownership was linked to military service in mediaeval times.[10] But

[3] Mari Takayanagi, 'Sex Disqualification (Removal) Act 1919' in Rackley and Auchmuty (eds), n 1, 133.

[4] Law of Property Act 1925, s 37.

[5] Arthur Underhill, *A Concise Explanation of Lord Birkenhead's Act* (Butterworth & Co, 1922) 48.

[6] Herbert A Smith, 'The English Law of Property Act 1922' (1924) 30 *West Virginia Law Quarterly* 163.

[7] Rosemary Auchmuty, 'Whatever Happened to Miss Bebb? *Bebb v the Law Society* and women's legal history' (2011) 31 *Legal Studies* 175.

[8] **'First Published Law Textbooks on "Women and Law" Written by Women Lawyers in Great Britain, 1924–34'.**

[9] Maud I Crofts, *Women under English Law* (National Council of Women of Great Britain, 1925) 36–38.

[10] AD Hargreaves, *An Introduction to the Principles of Land Law*, eds George A Grove and JF Garner (4th edn, Sweet & Maxwell, 1963) 13.

England did not have the Salic law, and daughters were not necessarily excluded. If there were daughters but no son, they shared the land equally as *coparceners* (which were similar to tenants in common). Property passed to direct issue (children, grandchildren, great-grandchildren) if there were any. The general rule was that females of the same degree were preferred to males of more distant degrees. Thus, if the eldest son had predeceased his father, the land would pass, in the absence of a son, to his daughters rather than to his younger brothers. But while an eldest son took the whole of the estate, in the absence of sons, daughters shared it equally.

A widow's entitlement to dower, a life interest in one-third of her deceased husband's estate, was no longer automatic – since the Dower Act 1833 it could be barred by an inter vivos (that is, during his lifetime) gift or will – but she would still get it on an intestacy. If childless, she would get half his personal estate plus £500 or the whole of the personalty, whichever was the larger. If there were children, she got only one-third of the personalty.

What widowers got was different, thanks to men's different history with respect to their wife's property. Under coverture – that is, before the MWPAs – a man owned his wife's personal property absolutely but only *managed* her real property. He could dispose of it, but only with her consent. Once the couple had a child, a father came to be seen as life tenant in his wife's real property 'by curtesy', holding it for the eventual benefit (on his death) of that child. It followed that, should the wife predecease him, he took all her personal property absolutely (which included leaseholds) and had a right of *tenancy by curtesy* to a life interest in his deceased wife's land, provided she had not made any disposition of it elsewhere in her will or (after the MWPA 1882) inter vivos.[11]

II. The Landmark

The provisions of the Administration of Estates Act 1925 were initially enacted in the LPA 1922, which, covering the whole set of property law reforms, was the biggest Bill ever introduced into Parliament.[12] That statute was supposed to come into force on 1 January 1925, but the date was postponed to 1 January 1926 because of the huge practical upheaval it was causing, by which time the reforms had been broken up into subject-specific statutes that did come into force on that date. There was no debate on the Administration of Estates Act itself, since the provisions had been comprehensively aired in the debates on the LPA 1922.

The new intestacy rules, which remain largely in force today, were still complicated, but basically gave preference to a spouse and children if there were any, and to the spouse alone if there were not; to children if there was no surviving spouse; thence to parents; thence to siblings; thence to half-siblings and step-siblings;

[11] ibid 74–75.
[12] HC Deb 15 May 1922, vol 154, col 90.

thence to grandparents; thence to aunts and uncles; thence to step-aunts and step-uncles. If a person in the relevant class was dead, his or her children took the share equally. The widow of a man who died from 1926 onwards, who had children, would receive all her husband's chattels, a fixed sum of £1,000 absolutely and a life interest in one-half of the rest of the estate; the children would have a life interest in the other half. Spouses were also given an option to buy the family home at the valuation at the deceased's death. When each child reached the age of 21 (the age of majority at the time) or married, their share passed to them absolutely; and when the widow died, her share passed to the children equally, in trust for any under 21 and absolutely for those of 21 and over. Only if none of the above relatives existed, nor their children, did the surviving spouse take the whole estate. And if no spouse existed either, the Crown took it.

The amount of £1,000 was arrived at after an extensive scrutiny of wills at Somerset House that showed that about 98 per cent of intestacies were worth less than £1,000.[13] Even in larger estates, it would almost certainly be enough to allow a widow to keep her home. In such cases, nothing would be left for the children, thus establishing, as Stephen Cretney points out, a decisive preference in intestacy law for the spouse of a deceased over blood kin. That this was a policy decision designed to benefit women is clear:

> The 1925 legislation thus established the related policies of allowing the whole of all but the largest estates to pass to the widow and ensuring that she should be able to go on living in the family home after her husband's death.[14]

This would seem to contradict the observation of Helena Normanton in her *Everyday Law for Women* that '[t]he new law … is at any rate theoretically equal as between the sexes, although in practice it quite often works out more disadvantageously to widows than did the former system'.[15] She could only have been talking about large estates.

There was another indirect consequence of the land-law reforms that could benefit women on intestacy. As explained by Sir Thomas Bramsdon MP, an elderly lawyer, in the debates on the LPA 1922:

> Tucked up in the Bill is a Clause which provides that where two people die by accident, and it is not possible to say which is the survivor, as in the case of a shipwreck, the younger will be declared to have survived. Lawyers often have these cases cropping up, and a great deal of litigation follows in order to ascertain who is the survivor, but our friends the ladies will, perhaps, be pleased with this proposal, because generally in those cases the survivors will be women, as the younger of the two, and so we may have land going in a direction which we did not anticipate.[16]

[13] ibid col 99.

[14] Stephen Cretney, *Law, Law Reform and the Family* (Clarendon Press, 1998) 249.

[15] Helena Normanton, *Everyday Law for Women* (Ivor Nicholson and Watson, 1932) 176; and **'First Published Law Textbooks on "Women and Law" Written by Women Lawyers in Great Britain, 1924–34'**.

[16] HC Deb 15 May 1922, vol 154, col 136.

III. What Happened Next

Under the Administration of Estates Act 1925, widows and daughters received a certain share of an intestate man's property. But when a man made a will, there was nothing to stop him making little or no provision for them because of the principle of freedom of testation in English law. Feminists were prompt to realise the inconsistency in the different treatment of the families of an intestate and those of a testator, recognising the injustice of a law that allowed men to disinherit their families, often in favour of a mistress or illegitimate children. The Government too was not keen to have to find public funds to support a destitute widow and children. This led to the passing, in the face of considerable male opposition, of the **Inheritance (Family Provision) Act 1938**.

After the Second World War, it was recognised that the intestacy rules had not kept pace with inflation; £1,000 was no longer adequate to enable a widow to stay in her home. Lord Morton, a Lord of Appeal in Ordinary, was appointed in 1950 to chair a Committee on the Law of Intestate Succession, which took evidence from a wide range of individuals and organisations, including the **Married Women's Association** and the National Council of Women of Great Britain. Following its recommendations, the Intestates' Estates Act 1952 raised the £1,000 fixed sum to £5,000 (and it has been further increased several times since then), the intention being to keep parity with the increasing prices of family homes, which it has patently not done.[17] The idea of allowing the spouses of intestates to purchase the family home at the valuation of the deceased's death was abandoned; concerns had been raised in Parliament about encouraging 'old ladies to insist on going on living in houses that were far too large for them'.[18] Instead, powers were allocated to personal representatives (those who distributed the property) to redeem it for the spouse.

During the debates on the 1952 statute, there were jokes in Parliament about 'elderly gentlemen who marry little blonde creatures much younger than themselves'[19] and whose property would pass to the young bride's family if they failed to make a will, rather than to their own blood relatives. This demonstrated an increasing post-war recognition that family forms were changing, that divorce was becoming more common and that the surviving spouse might have nothing to do with the surviving children. Indeed, a divorce reform bill had been introduced in 1951 and only withdrawn on the promise of a Royal Commission on Marriage and Divorce, which subsequently took place, also chaired by Lord Morton.

The Matrimonial Proceedings and Property Act 1970 enabled divorcing spouses for the first time to benefit from capital transfers on the basis of their contribution to the marriage.[20] The Law Commission, in a series of reports in

[17] It stands at £270,000 at the time of writing.

[18] Quoted in Cretney, n 14, 261.

[19] Quoted ibid 263.

[20] Rosemary Auchmuty, 'Feminism, Property, and Divorce Law Reform in the 1960s' in Joanna Miles, Daniel Monk and Rebecca Probert (eds), *Fifty Years of the Divorce Reform Act 1969* (Hart Publishing, 2022) 71.

the 1970s, acknowledged that spouses of people who died intestate should have at least a similar claim on their deceased spouse's property. This led to the enactment of the Inheritance (Provision for Family and Dependants) Act 1975. More recent reforms include the assimilation of civil partners to the spousal rules and the abolition of the presumption on intestacy succession noted above, that when two people die together in circumstances where it is impossible to know who died first, the younger should be assumed to have lived longer. For deaths on or after 1 January 1996, a surviving spouse or civil partner is only entitled on intestacy if he or she has survived the deceased by at least 28 days.[21]

More recently, the increasing number of cohabiting couples and their children who do not fall within the intestacy rules has led to increasing concern. Since 1995, cohabitants have been to able apply for provision under the Inheritance (Provision for Family and Dependants) Act 1975, but only if they fall within the definition of 'dependant'. In 2011, the Law Commission recommended that specific rules be drawn up for cohabitants.[22] This was reiterated by the Women and Equalities Committee of the House of Commons in 2022.[23] It has not, however, been taken up by the Government.

IV. Significance

The significance for women of the Administration of Estates Act 1925 was that, as the Solicitor-General of the time, Sir Leslie Scott, explained:

> [W]omen will, for the future and for the first time in English history, be placed on a footing of complete equality with men regarding succession on an intestacy. A surviving wife or mother, for instance, will have the same rights and privileges of inheritance and succession as a surviving husband or father.[24]

A commentator in the *American Bar Association Journal* observed that the reform was not really so radical, because '[s]ocial custom has in practical effect long since substituted the disposition by will or settlement for the law of descent'[25] – and most men left property to their wives and daughters. But the *symbolic* significance of the new intestacy rules should not be underestimated, when distinctions in the treatment of married women in other parts of the law still survived.[26]

[21] Law Reform (Succession) Act 1995.

[22] Law Commission, *Intestacy and family provision claims on death* (2011). Other recommendations by the Law Commission were implemented in the Inheritance and Trustees' Powers Act 2014.

[23] House of Commons Women and Equalities Committee, *The Rights of Cohabiting Partners*, 2nd Report of the session 2022–23, HC 92 (2022).

[24] HC Deb 15 May 1922, vol 154, col 92.

[25] Orrin K McMurray, 'The English Law of Property Act 1922' (1922) 8 *American Bar Association Journal* 485.

[26] **Law Reform (Married Women and Tortfeasors) Act 1935**.

In 1927, Dorothy L Sayers published a novel, *Unnatural Death*, that turned precisely on the provisions of the Administration of Estates Act 1925. Miss Whittaker, a grandchild of Miss Dawson's dead sister, was presumed to be the nearest living relative of elderly Miss Dawson. Under the old intestacy rules, which allowed property to pass down through direct 'issue' or descendants, she would have received her grandmother's share if Miss Dawson died intestate. Then she discovered that the new statute, not yet in force, only permitted the *children* (not grandchildren) of a dead relative to benefit. So she killed Miss Dawson before the introduction of the Act to benefit under the old rules.

In reality, it was *widows* who overwhelmingly benefited from this Act, since women tend to live longer than men. *Daughters* also benefited from the incorporation of real property into the whole estate and the gender-neutral rules that replaced the old preference for males.

Sex equality on intestacy looks exactly like the kind of reform that 'equality' feminists like the **Six Point Group** would have espoused. There is no evidence, however, that they had to campaign for it. This appears to have been one of those rare legal reforms that were handed down by male lawmakers whose goal was primarily to simplify and standardise the rules of property transfer. Land lawyers have always been keen on consistency and certainty in legal rules, often at the expense of principle[27] – as we see from the many equitable interventions in property law dealings – but here the two coincided. There was evidence of considerable resistance by the legal profession to the reforms, but this was not because of the sex equality; rather, their concern was with the introduction of simplified conveyancing and succession rules that would render their conveyancing services, if not entirely redundant, certainly less remunerative.[28] The land-law reforms of 1925 removed all provisions in English land law in which women or married couples were treated differently from anyone else. The result is that, since then, English land law has recognised neither sex nor marriage, and the formal rules, not just in this Act but in the entirety of English land law, are completely gender-neutral in their application.

Formal equality and sameness do not inevitably guarantee justice, however. In making their break with the past, the drafters of the 1925 Acts did not foresee how the social landscape was to change in the future. Ever since 1925, land law and the succession laws have repeatedly been challenged by the unexpected democratisation of home ownership; the rise in divorce, illegitimacy and cohabitation; and, above all, the enduring conflict between men's power to define the laws and justice for women.

[27] J Stuart Anderson, *Lawyers and the Making of English Land Law, 1832–1940* (Clarendon Press, 1992) 331.

[28] ibid; Avner Offer, 'The Origins of the Law of Property Act 1925' (1977) 40 *Modern Law Review* 505.

Further Reading

- Stephen Cretney, *Law, Law Reform and the Family* (Clarendon Press, 1998).
- Maud I Crofts, *Women under English Law* (National Council of Women of Great Britain, 1925).
- AD Hargreaves, *An Introduction to the Principles of Land Law*, eds George A Grove and JF Garner (4th edn, Sweet & Maxwell, 1963).

20

Short v Poole Corporation (1926)

HARRIET SAMUELS

Short v Poole Corporation[1] involved a legal challenge to the marriage bar that prevented married teachers from working in schools. The marriage bar had been reintroduced by many local authorities after the First World War with the encouragement of the Board of Education, the government department responsible for education policy.[2] It led to the sacking of many married women teachers', often with little notice and sometimes without being able to qualify for their pensions.[3]

The challenge in *Short* was brought by Ethel Florence Short, a long-serving married teacher and one of 22 married women teachers working in elementary schools in Poole, Dorset. Although she was successful at first instance, a unanimous Court of Appeal took a very deferential approach to the local authority, holding that '[a] mere decision to discontinue the employment of married women teachers, or of any women teachers at all, or a decision to employ women teachers only, could not … be interfered with by the courts'.[4] It concluded that the local authority had exercised its statutory discretion lawfully, therefore leaving it open for local authorities to bar married women from working in state schools across England and Wales. Despite the failure of the claim, the legal strategy in *Short* energised the political activity of the women's movement at the time. It was part of a decades-long chain of events that led to the eventual ending of the marriage bar in 1944.

I. Context

During the First World War, women made up a valuable part of the workforce, often taking on jobs typically carried out by men. Women teachers were employed in increasing numbers in schools throughout the conflict, since about half of the

[1] *Short v Poole Corporation* [1926] Ch 66 (hereinafter *Short*). Poole Corporation refers to the local governing body for the Poole area. Such bodies are more usually described as local councils or local authorities. Poole is now part of the Bournemouth, Christchurch and Poole Council.

[2] Alison Oram, *Women Teachers and Feminist Politics 1900–39* (Manchester University Press, 1996) 26.

[3] See the facts in *Price v Rhondda Urban District Council* [1923] 2 Ch 372.

[4] *Short* at 94 (per Sargant LJ).

male workforce, and some women teachers, had left to join the forces.[5] Married women and retired teachers were encouraged to return to work in schools.[6] Despite their invaluable contribution, after the war, married women were expected to resume their role as homemakers.[7] Various economic, social and cultural reasons have been offered for the abrupt change in attitude towards women in the post-war period. A brief economic upturn had been followed by recession and unemployment, as soldiers returned from the fighting.[8] It was believed that excluding married women from the workforce would free up jobs for those men. Culturally, the (predictable) backlash against women's progress toward greater equality was growing. Many people, including trade unions, supported the notion that men should earn a 'family wage' and take responsibility for keeping their wives,[9] while for others there was a desire to return to the 'natural' order that had been disrupted by the war.[10]

At the same time, there was a growing sense within the teaching profession that moves towards women's equality were stalling. In 1924, an editorial in *The Woman Teacher* noted that, despite the many positive – though limited – changes that had occurred elsewhere (including the vote for women over 30[11] and the ability of women to stand for Parliament[12] and to enter the professions),[13] the teaching profession was lagging behind.[14] The editors expressed their frustration with the absence of equal pay and opportunity. Continuing prejudice, and a sense or 'feeling' that men viewed women teachers as inferior, were proving stubborn obstacles to further progress. Although the marriage bar was applied in other institutions such as the Civil Service, it was teachers who appear to have put up the most resistance. They had a track record of engaging in feminist politics – for example, many were strong supporters of the suffrage movement – and they had consistently fought for equality in the workplace. Their professional identity included the notion that their lives should be determined by their intellect and ability as teachers rather than their gender.[15]

It was against this backdrop that the legal conflict arose between married women teachers and local councils. Many councils had re-introduced the marriage

[5] Oram, n 2, 59.

[6] ibid.

[7] Noreen Branson, *Britain in the Nineteen Twenties: The History of British Society* (Weidenfeld and Nicolson, 1975) 211.

[8] ibid 13.

[9] Cheryl Law, *Suffrage and Power: The Women's Movement 1918–28* (IB Taurus, 1997) 76.

[10] Susan Kingsley Kent, 'The Politics of Sexual Difference: World War I and the Demise of British Feminism' (1988) 27(3) *Journal of British Studies* 239.

[11] See Mari Takayanagi,' Representation of the People Act 1918' in Erika Rackley and Rosemary Auchmuty (eds), *Women's Legal Landmarks: Celebrating the History of Women and Law in the UK and Ireland* (Hart Publishing, 2019) 113.

[12] See **'Parliament (Qualification of Women) Act 1918'**.

[13] See Mari Takayanagi,' Sex Disqualification (Removal) Act 1919' in Rackley and Auchmuty (eds), n 11, 133.

[14] 'The Outlook for Women Teachers in 1925' *The Woman Teacher* (11 April 1924) 220.

[15] Oram, n 2, 9.

bar, claiming that they wanted to help younger single women who had recently completed their teacher training.[16] Reports that young women were unable to find teaching positions allowed local authorities to claim that parents would not support their daughters' teacher training if they were unable to find work, so it was necessary to dismiss the married women teachers to provide the younger women with job opportunities.[17]

The first reported legal challenge to the marriage bar was the case of *Price v Rhondda Urban District Council* (1923).[18] This was a test case, brought by Elizabeth Price on behalf of 57 women, and funded by the women themselves after the National Union of Teachers (NUT) refused to support them.[19] The claim failed on various grounds, the most disappointing of which was the judge's ruling on section 1 of the Sex Disqualification (Removal) Act 1919, which provided:

> A person shall not be disqualified by sex or marriage from the exercise of any public function, or from being appointed to, or holding any civil or judicial office or post, or from entering or assuming or carrying on any civil profession or vocation.

The judge held that the legislation removed disqualifications but did not prevent a public authority from inviting job applications from one sex only, and did not therefore prohibit the dismissal of the women teachers on marriage.[20] *Short*, the second reported claim, was backed by the NUT after considerable pressure had been placed on the union by its members.[21] It relied not on the disappointing 1919 Act but on the abuse of the local authority's statutory powers.

II. The Landmark

Poole Corporation, on the recommendation of its Education Committee, had dispensed with the services of married women teachers in its elementary (now known as primary) schools, only making an exception on compassionate grounds for married women whose husbands were incapable of supporting them. The reason for the decision to dismiss the married women teachers was a matter of dispute. The recommendation of the Education Committee had simply stated that 'the retention of married women teachers is inadvisable'.[22] However, a letter from the Town Clerk conveying the decision to the managers of some local schools was put in evidence. This letter explained that the Education Committee had taken the decision because it considered that 'the duty of the married woman is primarily to look after her domestic concerns', that it was impossible for her to do this and be an effective

[16] ibid 60.
[17] *Short* at 78 (per Romer J).
[18] *Price v Rhondda Urban District Council* [1923] 2 Ch 372 (hereinafter *Price*).
[19] Oram, n 2, 168.
[20] *Price* at 391 (per Eve J).
[21] Oram, n 2, 168.
[22] *Short* at 83.

teacher, and that it was unfair to the large number of young unmarried teachers who were looking for work if the positions were occupied by married women.[23]

After receiving her notice, Ethel Short wrote a letter to the Town Clerk to persuade the Corporation that she was capable of managing her household and working. When this failed, she challenged her dismissal on the basis that the council had acted unlawfully in exceeding its statutory powers under section 17 of the Education Act 1921. This required the council to 'maintain and keep efficient' the elementary schools in its areas. Short's counsel argued that the council's powers were therefore limited to educational purposes and that it had exceeded its statutory powers by acting for reasons of social policy – that is, the belief that married women were not efficient teachers and desiring to provide jobs for newly trained single women.

At first instance, Romer J accepted the arguments made above by Ethel Short's counsel. His judgment is scathing about the council's reasons for the dismissals. He held that the council had not acted for the 'best reasons of education', as required by the statute, but for the irrelevant purposes of inducing married women to stay home and to provide work for the unmarried teachers.[24] He also held that the exemption to the policy for married women whose husbands could not support them made little educational sense – not least because a woman with a sick husband was likely to be more distracted by her domestic commitments and less efficient than other married women.[25] He noted that Ethel Short, as a married woman with no children, who employed someone to do her domestic work, and whose mother lived with her and helped out, was 'exceptionally free from ties that might interfere with the discharge of her duties as a teacher'.[26]

Poole Corporation appealed. A unanimous Court of Appeal overturned Romer J's judgment, holding that the council had acted for an educational purpose. Its legitimate concerns about the efficiency of employing married women as teachers, given their heavy domestic responsibilities and genuine anxiety about the drying up of the supply of new teachers, were not 'alien and irrelevant' matters but relevant educational considerations. Warrington LJ explained that 'if the defendants were to dismiss a teacher because she had red hair, or for some equally or frivolous and foolish reason, the court would declare the attempted dismissal to be void'.[27] In so doing, he set the test for 'irrelevance' in the realms of the ridiculous (such as being dismissed for having red hair) rather than, for example, making a decision on the basis of prejudice or supposition (such as assuming, without evidence, that married women teachers were unable to perform their duties). The Court also rejected the suggestion, accepted by Romer J, that the exception to the marriage bar for married women whose husbands could not support them showed

[23] ibid 84.
[24] ibid 77.
[25] ibid 73.
[26] ibid 74.
[27] ibid 91.

that married women could be perfectly efficient teachers. Rather, the Court of Appeal contended that it demonstrated that the council was acting benevolently by making an exception in situations where 'grievous hardship would be caused'.[28]

Ultimately, the Court of Appeal refused to intervene in the council's decision, employing notions of judicial restraint to justify its position. The Court stated that it was not sitting in judgment on the merits of the policy and that it was a matter for the democratically elected council. But the sympathy of the judges for the marriage bar was reflected in the language they used. Warrington LJ, for example, suggested that it was not his role to determine whether the decision was 'wise or foolish' but rather to determine the relevance of a decision to employ only those who 'devoted' their entire energies to teaching 'without assuming the privilege and burden of domestic ties'.[29] Ethel Short's claim failed because the Court of Appeal, unlike the judge at first instance, was unwilling to accept the evidence in the Town Clerk's letter, mentioned above, that the Corporation had acted because it believed that married women should remain at home.[30]

III. What Happened Next

Shortly after the judgment in *Short* was handed down, the ruling was given in the final case in the so-called 'marriage bar trilogy', *Fennell v East Ham Corporation* (1926),[31] funded by the National Union of Women Teachers (NUWT). Inevitably, Lawrence J followed the decision in *Short*, holding that East Ham Corporation had acted lawfully in dismissing its married women teachers.[32] After this there are no reported legal challenges to the marriage bar in the courts. But as feminist activist Crystal Eastman commented after attending the court to hear the ruling in *Fennell*, 'British Feminists' did not take 'the decision lying down'.[33] Indeed, the case underlined the fact that new legislation was needed. The Sex Disqualification (Removal) Act 1919 had not prevented discrimination on the ground of marriage as women had hoped. Two Bills – the Married Women (Employment) Bill 1927 and Married Women Teachers (Employment) Bill 1930 – were introduced in Parliament, and even though both were unsuccessful, they provided an opportunity for activists to make the arguments against the marriage bar in Parliament and promote women's equality. The second reading debate on the 1927 Bill demonstrates the rancour that women's rights raised. Several MPs including Frederick Pethick Lawrence, a well-known suffrage campaigner,

[28] ibid 92.
[29] ibid 91–92.
[30] ibid 84.
[31] *Fennell v East Ham Corporation* [1926] Ch 641.
[32] ibid 655.
[33] Crystal Eastman, 'London Letter – The Married Teacher, 30 January 1926' in Blanche Wiesen Cook (ed), *Crystal Eastman: On Women and Revolution* (Oxford University Press, 1978) 172.

spoke in favour of the Bill, explaining that the Government had agreed to extend the franchise to women on the same terms as men so that women would have equal political rights, and removing the marriage bar was simply giving married women equal economic rights.[34] The objections to the Bill were that married women were not capable of being efficient teachers, their husbands should keep them and that their place was in the home. **Lady Astor** ridiculed these arguments, stating that 'I know women who could have twins every year and still be more efficient than some Members of Parliament'.[35] Nevertheless, the tenor of the debate showed the hostility that feminists had to overcome.

There was also intense campaigning at the local level, concentrating on persuading individual local authorities to eliminate the marriage bar. In London, for example, the NUWT's president, Agnes Dawson, was elected to the London County Council and had made the abolition of the marriage bar a key part of her election campaign. Once elected to the Labour-run council, she threatened to resign from the prestigious committee she chaired unless the bar was removed. After considerable effort by Dawson and others, the marriage bar for teachers and doctors was lifted by the London County Council in 1935.[36] At the national level, the marriage bar for women teachers was not lifted until the enactment of the Education Act 1944.[37]

IV. Significance

Short represents a key landmark in a determined struggle to overturn a pernicious policy. Ethel Short, as a married woman teacher, objected to a measure undermining her equality and ending her economic independence. She was sufficiently indignant at her treatment to enlist the help of her trade union and to endure having her name, face and personal details appearing in the national press.[38] Her farewell party was reported locally in the *Bournemouth Daily Echo*. It was attended by supportive members of the council, who expressed disapproval at her dismissal and commented that 'the children were most unfortunate in losing Mrs Short' and that 'the country could ill afford to lose such a good teacher'.[39]

The decision was also significant as part of a wider feminist campaign. As a test case it had consequences that went beyond the parties to the litigation in raising awareness and attempting to frame the legal and political debate. Legal hearings are performative events and have an impact outside the court room irrespective

[34] HC Deb 29 April 1927, vol 205, cols 1179–86.
[35] ibid cols 1196–1200.
[36] Helen Glew, *Gender, Rhetoric and Regulation: Women's Work in the Civil Service and the London County Council 1900–55* (Manchester University Press, 2016) 198.
[37] See further Harriet Samuels, 'Education Act 1944' in Rackley and Auchmuty (eds), n 11, 219.
[38] See, for example, 'Married Teacher: Challenges Right to Dismiss Her' *The Daily News* (14 July 1925).
[39] 'Tributes to a Teacher: Echo of the Poole Dismissal' *The Bournemouth Daily Echo* (26 December 1925).

of their result. During the litigation, a feminist counter-narrative to the prevailing view of married women was presented in the national and local press. This resisted the traditional picture of women's place in society. Ethel Short's situation as a married woman who earned more than her husband defied the wifely stereotype of the time.[40]

The legal challenge also held the local authority to account. It exposed the prejudice of Poole Corporation that had to own and justify its sex discrimination publicly. Although the Court of Appeal accepted the council's version of events, the evidence of the Town Clerk's letter spoke for itself and showed that the council took a narrow-minded view of married women's place in society, and it was this that guided its actions. In addition, the Court's decision in *Short* made it painfully clear that the current law did nothing to protect women from the marriage bar. After testing the law in this manner, the women were able to turn to political lobbying of Parliament and local authorities. Nevertheless, law is an important site of power, and the use of the courts showed that the women teachers were willing to mobilise every possible tool available in an attempt to shape the law.

The role of feminist resistance in undermining the marriage bar was vital. The reversal of the marriage bar in the Education Act 1944 is often attributed to the post-war shortage of teachers. And certainly government ministers, fearful of further demands for equal pay and other women's rights, did not present the end of the marriage bar as a step towards equality for women to the public, relying instead on misogynist arguments of the undesirability of the teaching of children by spinsters and stressing the benefits of married women's experience of domesticity.[41] Moreover, while some historians accept that feminist lobbying played an important role, they do not always stress that it was feminist activists' insistence that married women could be competent teachers and their constant resistance of enforced domesticity that allowed the argument for ending the marriage bar to gain traction.[42] After the Second World War, when there was an opportune moment, the legislation was passed, permanently ending the marriage bar in teaching.

Crediting the litigation in *Short* as an integral part of the struggle to end the marriage bar sees social change as a process and not a one-off event. Legal challenges are part of the process drawing attention to the inadequacy of the law, providing evidence of hardship and illustrating the urgent need for action. Women resilient enough to stand up for themselves and others, in an intimidating court environment to demand equality, deserve to be remembered by future generations as part of a feminist project that transformed women's lives.

[40] 'Married Teacher Wins her Case' *The Yorkshire Evening Post* (31 July 1925).

[41] Harold L Smith, 'The Womanpower Problem in Britain During the Second World War' (1984) 27(4) *The Historical Journal* 925, 942.

[42] Harold Smith, 'British Feminism in the Second World War' in Philippa Levine and Susan R Grayzel (eds), *Gender, Labour, War and Empire: Essays on Modern Britain* (Palgrave Macmillan, 2009) 93, 106.

Further Reading

- Alison Oram, *Women Teachers and Feminist Politics 1900–39* (Manchester University Press, 1996).
- Alison Oram, 'Serving Two Masters? The Introduction of a Marriage Bar in Teaching in the 1920s' in The London Feminist History Group (ed), *The Sexual Dynamics of History: Men's Power, Women's Resistance* (Pluto Press, 1983) 134.
- Mari Takayanagi, 'Sacred Year or Broken Reed? The Sex Disqualification (Removal) Act 1919' (2020) 29 *Women's History Review* 563.

21

Adoption of Children Act 1926

FRANCES BURTON AND ROSEMARY AUCHMUTY

The Adoption of Children Act 1926 was the first legislation enabling the legal adoption of children in England and Wales, with equivalent legislation passed in Ireland in 1929 and in Scotland in 1930. While it had general benefit, especially to children, in three respects it was of particular significance for women. First, it allowed them to adopt their own illegitimate children, and thus to legitimise them – and often also to conceal the circumstances of their birth. Second, it allowed women to adopt children by themselves if they had no husband – the situation of increasing numbers of women after the carnage of the First World War. Third, in an age before assisted reproduction, it offered married couples a way of having a family if they were unable to have children naturally.

I. Context

Prior to the 1926 Act, all adoptions in Britain were informal practices, employed to place illegitimate, orphaned or care-needing children with new parents or guardians, or, particularly in the upper classes, to provide childless adults with an heir. This latter practice often required adoptees to change their name by deed poll or to hyphenate the old and new surnames, sometimes creating the multiple-barrelled names recorded in the volumes setting out the lineage of the peerage and landed gentry.[1] It was not uncommon for well-to-do men to father children with women outside their social circle to whom they were not married, nor was it unknown for well-to-do women to bear children in similar circumstances, especially during the upheaval of the First World War. The period television drama *Downton Abbey* features two instances of members of Lord Grantham's family in this situation, mirroring the way that real-life examples were carefully masked through fear of social isolation. After the war, such incidents were certainly drivers of the movement towards legal adoption, which could sanitise such extra-marital births.

[1] Stephen Cretney, *Family Law in the Twentieth Century* (Oxford University Press, 2003) 596.

At the other end of the social scale there were what were called 'Poor Law' adoptions, where Poor Law Guardians (predecessors of the local authority system familiar today) would arrange new family placements for orphans and children who were deserted or ill-treated. The most usual reason for intervention was obvious child neglect, or some disability or impairment that rendered the birth parent(s) unable or unfit to bring up their families. The new parents were in practice only foster parents under the supervision of the Poor Law Guardians, who were supposed to visit the family twice a year. By the 1920s, however, that system was already falling apart, largely because of the shortage of adequate potential new 'parents'.[2]

In law, an illegitimate child was *filius nullius* (child of no one), but unmarried mothers (unlike their married counterparts) had custody rights, though these fell short of the guardianship rights of married fathers.[3] But the fact that pregnancy outside marriage was seen as shameful, to be concealed as far as possible, militated against unmarried women keeping their babies. At the same time, some married couples who were unable to have children must have felt the pressure to conform to the social norm of the nuclear family – married couple plus two or three children – that was mercilessly promoted in this period. For them, the exchange facilitated by adoption of an unmarried mother's baby presented a respectable and normalising solution for both parties.

One problem with unregulated adoption was that a birth parent could reclaim her child at any time, often when the child was old enough to earn money, leaving the adoptive parents, as well as the child, without any redress. As early as 1889, the Earl of Meath introduced an Adoption of Children Bill into the House of Lords that would prevent parents from recovering their children. Though it failed to proceed, the Custody of Children Act 1891 made it more difficult for them to do so. But the problem persisted: in 1925, Sir Geoffrey Butler (Conservative MP for Cambridge University), moving the second reading of an Adoption of Children Bill in the House of Commons, warned:

> The person who adopts a child, supposing it to have been a woman, possessing no rights over the child whom she may have adopted, to whom she may have given great care, for whom she may have even conceived profound affection, may find that a relation suddenly appears – worst of all, perhaps, some formerly neglectful parent – and claims to resume control of the child.[4]

Sir Henry Slessor, seconding, drew attention to the thousands of children ('of all classes of society') left after the war without parents to look after them and taken into homes run by adoption agencies or by private arrangements: 'Owing to the

[2] Jenny Keating, *A Child for Keeps: A History of Adoption in England 1918–1945* (Palgrave Macmillan, 2009) 25–26.

[3] As explained by **Monica Geikie Cobb**, 'Parent and Child' in G Evelyn Gates (ed), *The Woman's Year Book 1923–24* (Women Publishers, 1923) 182. See also **'Guardianship of Infants Act 1925'**.

[4] HC Deb 3 April 1925, vol 182, col 1708.

gap in our legislation those children to this day have not got any proper legal status, and no recognised parents.'[5]

Concerns were also raised about the activities of 'baby farmers' – people who 'adopted' children but took no care of them – which, familiar to nineteenth-century crusaders, were by no means a thing of the past. In the debate on a Private Members' Bill of 1924, Viscount Knutsford instanced a case he had come across where 'the poor little child was indecently assaulted by her adopted father – I hate to use the word father in such a connection – and she was too frightened to give evidence in court'.[6] Labour MP Ellen Wilkinson in the debate on the final Bill in 1926 also cautioned against allowing 'empty-headed women' to adopt pretty babies and then, tiring of them when they ceased to be playthings, returning them to the workhouse or elsewhere.[7]

A further impetus for the regulation of adoption was the devastating death rate in the Great War, resulting in a dearth of single men,[8] leaving many women who had been raised to believe that marriage and motherhood were their primary goals with little prospect of finding a husband and father for their children. An adoption law that enabled single people as well as married couples to adopt would allow these women to access motherhood.

Other casualties of the war were orphaned British and refugee children. In 1917, activist Clara Andrew founded the National Children Adoption Society to match childless couples with such children. From hostels all over the country, in the years 1917–32 almost 4,000 babies were thus placed with couples, including some in the former colonies.[9]

But the most pressing factor was the rising illegitimacy rate during and after the war that led to the founding in 1918 of the National Council for the Unmarried Mother and Her Child (NCUWC), with Lettice Fisher (an Oxford social economist from a political family, and wife of the historian HAL Fisher) as its president. For practical reasons, many mothers could not keep their babies, and the social opprobrium attached to unmarried pregnancy forced many others to give them up for adoption. It was a significant feature of the adoption movement at this stage that it was the interests of the unmarried mother, rather than those of her child, that provided the main justification for adoption reform at this time, even if the NCUWC in fact preferred to work for ways in which mothers could keep their children.[10] Agencies like Dr Barnardo's and the Salvation Army, as well as informal adoption committees, provided appropriate philanthropic engagement for middle-class women.

[5] ibid col 1720.

[6] HL Deb 18 March 1924, vol 56, col 813.

[7] HC Deb 26 February 1926, vol 191, col 950.

[8] The 1921 Census revealed that there were more women than men across all ages – 19.8 million females and 18 million males – with the greatest disproportion existing among those in their 20s and 30s (Office for National Statistics, *Census Unearthed: Population, widows and orphans in 1921* (12 April 2022)).

[9] See the *Wikipedia* entry for Clara Andrew, and compare with Jenny Keating, 'Clara Andrew 1862–1939', *Oxford Dictionary of National Biography* (8 August 2019).

[10] Pat Thane and Tanya Evans, *Sinners? Scroungers? Saints? Unmarried motherhood in twentieth-century England* (Oxford University Press, 2012) 27.

Opposition to reform took two main forms. The first was practical: many government officials and civil servants, as well as legal men generally, believed that the reforms proposed paid insufficient attention to how any adoption scheme could be implemented. The second was moral: it was argued that legalised adoption would be an unwarranted interference with private and family life. 'I strongly object to legalising the handing over by parents themselves of their own children to other people,' declared Lieutenant-Commander Kenworthy in the debate on the 1925 Bill,

> making that an irrevocable act, and giving the adoptors [*sic*] all the privileges of parenthood with regard to the children. I look upon this as a dangerous precedent, and as one among many tendencies which must be stopped if we are to preserve the whole structure of family life.[11]

Among the landed classes, a particular concern was the effect of adoption on inheritance arrangements, both of property and of titles. This mattered so much to them that the Act finally passed did not permit adopted children to succeed to property on an intestacy or a title.

But desire for adoption reform was strong across all parties and both Houses. The women MPs all supported it, though Ellen Wilkinson less enthusiastically than the others. **Lady Astor** spoke passionately on behalf of the childless woman: '[T]here are some people who never have children, and yet the maternal instinct in them is far stronger than in some who do have them. It is really one of the tragedies of life.'[12] Adoption, she contended, offered such women the chance of a family, while also providing a loving home for a child without one. But Labour MP Arthur Hayday, speaking against the Bill, objected to the idea that poor women should willingly give up their children for adoption by wealthier, childless couples: 'Why should the offspring of the poorest people be bartered as a piece of merchandise to people who may or may not have a family; to people who may think the encumbrance and risk of child-birth is too much for them?'[13]

II. The Landmark

Britain was late to regulate adoption legally. In the United States, legislation had been introduced across various States from 1851; in New Zealand from 1896; in Western Australia from 1896; and in British Columbia in Canada from 1920.[14] In Britain, however, even allowing that during and immediately after the war the Government was occupied with matters considered more pressing and important,

[11] HC Deb 3 April 1925, vol 182, col 1732.
[12] ibid col 1736.
[13] ibid col 1740.
[14] Jean-Francois Mignot, 'Full adoption in England and Wales and France: a comparative history of law and practice (1926–2015)' (2017) 41 *Adoption and Fostering* 107.

there was also perceptible resistance to the legal regulation of adoption. In 1920, however, the Government bowed to public pressure and appointed a Committee, chaired by Sir Alfred Hopkinson KC, to consider whether legal regulation of adoption might be desirable or feasible. The Committee gathered evidence from organisations involved in placing children with families and from women's organisations, and came to the conclusion that legislation was required to give binding effect to adoption arrangements for children. This recommendation was not welcomed by the Lord Chancellor's Office, the Ministry of Pensions, the Ministry of Health and the Board of Education, who all raised concerns about the administrative difficulties of implementation.[15]

The consequence was a flurry of Private Members' Bills – eight in all – from members of both Houses and all parties. The Government's delaying tactic was to set up a further Committee, headed by a judge of the Chancery Division, Tomlin J, whose members included the Duchess of Atholl, a Scottish Unionist MP whose husband had introduced an Adoption Bill into the House of Lords in 1924.[16] Its report was cautious, but it did recommend legislation, and it drafted the Bill that was to pass in almost unchanged form into law as the Adoption of Children Act 1926.

It was a short enabling Act of only 12 sections. Section 1 allowed both couples and individuals to adopt an infant (a person under the age of 21). Under section 2, adopters had to be over 25 years of age and at least 21 years older than the adoptee, unless the latter was a blood relative. Sole males were not permitted to adopt females unless there were special circumstances, an evident gesture to feminists concerned about the potential for sexual abuse by men. The child's parents or guardians had to give consent, unless unable to do so. Section 9, intended to deter baby farming, specified that no money was to change hands. A concession to property concerns was the provision that though the child would thenceforth be treated in almost every respect as if the legal child of the adopters, where an adoptive parent died intestate, the adopted child could not inherit.

In an associated measure, the Legitimacy Act 1926 enabled children to be legitimised following the marriage of their parents, provided that both parents had been free to marry at the time of the birth. They could inherit property but not titles. Five thousand children were thus legitimised in the first year of the Act's operation.[17]

III. What Happened Next

A survey conducted in the first year of the Adoption Act's operation revealed that, of 3,548 adoptions, 150 were to single women (and 450 to single men). Two-thirds of the children adopted were illegitimate.[18] Suffragette Mary Richardson and

[15] Cretney, n 1, 600.
[16] HL Deb 18 March 1924, vol 56, cols 808–17.
[17] Keating, n 2, 37.
[18] Thane and Evans, n 10, 43.

journalist Martha Gellhorn are instances of single women who adopted a child, while Dorothy L Sayers and Rebecca West adopted their own sons to make them legitimate.[19] Though informal adoption continued, by 1936 there were over 5,000 legal adoptions annually.[20] That said, the number of illegitimate births always exceeded the number of adoptions, suggesting that some unmarried mothers (or their families) kept the child.[21]

Secrecy permeated the process, even though it was not required, indicating that although the Act enabled many people to adopt children formally, it did nothing to challenge the stigma of illegitimacy or to make birth outside marriage socially acceptable. There is much evidence in women's magazines of the period before and after the Second World War to suggest that people did not usually reveal that their adopted child was not their own, creating an impression that adoption was somehow inferior or shameful. At the same time, the continuing association with immorality and shame put pressure, sometimes amounting to force, on single mothers to surrender their babies for adoption.

By the mid-1930s, concern was mounting over casual practice in implementation of the Act, problems that had been foreseen in the debates, including the rudimentary nature of checks on prospective parents, together with publicity given to notorious maternity homes that charged fees and children who were sent overseas without any safeguards. This led local authorities and voluntary organisations like the National Society for the Prevention of Cruelty to Children to call for further regulation. A national committee chaired by Florence Horsbrugh, Conservative MP for Dundee, made recommendations to curb abuse that resulted in further legislation in 1939 and 1943. With illegitimacy on the rise again during the Second World War, the new laws revealed a shift in focus to the welfare of the child, rather than the interests of parents, and so provided the foundation for the modern approach that underpins contemporary law-making. The Children Act 1948 reorganised children's services under local authorities. The Adoption of Children Act 1949 finally allowed an adopted child to inherit as if he or she were legitimate. Subsequent legislation – the Children Act 1975 and the Adoption Act 1976 – further regularised the adoption process, giving adopted children the right to see their original birth certificates and trace their mothers.

From the 1960s onwards, the number of babies available for adoption began to decline. The Legitimacy Act 1976 gave the same rights to legitimated children as those enjoyed by people born legitimate. Finally, in recognition of the fact that sex outside marriage was no longer regarded as sinful, the marriage rate was in swift decline and the divorce rate rising, and more and more children were being born out of wedlock, to the point where it was regarded as normal, the Family Law Reform Act 1987 removed all remaining distinctions between children born within and outside marriage, thus bringing an end to the very concept

[19] Keating, n 2, 140–42.
[20] ibid 117.
[21] ibid 32.

of illegitimacy. This meant that single women no longer had to give away their babies, much less adopt them; and that there were fewer such babies for other people to adopt. Today, more than half of all babies are born to parents who are neither married nor in a civil partnership.[22] And today, most adoptions are of children in care.[23]

At the same time, advances in genetics have meant that many couples or individuals who in the past were unable to have their own biological children can now do so, while others, including lesbians, can bear children with the assistance of donor insemination.

IV. Significance

The Adoption of Children Act 1926 is primarily significant for making adoption a legally recognised status that provided for a permanent and irrevocable transfer of parentage. Commentators tend to locate the impetus for regulation in concern about the casualties of the First World War (orphans, refugees, illegitimate children and partnerless women) and, especially, the work of Clara Andrew and other workers in voluntary organisations dealing with adoption.[24] But the Adoption of Children Act also sits comfortably within the stream of 1920s legislation that dealt with 'women's issues' and, especially, issues concerning women's role as wife and mother.[25] This body of legislation has been attributed to the effect of women's entry into Parliament and their diligence in pushing through 'women's issues'. But it can also be seen as part of the backlash against more radical reforms that would further challenge men's domination of the public sphere.[26]

The 1926 Act, therefore, while not at first sight an overtly feminist statute, does exemplify feminists' concern with women's *actual* (rather than desired) lives, which were increasingly being reduced to domesticity through formal and informal restrictions and media pressure. This concern was shared by new and old feminists[27] alike, but was particularly felt by new feminists, who recognised that, for women inculcated with the idea that the attainment of marriage and motherhood was their primary goal, being able to *have* a family was important. The Adoption Act was of significant benefit to women who could not or did not bear children in socially acceptable ways. Until the advent of assisted reproduction, the Act offered couples who could not have children naturally, as well as single women

[22] Office for National Statistics, *Births in England and Wales: 2022* (17 August 2023).
[23] Cretney, n 1, 597.
[24] 'Clara Andrew', *Wikipedia*, n 9.
[25] Other examples include the Matrimonial Causes Act 1923, the Guardianship of Infants Act 1925, the **Widows', Orphans' and Old Age Contributory Pensions Act 1925** and the **Age of Marriage Act 1929**.
[26] Martin Pugh, *Women and the Women's Movement in Britain 1914–1959* (Macmillan, 1992) 114.
[27] One of the six 'points' of the **Six Point Group**, normally viewed as 'old' feminists, was 'Satisfactory legislation for the unmarried mother and her child'.

without a male partner and, especially, lesbians, the only formally legal way to acquire and bring up children as their own, and for unmarried mothers to keep and legitimise their own children.

Further Reading

- Stephen Cretney, *Family Law in the Twentieth Century* (Oxford University Press, 2003) ch 17.
- Jenny Keating, *A Child for Keeps: A History of Adoption in England 1918–1945* (Palgrave Macmillan, 2009).
- Pat Thane and Tanya Evans, *Sinners? Scroungers? Saints? Unmarried motherhood in twentieth-century England* (Oxford University Press, 2012).

22

Representation of the People (Equal Franchise) Act 1928

MARI TAKAYANAGI

The Representation of the People (Equal Franchise) Act 1928 gave women the parliamentary vote on the same terms as men for the first time. It removed the qualifications of the Representation of the People Act 1918, which had given women who met minimum property qualifications the vote at age 30. The Equal Franchise Act swept these restrictions away to give women the vote at age 21 with no property or other qualifications. As the culmination of the long campaign for votes for women, it is perhaps the most significant of women's legal landmarks in terms of political equality, and a great victory for feminist campaigning organisations and the early women MPs in the interwar period.

I. Context

Following decades of campaigning by suffrage organisations led by Lydia Becker, Millicent Fawcett, Emmeline Pankhurst and others, and a Speaker's Conference on Electoral Reform in 1916–17, which recommended some measure of women's suffrage, the Representation of the People Act gave the parliamentary vote to the first women in February 1918. However, this was not on equal terms with men. Men could vote at age 21 (or 19 if on military service) while women had to be 30. Unlike men, women additionally had to meet the minimum property qualifications for the local government franchise. This meant occupying either a dwelling-house of any value, or land or premises of a yearly value of not less than £5. Women were also given the university franchise,[1] provided they were 30 years

[1] From 1603, some universities had separate representation in Parliament, meaning people affiliated with universities could potentially vote twice in elections – in their university constituency and in the constituency where they were resident. The university franchise was abolished in 1948 (see further Neil Johnston, *The History of the Parliamentary Franchise* (House of Commons Library Research Paper, 2013)).

old and would be entitled to be so registered if male, but were excluded from the business franchise,[2] which applied only to men. Overall, the 1918 Act gave the vote to 8.4 million women, approximately two-thirds of the adult female population.[3]

The restrictions were put in place to avoid women's becoming the majority of voters, as would have otherwise happened in 1918 because of the loss of men during the First World War. There was much apprehension about the new women voters and how they would behave, and it was not politically acceptable for them to outnumber male voters at this time. The 1918 Act left obvious gender inequalities, and also a strange anomaly with regard to age, as the **Parliament (Qualification of Women) Act**, passed in November 1918, allowed women to stand as MPs without any special restrictions as to age or property. Women could therefore stand for election from the age of 21 years, the same as men, while being simultaneously too young to vote themselves.

Feminist organisations that had previously campaigned mainly on the right to vote identified a host of other issues to focus on from 1919 onwards. The National Union of Women's Suffrage Societies (NUWSS) renamed itself the National Union of Societies for Equal Citizenship (NUSEC), demonstrating its wider remit and concern for broader social and economic issues affecting women. These included equal pay for equal work, an equal standard of sex morals between men and women, widow's pensions, equal guardianship and the opening of professions to women, as well as equal franchise. Other continuing organisations included the Women's Freedom League[4] and the National Council of Women,[5] and new feminist organisations were formed, such as the **Six Point Group**. Collectively, their campaigning led to some legislative successes, such as the **Widows', Orphans' and Old Age Contributory Pensions Act 1925** and the **Guardianship of Infants Act 1925**. However, the vote was never forgotten, and there was a decade of continued campaigning, in particular by lobbying sympathetic male MPs in Parliament to introduce Private Members' Bills and ask questions. The Labour and Liberal parties supported equal franchise, but most Conservative MPs were opposed, fearing that younger, poorer female voters would not vote Conservative.

[2] As the vote was historically based on property ownership, some men were eligible for a vote both for the property where they were resident and for their business property. The Reform Act of 1832 established that men could vote in their residence and either in their university or business, but not both. The 1918 Act stated that men occupying a business premise of £10 for more than six months were eligible for the business franchise, and this had to be in a different constituency from their residential vote. The business franchise was abolished in 1948.

[3] See Mari Takayanagi, 'Representation of the People Act 1918' in Erika Rackley and Rosemary Auchmuty (eds), *Women's Legal Landmarks: Celebrating the History of Women and Law in the UK and Ireland* (Hart Publishing, 2019) 113.

[4] The Women's Freedom League was formed in 1907 as a breakaway group from the Women's Social and Political Union. It focused on many equality issues, including equal franchise. It dissolved in 1961.

[5] The National Council of Women of Great Britain was founded in 1895 as the National Union of Women Workers to campaign on social reform and working conditions for women. It changed its name in 1918, reflecting broader concerns such as women police, public health, women justices, juvenile courts, traffic of women and representation of women in the League of Nations, as well as equal franchise. It still exists today.

The Government elected in December 1918 was a Conservative-dominated coalition led by Liberal Prime Minister David Lloyd George. The first Private Member's Bill on equal franchise followed swiftly; this was the Women's Emancipation Bill 1919 introduced by Benjamin Spoor (Labour), which passed the House of Commons but fell in the Lords due to Government opposition, replaced by the Sex Disqualification (Removal) Bill, which did not include the franchise.[6] The Women's Emancipation Bill demonstrated an early majority in the Commons for equal franchise, even before **Nancy Astor** became the first woman MP to sit at Westminster, but without government support it stood no chance of success.

Further Private Members' Bills over the next few years led to discussion and debate but no parliamentary progress. Sympathetic male MPs were gradually joined by women, although only 10 women MPs were elected and took their seats before 1928. Some were strong supporters of equal franchise regardless of party, including Astor (Conservative), Margaret Wintringham (Liberal) and Ellen Wilkinson (Labour). Other Labour women, such as **Margaret Bondfield** (who had supported adult suffrage all her life), were supporters but wanted to give priority to relieving poverty and other issues affecting the lives of working people; while Conservative women other than Astor (Mabel Philipson, the Duchess of Atholl and the Countess of Iveagh) doubted the wisdom of equal franchise, including its possible effect on their party, and remained loyal to their party's position.[7] In January 1924, a Labour minority government came to power but did not introduce an equal franchise bill. A Private Member's Bill was duly introduced in February 1924 by William Murdoch Adamson (Labour), with a woman MP leading debate on both sides for the first time; it was seconded by Dorothy Jewson (Labour) and opposed by the Duchess of Atholl, who recognised grievances from the 1918 Act but argued in favour of a new Speaker's Conference to consider the issue, a delaying tactic. Despite Cabinet support and a huge amount of work by Susan Lawrence (Labour) to get the Bill through a hostile standing committee, the Bill fell along with the Labour Government later that year.[8]

By now, women had voted in three general elections as well as numerous by-elections without great societal upheaval. The Conservative party, continuing to fear the electoral effect of young women voters, remained opposed, but its leadership began to move towards supporting equal franchise. As early as 1922, Andrew Bonar Law declared in an election leaflet aimed at women voters that 'even at the time that the Franchise Bill of 1918 was passed I felt that the discrimination in age between men and women could not be permanent' – a personal opinion but a significant one nonetheless, coming from the party leader.[9] The

[6] See Mari Takayanagi, 'Sex Disqualification (Removal) Act 1919' in Rackley and Auchmuty (eds), n 3, 133.

[7] Mari Takayanagi, '"Does the right hon Gentleman mean equal votes at 21?" Conservative Women and Equal Franchise, 1919–1928' (2019) 28(2) *Women's History Review* 194.

[8] Mari Takayanagi, 'Women and the Vote: the Parliamentary Path to Equal Franchise 1918–1928' (2018) 37(1) *Parliamentary History* 168.

[9] See Takayanagi, n 7.

next party leader, Stanley Baldwin, appears to have been personally committed to equal franchise but lacked Cabinet support to change policy. He did go so far as to write, in a published election address to Caroline Bridgeman, chairman of the Women's Unionist Organisation (WUO) in October 1924, that 'The Conservative and Unionist Party are in favour of equal political rights for men and women and desire that the question of an extension of the franchise should be settled by a Conference of all the political parties.'[10] Although not in the party manifesto, this was interpreted by some as a pledge.

The Conservatives came to power in the election of October 1924, and another Private Member's Bill was introduced in February 1925 by William Whiteley (Labour). It was opposed by the Government, who argued for delay. However, following a crucial intervention by Nancy Astor, the Home Secretary William Joynson-Hicks stated during the House of Commons debate that 'no difference will take place in the ages at which men and women will go to the poll at the next election'.[11] Baldwin was present, and did not contradict him, meaning this statement was subsequently seen as an undertaking by the Government. Joynson-Hicks and Baldwin were not yet ready to change policy, however. Astor voted in favour of equal franchise against her party in the subsequent division. This was a major rebellion on her part, and she wrote privately that she felt it justified as the government action was 'an evasion of the undertaking that had been given at the election'.[12]

Although women's organisations had never stopped campaigning on equal franchise, the indirect support from Baldwin and Joyson-Hicks encouraged them to lobby this particular government to introduce equal franchise before the next election. The Equal Rights Political Campaign Committee was formed to actively focus on the issue, with marches and mass demonstrations. The *Daily Mail* opposed equal franchise, its proprietor Lord Rothermere fearing that young women would all vote Labour, with a campaign to 'Stop the Flapper Vote Folly'.[13] Serious discussion was given to introducing equal franchise at age 25 for both sexes; Violet Markham, a previous opponent of votes for women, wrote 'Why not universal suffrage at the age of 25? … surely the next revision should aim at giving us not a mere increase in numbers, but better quality in our electorate'.[14] The prospect of removing the franchise from men aged 21–24, however, made this a difficult proposal politically.

An Equal Franchise Cabinet Committee was set up in October 1926. By now opinion was starting to change in the wider Conservative party, as Viscountess Elveden, chairman of the Conservative party's Women's Advisory Committee, wrote to the Home Office on 19 November 1926 that they had passed a resolution

[10] Shropshire Archives, Bridgeman papers, 4629/1/4/9.
[11] HC Deb 20 February 1925, vol 180, cols 1500–03.
[12] Letter to Lady Trustram Eve, 25 February 1925 (Astor papers, University of Reading, MS1416/1/1/261). See further Takayanagi, n 7.
[13] Adrian Bingham, '"Stop the Flapper Vote Folly": Lord Rothermere, the *Daily Mail*, and the Equalization of the Franchise 1927–28' (2002) 13(1) *Twentieth Century British History* 17.
[14] Letter to *The Times* (21 February 1925).

that, unless there was action on equal franchise, 'Great discontent will ensue among the women of the country with results prejudicial to the interests of the Party at the next General Election.'[15] Meanwhile, public pressure was maintained by non-party women's organisations, supported by Astor in particular.

Despite opposition to the end by Winston Churchill,[16] the full Cabinet finally agreed to introduce a Bill the following session for equal franchise at age 21 in April 1927. The Equal Rights Political Campaign Committee continued to keep pressure on the Government with deputations and letter-writing.

II. The Landmark

The Equal Franchise Bill was introduced in February 1928, its title 'An Act to assimilate the franchises for men and women in respect of parliamentary and local government elections; and for purposes consequential thereon.' NUSEC did not rest on its laurels, holding two mass equal franchise meetings on 8 March. Astor was prominent on the platform, and now this was government policy, the Duchess of Atholl also lent her name in support.

The Bill had its second reading on 29 March. It was introduced by Joyson-Hicks 'with a gay carnation in his button-hole',[17] who presented equal franchise as the logical culmination of reform bills since 1832. The debate went on for more than seven hours, with something of a celebratory carnival atmosphere. Women MPs speaking in favour included Nancy Astor, Gwendolen Guinness (formerly Viscountess Elveden, now the Countess of Iveagh), Ellen Wilkinson and Margaret Bondfield. Iveagh's support was particularly significant, as she had been doubtful about the wisdom of equal franchise only a year before,[18] but sexist remarks by George Cockerill MP (for example that he 'would prefer to see, quite frankly, men put in the supremacy')[19] in the debate spurred her on.

Although there was almost no opposition in the Commons, with 387 in favour and just 10 die-hard MPs voting against, it was noticed that many opponents chose not to attend, including Churchill. Overall attendance at the debate was above average,[20] however, and Churchill's correspondence indicates he was not deliberately evading voting. His wife Clementine wrote to him about 'your abstention in the Flappers Vote Division! … [R]eally as it was bound to go thro' it was naughty of you not to vote,' to which Churchill replied, '[n]obody expected there

[15] TNA, HO 45/13020.

[16] Churchill asked that his dissent be placed on record, which it was in a secret Cabinet minute, opened in the 1950s (TNA, CAB 23/90B).

[17] *Evening Standard* (29 March 1928) in Women's Library at LSE, 7AMP/D/5/1.

[18] Lady Iveagh to Baldwin, on standing in the Southend-on-Sea by-election, 14 November 1927 (Cambridge University Library, Baldwin Papers, 49).

[19] HC Deb 29 March 1928, vol 215, cols 1379–80.

[20] Mari Takayanagi, 'Parliament and Women c 1900–1945' (PhD thesis, King's College London, 2012) 137–38.

would be a division, as only about ten people were known to have the courage of their convictions'.[21] The detail of the Bill was discussed at committee stage in April, when Churchill did attend and supported the Government during a division on age 21 versus age 25.

The Act as passed gave women the vote on the same terms as men, at age 21. Men and women now had the same qualifications for the parliamentary vote, based on residence, business premises, or being the husband or wife of a person with a business premise qualification, and the university franchise. Some Labour MPs tried to use the Act to introduce further electoral reform, such as abolishing plural voting, but the title of the Bill had been carefully drafted to 'assimilate' existing law rather than amend.[22] One consequence of the new equality was that a husband gained a vote if his wife qualified for the business vote, meaning an estimated 16,000 *men* in England and Wales gained a second vote in respect of their wives' occupation of business premises. The Act also equalised the local government franchise and made provision for consequential issues on election expenses and the electoral register.

III. What Happened Next

Feminist organisations celebrated the passage of the Act. The NUSEC annual report for 1928 declared '[t]his report marks the close of a momentous ten years in the history of the women's movement'.[23] Effort then switched to educating new female voters as to how to register to vote and explaining why it was important. There was a short period before the Act was implemented, during which time Jennie Lee was elected as an MP in a by-election despite being too young to vote herself. Lee was aged 24 when elected as Labour MP for North Lanark on 21 March 1929, and remarked in her autobiography, 'The Tories could not attack me on account of my youth for all the political parties were angling for the flapper vote.'[24]

Two months later, women were allowed to vote at 21 for the first time in the general election on 30 May 1929. A record total of 14 women MPs were returned, including Margaret Bondfield, who was appointed the first female Cabinet Minister in a Labour Government. Some put the blame for Conservative failure on the 'flapper' vote; however, financial crisis meant the next general election only two years later returned a Conservative-dominated Coalition led by Ramsay MacDonald, with a new record total of 16 women MPs. Baldwin took over again as Prime Minister in 1935, and Churchill's fear that equal franchise would lead to the destruction of the Conservative party was unfounded.

[21] Winston Churchill, *Winston S Churchill*, vol 5, Companion pt 1: *Documents – the Exchequer years 1922–1929*, eds Martin Gilbert and Randolph S Churchill (Heinemann, 1979) 1245, 1247.

[22] TNA, HO 45/13153.

[23] Women's Library at LSE, 2NSE/C/11.

[24] Jennie Lee, *My life with Nye* (Jonathan Cape, 1980) 66.

The next major piece of legislation affecting the franchise was the Representation of the People Act 1948. This set out that a voter could vote only once in one constituency by residence, abolishing the business franchise, university constituencies and multi-member constituencies. The parliamentary franchise was then unchanged until the Representation of the People Act 1969 lowered the age of voting from 21 to 18, where it remains today.

IV. Significance

The Equal Franchise Act directly led to the enfranchisement of 5,250,000 women, of whom 1,800,000 (34 per cent) were over the age of 30 years. This also meant women voters outnumbered men for the first time, by some 2 million.[25] The Act was the result of a decade of lobbying by feminist campaigners outside Parliament, along with crucial support by some of the early women MPs, especially Nancy Astor.

However, it is also the genuine culmination of the much longer suffrage struggle. Equal franchise is often portrayed as a footnote or postscript to the 1918 Act, the necessary tidying-up work 10 years after the principle of votes for women was won. But parliamentary debates in 1928 show great awareness of the place of equal franchise in history. Much credit was given to previous generations of suffrage campaigners, vindicated after decades of opposition. Namechecks included Mary Wollstonecraft, John Stuart Mill, Constance Lytton (whose brother the Earl of Lytton spoke in the Lords of 'placing a wreath on the tombs of these early champions'),[26] Lydia Becker, Josephine Butler, Millicent Fawcett and Emmeline Pethick Lawrence. The last's husband, Frederick, was present as an MP and declared, 'I have never given a vote in this House that has given me greater pleasure than I shall derive from the vote which I propose to give tonight'.[27]

Of the great suffrage leaders who were still alive in 1928, Emmeline Pankhurst watched the second reading of the Equal Franchise Bill from the House of Commons gallery in February. She died in June before its final passage, aged 69, and only two years later Stanley Baldwin unveiled her statue in Victoria Tower Gardens in 1930 – equal franchise ushering in the ultimate seal of establishment approval. Millicent Fawcett, having witnessed the very first women's suffrage debate in the Commons in 1867, took great pleasure in seeing the struggle through from beginning to end. She went to watch the Bill gain Royal Assent in the Lords in July 1928, arriving a minute too late. She died the following year, aged 82, and had to wait until 2018 for her statue at Westminster.

[25] HC Deb 29 March 1928, vol 215, cols 1366–1369.
[26] HL Deb 22 May 1928, vol 71, col 227.
[27] HC Deb 29 March 1928, vol 215, col 1430.

The Equal Franchise Act did not make women equal citizens, and there were many issues for feminist organisations to continue to campaign on. For example, British women continued to lose their nationality (and therefore also their right to vote and to stand as MPs) on marriage to non-British men until 1948.[28] But equal franchise was a huge and necessary step in giving women equal political rights and responsibilities: a true legal landmark.

Further Reading

- Cheryl Law, *Suffrage and power: the women's movement, 1918–1928* (IB Tauris, 1997).
- Mari Takayanagi, '"Does the right hon Gentleman mean equal votes at 21?" Conservative Women and Equal Franchise, 1919–1928' (2019) 28(2) *Women's History Review* 194.
- Mari Takayanagi, 'Women and the Vote: the Parliamentary Path to Equal Franchise 1918–1928' (2018) 37(1) *Parliamentary History* 168.

[28] Helen Kay and Rose Pipes, 'British Nationality Act 1948' in Rackley and Auchmuty (eds), n 3, 233.

23

Age of Marriage Act 1929

LAURA LAMMASNIEMI AND KANIKA SHARMA

Section 1 of the Age of Marriage Act 1929 ('1929 Act') stated that 'A marriage between two persons either of whom is under the age of sixteen shall be void …'. It created an equal age of consent to marriage for both sexes, and significantly raised the age of marriage for girls. Prior to the Act, the minimum age of marriage was set in common and canon law, a system of laws and ordinances originating from the Christian Church, at 12 for a girl and 14 for a boy with parental consent, and 21 without. The Act further strengthened that protection by making underage marriages void not only voidable, as they had previously been. The debates leading to the 1929 Act were particularly important as they were influenced by international and imperial concerns, and themselves came to influence the discourse around child marriage in the British colonies. The reform in the UK was, for instance, closely related to similar attempts in India, where women's rights groups were also seeking to introduce a minimum age of marriage, culminating in the Child Marriage Restraint Act in India, also passed in 1929.

I. Context

In the early twentieth century, the issue of the reform of the age of marriage came to be influenced by Britain's moral concerns at home and its imperial ambitions abroad. The Age of Marriage Act 1929 must be read and understood in the context of the increased national and international focus on the rights of women and children in the interwar years, women's rights activism and the interventions of the League of Nations during this period.

The age of consent for girls for sex outside marriage had been raised several times in the nineteenth century and had been set at 16 in 1885.[1] The age of marriage, however, had remained 12 for girls and 14 for boys under common and

[1] Laura Lammasniemi, '"Precocious Girls": Age of Consent, Class and Family in Late Nineteenth-Century England' (2020) 38(1) *Law and History Review* 241. See also **'Criminal Law Amendment Act 1922'**.

canon law. Until 1929, marriages were voidable if the girl had not reached the age of 12, but such marriages could be ratified upon her reaching that age, although examples of such early marriages were rare.[2] Parental consent had been required for anyone under the age of 21 to marry since Lord Hardwicke's Marriage Act passed in 1753, and even after the 1929 Act, marriages below the age of 21 could only be entered into with parental consent, except in Scotland.

Marriage had traditionally been seen as a protective institution that ought not to be denied to two people capable of conceiving a child.[3] In the nineteenth century, women's rights activists, such as Josephine Butler, had already questioned the low age of consent while doubting whether a girl aged 12 had the intellectual maturity to understand and consent to marriage and sexual intercourse within it, and also whether she had the physical maturity to consummate the marriage and bear children. While attitudes towards unmarried mothers were not as isolating and devastating in the interwar years as they once had been, the institution of marriage remained of great social importance in the early twentieth century, and life was exceedingly difficult for unmarried mothers.[4] During the interwar years, women's rights groups such as the **Six Point Group** campaigned for several family law issues intended to improve the lives of women and to promote gender equality, such as increased protection for the unmarried mother and equal guardianship rights. The age of marriage reform was specifically supported and campaigned for by the National Union of Societies for Equal Citizenship (NUSEC) led by Eleanor Rathbone. In 1927, Rathbone led a delegation on the matter to the Home Secretary to argue for an increase in the marriage age, supported by members from the National Council of Women, the Union of Jewish Women and the British Social Hygiene Council. Rathbone contended that a bad example set by Britain had repercussions in places like India, demonstrating that the domestic campaign was never distinct from the international and Indian one.[5]

These concerns over women's rights gained further international attention in the 1920s when the League of Nations turned its attention to the protection of women and girls. In 1928, the League of Nations' Advisory Commission for the Protection and Welfare of Children and Young People published a groundbreaking report, *The Age of Marriage and the Age of Consent* ('the Report'). The Report was part of a wider attempt by the League's Child Welfare Committee (CWC) to recognise childhood as a special part of the life cycle that ought to be protected from labour, early marriages and all forms of harm, including sexual

[2] Rebecca Probert, *Marriage Law and Practice in the Long Eighteenth Century: A Reassessment* (Cambridge University Press, 2010).

[3] *Report of the Royal Commission on the Laws of Marriage* ['Chelmsford Commission'] (C (1st series) 4059, 1868).

[4] Pat Thane, *Sinners? Scroungers? Saints?: Unmarried Motherhood in Twentieth-Century England* (Oxford University Press, 2012).

[5] 'The marriage age' *The Times* (9 November 1927) 11.

harm. Once published, the Report placed Britain with the countries that had the lowest age of consent to marriage for girls around the world.[6] The CWC action against early marriages was influenced by concern over the trafficking of women and girls, and the Report identified promises of marriage as one of the key avenues by which girls were lured into sexual exploitation and sex work.

Meanwhile in India, since the late nineteenth century, social reform had emerged as a 'site for rehearsal' of the mobilisational capacities of the national movement in anticipation of self-governance.[7] In particular, the national movement had sought to resolve the 'women's question', which child marriage predominantly came to be seen as, by isolating it from any intervention by the colonial state.[8] For its own part, although the colonial state sought to claim ideological legitimacy by positioning itself as an agent of modernity, its deepest alliances lay with Hindu and Muslim orthodox groups that opposed the reforms.[9] In light of the increasing popularity of the nationalist movement, it was also reluctant to champion radical reform for Indian women, in order to pre-empt the possibility of social revolution and the end of the colonial state altogether.[10]

The reform of child marriage in India gained increased legislative enquiry in the 1920s, and in the three years before the Child Marriage Restraint Bill was introduced in the central legislature, at least four other Bills on child marriage (besides those seeking to regulate the age of consent) were in circulation at the central and provincial levels.[11] Support for reform came through various activist groups, including newly formed women's organisations such as the Women's Indian Association, the National Council of Women in India and the All-India Women's Conference, which actively campaigned against child marriage, commented on proposed Bills and lobbied for what came to be the Child Marriage Restraint Act 1929.[12] In fact, the popularity of the Indian campaign on behalf of child marriage reform in the 1920s threatened to embarrass the colonial state by exposing its obstructionist nature on the issue.[13]

[6] League of Nations' Advisory Commission for the Protection and Welfare of Children and Young People, *The Age of Marriage and the Age of Consent* (League of Nations, 1928) 5.

[7] Janaki Nair, '"Imperial Reason", National Honour and New Patriarchal Compacts in early twentieth-century India' (2008) 66 *History Workshop Journal* 208, 210.

[8] Partha Chatterjee, 'The Nationalist Resolution of the Women's Question' in Kumkum Sangari and Sudesh Vaid (eds), *Recasting Women: Essays in Colonial History* (Zubaan, 2003) 306. For a discussion on proposed child marriage bills focusing on a minimum age of marriage for males in India in the 1920s, see Ishita Pande, *Sex, Law, and the Politics of Age Child Marriage in India, 1891–1937* (Cambridge University Press, 2020) ch 3.

[9] Mrinalini Sinha, 'Refashioning Mother India: Feminism and Nationalism in Late-Colonial India' (2000) 26 *Feminist Studies* 623, 632.

[10] Nair, n 7, 210.

[11] Pande, n 8, 149.

[12] Geraldine Forbes, *Women in Modern India* (reprint, Cambridge University Press, 2004) 83–90.

[13] Sinha, n 9, 629–30.

II. The Landmark

The Age of Marriage Bill 1929 was influenced by the League of Nations' Report and introduced in the House of Lords by Lord Buckmaster, a former Liberal Lord Chancellor and supporter of women's rights, who argued that there was an urgent need to raise the age of consent for marriage for the protection of young girls, who were left vulnerable to sexual exploitation within marriages and by traffickers.[14] One of the key features in the Bill was that underage marriages were to become void, not merely voidable. Despite opposition from many parliamentarians who felt such marriages should have been merely voidable, the Bill passed into law. Many supporters of the Bill made comparisons to early marriages elsewhere in the British Empire, and there was a particular concern over child marriages in India.[15] Referring to the American journalist Katherine Mayo's controversial and much criticised 'exposé' on child marriage in India,[16] which had recently stirred public consciousness in the UK, Lord Buckmaster also brought to the attention of the House of Lords that the law in UK on the issue 'in some respects was identical, and in one marked instance was worse' than the Indian regulations.[17] He emphasised the need for the UK to maintain moral leadership over India by leading the way in reform.

So it was that in 1929, the UK increased the minimum age of marriage and India introduced a minimum age of marriage for the first time. The 1929 Act applied across the UK, except in Northern Ireland where canon law continued to prevail until 1951, increasing the age of marriage to 16 and making underage marriages void. The Child Marriage Restraint Act 1929 in India set the minimum age of marriage as 18 for men and 14 for girls, and sections 3 to 6 introduced a punishment of up to three months' imprisonment and/or a monetary fine to be imposed upon the adult groom, the parents or guardians of the underage bride or groom, and 'whoever performs, conducts or directs any child marriage'.

III. What Happened Next

The Child Marriage Restraint Act 1929 had been fiercely lobbied for by Eleanor Rathbone, who had been elected as an independent Member of the UK Parliament in 1929. Though an initial supporter of the colonial state and its interventions on the matter, Rathbone soon came to recognise that the Indian Act was a 'dead letter'.[18] For instance, the most radical recommendation of the Bill – provisions for

[14] HL Deb 12 March 1929, vol 73, cols 397–425.

[15] HL Deb 28 February 1929, vol 72, cols 1203–19.

[16] Katherine Mayo, *Mother India* (Jonathan Cape, 1927). For an analysis of the book, Mrinalini Sinha, *Specters of Mother India: The Global Restructuring of an Empire* (Duke University Press, 2007).

[17] HL Deb 19 February 1929, vol 72, col 963.

[18] Eleanor Rathbone, *Child Marriage: The Indian Minotaur* (George Allen and Unwin, 1934).

the annulment of underage marriages – was dropped before the Act was passed. Rathbone used her position in Parliament to question the Secretary of State for India on the Government's plans to strengthen the law, memorably raising the issue 11 times in the House of Commons in her first 39 months.[19] However, Rathbone's interventions on India often drew the ire of Indian women who were also championing reform, because of her failure to consult them.[20] This failure to consult Indian women, to cast them as helpless and voiceless victims of backward or uncivilised cultural and religious practices, was the hallmark of what has come to be known as imperial feminism.[21] Popular from the mid-nineteenth century onwards, such feminists aimed to gain recognition as imperial citizens and more rights in the domestic sphere for British women by highlighting their difference from colonial women, and emphasising their contribution to the imperial project for shouldering 'the White woman's burden'. However, by the 1920s, an emergent Indian feminist movement was championing domestic reform on a number of issues, including women's education and empowerment, challenging Indian social and religious norms on dowry and widowhood, and increasing property, employment, marriage and maternal rights for women, as well as establishing a minimum age of marriage.[22] The Indian feminist movement was also supportive of the larger national movement for independence from British colonial rule, and as a result was critical of 'an old suffragist' like Rathbone, who championed reform within the existing imperial legal and political structures.[23]

In England, the 1929 Act was less politicised, yet it did not immediately put a stop to all underage marriages. There are press reports in the 1930s and 1940s of decrees *nisi de nullity* being awarded on the grounds that marriage took place when the girl had been under the age of 16. The first reported nullity case was *Carr (otherwise Fowler) v Carr* from 1936, where a marriage was declared void after six years when the bride admitted she had lied about her age to the vicar and to her husband.[24] Although these marriages were declared void, the decree usually came after some years of marital life, when one of the spouses was seeking to separate. In one case, the marriage was declared void after 18 years of cohabitation.[25] These cases demonstrate that in the years following the 1929 Act, despite the change in the law, people continued to marry before reaching 16, and continued their marital life without interference from the authorities until one or both of the parties wished to end the relationship.

[19] HC Deb 26 July 1933, vol 280, cols 2585–86.

[20] Sumita Mukherjee, *Indian Suffragettes: Female Identities and Transnational Networks* (Oxford University Press, 2018) 105.

[21] Valerie Amos and Pratibha Parmar, 'Challenging Imperial Feminism' (1984) 17 *Feminist Review* 3; Antoinette Burton, *Burdens of History: British Feminists, Indian Women, and Imperial Culture 1865–1915* (University of North Carolina Press, 1994).

[22] Padma Anagol, *The Emergence of Feminism in India, 1850–1920* (Ashgate, 2006).

[23] Shampa Roy, 'Cross-Cultural Sisters? Eleanor Rathbone and the Indian Feminist Movement in the 1930s' (2006) 12 *Asian Journal of Women's Studies* 7.

[24] 80 SJ 57 HC PDAD; *The Times* (14 January 1936).

[25] 'Marriage declared void after 18 years' *Cheshire Observer* (28 July 1951).

In Scotland, the 1929 Act was arguably weaker, as the Act had no impact on any right or capacity of legitimation *per subsequens matrimonium* under Scots law.[26] This meant that couples who married in Scotland could have their marriage confirmed after the parties turned 16, if they still wished to continue living together as husband and wife in Scotland.

Nor did the 1929 Act address the control parents had over the marriages of their children. While it increased the minimum age for marriage to 16 under parental consent, the age was still considerably lower than the minimum age without parental consent. Without parental consent, the age of marriage was set at 21 until the Family Law Reform Act 1969 reduced it to 18. It was only in 2023 that the requirement for parental consent was removed when the Marriage and Civil Partnership (Minimum Age) Act 2022 came into force. As the 2022 Act raised the age of marriage to 18, it has also been hailed as a breakthrough in the fight against forced marriages.[27]

In Scotland, the requirement for parental consent for marriage between the ages of 16 and 21, as stipulated by the 1929 Act, did not apply, and 'regular' marriages did not have to take place within a church building or require parental consent.[28] Scots law continued to recognise 'irregular marriages' that were conducted without the reading of marriage banns or in the absence of a minister.[29] As a result, runaway marriages from England were not unusual, and small industries catering to the needs of the runaway bride and groom sprouted in Scottish border towns such as Gretna Green. While their popularity may have been more cultural than legal,[30] the 1920s and 1930s saw a resurgence of such marriages,[31] encouraged by the 1929 Act and the improvement in motor transport,[32] until the Marriage (Scotland) Act 1939 put an end to on-the-spot marriages.

IV. Significance

Despite its mixed implementation, the 1929 Act is significant as it came into existence as part of transnational and international feminist campaigning and

[26] Scottish Law Commission, *Reform of the Law Relating to Legitimation per subsequens matrimonium* (Scottish Law Commission, 1967).

[27] Alexandra Topping, 'Campaigners hail law raising age of marriage to 18 in England and Wales' *The Guardian* (27 February 2023).

[28] Eleanor Gordon, 'Irregular Marriages: Myth and Reality' (2013) 47 *Journal of Social History* 507, 509.

[29] 'Marriage' in *Scottish Way of Birth and Death*, A Project by the Centre of History of Medicine, University of Glasgow at www.gla.ac.uk/schools/socialpolitical/research/economicsocialhistory/projects/scottishwayofbirthanddeath/marriage/ [last accessed 14 September 2023].

[30] They constituted less than 10% of registered irregular marriages: Eleanor Gordon, 'Irregular Marriage and Cohabitation in Scotland, 1855–1939: Official Policy and Popular Practice' (2015) 58 *The Historical Journal* 1059, 1066. Gordon argues that many eager runaway couples were thwarted by the absence of witnesses, and those that did marry overlooked the need to register such marriages in Dumfries, 25 miles away.

[31] Gordon, n 28, 510.

[32] 'Marriage', n 29.

consciousness raising on the rights of women and girls. Lord Buckmaster was influenced by the CWC of the League of Nations and campaigning by NUSEC. These international and transnational feminist campaigns forced Parliament to evaluate the rights of girls and women at home in order to catch up with the rest of the world, where higher protection was awarded to girls.

It is impossible to assess the impact the 1929 Act had on the trafficking of women and girls, but its impact on how consent and capacity to enter marriages were perceived is clear. In the aftermath of the 1929 Act, the courts were finally forced to recognise the harm that was involved in early marriages. In *Pugh v Pugh* (1951), a case that confirmed that marriages to minors in other jurisdictions would also be void in England, Pearce J held that in

> modern thought it is considered socially and morally wrong that persons of an age, at which we now believe them to be immature and provide for their education, should have the stresses, responsibilities and sexual freedom of marriage and the physical strain of childbirth. Child marriages are by common consent believed to be bad for the participants and bad for the institution of marriage.[33]

He was firm in his ruling that people cannot evade the law and enter into marriages with underage girls by simply going to another jurisdiction, including Northern Ireland, and emphasised that the 1929 Act was founded on social and moral grounds, not on Christian doctrine, in an important recognition of how family law had transformed.

If the 1929 Act in England was broadly enforced, the Child Marriage Restraint Act in India was a failure even before it took effect. The anticipation of its application led to a sharp increase in the number of child marriages in the six months after the law was passed.[34] But even after the law came into effect, Indians dodged the age limits by travelling short distances to territories that were not directly controlled by the British. In any event, in the absence of compulsory birth registration or reliable birth records, courts were unwilling to impose punishment unless it could be established *beyond doubt* that the child was below the minimum age.[35] As a result, the Indian Act resulted in very few legal cases and even fewer convictions, with many of those found guilty soon pardoned.[36] Though a failed law, the Child Marriage Restraint Act had a 'profound effect' on the first Indian women's organisations that had formed in India in the interwar period.[37] Child marriage became a unifying issue for women from different regions, religions and communities across the country.

The Child Marriage Restraint Act has remained on the books, with periodic increases in the minimum age of marriage for both girls and men across postcolonial South Asia, even as child marriage itself continues to be widely

[33] *Pugh v Pugh* [1951] P 482.
[34] Rathbone, n 18, 47.
[35] Pande, n 8, 72–120.
[36] Forbes, n 12, 89.
[37] ibid.

practised.[38] While Pakistan and Bangladesh continue to retain the Child Marriage Restraint Act, India finally replaced it with the Prohibition of Child Marriage Act 2006, which makes underage marriages voidable at the wife's option. All three countries retain a higher minimum age of marriage for men, and lower ages for women/girls.

Despite the varied success of the legislative reform in the 1920s on the age of marriage in England and in the British Empire, these interventions were significant. Beyond the impact of transnational movements on women's rights, they were also instrumental in shifting the focus onto childhood and girlhood, and establishing childhood as a special part of the life cycle that ought to be protected.[39]

Further Reading

- Advisory Commission for the Protection and Welfare of Children and Young People, League of Nations, *The Age of Marriage and the Age of Consent* (1928).
- Stephen Cretney, *Family Law in the Twentieth Century: a History* (Oxford University Press, 2005).
- Ishita Pande, *Sex, Law, and the Politics of Age Child Marriage in India, 1891–1937* (Cambridge University Press, 2020).

[38] In 2010, nearly 46% of women (about 24.4 million women) aged 20–24 years in South Asia reported being married before the age of 18. S Daarwin Subramanee et al, 'Child Marriage in South Asia: A Systematic Review' (2022) 12(22) *International Journal of Environmental Research and Public Health* 15138.

[39] Pande, n 8, 75.

24

A Room of One's Own, Virginia Woolf, 1929

MADELEINE DAVIES

Virginia Woolf's *A Room of One's Own* was first published on 24 October 1929, and over the course of the following decades established itself as the 'foundation stone' of twentieth-century literary feminism. A hybrid text (part essay, part lecture, part fiction), *A Room of One's Own* proposes that women's freedom is a material matter entirely dependent upon money, space and bodily autonomy: 'Intellectual freedom depends on material things.'[1] Amongst other arguments, the book demonstrates with excoriating clarity how men respond to legal reforms that benefit women but that challenge their own power, and it suggests how women may model new freedoms within the stubborn, if weakening, dominant patriarchy.

I. Context

The year 1928 had been significant for women's rights in the UK, because the **Representation of the People (Equal Franchise) Act** extended the franchise to women on equal terms with men, a decade after the first Representation of the People Act. This Act itself connected with a raft of sex equality reforms, including the Sex Disqualification (Removal) Act 1919, which granted women at least nominal access to the professions and membership of professional bodies.[2]

The result of such equality reforms was not, however, the creation of a level playing field nor the sudden reconsideration of long-held prejudices against, and attitudes towards, women. Indeed, the contrary seems to have been the case, if Woolf's perspective in *A Room of One's Own* is even broadly accurate. Against the backdrop of a looming economic depression (by 1930, unemployment had almost

[1] Virginia Woolf, *A Room of One's Own & Three Guineas* (Vintage, 2001 edn) 93.

[2] See further Mari Takayanagi, 'Sex Disqualification (Removal) Act 1919' in Erika Rackley and Rosemary Auchmuty (eds), *Women's Legal Landmarks: Celebrating the History of Women and Law in the UK and Ireland* (Hart Publishing 2019) 133.

doubled to reach 20 per cent),[3] heightened anxieties about women's increasingly visible role in society and about women 'stealing' 'men's jobs' appear to have energised misogynistic push-back.

Also crucial to the context surrounding the genesis of this landmark text is the recent advent of more widely-available contraception. One of the female names mentioned in *A Room of One's Own* is 'Mary Carmichael', which clearly evokes the birth-control pioneer and eugenicist, Marie Stopes (Stopes had published a novel as 'Marie Carmichael', entitled *Love's Creation* (1928)). Also noteworthy is the fact that Stopes's mother was Charlotte Carmichael Stopes, author of a searing feminist critique of received legal history entitled *British Freewomen: Their Historical Privilege* (1894).[4] The formidable arguments of *A Room of One's Own*, which demonstrate, for example, the absence of women from the male-authored canon of 'History', strongly suggest that Woolf would have been familiar with this text and fully aware of its contemporary influence on the fight for women's emancipation.

II. The Landmark

The text published as *A Room of One's Own* began life as a series of lectures Woolf delivered at Newnham College and Girton College, Cambridge University, in October 1928. Originally titled 'Women and Fiction', the lectures aimed to map the relationship between women and literature. The research for the lectures drew Woolf's attention to women's exclusion from the historical records, the professions and the literary canon. Her further thinking around these issues is extended in the long-form version of the lectures that we know as *A Room of One's Own*. In this more spacious 'room', Woolf expands upon issues of money, creativity, education, authorship, and freedom of speech, movement and thought. The text both begins and ends with the famous declaration that women's freedom depends on two things to which only a rarified few had ever had access: a room of their own and an independent income. Woolf uses both to represent freedom itself.

Woolf argues in *A Room of One's Own* that the advent of the equal franchise 'triggered' patriarchy, which felt its grip on power loosening. Its response to the threat was, Woolf argues, registered in frenzied attempts by men to confirm male superiority by insisting upon female inferiority. *A Room of One's Own*, amongst its many different types of argument, drags into the light this pervasive atmosphere of 'anger' against women and holds it up for analysis. In a sequence of 'scenes', she provides evidence for her position that men's fear of women (and their determination to retain power) has most frequently been manifested in men's determination

[3] 'The unemployment rate doubled from the end of 1929 to the end of 1930, reaching a peak of 23% in January 1933': Meredith M Paker, 'Industrial, regional, and gender divides in British unemployment between the wars' (SSRN Working Paper, July 2023).

[4] Charlotte Carmichael Stopes, *British Freewoman: Their Historical Privilege* (Swan Sonnenschein, 1894).

to exclude women to the point of erasure. Threat is eliminated: power and money are preserved in male hands.

One such scene involves the narrator's survey of a random newspaper; characteristically witty, the section nevertheless lays bare the quotidian nature of repressive male power and its diminishment of women:

> Some previous luncher had left the lunch edition of the evening paper on a chair, and, waiting to be served, I began idly reading the headlines. A ribbon of very large letters ran across the page. Somebody had made a big score in South Africa. Lesser ribbons announced that Sir Austen Chamberlain was at Geneva. A meat axe with human hair on it had been found in a cellar. Mr Justice —— commented in the Divorce Courts upon the Shamelessness of Women … The most transient visitor to this planet, I thought, who picked up this paper could not fail to be aware, even from this scattered testimony, that England is under the rule of a patriarchy. Nobody in their senses could fail to detect the dominance of the professor. His was the power and the money and the influence. He was the proprietor of the paper and its editor and sub-editor. He was the Foreign Secretary and the judge. He was the cricketer; he owned the racehorses and the yachts. He was the director of the company that pays two hundred per cent to its shareholders. He left millions to charities and colleges that were ruled by himself … With the exception of the fog he seemed to control everything.[5]

It is a key function of the text to hold a mirror to society and to reflect its true dynamics back at the reader, and it is a related function to map the matrix of forces that impoverish women materially and creatively. The text rarely provides solid answers to the questions it raises, but it explores a variety of potential theories; it suggests rather than asserts. The embedded reference to birth-control pioneer Marie Stopes via 'Mary Carmichael' points towards a central argument of the text that the 'room' that is most important for women to 'own' is the 'womb-room' itself, for how is a woman to win freedom and space if she cannot control the female body's tendency to produce an annual baby during the years of her peak creative productivity? Birth control disrupts the 'automatic destiny' of women, and it is through the oblique reference to Marie Stopes that Woolf positions the possibility of a choice for women between giving birth to books or to babies.[6]

Control over reproduction, suggests *A Room of One's Own*, joins financial autonomy and physical space as key to women's freedom. The massive families of the pre-birth control era trapped women within the domestic role and domain. With the other barriers of scant higher-education opportunities, with the Sex Disqualification (Removal) Act still inadequate and with socio-cultural expectation forming yet another obstacle, women had never been able to earn the money necessary to achieve either agency or autonomy. This situation kept women subservient to men on whom their continued survival, and the survival of their children, depended. If performing the role of the 'Angel of the House' was what was required to ensure this survival, women had no choice other than to

[5] Virginia Woolf, *A Room of One's Own and Three Guineas* (Penguin, 1993 edn) 30.
[6] See further **'Ministry of Health Memorandum 153/MCW (1930)'**.

conform to that disabling model of compliance.[7] There is no space in this dynamic for independent thought, for contradicting a male opinion, for challenging male orthodoxy. Biology and the law thus conspire to keep women's bodies busy and their minds locked up.

A Room of One's Own can, however, be criticised for lacking nuance in relation to the difference to women's lives made by class. But this criticism has a defence. Woolf's relationship to her class position is contradictory because, while she could be a thundering snob, she rarely ducks the issue of her own privilege and seems to appreciate the difference it makes to her analysis of literature, politics, money and social relationships. In the Preface known as 'Memories of a Working Women's Guild',[8] for example, upper-middle-class Woolf does not attempt to occlude her class position (far from it), nor does she apologise for the fact that her remit is literature, her profession is literature and her expertise is in literature. In *A Room of One's Own*, she is clear that to regard this field as being somehow separate from economic forces, ideology and fundamental questions of freedom is an unsustainable position; after all, if the first implicit question of *A Room of One's Own* is 'Where are the books written by women?', the second, intimately related question of the text is 'Why [is] one sex so prosperous and the other so poor?' The underpinning position of *A Room of One's Own* is that though class privilege and deprivilege means that not all women are disempowered and impoverished in precisely the same way, they are nevertheless all disempowered and impoverished within patriarchy. Woolf's 'status' as the member of an intellectual elite means very little when, as a woman, her citizenship of England is a contingent matter,[9] when access to the professions is strewn with obstacles and when elite universities such as Cambridge refuse to allow women to graduate.[10]

As she states in the later text *Three Guineas*:

> All these facts will convince her reason (to put it in a nutshell) that her sex and class has very little to thank England for in the past; not much to thank England for in the present; while the security of her person in the future is highly dubious.[11]

It is, after all, as Woolf's narrator points out in *A Room of One Own*, 'only for the last forty-eight years' that women have had 'a penny' of their own (thanks to the

[7] 'The Angel of the House', the tile of a poem by Coventry Patmore, is referenced in Woolf's essay, 'Professions for Women' in David Bradshaw (ed), *Virginia Woolf: Selected Essays* (Oxford University Press, 2008).

[8] Virginia Woolf, 'Memories of a Working Women's Guild' (a preface to the Women's Co-operative Guild's, *Life as We Have Known It* (1931)) in Bradhsaw (ed), n 7.

[9] Woolf explains in *Three Guineas*, written 10 years after *A Room of One's Own*, that as a woman her citizenship is revoked if she marries a foreigner: '[S]he will reflect that for her there are no "foreigners", since by law she becomes a foreigner if she marries a foreigner … "Our country" still ceases to be mine if I marry a foreigner … as a woman I have no country' (Virginia Woolf, *A Room of One's Own and Three Guineas* (Penguin, 1993) 233–34).

[10] Cambridge University finally allowed women to graduate with a degree in 1948. The first woman to receive a degree from the University was the Queen Mother, who was awarded an honorary degree.

[11] Woolf, n 9, 233.

Married Women's Property Act 1870): '[T]he law denied [women] the right to possess what money they earned. … For all the centuries before that it would have been [a woman's] husband's property …'[12]

III. What Happened Next

An important phase of the argument of *A Room of One's Own* involves the narrator's careful re-positioning of historical women writers whose work had been overlooked for centuries: 'we think back through our mothers if we are women' refers to literary 'mothers' who show women who come after them the path towards writing.[13] This re-positioning work is necessary because, as Germaine Greer points out, despite a chain of successful female writers who managed (against all odds) to overcome male hostility and to achieve recognition in their own era, the records delete such women in the years following: '[A]lmost uninterruptedly since the Interregnum, a small group of women have enjoyed dazzling literary prestige during their own lifetimes, only to vanish without trace from the records of posterity.'[14] Endorsing Greer's observation, Elaine Showalter adds 'the result is that each generation of women writers has found itself, in a sense, without a history'.[15] The damage caused by this situation is noted throughout *A Room of One's Own* and in chapter 4 in particular: '[f]or masterpieces are not single and solitary births; they are the outcome of many years of thinking in common'.[16]

With grim irony, despite the success of *A Room of One's Own* upon its publication, and despite the success of her writing career, Woolf herself was 'disappeared' following her death in 1941. Her work was unread and unstudied in the 1940s and 1950s. It was not until the 1970s that she was rediscovered by an emergent feminist literary industry, which found in her writing a rigorous template through which to theorise women's writing, voice and agency. Woolf had been anxious about the reception of *A Room of One's Own*, and was nervous of being labelled a feminist (Hermione Lee points out that 'Woolf was notoriously edgy about the F-word'),[17] so a second irony is that Woolf became the 'mother' of a second-wave feminist movement through this text.

It is not just her central argument that proved so important to later-century feminist thinking; it is also her methodologies. Woolf does not originate but develops a project known later as 'Herstory', the building of a female writing tradition to restore women to their rightful places in the 'herstory' of literature.

[12] ibid 20.

[13] Woolf, n 1, 65.

[14] Germaine Greer, quoted by Elaine Showalter in *A Literature of Their Own: from Charlotte Brontë to Doris Lessing* (Virago, 1979) 7.

[15] ibid 8.

[16] ibid 56.

[17] Hermione Lee, 'Introduction' to Virginia Woolf, *A Room of One's Own & Three Guineas* (Vintage, 2001 edn) viii.

The cultural inheritance of this project is registered (among other places) in the syllabuses of English Literature degree programmes, which now feature a wide range of women authors from Æmelia Lanyer, through to Aphra Behn, to Woolf herself. Further, it was Woolf who developed a post-structuralist analyses of 'History' decades before influential critics such as Hayden White developed related arguments:[18] the famous 'Shakespeare's Sister' section of *A Room of One's Own* not only identifies the fact that the story *not* told constitutes the story that *is* told, but also lays bare the false equivalences between 'history' and 'fact' and between 'literature' and 'fiction'.

Modern readers of *A Room of One's Own* not only respond to the logic of the arguments presented but find themselves shocked that so little appears to have changed in the intervening 100 years. In relation to the description of the 'lunch edition of the evening paper', for example, journalism (or what passes for it) still leads with the male priorities of sport and politics, and newspaper barons still only come in one sex; wealth is owned by a billionaire class of men and the gender pay gap persists; the glass ceiling refuses to shatter, or not enough and not for enough women; women's writing is too often, too glibly, denigrated as 'chick lit'; women who 'speak out' against the grain of received wisdom are 'cancelled' (an updated version of exclusion) with more rage and glee than their male counterparts; women remain blamed and shamed for a host of baffling breaches of one unspoken code or another (how easy it remains to err as a woman).

Above all, Woolf launches in this text a thousand debates about women's relationship to (and contested sovereignty over) their own bodies, about gender and androgyny, about money and about 'the word' itself. Every page of the text is packed with by-ways of thought later seized on by later-century feminism: is 'the sentence' 'male', asks Woolf, and does it both articulate and perpetuate the terms of patriarchy, an argument further developed by Dale Spender in *Man Made Language*.[19] Do women write from their bodies, asks Woolf, an argument further developed by Hélène Cixous in 'The Laugh of the Medusa'.[20] What is at stake in a woman's 'room', in a space of her own, a question further developed in feminist classics such as Marilyn French's novel *The Women's Room*, and still discernible in the fraught debates around single-sex spaces.[21]

A decade after *A Room of One's Own*, Woolf published *Three Guineas*, building upon some of the central issues of the earlier text (for example, the remodelling of women's education and women's exclusion from the professions).[22] This later text, however, failed to achieve either the cultural penetration or the positive reception of its elegantly persuasive sister text. By 1938, in the face of aggressive European

[18] Hayden White, 'The Historical Text as Literary Artefact' in *Tropics of Discourse: Essays in Cultural Criticism* (John Hopkins University Press, 1978).
[19] Dale Spender, *Man Made Language* (Routledge & Kegan Paul, 1980).
[20] Hélène Cixous, 'The Laugh of the Medusa', trs Keith Cohen and Paula Cohen (1976) 1(4) *Signs* 875.
[21] Marilyn French, *The Women's Room* (Simon & Schuster, 1977).
[22] Virginia Woolf, *Three Guineas* (Hogarth Press, 1938).

fascism, the contexts had changed and there was little appetite for a feminist, pacifist invective of the flavour Woolf delivers here. Furious and not afraid to show it, *Three Guineas* makes a series of stunning arguments but, despite its intellectual rigour, it is the more sophisticated *A Room of One's Own* that stands as the landmark of twentieth-century feminist literary argument.

IV. Significance

A Room of One's Own is itself a textual 'room' created for thinking, a space in which to chart the roots of women's exclusion and the path towards women's freedom. The first sentence of the text locates 'space' as key: 'But you may say, we asked you to speak about women and fiction – what has that got to do with a room of one's own?'[23] Of equal significance is the fact that the first word, 'But', exemplifies the text's landmark status via its head-on intervention in (and implicit objection to) male-led contemporary debates about women: 'But' signals that here women talk back. *A Room of One's Own* thus marks a crucial 'turn in the road' in the debate around women's equality, which is one of the reasons why Hermione Lee terms it 'probably the most influential feminist essay of the twentieth century'.[24]

Despite its flaws and blind-spots, *A Room of One's Own* reminds us that the fight for the right to write, to speak and to be heard is nothing new for women; generations have gone through this before. Sometimes small steps forward in the fight for equality are achieved, and some steps backwards produce setbacks too; all over the world, new battles need to be fought to assert women's fundamental rights. But it is in texts such as *A Room of One's Own* that 'landmarking' is achieved, because it is in such moments of 'speech' that a line in the sand is drawn. That opening 'But' launches a multivocal talking back to patriarchy, and it is this female chorus that speaks so clearly and so directly to the women of subsequent generations.

Woolf suggests in *A Room of One's Own* that 'all women together ought to let flowers fall upon the tomb of Aphra Behn[25] for it was she who earned them the right to speak their minds'.[26] Precisely the same is true, of course, of Woolf herself, particularly in this text. Despite later-century criticisms about her silences around class and race, it was Woolf who gave women a critical vocabulary in which to understand the links between patriarchy and women's poverty, between writing and sex, between 'rooms' and agency, between articulation and freedom. Via the

[23] Woolf, n 1, 1.
[24] Lee, n 18, vii.
[25] A 17th-century English playwright who was one of the first English women to earn a living by her writing.
[26] Woolf, n 1, 56.

winding pathways of *A Room of One's Own*, via the dead ends and retraced steps, via wit laced with glistening intellect, this issue of women's freedom runs like a vein through every word of the text: 'Lock up your libraries if you like; but there is no gate, no lock, no bolt that you can set upon the freedom of my mind.'[27]

Further Reading

- Rachel Bowlby, *Feminist Destinations and Further Essays on Virginia Woolf* (Edinburgh University Press, 1997).
- Julia Briggs, *Reading Virginia Woolf* (Edinburgh University Press, 2006).
- Susan Sellers (ed), *The Cambridge Companion to Virginia Woolf* (2nd edn, Cambridge University Press, 2010).

[27] ibid 64.

25

Margaret Bondfield, First Woman Cabinet Minister, 1929

JACQUI TURNER

Margaret Bondfield was a political trailblazer and a woman of many 'firsts'. She was a founding member of the Adult Suffrage Society (ASS) in 1904 and of the Women's Labour League in 1906. She became the first female president of the Trade Union Congress (TUC) in 1923, following a long tenure in the Shop Assistant's Union. She was a lifelong socialist and pacifist, committed to improving women's social and political workplace rights alongside a deep ideological conviction motivated by her own experience in the workplace and her commitment to trade unionism. She was also motivated by class and experiences of poverty. But it was as a Minister in the second Labour Government, when she became the first woman to be appointed a Cabinet Minister and the first woman Privy Counsellor, that her political career reached its pinnacle.

I. Life

Bondfield was born in 1873 in Somerset to a large working-class family, the 10th of 11 children. Her father supported the rights of working women and encouraged independence in his daughters. She began a drapery apprenticeship in Hove in 1887, and also attended meetings held by Liberal suffragist and women's rights activist Louisa Martindale in Brighton. In 1894, she left the south coast for London. Here, poor living and working conditions for shop workers were intensified by increasing demand in terms of opening hours (often 8am until midnight). She experienced low wages, poor dietary provision and insecurity of work, where a mistake meant dismissal on the employer's terms.

Mary Agnes Hamilton described Bondfield's route into labour politics as stemming from her commitment to trade unionism, but also a desire for belonging or companionship.[1] In 1896, Bondfield began to write from her personal experience

[1] Mary A Hamilton, *Margaret Bondfield* (Leonard Parsons, 1924) 29–33. Hamilton was a writer and broadcaster, and Labour MP for Blackburn between 1929 and 1931.

about the precarity of employment coupled with living and working conditions for shop workers, under the pseudonym Grace Darer. She was published by the *Daily Chronicle* and the journal of the National Amalgamated Union of Shop Assistants, Warehousemen and Clerks (NAUSAWC), *Shop Assistant*. In 1898 she joined the newly formed NAUSAWC, a predominantly male organisation. Bondfield encouraged women shopworkers to join, delivering leaflets directly to the sales counters of their workplace. In 1898 she was appointed assistant secretary and, in 1899, became the only female delegate at the TUC annual conference.

Influenced by Bondfield's activism and vigorous lobbying, the Shop Hours Act was passed in 1904. The Act enabled local authorities to regulate or fix local shop closing hours by 7pm, or on one day a week, at 1pm.[2] However, while the aim may have been to reduce the working hours of shop assistants and promote their health and welfare, the law was often unenforced, as most shops were small businesses whose owners were reluctant to change.

Bonfield supported adult suffrage and presided over the ASS, formed in 1904. Her position was that the franchise should be extended to all adults regardless of gender or property, rather than the limited 'on the same terms as men' agenda of many women suffragists and suffragettes, which would have enfranchised only certain women thus disenfranchising the working class, including men. On 3 December 1907, Bondfield engaged in a debate of adult suffrage versus sex equality with Teresa Billington-Greig, co-founder of the Women's Freedom League, who had struggled to promote women's suffrage at trade union meetings. Bondfield said:

> I work for Adult Suffrage because I believe it is the quickest way to establish a real sex-equality … I have always said in my speeches and in conversation that these women who believe in the same terms as men Bill have a perfect right to go on working for that Bill, and I say good luck to them and may they get it! But don't let them come and tell me that they are working for my class.[3]

The presence of Bondfield encouraged other socialist women into the organisation, such as Ada Nield Chew and Dora Montefiore, who became secretary in 1919. However, the ASS was not a success and was criticised by Charlotte Despard, a prominent suffrage campaigner, and Keir Hardie, Labour Party founder, for inertia.[4] Bondfield herself admitted that the group was marginal and had little influence.

In 1906, along with Mary Macarthur,[5] she founded the Women's Labour League, and by 1908 she had left her trade union role to become the League's

[2] Shop Hours Act 1904. The Act had some exemptions including tobacconists, chemists, newsagent, and post offices and was amended and extended by the Shops Act 1911 which included half-day closing.

[3] JF(42)/D180, 'Sex Equality (Teresa Billington-Greig) versus Adult Suffrage (Margaret Bondfield), Verbatim report of debate on Dec 3rd 1907', *Women's Freedom League* (Manchester, 1908). Isabella Ford was in the Chair.

[4] Krista Cowman, *Women in British Politics, c 1689–1979* (Bloomsbury, 2010) 109–110.

[5] Mary Macarthur was a trade union leader and adult suffragist. She was the secretary of the Women's Trade Union League from 1903 and founded the National Federation of Women Workers in 1906.

secretary before becoming women's officer for the National Union of General and Municipal Workers (NUGMW). In 1918 she was elected to the General Council of the Trades Union Congress, becoming the first female chair in 1923.

In December 1923, she was elected to Parliament as MP for Northampton. Together with Dorothy Jewson and Susan Lawrence, she was one of the first three Labour women MPs. Bondfield served as a junior Minister, Parliamentary Secretary to the Ministry of Labour, in the minority Labour Government of 1924. She lost her seat in the general election later that year, which brought in a Conservative Government with a large majority. Bondfield was re-elected to Parliament at a by-election in Wallsend in 1926.

Adult suffrage was finally achieved with the passage of the **Representation of the People (Equal Franchise) Act 1928**. Bondfield welcomed the Act in terms of humanity rather than gender equality, saying in Parliament, '[s]ince I have been able to vote at all, I have never felt the same enthusiasm because the vote was the consequence of possessing property rather than the consequence of being a human being'.[6]

In 1929, Bondfield reached arguably the pinnacle of her political career when she was appointed Minister of Labour in the second Labour minority government, the first woman to hold a senior Cabinet position while sitting in the UK Parliament.[7] It was, however, a short and tumultuous term during a politically and economically turbulent time. Bondfield had previously been accused of betraying the working-classes as a member of the Blanesburgh Committee, which had recommended cuts in unemployment insurance in 1927.[8] Now, as Minister of Labour, Bondfield herself had ultimate responsibility and came under enormous pressure to cut unemployment benefit. Her willingness to contemplate cuts alienated her from many in the Labour movement.

The financial crisis split the Labour party two years later, when nine Cabinet Ministers resigned rather than accepting cuts in unemployment benefits and the salaries of state employees in August 1931. The Labour Government fell, caused by a lack of public confidence after a failure to balance the budget and with no prospect of economic recovery in sight. It was replaced by Ramsay MacDonald's National Government.[9] Bondfield did not join the National Government. She lost her seat in the general election of October 1931 to Irene Ward (Conservative), which marked the end of her career in national politics.

[6] HC Deb 29 March 1928, vol 215, col 1415.

[7] **Constance Markievicz** had previously become the first woman Cabinet Minister in Ireland in 1919, sitting in the Dáil Éireann.

[8] The Blanesburgh Committee recommended some cuts in benefits and a requirement for claimants to have made 30 contributions in the previous two years. These recommendations were included in the Conservative Government's Unemployment Insurance Act 1927.

[9] The National Government introduced an emergency budget increasing taxes on those in work and reducing unemployment benefits and Civil Service pay. More broadly, Britain abandoned free trade, adopting a nationalistic, protectionist policy while also leaving the gold standard.

Bondfield remained active in the trade union movement and the NUGMW until 1938, and carried out investigations for the Women's Group on Public Welfare during the Second World War. She died in 1953 in Surrey, aged 80. Bondfield never married, stating:

> I concentrated on my job. This concentration was undisturbed by love affairs. I had seen too much – too early – to have the least desire to join in the pitiful scramble of my workmates. The very surroundings of shop life accentuated the desire of most shop girls to get married. Long hours of work and the living-in system deprived them of the normal companionship of men in their leisure hours, and the wonder is that so many of the women continued to be good and kind, and self-respecting, without the incentive of a great cause, or of any interest outside their job … I had no vocation for wifehood or motherhood, but an urge to serve the Union.[10]

Her obituary in *The Times* paid tribute to her as 'one of the most notable women' of the British Labour movement, recognising her pioneering spirit, generous nature, selfless devotion to practical causes and success as a public speaker.[11] Tributes were led in the House of Commons by the Lord Privy Seal:

> She was not a Member for very long, but she will always have a unique place in the history of Parliament. She was the first Lady to be admitted to the Privy Council and the first right hon Lady to be a Cabinet Minister. She was Minister of Labour at a very difficult period, but she was a good Parliamentarian. As one who had constantly to cross swords with her, I know that she was always a courteous and generous opponent.[12]

Clement Attlee added, 'She was a very distinguished Member of this House and she gave unwearied service for very many years to the cause of women workers. She was a very old friend and colleague of mine. She was a very fine character.'[13]

II. Context

Bondfield came from a trade union background. Trade unions were historically male-dominated and conservative in attitudes to any state interference in family life. A substantial proportion of women in paid work worked in domestic service, difficult to unionise. However, in industries where women were present in large numbers they could effect change, such as the match women's strike of 1888,[14] and in Bondfield's area of shop work. She worked closely with other pioneering women trade unionists who might also have become leading politicians, such as Mary Macarthur, who was one of the first women to stand following the **Parliament**

[10] Margret Bondfield, *A Life's Work* (Hutchinson, 1948) 36–37.
[11] *The Times* (18 June 1953).
[12] HC Deb 18 June 1953, vol 516, col 1187.
[13] ibid.
[14] Jacqueline Lane, 'Match Women's Strike 1888' in Erika Rackley and Rosemary Auchmuty (eds) *Women's Legal Landmarks: Celebrating the History of Women and Law in the UK and Ireland* (Hart Publishing, 2019) 91.

(Qualification of Women) Act 1918; Macarthur did not have the chance to stand again before her death in 1921.

As one of the earliest Labour women MPs, Bondfield's election in Northampton (a working-class seat held by Liberals for many years previously) was to an extent a party-political response to the elections of **Nancy Astor** (Conservative, 1919), Margaret Wintringham (Liberal, 1921) and Mabel Philipson (Conservative, 1923), which had a profound effect on the Labour party. In 1918, the first women voters had been assured that 'The Labour party is the woman's party',[15] but despite having been able to join the party on equal terms to men since its inception, the party had not yet returned a female MP. Bondfield benefited from a programme reconsidering constituencies to provide women candidates with winnable seats and strong grassroot support. Bondfield never underestimated her appeal to the working classes but said little about her own background beyond her work experiences, nor that of other Labour women MPs, focusing instead on their qualifications that fitted them for the role.[16] But even so, she won her seat only after two unsuccessful attempts in 1920 and 1921. The number of female candidates remained tiny and successes even fewer throughout the interwar period.

With such a small pool of female MPs across all parties, there was no prospect of a woman Minister, let alone Cabinet Minister, before Bondfield. The traditional route to Cabinet is to first become a Parliamentary Private Secretary (PPS), effectively an apprenticeship to becoming a junior Minister and then a Cabinet Minister. However, male Ministers in this period were reluctant to accept a woman as their PPS, as this required access to gossip and discussion in spaces such as bars, smoking rooms and cloakrooms in Parliament, from where women were either formally or informally excluded.[17] Bondfield's appointment as a junior Minister immediately after her election reflected her long service to the trade union movement and the party, and also that Labour arrived rather suddenly and unexpectedly as a party of government, and with a large number of new MPs.

Bondfield's appointment in 1924 increased pressure on the Conservatives to find a woman Minister when they took power later that year. Stanley Baldwin duly appointed the Duchess of Atholl as a junior Minister between 1924 and 1929, but Atholl never rose to Cabinet level.[18] By the time Labour returned in 1929 Bondfield was 56 years old; with her previous ministerial experience in the Ministry of Labour, as well as her extremely impressive trade union credentials, she was a clear choice to be the new Minister of Labour.

[15] Labour Party general election manifesto, 1918.

[16] 'Margaret Bondfield introduces Labour women MPs 1929', *British Movietone* at www.youtube.com/watch?v=4KUvSZkgjSk.

[17] Paula Bartley, *Labour Women in Power: Cabinet Ministers in the Twentieth Century* (Springer, 2019) 8.

[18] Katharine Murray Stewart (Scottish Unionist MP for Kinross and West Perthshire, 1923–38), Duchess of Atholl, was the first woman in Scotland to be elected to Parliament. She became Parliamentary Secretary to the Board of Education in 1924, and the first woman to serve in a British Conservative Government – but not in Cabinet.

III. What Happened Next

Bondfield's term in Cabinet was dominated by the backdrop of global economic turmoil caused by the Wall Street Crash and the ensuing Great Depression, an economic decline that provided a sharp contrast to the relative economic growth of the 1920s. The lack of a majority put the Labour Government in thrall to the Liberals, to the disappointment of the many on the left of the party. As the economic climate worsened and unemployment increased, it became clear that government spending would need to be rationalised, but many Labour MPs were vehemently opposed to the working classes' bearing the brunt of any punitive measures.

Bondfield believed unemployment insurance should be a contributory benefit funded by an insurance fund, rather than more generous benefits from general taxation. However, as Minister of Labour she faced an impossible task, trying to contain the fund's deficit while also massively increasing borrowing.[19] She was fiercely criticised by both sides either for betraying the unemployed or for being too soft on them.[20] Under enormous pressure from the Treasury to cut costs, amongst the economies she took were cutting benefits for married women.

Although some women MPs worked together within and across parties, it would be wrong to pigeonhole women MPs into a homogeneous group motivated primarily by their sex. As Krista Cowman has observed, women on the left of the Labour Party, such as Jennie Lee and Ellen Wilkinson,

> felt no solidarity as women with the Minister of Labour Margaret Bondfield, as she struggled to keep unemployment relief within affordable levels during the economic crisis of the 1920s. For Lee and Wilkinson the privations of their working class constituents were more important than government policy or any other woman MPs.[21]

Despite this, along with most women MPs of the interwar period, Bondfield did much to advance the interests of women. The agenda she pursued in Parliament was motivated by her commitment to addressing the causes of gender inequality in the workplace, poverty and unemployment, much of which she described in terms of the disproportionate impact on women. Bondfield believed her greatest contribution was to connect the Labour movement 'with women's work'.[22] That said, there remained an ambiguity in the Labour party's attitude to feminism. While feminists demanded 'equal opportunity of employment … trade unionists wanted discriminatory legislation on working hours and conditions: to protect the health of mother and child, and to promote the full employment of men at a "family wage"'.[23]

[19] As unemployment soared, Bondfield had to repeatedly return to Parliament to ask for increases, which also soared, from £40 million in April 1930 to £131 million in June 1931.

[20] Philip Williamson, 'Bondfield, Margaret Grace (1873–1953), trade unionist, campaigner for women's interests, and politician', *Oxford Dictionary of National Biography* (23 September 2004) (rev 6 January 2011).

[21] Cowman, n 4, 109–26.

[22] Bondfield, n 10, 329.

[23] Brian Harrison, *Prudent Revolutionaries: Portraits of British Feminists Between the Wars* (Oxford University Press, 1987) 127.

After Bondfield's departure from Cabinet in 1931, the UK had to wait 14 years for its next woman Cabinet Minister – Ellen Wilkinson, Minister of Education in Clement Attlee's Labour Government of 1945. The first Conservative woman Cabinet Minister was Florence Horsbrugh, who was appointed Minister of Education in 1953. As of March 2023, there were just seven women full Cabinet Ministers (30 per cent) and only 55 women have *ever* been Cabinet Ministers.[24]

IV. Significance

Margaret Bondfield's career spanned first-hand experience of the dismal conditions experienced by shop workers fueled by an increasing consumer society, to her reign as Britain's first female Cabinet Minister overseeing employment issues at a time of greatest depression. Her commitment to trade unionism was exemplary. Indeed, her obituary in *The Times* called her 'first and foremost a trade unionist rather than a politician', with her essential work for social betterment carried out elsewhere than Westminster.[25]

However, this should not overshadow her achievements as a female pioneer in parliamentary politics and government. When Bondfield was first elected to Parliament in 1923, full adult suffrage had not yet been achieved, and many poorer and younger working-class women could not vote. Women had been in Parliament for less than a decade when Bondfield became a Cabinet Minister in 1929.

Her support for adult franchise rather than women's suffrage on the same terms as men, alongside her decision to deny married women the 'dole' in an effort to balance the national books, has undermined her position as a feminist pioneer. But when she was appointed Minister of Labour, her contribution to British parliamentary democracy was sealed as a crucial female first. She believed her appointment was 'part of the great revolution in the position of women which had taken place in my lifetime and which I had done something to help forward'.[26]

Further Reading

- Margaret Bondfield, *A Life's Work* (Hutchinson, 1948).
- June Hannam and Karen Hunt, *Socialist Women Britain, 1880s to 1920s* (Routledge, 2002).
- Tony Judge, *Margaret Bondfield First Woman in the Cabinet* (CreateSpace Independent Publishing Platform, 2018).

[24] House of Commons Library Research Briefing, *Women in politics and public life*, Standard Note 1250, March 2023.

[25] *The Times*, n 11.

[26] Bondfield, n 10, 276.

26

Ministry of Health Memorandum 153/MCW, 1930

JOANNE BESWICK

In July 1930, 'responding to a widespread and responsible demand', the Ministry of Health issued Memorandum 153/MCW, permitting local authorities to give birth-control advice to married women for whom a further pregnancy would be detrimental to health.[1] Having regard to the 'acute division of public opinion' on the issues of birth control,[2] the Memorandum was clear that such advice would not be given to anyone falling outside this small group – that is men, whether married or otherwise, and unmarried women. Despite its limited remit, the Memorandum 153/MCW was an important recognition of the fact that 'while the right number of children means happiness in the home, more than that number is just the reverse'.[3]

I. Context

After the Boer War (1899–1902) had exposed the poor state of health of the recruits, largely due to inadequate nutrition and sanitation, there was general recognition that infant and maternal mortality rates were also high, in part for the same reasons. In consequence of this understanding, women's associations set up child-welfare clinics as exemplars for the Government to follow. This voluntary provision led to the Maternity and Child Welfare Act 1918, to improve the care provided to mothers and young children. It made local authorities in England and Wales responsible for 'attending to the health of nursing mothers and children under five' and provided government subsidies to enable this to happen.[4]

[1] Ministry of Health and Birth Control [post issue of circular MCW/153] (Wellcome Collection PP/EPR/B.4).

[2] ibid 1.

[3] 'What Birth Control Means' (1931) 3 (Wellcome Collection PP/EPR/B.4).

[4] See Hazel Biggs, 'Maternity and Child Welfare Act 1918' in Erika Rackley and Rosemary Auchmuty (eds), *Women's Legal Landmarks: Celebrating the History of Women and Law in the UK and Ireland* (Hart Publishing, 2019) 119.

A major concern was the influence of family size on the health of mothers and infants. Ernest Thurtle, Labour MP for the east London constituency of Shoreditch and Finsbury, pointed out that families tended to be larger in poorer areas, and health correspondingly more seriously compromised. As he explained in the House of Commons debate on the Local Authorities (Birth Control) Bill in 1926:

> In those districts where overcrowding is most intense, where poverty is most acute, where all the elemental necessities for healthy child life are most conspicuous by their absence, you get a very high birth rate and in other districts, where conditions are infinitely better, you have a comparatively low birth rate. No Members of the House are going to contend that that state of affairs is satisfactory, either from a national or a human standpoint.[5]

Although there was never any statutory prohibition on providing information on birth control by Public Health Authorities in England and Wales,[6] discussion of controlling family size by the use of contraception had always been extremely controversial. In 1877, Annie Besant and Charles Bradlaugh were put on trial for re-publishing *Fruits of Philosophy* by Charles Knowlton, a pamphlet dating from 1832, that provided instructions on birth control as a means of combatting over-population.[7] It was alleged that the pamphlet was contrary to the Obscene Publications Act 1857, which outlawed salacious literature. Besant and Bradlaugh were charged with publishing material that was 'likely to deprave or corrupt those whose minds are open to immoral influence'.[8] In their defence, they argued in court that 'children were half-starved because there is food enough for two but not twelve'.[9] Besant and Bradlaugh were both found guilty of publishing an 'obscene libel' and sentenced to six months in prison.[10]

After the court case, Annie Besant published her own book advocating birth control, *The Laws of Population*. The idea of a woman advocating birth control received wide and critical publicity.[11] Besant lost custody of her child to her estranged husband because, as she bemoaned in a subsequent case, the authorities felt that there

> cannot be a doubt that the future welfare of this child will be prejudiced by her being brought up in association with persons who hold the opinions which her mother professes and advocates – opinions which are looked upon by most people as wrong, and by her own sex as perfectly shocking.[12]

[5] HC Deb 9 February 1926, vol 191, col 850.

[6] Unlike the USA, where the so-called Comstock Laws 1873 were in force.

[7] 'The Trial of Annie Besant and Charles Bradlaugh' at https://editions.covecollective.org/chronologies/trial-annie-besant-and-charles-bradlaugh [accessed 26 October 2023].

[8] *The Queen v Charles Bradlaugh and Annie Besant (Specially Reported)* (Freethought Publishing Company, 1877) 28 quoted in Mytheli Sreenivas, 'Birth Control in the Shadow of Empire: The Trials of Annie Besant, 1877–1878' (2015) 41(3) *Feminist Studies* 509, 515 (special edition on *Gendering Bodies, Institutional Hegemonies*).

[9] ibid 519.

[10] The Court of Appeal later quashed the sentence for a procedural reason: *Charles Bradlaugh and Annie Besant v The Queen* (1878) 3 QBD 607.

[11] Carol Hanbery Mackay, 'A Journal of Her Own: The Rise and Fall of Annie Besant's Our Corner' (2009) *Victorian Periodicals Review* 324.

[12] *In re Besant* (1878) 11 ChD 508.

Just over 40 years later, Marie Stopes had published *Wise Parenthood: A Treatise on Birth Control or Contraception*. A sequel to her widely-read *Married Love*, the book upset the leaders of the Church of England, which, along with the Catholic Church, was totally opposed to the use of birth control. Other critics claimed, without evidence, that artificial prevention of conception was dangerous. Stopes sought to defend her ideas by bringing a libel action against one such author, Dr Halliday Sutherland, a doctor working on anti-tuberculosis treatments and author of *Birth Control: A Statement of Christian Doctrine against the Neo-Malthusians*.[13] Defending the claim, Sutherland argued that: (i) the words complained of consisted of allegations of fact that were true in substance; and (ii) the words were fair comment made in good faith and without malice on a matter of public interest. At trial, the jury, somewhat problematically, found that while the words were true in substance and fact, they were not fair comment. Both sides claimed to have won. In the end, judgment was given for the defendant. Stopes successfully appealed, but this was overturned by the House of Lords, Viscount Cave, then Lord Chancellor, making it clear that in so doing the Lords were 'not concerned with any question as to the desirability of the use of contraceptives, or as to the propriety of encouraging such use by the circulation of printed matter or in any other way', but simply on the intracies of libel law.[14]

Stopes further attempted to disseminate her ideas by writing a play, also entitled *Married Love*, under the pseudonym George Dalton. Its theme was the impotence of a husband and the ignorance of a wife about how to conceive a child. The play failed to obtain a licence to be performed at the Royal Court Theatre in November 1923, with the Lord Chamberlain, George S Street, stating that 'no excuse is sufficient for inflicting such an unnecessarily disgusting play on the public'.[15]

Despite this opposition, Stopes continued her campaign. In 1921 she had founded the Society for Constructive Birth Control. With financial help from her second husband, Humphrey Roe, she opened the first of her birth-control clinics in Holloway (north London) on 17 March 1921.[16] A second was opened in Walworth (south London), in the same year, by the Malthusian League, which was a long-time supporter of birth control because they saw over-population as the main cause of poverty.[17]

It is clear that Stopes's advocacy of birth control was linked, in part, to her support for eugenics.[18] She was not alone.[19] In 1922, a health visitor who shared

[13] *Sutherland v Stopes* [1925] AC 47.

[14] ibid 55.

[15] Memorandum by George S Street, Ceremonial Department, St James's Palace, 9 October 1923.

[16] University of London, 'Women's History Month: The Centenary of Britain's First Birth Control Clinic' at www.london.ac.uk/senate-house-library/blog/100yearsFirstBirthControlClinic [accessed 26 October 2023].

[17] Madeline Simms, 'Parliament and birth control in the 1920s' (1978) 28(187) *Journal of the Royal Society of General Practitioners* 83, 84.

[18] Agnes Arnold-Forster, 'Marie Stopes opened the UK's first birth control clinic 100 years ago – she was also a eugenicist' *The Conversation* (16 March 2021).

[19] Ann Taylor Allen, 'Feminism and Eugenics in Germany and Britain, 1900–1940: A Comparative Perspective' (2000) 23(3) *German Studies Review* 477.

her views, Miss ES Daniels, was dismissed by Edmonton (north London) Council in 1922 for advising mothers attending the council-run maternity centre that they could obtain birth control by visiting the Marie Stopes clinic.[20] Although 500 people signed a petition in her support, her dismissal was upheld by the Ministry of Health.[21]

Nor was she alone in advocating for birth control. In 1923, Guy Aldred and his wife Rose Witcop were found guilty of selling a pamphlet, *Family Limitation*, by American feminist Margaret Sanger, which included information on birth control. Dora Russell, a feminist and socialist campaigner, and economist Maynard Keynes paid their legal costs to allow them to go free. Russell also campaigned within the Labour party for birth-control clinics. In 1924, Russell was one of a group of Labour women who set up the Workers' Birth Control Group along with Katharine Glasier, Susan Lawrence, **Margaret Bondfield** and Dorothy Jewson, and with the support of some men, such as HG Wells. This group specifically framed birth control as a working-class issue, arguing that birth-control methods would improve the health of working-class mothers. They campaigned for local authorities to provide information about birth control. At the same time, socialist Stella Browne toured the country, giving women information about women's health, birth control and sexuality.[22] At the 1926 Labour Party Conference, Russell shocked the audience by declaring that it was four times as dangerous for a woman to bear a child as for a man to work in a mine (then considered the most dangerous occupation), but the party officials refused to adopt the policy as they feared losing the Catholic vote.[23]

At first, many women's organisations were wary of associating themselves with such a controversial cause. The National Union of Societies for Equal Citizenship (NUSEC), for instance, presented arguments on either side of the debate but refused to commit to its own opinion. The National Council for the Unmarried Mother and her Child was afraid of damaging its already controversial cause, even though, as Pat Thane and Tanya Evans explain, it mostly supported birth control covertly.[24] But socialist radicals like Browne and Russell presented it in the context of healthy motherhood, while middle-class 'old' feminists like Cicely Hamilton, Vera Brittain and Winifred Holtby saw it as 'widening the scope of human freedom and choice'.[25] The working-class Women's Cooperative Guild, which had published the book *Maternity* in 1916, passed a resolution in 1925 asking the Ministry of Health and Municipal Authorities to make adequate

[20] Clare Debenham, 'Grassroots Feminism: A study of the campaign of the Society for the Provision of Birth Control Clinics' (PhD thesis, University of Manchester, 2010).

[21] Simms, n 17, 84.

[22] Sheila Rowbotham, *A new world for women: Stella Browne – socialist feminist* (Pluto, 1977).

[23] Debenham, n 20, 60.

[24] Pat Thane and Tanya Evans, *Sinners? Scroungers? Saints? Unmarried motherhood in twentieth-century England* (Oxford University Press, 2012) 23.

[25] Susan Kingsley Kent, 'Gender Reconstruction after the First World War' in Harold L Smith (ed), *British Feminism in the Twentieth* Century (Edward Elgar, 1990) 66, 76–77.

provision for maternity and infant welfare centres where doctors would be free to give birth-control information.[26] In the same year, NUSEC changed its stance and called on the Ministry of Health to allow doctors in such centres to give birth control where a woman asked for it or where it would be beneficial to her health.[27]

Meanwhile, there was growing support within the medical profession for family limitation, especially from women doctors.[28] Most male doctors, except for those involved in the neo-Malthusian and eugenics movements, held to the view that their role was limited to curing illness; for them, abstinence was the best way to limit family size.[29] It was women practitioners, alongside a few significant male doctors, including Lord Dawson of Penn (the King's doctor), Norman Haire and CP Blacker, who tried to convince their medical colleagues that 'birth control was a legitimate, effective and medically harmless means for preventing conception in order to fight poverty and reduce the incidence of abortion'.[30] Helena Wright, who had been a student of Winifred Cullis, Professor of Physiology at the University of London and a future member of the Birth Control Investigation Committee, made the point that 'women clients came to us because we were all women. Women doctors, women nurses, women running clinics …'[31] and, perhaps most importantly, because they provided efficient female-centred birth control. Women doctors also tried to educate mothers: Dr Alice Vickery started outreach work by giving talks to working-class mothers on methods of birth control; she also donated funds for the women to purchase contraceptive materials.[32]

II. The Landmark

The Ministry of Health did not actually prohibit the giving of contraceptive advice, but it did nothing to make it accessible. Local authorities were free to offer it, but most held back through fear of losing government funding. Thus, on 9 February 1926, Ernest Thurtle moved the Local Authorities (Birth Control) Enabling Bill in the House of Commons, aiming to authorise local authorities to give birth-control information to married women who asked for it. He made the socialist point that wealthy women had access to this knowledge but that working women, who needed it more, were denied it. He also made the feminist point that birth control was important for women's health and equality of oportunity.

[26] 'Ministry of Health, Public Health authorities and Birth Control by Future Citizen [Edith How-Martyn]', 7 (Wellcome Collection PP/EPR/B.4).

[27] Kingsley Kent, n 25, 77.

[28] Caroline Rusterholz, *Women's Medicine: Sex, family planning and British female doctors in transnational perspective, 1920–70* (Manchester University Press, 2020) 37–84.

[29] ibid.

[30] ibid.

[31] ibid 41.

[32] Debenham, n 20.

Although the Bill would not have compelled authorities to act, but only to enable them to do so, it was opposed by twice as many MPs as supported it, most of the opposition coming from within Thurtle's own Labour party.[33]

A few months later, on 28 April 1926, Lord Buckmaster, drawing on eugenic, socialist and feminist views, moved a resolution in the House of Lords that local authorities should be empowered to give information about family limitation to married women.[34] It passed, and the House of Lords became the first legislative chamber in the world to endorse birth control. Within a few months, 37 local authorities and 74 other organisations had sent resolutions to the Prime Minister asking for birth-control advice to be made available at maternity and infant-welfare clinics, of which there were amost 2,500 across the country.[35] Still the Government failed to act.

Following the general election in 1929, when Labour came to power with nine women MPs elected, feminists intensified their lobbying. A special committee was set up to consider the provision of birth-control information and assistance. This was followed by a Conference on Birth Control in April 1930. In the end, although successive Ministers of Health had excused their inactivity on this matter by declaring that this was a political question that required a vote in Parliament,[36] once sufficient pressure had been applied by birth controllers and local authorities, the Minister was emboldened to abandon the excuse of politics and lift the prohibition against birth control by simple departmental regulation: Memorandum 153/MCW.

III. What Happened Next

The next challenge was that Public Health Authorities had to be encouraged to use their powers. Five separate birth-control societies that had been formed in the 1920s to open clinics throughout England came together in 1930 to become the National Birth Control Council (NBCC). With the slogan 'Children by choice, not chance', the Council immediately started to put pressure on local health authorities to implement the circular.[37] Since the Memorandum had not been publicised – copies had not even been sent to all authorities, only to those that had asked for it – it set about reprinting and distributing them.[38] A list drawn up by the director of the Birth Control International Information Centre, Edith How-Martyn, showed 72 areas that had approved the Memorandum in principle, with just 30 of

[33] Simms, n 17, 85.
[34] HC Deb 28 April 1926, vol 63, col 996.
[35] Simms, n 17, 86.
[36] ibid 87.
[37] Family Planning Association, 'History of Family Planning' factsheet at www.fpa.org.uk/medical-professional/factsheets/ [accessed 26 October 2023]. The National Birth Control Council changed its name to the National Birth Control Association (NBCA) in 1931, and then to the Family Planning Association (FPA) in 1939.
[38] Simms, n 17, 87.

those areas actually such taking action.[39] By 1933, however, almost 80 were giving out birth-control advice.[40] An Addendum added in 1934 allowed local authorities to provide birth-control information to married women with any kind of medical indication.[41] In 1937, following concerns about the rate of maternal mortality, local health authorities were encouraged to establish post-natal clinics that would also provide contraceptive advice.[42]

In 1949, the Royal Commission on Population, which had been appointed in 1943, recommended in its report that 'the giving of advice on contraception to married persons who wanted it should be accepted as a duty of the National Health Service [NHS]' and 'the initial duty to give advice should rest with the family doctor'.[43] The recommendation was accepted. So although now a duty, it was still (theoretically at least) restricted to married persons and did not necessarily represent the beliefs of the profession on whom the duty was placed. This was borne out by the finding in a survey conducted in 1961 that fewer than 50 per cent of GPs believed that contraceptive advice should be a part of the services they provided.[44] During the 1960s, the Minister of Health left it to GPs to decide on medical grounds who should receive the new contraceptive pill, implying that it was not dependent on marital status.[45] With the increasing use of 'the pill' and changes in social attitudes, in 1967 local authority-funded family health clinics were explicitly allowed to give contraceptive advice to unmarried women on both medical and social grounds. Only in 1974 did the NHS Reorganisation Act 1973 *require* the provision of family-planning services on the NHS.[46]

IV. Significance

The immediate significance of this landmark was that it opened the door to the legal provision of contraception, albeit to a limited number of women to begin with. It marked an important departure from the idea that children were always a blessing, no matter the effect on the woman's health or opportunities or the family's poverty. By allowing women to control the size of their families, access to birth-control information gave them a considerable amount of autonomy over their bodies. It marked the separation of sex from reproduction, in an era when

[39] 'The Ministry of Health and Birth Control', n 1, 2.
[40] Simms, n 17, 87.
[41] ibid.
[42] Ministry of Health, *Maternal Mortality Circular 1622*, 7 May 1937.
[43] *Report of the Royal Commission on Population* (Cmd 7695, 1949) 259.
[44] The Health Foundation, 'Formal birth control services for married women' at https://navigator.health.org.uk/theme/formal-birth-control-services-married-women [accessed 26 October 2023].
[45] ibid.
[46] ibid.

the enjoyment of sexual relations was increasingly being promoted as the basis of a happy marriage.[47] It had an important impact on the health of the women themselves, as well as on their families, including their existing children, who would be able to enjoy a higher standard of living. In the long term, women would not only be freer to enjoy sex in marriage but would have freedom to experiment before marriage without suffering an unwanted pregnancy.

The ability to control their childbearing gave women greater opportunity to enter the labour market and become financially independent and potentially more fulfilled. That said, the desire by patriarchal governments, jurisdictions and individual men to control women's bodies has not gone away, as we see from today's restored or continuing restrictions on access to abortion.[48]

Further Reading

- Ministry of Health and Birth Control [post issue of circular MCW/153], Wellcome Collection PP/EPR/B.4 at https://wellcomecollection.org/works/rcpfwtnx/items.
- Madeline Simms, 'Parliament and birth control in the 1920s' (1978) 28(187) *Journal of the Royal Society of General Practitioners* 83.
- Caroline Rusterholz, *Women's Medicine: Sex, family planning and British female doctors in transnational perspective, 1920–70* (Manchester University Press, 2020).

[47] See, for example, Stopes, *Married Love* (1918), Theodor Van de Velde, *Ideal Marriage, Its Physiology and Technique* (1928), Isabel Emslie Hutton, *The Sex Technique in Marriage* (1932) and Helena Wright, *The Sex Factor in Marriage* (1931). All sold widely.

[48] Adelaide Wood, 'Women and Their Fight For and Against Contraceptives and Rights in the 1920s' in Mir Yarfitz (ed), *Gender & Sexuality in World History* (2022) Section A at https://genderhistory.pubpub.org/pub/women-and-their-fight-for-and-against-contraceptives-and-rights-in-the-1920s [accessed 26 October 2023].

27

Stella Thomas, First Black Woman to be Called to the Bar of England and Wales, 1933

JUDITH BOURNE

Stella Jane Thomas (1906–74) was the first West African woman to be called to the Bar of England and Wales at the Middle Temple. Called on 10 May 1933, by 1935 she had returned to West Africa and registered as a barrister at the Supreme Courts of both Sierra Leone (October 1935) and Nigeria (November 1935), thus enshrining her in history as the first woman lawyer in West Africa. Practising in her brother's chambers until 1942/3, she then became the first woman in West Africa to accept a (quasi-) judicial appointment, when she was appointed as a magistrate.[1]

I. Life

Thomas can be described as having been born in Lagos (Nigeria) of Sierra Leonean descent, although these countries had been artificially created by the colonial powers for control, exploitation and profit. She was one of the Yoruba people,[2] an African diaspora who reached from Nigeria to Benin.[3] Her parents were Josetta Mary Thomas and Peter Claudius Thomas, a successful businessman and trail-blazer as the first African President of the Lagos Chamber of Commerce, and the first African to have European employees.[4]

Schooled in Freetown (the capital of Sierra Leone),[5] Thomas travelled to England in 1926, behaviour described as 'rare': an unmarried black woman

[1] Christopher Fyfe, *Sierra Leone, 1787–1987, Two Centuries of Intellectual Life* (Manchester University Press, 1987) 446; and *The Colonial Review*, vols 3–4 (1943) 35 and 116.

[2] Adedapo Adeniran, *Nigeria The Case for Peaceful and Friendly Dissolution* (The Futility of the Land Use Publisher, 2010) 40.

[3] Samuel Johnson, *The History of the Yorubas, From the Earliest Times to the Beginning of the British Protectorate* (Cambridge University Press, 1966) xix.

[4] *The Colonial Review*, vols 3–4 (1943) 116.

[5] Fyfe, n 1, 446.

travelling to England as a student.[6] Many texts describe her as having studied at the University of Oxford and being a member of the West African Student Union. However, the Bodleian Library does not record Thomas as having matriculated in its indexes up to and including 1932; further, her 1933 Middle Temple 'Call Form' leaves her university education as blank, and her Middle Temple admission application describes her as having passed the Cambridge Schools Certificate.[7] However, there are many inconsistencies in the numerous, but mostly one paragraph, records of her life in other histories.

On 12 December 1929, she was admitted to the Middle Temple for the fee of just over £157. Her form described her as her father's second daughter. Having passed her final Bar exams in December 1932, she was later called to the Bar alongside her elder brother Stephen, who would later become the first Chief Justice of the Mid-Western region in Nigeria. Another brother, Emanuel, was also a member of Middle Temple, but he was never called, later becoming the first RAF-commissioned African; he flew for Britain in the Second World War.[8] By 1935, Thomas had returned to Lagos, joining her brother Stephen's chambers.[9]

She was made a magistrate in either 1942[10] or 1943,[11] and retired from this role either upon her marriage[12] or in 1971.[13] There is evidence of her magistracy: she sentenced Alice Ewo to a fine of £5 and 10 shillings, or one month's imprisonment with hard labour, for selling six cigarette sticks for 6d instead of the fixed price of five cigarette sticks for 4d.[14] In November 1943, Thomas married a fellow Nigerian barrister, Richard B Marke, who was also of Sierra Leonean descent and with whom she had studied.[15] Thereafter known as 'Mrs Marke',[16] her marriage and profession gave her an influential status in social and civic public life.[17]

II. Context

Thomas was born into a constantly changing political landscape: Nigeria and Sierra Leone were two British colonies under indirect rule. Before 1903, there was

[6] Delia Jarret-Macauley, *The Life of Una Marson, 1905–1965* (Manchester University Press, 1998) 48.
[7] MT/3/AHC/33.
[8] *United Empire*, vols 34–35 (1943) 48.
[9] AN Henry and AF Evarista, 'The Emergence and History of the "Gentlewomen of the Bar" into the Legal Profession in the South West Geopolitical Zone of Nigeria' (2017) 8(1) *Arts and Social Sciences Journal* 3.
[10] Mbonu Ojike, *My Afrika* (John Day Publisher, 1946) 174; and *The Crisis* 'International' (November 1942) 344.
[11] Fyfe, n 1, 446.
[12] Ojike, n 10.
[13] Emeka Keazor, 'Notable Nigerians: Stella Thomas' NSIBIDI Institute (4 November 2014).
[14] Chima J Korieh, *Nigeria and World War II, Colonialism, Empire, and Global Conflict* (Cambridge University Press, 2020) 164.
[15] Robert Wellesley Cole, *An Innocent in Britain: or, The Missing Link* (Campbell Matthews Publishers, 1988) 81.
[16] Fyfe, n 1, 446.
[17] ibid.

little white administration due to cost and health implications,[18] and so Africans were governed by their fellow Africans, men like Thomas's father: from Sierra Leone, Christian, English-speaking and literate.[19] However, by 1913, racist theories and medical advances[20] enabled white men to work in West Africa; these theories were convenient colonial tools for racial segregation and the restriction of influence of educated Africans. These strained relations were further exacerbated by the First World War, in which many Africans had fought for the British.[21] New opportunities were created for Africans after 1918, as the war and global influenza pandemic's death toll meant a lack of suitable colonial white men, enabling Africans again to enter the higher Civil Service. From 1922, limited franchise was introduced,[22] and by the 1930s Africans had begun to think of not sharing colonial power but ending it.[23]

Thomas was also born during a time of limited educational opportunities for Africans. For most, schooling ended at the age of 13 or 14[24] and was mostly vocational.[25] Fourah Bay College opened in Sierra Leone in 1827, becoming the first university in sub-Saharan Africa. This helps to explain the British use of Sierra Leonean men for colonial positions: they were the few who were educated. Not until 1948 did Nigeria establish its own institution of higher education, University College Ibadan. As a result of these educational limitations, West African students tended to travel to England to study, and consequently by the 1920s there were some 60 African lawyers in Nigeria and seven doctors.[26] This route into the professions was, of course, only open to the wealthy. Sending Thomas to train in England would have been a risk for her family, but a calculated risk. Her parents clearly realised that Nigeria would need British-educated professional Africans to change the colonial system and/or to gain independence.

Thomas was not required to have been called to the English Bar in order to practise law or sit as a magistrate. Unlike England, Nigeria had a fused profession; any legal training in England would not have prepared Thomas for life as a Nigerian lawyer, as England had a dual profession, and there was no teaching of indigenous Nigerian law.[27] She would, however, have needed a grounding in English law in

[18] Judith Brown and Wm Roger Louis (eds), *The Oxford History of the British Empire*, vol IV: *The Twentieth Century* (Oxford University Press, 1999) 517.

[19] ibid.

[20] For the manufacture of quinine for malaria, see Lars Berge and Irma Taddia, *Themes in Modern African History and Culture, Festschrift for Tekeste Negash* (Libreriauniversitaria.it edizioni Publishers, 2013) 79.

[21] Kinshasha Holman Conwill, *We Return Fighting, World War I and the Shaping of Modern Black Identity* (Smithsonian Publishers, 2019); Brown and Louis, n 18, 519.

[22] Brown and Louis, n 18, 519.

[23] ibid 521.

[24] AD Roberts, JD Fage and Roland Anthony Oliver, *The Cambridge History of Africa*, vol 7 (Cambridge University Press, 1975) 227.

[25] ibid 228.

[26] Ibid 229.

[27] JO Fabunmi and AO Popoola, 'Legal Education in Nigeria: Problems and Prospects' (1990) 23(1) *Verfassung und Recht in Übersee/Law and Politics in Africa, Asia and Latin America* 34, 37.

order to practise law and to sit as a magistrate. Nigeria administered two forms of law: English law, administered in the Supreme Court and magistrates' courts; and 'native' and customary law, administered in the 'native' courts.[28] There was a resulting tension within the colonial courts about how to uphold uniform colonial justice based on the common law whilst also allowing customary indigenous law.[29]

There was a community of indigenous lawyers in Nigeria that she could have joined, but they struggled against British dominance.[30] It has been estimated that of 110 district magistrates in Nigeria in 1940, only 13 men were professionally qualified.[31] Expatriate lawyers sat as judges in the higher courts,[32] although some of these judges were Africans.[33] There has been some debate as to whether they were 'villainous collaborators' or 'intellectual middlemen'.[34] The Second World War saw an increase in the number of magistrates because of staff shortages due to the war. The Administrative Service found it hard to find suitable people, and there was an increase in crime and litigation.

We know that early women barristers in England found establishing and maintaining practice difficult. Formal admission to the legal profession in 1919 did not end substantive discrimination: clients were wary of briefing women; men in general held discriminatory views about women's professional ability and behaved misogynistically. Racism was rife in England: there was a colour bar, although not an explicit one,[35] and London was one of the principal places where it was practised. In 1929, for example, the actor and musician Paul Robeson was refused service at the Savoy Grill.[36] Even Helena Normanton, the first woman to join an Inn of Court, a woman who left the teaching profession because she could not advocate the nobility of Empire and who called for home rule for India, described Africans as a 'child race', who needed manual qualifications to fall back on if they could not succeed in the professions.[37]

Thomas was one of the founding members of the League of Coloured Peoples, a civil rights organisation open to all races.[38] The League advocated for the end of the colour bar.[39] It had 12 centres, a journal called *The Keys*, organised social activities and lobbied for change.[40] Thomas performed in a play at the YMCA, *What a Price* by Una Masson, the first black woman to be employed by the BBC.

[28] Great Britain. Colonial Office, *Annual Report on Nigeria* (HM Stationery Office, 1949) 66.
[29] Bonny Ibhawoh, *Imperial Justice, Africans in Empire's Court* (Oxford University Press, 2013) 44.
[30] ibid 40.
[31] Atul Kohli, *Imperialism and the Developing World How Britain and the United States Shaped the Global Periphery* (Oxford University Press, 2020) 185.
[32] Ibhawoh, n 29, 41.
[33] ibid 42.
[34] ibid 41.
[35] Caroline Bressey, *New Geographies of Race and Racism* (Taylor and Francis, 2016) 31–32.
[36] Eve Rosenhaft and Robbie John Macvicar Aitken (eds), *Africa in Europe, Studies in Transnational Practice in the Long Twentieth Century* (Liverpool University Press, 2013) 76.
[37] Helena Normanton, 'Teaching a Child Race' *Child Education Journal* (November 1926).
[38] Peter Fryer, *Staying Power, The History of Black People in Britain* (Pluto Press, 1984) 327.
[39] Bressey, n 35, 32.
[40] Colin Chambers, *Black and Asian Theatre In Britain, A History* (Taylor and Francis, 2020).

The Guardian commented on Thomas's sheer beauty as she walked across the stage in an orange dress. While the play failed to make money, it brought home to the British public that the Africans could manage their own affairs.[41] In 1934, Thomas openly challenged Dame Margery Perham's 1934 lecture at the Royal Society of Arts. The only African woman to participate in the discussion, Thomas argued that Africans should be involved and consulted in the process of seeking to resolve the problem of Africa. She criticised Lord Lugard's dual mandate policy, stating that it made puppets out of traditional rulers and chiefs.[42]

On her return to Nigeria, she would have continued to suffer discrimination from living under a colonial power and discrimination by virtue of her sex. The majority of women at this time worked in agriculture, with some teaching or nursing, but they were discouraged from entering the legal profession, considered a man's job. Only one in eight women received an education in the 1930s,[43] and women from the north of Nigeria only obtained the vote in 1979.[44]

III. What Happened Next

We know nothing of Thomas's life after her marriage. Her trailblazing would have been lonely, as change was slow. It was not until 1947 that Mrs Renner (Modupe Alakija) became the second female lawyer in Nigeria. From 1949 to 1960, another 18 women would join them as women lawyers, compared to over 300 male lawyers.[45] Modupe Omo-Eboh, called to the Bar at Lincoln's Inn, went on to become the first female judge in Nigeria when she was appointed a Judge of the High Court in Nigeria in 1969.[46] By 2015 there were just 10 senior women judges.[47] There has only been one woman Nigerian Bar Association President, and of 475 Senior Advocates, approximately 20 are women.[48] Women lawyers in Nigeria, like women in the UK, continue to suffer from discrimination both in and out of the courtroom.[49]

[41] ibid.

[42] Helen Tilley, *Africa as a Living Laboratory, Empire, Development, and the Problem of Scientific Knowledge, 1870–1950* (University of Chicago Press, 2011) 289.

[43] Amy Cassedy et al (eds), *Women and Work: A Handbook* (Taylor and Francis, 2013) 500.

[44] Epiphany Azinge, 'The Right to Vote in Nigeria: A Critical Commentary on the Open Ballot System' (1994) 38(2) *Journal of African Law* 173.

[45] Henry and Evarista, n 9, 2.

[46] Gretchen Bauer and Josephine Dawuni, *Gender, and the Judiciary in Africa, From Obscurity to Parity?* (Taylor and Francis, 2015) 69.

[47] ibid.

[48] Jennifer Ugwu, 'Women lawyering in a man's world' *The Guardian* (29 May 2018); Josephine Jarpa Dawuni and Hon Akua Kuenyehia (eds), *International Courts and the African Woman Judge, Unveiled Narratives* (Routledge, 2019).

[49] Ugwu, n 48.

IV. Significance

The significance of Thomas's call to the Bar cannot be overestimated. Empire and colonial rule deprived most Africans of educational and professional advantages. They also encouraged negative attitudes and stereotypes about Africans. Her call broke down some barriers and stereotypes. However, she needed the help of enabling men to achieve this: her father (by his encouragement and the investment of his wealth) and her brother (by his offer of a seat in his chambers). Her story demonstrates how important wealth, networks and connections are to success in the practise of law.

Thomas is an important figure for diversity. Her life demonstrates that Africans have a long tradition at the Bar of England and Wales. By practising as a barrister and sitting as a magistrate, she broke the mould in England, Nigeria and Sierra Leone. This engagement with her history gives context to the discrimination faced by Africans then and now. However, it enables us to go beyond narratives of discrimination and slavery, showing achievement, success and trailblazing. Her life also shows us the value and power of education.

Thomas's story speaks to processes that discriminated against her then and now: why did it take a West African woman a decade longer to be called to the Bar than other women from British colonies, such as Cornelia Sorabji and sisters BH and BT Lim?[50] Why did it take so long for African women to follow in the footsteps of their fellow men, who had been joining Inns of Courts from the 1840s?[51] What was it that offended the establishment about African women? Why has Thomas's story not been fully recorded? What processes are still in place that discriminate against African women? Why has change been so slow?

Further Reading

- Gretchen Bauer and Josephine Dawuni, *Gender, and the Judiciary in Africa, From Obscurity to Parity?* (Taylor and Francis, 2015).
- AN Henry and AF Evarista, 'The Emergence and History of the "Gentlewomen of the Bar" into the Legal Profession in the South West Geopolitical Zone of Nigeria' (2017) 8(1) *Arts and Social Sciences Journal* 3.
- Emeka Keazor, 'Notable Nigerians: Stella Thomas' NSIBIDI Institute (4 November 2014).

[50] See further Patrick Polden, 'Portia's progress: women at the Bar in England, 1919–1939' (2005) 12(3) *International Journal of the Legal Profession* 293, 295–97.

[51] For example, Edward Cragg Haynes joined Middle Temple in 1842, Thomas Morris Chester was called at Middle Temple in 1870 and Christian Frederick Coles joined Inner Temple in 1883.

28

Law Reform (Married Women and Tortfeasors) Act 1935

JOANNE CONAGHAN

The Law Reform (Married Women and Tortfeasors) Act 1935 is well known among tort lawyers for abolishing the common law rule denying one tortfeasor the right to claim a contribution to damages from another. However, it is equally important for addressing the legal capacities and liabilities of married women. The Act clarified the law relating to married women's capacity to sue and be sued. In abolishing the liability of husbands for torts committed by their wives, the Act might be seen to be as much a legal victory for men as for women, and indeed, to a considerable extent, it was men's actions that drove this element of reform. Nevertheless, in taking yet a further step in the direction of formal equality between men and women under the law, the Act is rightly regarded as a landmark for women's rights.

I. Context

That husbands could be sued for civil wrongs committed by their wives was one of many consequences that flowed from the legal doctrine of coverture, also known as the 'doctrine of unity'. Thought to be a Norman import, coverture (from the Old French *couvert*, to cover) expressed the notion that, on marriage, a woman's legal identity became absorbed in that of her husband:

> By marriage, the husband and wife are one person in law: … the very being or legal existence of the woman is suspended during the marriage, or at least is incorporated and consolidated into that of the husband: under whose wing, protection, and cover she performs every thing.[1]

Practically speaking, coverture was the legal means by which a husband's authority over his wife was conferred. Moreover, it inflicted a host of legal incapacities

[1] David Lemmings (ed), *The Oxford Edition of Blackstone's Commentaries on the Law of England* (Oxford University Press, 2016) 1.15.430.

and disabilities on married women. At common law, and subject to any equitable settlements set up on her behalf, all the property a woman owned at the time of her marriage became her husband's, along with any subsequent property acquired by her. A wife did not even have the right to dispose of her own earnings. Her ability to make contracts or to sue or be sued in tort was entirely dependent upon joining her husband to the action, the wife having no procedural existence of her own. Towards the end of the nineteenth century, some of the worst effects of coverture were mitigated through the enactment of the Married Women's Property Acts (1870, 1882, 1893).[2] These statutes allowed a married woman to keep her own earnings and property, and to have the right to sue and be sued in relation to this 'separate property',[3] without the need to join her husband as a plaintiff or defendant. However, elements of the doctrine of coverture itself remained, successive legislative interventions addressing its effects in piecemeal, grudging fashion.

Among the many areas of legal doubt and uncertainty arose the question of whether a husband's liability for his wife's torts had survived the passing of the Married Women's Property Act (MWPA) 1882. According to section 1(2) of that Act:

> A married woman shall be capable of entering into and rendering herself liable in respect of and to the extent of her separate property on any contract, and of suing and being sued, either in contract or in tort, or otherwise, in all respects as if she were a feme sole, *and her husband need not be joined with her as plaintiff or defendant* …[4]

Four years after the Act was passed, a husband argued in court that the removal of the requirement to join him in an action against his wife extinguished his liability altogether. His argument was rejected, the court confirming that a husband could still be joined in an action against his wife, albeit now at the discretion of the plaintiff.[5]

This approach was not universally accepted. In 1900, the legal scholar T Cyprian Williams pronounced the decision to be 'of doubtful authority',[6] lamenting 'the perversely narrow spirit in which the Married Women's Property Act 1882 has been interpreted'.[7] In a subsequent Court of Appeal decision in 1909, Fletcher Moulton LJ dissented from a majority decision to follow the position adopted in previous cases.[8] Both Cyprian Williams and Fletcher Moulton LJ stressed the

[2] See further Andy Hayward, 'Married Women's Property Act 1882 in Erika Rackley and Rosemary Auchmuty (eds) *Women's Legal Landmarks: Celebrating the History of Women and Law in the UK and Ireland* (Hart Publishing, 2019) 73.

[3] The term 'separate property' was created by the Married Women's Property Act (MWPA) 1882, s 2, to denote any property a wife brought to or acquired during the marriage.

[4] MWPA 1882, s 1(2) (emphasis added).

[5] *Seroka v Kattenburg* (1886) 7 QBD 177, subsequently approved by the Court of Appeal in *Earle v Kingscote* [1900] 2 Ch 585.

[6] T Cyprian Williams, 'A Husband's Liability for his Wife's Torts' (1900) 16(2) *Law Quarterly Review* 191.

[7] ibid 193.

[8] *Cuenod v Leslie* [1909] 1 KB 880.

procedural nature of the original rule: the joinder of the husband was required *not* because he was believed to be personally liable for his wife's wrongful acts but to ensure that the plaintiff had someone from whom to obtain redress, a wife having no assets of her own. It followed that once a wife could legally hold her own property, the rationale for joining the husband to the action no longer held.

The issue continued to be debated in legal circles throughout the early decades of the twentieth century. While lawyers focused on narrow legal technicalities, feminist organisations raised broader issues of principle, including women's equality and freedom to participate fully in civil and political life. By the 1920s, a range of groups had sprung up to advance feminist concerns beyond the achievement of the vote and entry into the professions. Although these groups had their differences,[9] they were in broad agreement about the need to erase the effects of coverture from English law.

II. The Landmark

In 1925, *Edwards v Porter*, a case concerning a husband's liability for his wife's torts, came before the House of Lords for the first time since the enactment of the Married Women's Property Acts. By a bare majority, their Lordships upheld the continued existence of a husband's liability.[10] The decision attracted immediate political attention: Lord Danesfort, an advocate for law reform, put a question to the parliamentary House of Lords, asking whether 'in view of the wide legislative changes … made in recent years in the status and rights of married women', a select committee could be appointed to reconsider the matter.[11] The drafting of a Married Women's Torts Bill swiftly followed, and managed to reach its second reading before being dropped in late 1925 in the face of competing parliamentary business. The same Bill was introduced in 1930 but, again, lost out to other issues.

Meanwhile, a broader concern about the difficulties associated with getting practical law-reform measures to the forefront of parliamentary business led to the appointment in early 1934 of a Law Revision Committee (LRC) under the auspices of the Lord Chancellor's Office.[12] A precursor of our modern-day Law Commission, the LRC was tasked, among other things, with revisiting the question of a husband's liability for his wife's torts. In late 1934, the LRC produced a report recommending the abolition of husbands' liability, while also addressing some other anomalies in the law governing married women's property status and legal capacity.[13] Its recommendations were broadly welcomed. An editorial

[9] For example, see **'Formation of the Six Point Group'**; and the **'Formation of the Married Women's Association, 1938'**.

[10] *Edwards v Porter* [1925] AC 1.

[11] *The Times* (7 May 1925) 8.

[12] On the genesis and operation of the LRC, see generally Paul Mitchell, *A History of Tort Law 1900–1950* (Cambridge University Press, 2015).

[13] LRC, *Fourth Interim Report* (Cmd 4770, 1934).

in *The Times* in December 1934 hailed the report for its 'bold and important reforms', describing them as 'simple, logical and in accordance with the equalitarian spirit of the age'.[14]

It is true that conventional, male-centred legal and political processes provided both the initial impulse and the procedural pathway for this particular legal reform. At the same time, feminist organisations were neither unaware of nor uninterested in what was developing. For example, in the aftermath of the parliamentary debate prompted by Lord Danesfort in 1925, Crystal Macmillan, barrister, suffragist and, at that time, Chair of the Married Women's (Parliamentary Bills) Committee, a sub-committee of the National Union of Societies for Equal Citizenship (NUSEC),[15] published a letter in *The Times* objecting to a suggestion, previously reported, that women were not actively seeking abolition of a husband's liability for his wife's torts. Macmillan lamented the 'piecemeal' way in which reform of the law relating to married women had proceeded to date and drew attention to a Coverture Disability (Abolition) Bill recently drafted by NUSEC, expressing the hope that it would 'soon be introduced' in Parliament.[16]

Similarly, in 1934, after the LRC report was published, Eva M Hubback, writing on behalf of the National Council for Equal Citizenship (NCEC),[17] while expressing approval of the LRC report, noted that it was proposing changes that 'my council has been advocating for years'.[18] Hubback was at pains to point out that the husbands' liability rule was not only unfair to men (the most dominant concern in public argument and commentary) but also disadvantaged women by rendering them risky partners with whom to do business, 'where there are so many methods legally open to [the married woman] to escape her obligations'.[19]

These interventions evidence the long-held concerns of many feminist organisations with the continued legal anomalies attaching to married women's status. There is also evidence that women engaged directly with the reform process. In early 1935, a deputation comprising representatives from numerous women's groups met with the Lord Chancellor, to affirm their support for the LRC report and make the case for more wide-reaching reform.[20] A consortium of women's groups also submitted a written Memorandum to the LRC, supporting the abolition of husbands' liability while drawing attention to the need to address a range of laws with the cumulative effect of disadvantaging married women in their commercial and business dealings.[21] The Memorandum included a strong call for the abolition of coverture and its legal effects, denouncing the 'survival of many anomalies and complications … which have no foundation in good sense and are indeed mere legal lumber'.[22]

[14] Editorial, *The Times* (21 December 1934) 14.
[15] Previously the National Union of Women's Suffrage Societies, renamed in 1919.
[16] C Macmillan, letter to *The Times* (8 May 1925) 15.
[17] An offshoot of the NUSEC, formed in 1928.
[18] EM Hubback, letter to *The Times* (24 December 1934) 11.
[19] ibid.
[20] *The Times* (27 February 1935) 16.
[21] Equal Rights Memorandum (ERM), LCO 2/1969, 29 June 1934. My thanks to Paul Mitchell for providing me with a copy of this report.
[22] ibid 4.

The LRC declined to take the radical path advocated in the Equal Rights Memorandum. However, Paul Mitchell speculates that the Memorandum nevertheless influenced the LRC report.[23] Mitchell also describes the process by which the Lord Chancellor set about consulting female MPs before introducing the Bill.[24] The reason for consulting women MPs, including Eleanor Rathbone, who seems to have engaged most directly with the proposals at this point, appears to have been to prevent their opposition to the Bill on the ground that the proposed reforms did not go far enough. In this, the consultation succeeded. No female MPs spoke either for or against the Bill during parliamentary debate and it passed easily through both Houses, becoming law in August 1935.

III. What Happened Next

As well as abolishing a husband's liability for his wife's torts (section 3),[25] the Law Reform (Married Women and Tortfeasors) Act 1935 made two significant additional improvements to married women's legal status. These included the effective abolition of the concept of married women's 'separate property', enabling married women to acquire, hold and dispose of property on the same basis as unmarried women (section 1), and the prohibition of any future 'restraints upon anticipation' (section 2). A restraint upon anticipation was a legal device typically imposed on a married woman's property settlement, which prevented her from touching the capital property under restraint or any future income from it. The alleged purpose of such devices was to stop husbands from forcing their wives to give up property settled on them, but, as Rosemary Auchmuty has observed, it was also a technique which ensured that family property remained largely intact for the benefit of future heirs.[26] The power to impose restraints upon anticipation on married women's property settlements had been unaffected by the MWPA 1882 Act, notwithstanding that their use undermined the purported purpose of that Act, which was to give married women more control over their own property. While section 2 of the 1935 Act prohibited the creation of any new restraints upon anticipation, to the dismay of those advocating more wholesale reform, existing restraints upon anticipation were permitted to remain in place. This was notwithstanding representations from female MPs and feminist organisations. The Permanent Secretary to the Lord Chancellor's Office, Sir Claud Schuster, recorded that the lack of retrospectivity in relation to restraints upon anticipation met with 'some not very forcible criticism' from women MPs consulted on the contents of the Bill.[27] The tone of the

[23] Mitchell, n 12, 295.

[24] ibid 296–300.

[25] Section 3 abolished a husband's liability for his wife's torts, whether before or after marriage, as well as 'in respect of any contract entered into or debt or obligation incurred by her before the marriage'.

[26] Rosemary Auchmuty, 'Married Women's (Restraint upon Anticipation Act) 1949' in Rackley and Auchmuty (eds), n 2, 241.

[27] LCO 2/1977, Letter from Schuster to Lord Hanworth MR dated 20 February 1935, cited by Mitchell, n 12, 297.

representatives who met with the Lord Chancellor in early 1935 was certainly more forceful. *The Times* reports that the deputation pressed hard for the abolition of all restraints upon anticipation, including those already in existence, 'otherwise such restraints would continue to operate into the twenty-first century'.[28] In fact, existing restraints upon anticipation were not abolished until 1949, after the end of the Second World War.[29]

The abolition of a husband's liability for his wife's torts met with less controversy, even to the extent of being held to apply retrospectively to torts committed before the Act came into force.[30] Nevertheless, England (and Wales) was no legal frontrunner on this issue. The High Court of Australia had jettisoned the liability rule as early as 1909[31] in a judgment considered but not followed by the House of Lords in *Edwards*. Nor did the 1935 Act herald the arrival of full sexual equality in tort law. Many aspects of coverture, including legal limits on the ability of husbands and wives to bring tort actions against one another, continued for some decades.[32] Moreover, the traditional 'domestic' torts, such as enticement, harbouring and loss of consortium, which provided husbands but not wives with a remedy for 'interferences' in family relations, were not abolished until the late twentieth century.[33] Indeed, it was not until 1981,[34] in a case in which a husband and wife were sued for civil conspiracy and, by way of defence, argued they could not legally conspire because they constituted one person in law, that an English court finally and firmly consigned the doctrine of coverture to the annals of legal history.

IV. Significance

It might be said that the 1935 Act is of no broader significance than as another step in the direction towards full legal equality in English law between women and men. That, however, would be to underestimate its symbolic as well as practical importance. This reform, notwithstanding its justice and good sense, was a long

[28] *The Times* (27 February 1935) 16.

[29] Auchmuty, n 26.

[30] In *Barber v Pigden* (1937) 1 KB 664, the plaintiff joined a husband to a suit against his wife after the Act came into force but in relation to a tort committed prior to enactment. The suit was roundly rejected by the Court of Appeal.

[31] *Brown v Holloway* (1909) 10 CLR 880. In Ireland, the liability rule remained until the Married Women's Status Act 1957, which also abolished restraints upon anticipation. In Scotland, a husband's liability for his wife's 'debts' was not fully extinguished until the Law Reform (Husband and Wife) Act 1984.

[32] Spousal immunity in tort was eventually abolished in England and Wales in the Law Reform (Husband and Wife) Act 1962.

[33] In *Newton v Hardy* (1933) 149 LT 165, a court recognised the possibility that a wife might have an action where her husband was 'enticed' away from her. By contrast, in *Best v Fox* [1952] AC 716, the House of Lords declined to extend the action for loss of consortium to wives. The actions for enticement, seduction and harbouring were abolished by the Law Reform (Miscellaneous Provisions) Act 1970. Loss of consortium was abolished by the Administration of Justice Act 1982.

[34] *Midland Bank Trust Co Ltd and another v Green (No 3)* (1981) 2 All ER 744.

time coming. Every stage of the struggle to erase the doctrine of coverture was hard fought and won. Legal patriarchy did not go 'gentle into the good night', and indeed, even today, is still capable of emitting a recalcitrant last gasp.

Looking at the debate that the husband's liability rule generated during this period, it becomes clear that, as with most law-reform initiatives, and particularly those with a gendered component, different concerns mobilised different sets of actors. First, there was concern about the (in)justice of the liability rule. This, in the main, came from men, who saw the continued legal imposition of responsibility on husbands for their wives' torts as unfair to them. Sometimes, this produced sexist and misogynistic commentary in public discourse. The position of wives was frequently analogised to that of animals, to pet monkeys or rabid dogs, and not in a favourable way. For example, in his presidential address to the Law Society, reported in *The Times* in 1935, Sir Harry Pritchard commented that

> in future husbands would be able to sleep peacefully knowing that if their spouses chose to commit torts, they alone would be responsible. There would no longer be the same force in the saying that it is better to keep a dog with a savage temper than to marry a wife with a venomous tongue because he could kill the animal and could not even lock up the wife.[35]

Feminists readily acknowledged the unfairness to men,[36] but also drew attention to the injustice of the liability rule, along with the continued imposition of limitations on married women's ability to control their own property and conduct their own professional and commercial dealings, imposed upon women. The Equal Rights Memorandum (also drawing somewhat unfortunate allusions to women as animals) argued that the liability rule 'treat[s] a woman disrespectfully to make another, her husband, liable for her wrongful acts, as if she were his horse or his dog'.[37] More importantly the Memorandum stressed the economic consequences of the continued legal restrictions on married women. This was a period of feminist concern to advance women's economic independence and promote their employment, the issue of women's legal 'status' becoming harnessed to broader goals of economic and political equality. The issues here were complex and contested. For example, while most feminist organisations supported the abolition of the doctrine of coverture and its various disabling effects, women's groups were divided at this time about whether to support or oppose the continued operation of protective labour legislation that limited women's ability to work in factories and some other industries.[38] As always, the pursuit of sexual equality in law was neither straightforward nor necessarily to women's immediate advantage. Nevertheless, reflecting

[35] *The Times* (25 September 1935) 6. This comment is approvingly reproduced by pioneering tort scholar, Percy Winfield, in PH Winfield, 'The Law of Tort, 1885–1935' (1935) 51 *Law Quarterly Review* 249, 251.

[36] See Macmillan, n 16.

[37] ERM, n 21, 1.

[38] See generally Olive Banks, *Faces of Feminism: A Study of Feminism as a Social Movement* (Blackwell, 1986).

on the enactment of the Law Reform (Married Women and Tortfeasors) Act 1935 provides an opportunity to appreciate the hard choices and uphill battles that our feminist legal pioneers made and fought on our collective behalf.

Further Reading

- Paul Mitchell, *A History of Tort Law 1900–1950* (Cambridge University Press, 2015).

29

Matrimonial Causes Act 1937

PENELOPE RUSSELL

The Matrimonial Causes Act 1937 extended the grounds for divorce so that both women and men could end their marriage on the basis of desertion or cruelty, in addition to the existing single ground of adultery. Section 2 provided that a petition for divorce could be presented to the High Court by either the husband or the wife on one or more of four grounds: that the respondent since the celebration of the marriage had committed adultery; that they had deserted the petitioner without cause for a period of at least three years; that they had treated the petitioner with cruelty; or that they were incurably of unsound mind.[1] Although the reform did not bring about divorce by consent, the expansion of the grounds from one to four meant that fewer women and men were locked in loveless marriages and were now able to seek a divorce.

I. Context

Prior to the 1937 Act, divorce law in England and Wales was governed by the provisions of the Matrimonial Causes Act 1857, as amended by the Matrimonial Causes Act 1923. Under these Acts, there was only one ground for divorce, namely adultery, though before 1923 women had to prove an additional aggravating offence; after 1923, both women and men could rely on adultery alone.[2] However, the restriction to a single-fault ground for divorce caused hardship to separated couples, as it continued to be difficult to formalise new unions where adultery was not the reason for the ending of the relationship. In an era when marriage was the only respectable way for heterosexual couples to live together, the aim of the 1937 Act was 'to reduce, in future at least, the numbers of permanent "separations" and the formless lives which they produce'.[3]

[1] The Act also allowed a wife to petition on the basis that her husband had, since the celebration of the marriage, been guilty of rape, sodomy or bestiality.

[2] For further information, see Penelope Russell, 'Matrimonial Causes Act 1923' in Erika Rackley and Rosemary Auchmuty (eds), *Women's Legal Landmarks: Celebrating the History of Women and Law in the UK and Ireland* (Hart Publishing, 2019) 189.

[3] AP Herbert, *The Ayes Have It* (Methuen & Co Ltd, 1937) 137.

The principal campaigner for divorce reform was May Seaton-Tiedeman, who was the honorary secretary of the Divorce Law Reform Union (DLRU), the most important pressure group working for reform at that time.[4] When debating divorce reform 30 years later, Lord Chorley described her as 'a woman of tremendous dynamism and drive … who gave up the whole of her spare time and energies and carried the banner of this movement up and down the country in the most selfless and tireless way'.[5] Seaton-Tiedeman spoke at between 30 and 40 public meetings a year, wrote to the press and lobbied Parliament to bring about divorce reform.[6] She presented a case study to the Prime Minister in 1924,

> which she said was typical of thousands of cases that come to [the DLRU in which] … a woman asked if she could get a divorce from her husband, and obtain the custody of her two children.[7] She is 33, her husband has not co-habited with her since the birth of the second child, telling her that he has no further use for women, and boasting of his friendships with young men, but defying her to prove anything … Her health is breaking under this abominable cruelty …[8]

In 1935, a letter was published in the *Daily Mirror*, written by 'a victim', which said:

> For nearly thirteen years I, with my child, have been obliged to live apart from my husband. I have suffered degradation and embarrassment in abortive efforts to free myself from an impossible and ambiguous position. A normal, passionate and not unattractive woman, I have lived a lonely, unnatural and difficult life; and thanks to our iniquitous divorce laws, I must perforce continue to do so.[9]

Although a divorce hearing only took three minutes,[10] the courts imposed strict requirements for the proof of adultery, thus encouraging couples to collude with each other to take part in a staged 'adultery' known as a 'hotel bill case'. In these situations,

> a woman was hired for a free trip for a week-end to an expensive seaside hotel, with no duties to perform except to be seen in bed with the husband for a few minutes before breakfast, having spent the night either drinking and playing cards or sleeping in separate beds.[11]

The divorcing couple would pay for the services of the woman and private detective and the witness testimony of a chambermaid and hotel manager.[12] Thus divorce was possible, but only if both parties cooperated and if 'one were wealthy

[4] CA Moyse, 'Marriage and divorce law reform in England and Wales, 1909–37' (DPhil Thesis, University of Cambridge, 1996) 48.

[5] HL Deb 30 June 1969, vol 303, col 420.

[6] Moyse, n 4, 62.

[7] See further **'Guardianship of Infants Act 1925'**.

[8] Adam Macqueen, *The Prime Minister's Ironing Board and Other State Secrets: True Stories from the Government Archives* (Little Brown, 2013) 247.

[9] A Victim, 'Divorce Laws' *The Daily Mirror* (24 October 1935) 11.

[10] 'Speedy Divorces', *Derby Evening Telegraph* (18 March 1935) 8.

[11] Lawrence Stone, *Road to Divorce* (Oxford University Press, 1990) 397.

[12] C Langhamer, 'Adultery in Post-War England' (2006) 1 *History Workshop Journal* 101.

enough to pay the costs of hotel rooms, private detectives, witnesses' corroborative evidence, and legal and court fees'.[13] This meant that divorce was out of reach for most people.

Barrister Helena Normanton spoke at the 1934 conference of the National Council of Women to plead for divorce reform. She observed that

> in many of the cases … where divorce was impossible, one or both of the separated parties entered into some second domestic arrangement which was irregular in the eye of the law, though these unfortunate people would gladly regularise their position if the law permitted them to do so.[14]

Her resolution for reform was opposed by the Mothers' Union, the largest women's group in this period with over 500,000 members.[15] It sought to uphold Christian values such as the sanctity of marriage, believing that the interests of women and children were best served by permanent, monogamous marriage.[16]

In 1934, AP Herbert published a satirical novel entitled *Holy Deadlock*, which turned on the efforts of an imaginary husband and wife, John and Mary Adam, to seek a divorce, since they have found themselves incompatible and have met new partners whom they wish to marry. In the novel, John agrees to provide Mary with the necessary evidence for a divorce by taking part in a hotel bill case but, despite doing so twice, is ultimately unsuccessful because of the judge's suspicions about collusion. At the end of the novel, solicitor Mr Boom summarises the outcome of the divorce proceedings as follows:

> Two or three truthful people have been compelled to tell lies … Three decent people have been compelled to behave indecently … One chaste woman has been compelled to commit adultery. Four people have been prevented from marrying the person of their choice, and one man has lost his job.[17]

The novel was hugely popular, selling 90,000 copies.[18] It was mentioned in the House of Commons in 1934, when the Attorney-General was asked whether he proposed to take any action following the publication of the novel, in which the 'judges and courts, and the legal code which they administer in matrimonial causes, are held up to public ridicule and contempt'.[19] Herbert commented in a later edition of the book that it 'had softened the climate of public opinion in which Members of Parliament have their being, and so made it easier for many to support, or accept, a reform which had always been considered politically perilous'.[20] Evelyn Waugh's *A Handful of Dust*, also published in 1934, further poked fun at the absurdities of the divorce law. As Henry Kha has commented, 'Waugh and Herbert exposed the

[13] Colin Gibson, *Dissolving Wedlock* (Routledge, 1994) 97.
[14] 'Women Urge Law Reform' *The Leeds Mercury* (4 October 1934) 3.
[15] N Woods, President of the Mothers' Union, *The Times* (26 November 1936) 12.
[16] Moyse, n 4, 81, 98.
[17] AP Herbert, *Holy Deadlock* (Penguin Books, 1955) 315.
[18] Reginald Pound, *AP Herbert: A Biography* (Michael Joseph Ltd, 1976) 116.
[19] HC Deb 4 June 1934, vol 290, col 566.
[20] Herbert, n 17, 7.

impracticality and incoherence of upholding a Victorian law with societal values that had moved on by the 1930s'.[21]

Society had undoubtedly become more sympathetic towards divorce reform since the First World War. Viscount Dawson argued, in the parliamentary debates in 1937:

> With a changed sense of values, has not the view steadily progressed during the last twenty-five years that when the main purposes of marriage have been frustrated – frustrated beyond repair – that marriage ceases to have any spiritual meaning or any spiritual existence? Where the kernel of marriage has been lost, the tendency of the present age is to throw away the husk – and can we say that it is wrong?[22]

In the 1920s and 1930s, there was growing awareness of the unfairness of the law of divorce, following the sensationalistic reporting of the facts of the divorce case *Russell v Russell*,[23] which involved members of the aristocracy making allegations of rape, adultery and virgin birth. Historian Lucy Bland has written that the case involved 'not only sex, but also aristocrats behaving badly, court-room drama, sensation, revelation – everything in fact that sold newspapers'.[24] Even the Church of England began softening its attitudes towards divorce. In June 1935, the Convocations of Canterbury and York declared that the Church was ready to consider some proposals for the amendment of the divorce grounds, as it recognised that divorce reform was 'demanded by the circumstances of the day'.[25]

II. The Landmark

A year after the publication of *Holy Deadlock*, Herbert was elected as an independent MP for Oxford University on a ticket of divorce reform.[26] Three months later he presented a Private Member's Bill, based on the proposals in the majority report of the 1912 Royal Commission,[27] to expand the divorce grounds beyond adultery. Initially, Herbert was unsuccessful in the ballot for time for Private Members' Bills, but he managed to persuade a fellow MP, Rupert de la Bere, to present the Bill in the next session in 1936.[28] To bring about the passage of the Bill, he also relied upon the Government's 'stance of benevolent neutrality'.[29] Although the Coalition Government was not prepared to advance a reform that was considered a matter

[21] Henry Kha, 'The Spectacle of Divorce Law in Evelyn Waugh's *A Handful of Dust* and AP Herbert's *Holy Deadlock*' (2018) 30(2) *Law & Literature* 267, 281.
[22] HL Deb 28 June 1937, vol 105, col 825.
[23] *Russell v Russell* [1924] AC 687.
[24] L Bland, *Modern Women on Trial* (Manchester University Press, 2013) 176.
[25] 'Question of Divorce' *The Times* (7 June 1935) 18.
[26] Herbert, n 3, 11.
[27] *Report of the Royal Commission on Divorce and Matrimonial Causes* (Cd 6478, 1912).
[28] Herbert, n 3, 85.
[29] Sharon Redmayne, 'The Matrimonial Causes Act 1937: A Lesson in Art of Compromise' (1993) 13(2) *Oxford Journal of Legal Studies* 183, 186.

of private conscience, Prime Minister Stanley Baldwin agreed in Parliament, when prompted by Herbert, to consider supporting the Bill, provided it was 'non-controversial'.[30]

Despite changing social attitudes, the Bill still faced opposition from Anglican and Catholic MPs, as well as campaigning groups. According to Herbert, in his account of the passage of the Bill, the Mother's Union began a 'massive postal bombardment of members to block the reform'.[31] However, at the time of the second reading of the Bill, a letter was published in *The Times* urging the Government to support the Bill, signed by a consortium of women's groups: the National Council for Equal Citizenship, the National Council of Women of Great Britain, the Women's Cooperative Guild and the Women's Liberal Foundation.[32] The letter stated that divorce reform would 'enhance public respect for the institution of marriage' and 'discourage extra-marital relationships'. Mavis Tate MP spoke in support of the Bill at its second reading, expressing concern about the 'stigma of illegitimacy' and decrying the fact that 'adults should be prevented from bringing children into the world because they are legally tied to partners who are in prison or in an asylum'.[33]

Initially, Herbert had included within the Bill a provision abolishing decree nisi in order to avoid the six-month delay in the grant of divorce when the King's Proctor (an official of the Crown) might investigate allegations of collusion between the parties and possibly rescind the decree. This process was very unpopular: the founder of the DLRU, Edmund Haynes, had written in 1921 that 'the official activities of the King's Proctor are not merely degrading, un-English, and anti-social, but also expensive at a time when economy is or ought to be the order of the day'.[34] However, under pressure, Alan Herbert agreed to drop the provision for the abolition of decree nisi so that the Bill could proceed.[35]

In addition, at the committee stage, Herbert accepted an amendment that would impose upon the courts a duty to dismiss a divorce petition if not satisfied that there had been no collusion between the parties.[36] He agreed to this amendment because he wanted the support of vocal opponent MP, William Spens, in the passage of the Bill,[37] and thereafter Spens did indeed become a supporter of the Bill.[38] Herbert was aware that such compromises were needed in order to assuage fears about the sanctity of marriage prompted by the abdication crisis, which was at its peak during the committee stage.[39] After the final reading of the Bill in the

[30] HC Deb 20 May 1936, vol 312, col 1191.
[31] Herbert, n 3, 146.
[32] 'The Marriage Bill' *The Times* (20 November 1936) 12.
[33] HC Deb 20 November 1936, vol 317, col 2109.
[34] ESP Haynes, 'Lord Gorell's Matrimonial Causes Bill' (May 1921) *The English Review* 459, 462.
[35] Redmayne, n 29, 183, 193.
[36] Matrimonial Causes Act 1937, s 4.
[37] Herbert, n 3, 131.
[38] HC Deb 16 April 1937, vol 322, col 1380.
[39] Stephen Cretney, 'The King and the King's Proctor: the abdication crisis and the divorce laws 1936–1937' (2000) 116 *Law Quarterly Review* 583, 585.

House of Commons in July 1937, the expansion of the divorce grounds became law and Herbert was congratulated on having passed an Act 'of major importance full of difficulties and rich in controversy'.[40] After the Act received Royal Assent, the Chairman of the DLRU wrote to *The Times*, noting that although Herbert had received his due tribute, there was 'a strange silence of many newspapers on the long sustained work of May Seaton-Tiedeman':

> For 25 years, in season and out of season, by lectures and debates in many places (nearly every Sunday she has advocated her case in Hyde Park), by correspondence in the Press and by innumerable interviews, Mrs Seaton-Tiedeman has worked for divorce reform, sparing neither her health nor her purse.

Without her, the letter concluded, 'Mr Herbert's Bill might very well have miscarried'.[41]

III. What Happened Next

The Herbert Act (as it became known)[42] received Royal Assent on 30 July 1937 and came into effect on 1 January 1938. It remained in force for more than 30 years, until the Divorce Reform Act 1969 made provision for divorce by consent (though fault or long separation still needed to be evidenced).[43] The Divorce Reform Act, though supported by equality feminists, was opposed by others who feared the economic consequences of easier divorce on wives who depended on their husbands for economic support. Many separated wives had refused to divorce their husbands because by so doing they would lose their entitlement to their husbands' support and benefits. In consequence, the Matrimonial Proceedings and Property Act 1970 was enacted (and subsequently consolidated with the Divorce Reform Act in the Matrimonial Causes Act 1973) to allow the reallocation of property between former spouses on divorce.

No-fault divorce was finally enacted in the Divorce, Dissolution and Separation Act 2020, which came into force on 6 April 2022.

IV. Significance

This landmark statute made it easier for more of those in unhappy unions to seek a divorce. Women were no longer reliant on the cooperation of their husbands to admit adultery, because they now had alternative grounds available to them, although admittedly the liberalisation of divorce grounds also meant

[40] HC Deb 23 July 1937, vol 326, col 2632.
[41] Mr AD Howell Smith, 'Divorce Law Reform' *The Times* (4 August 1937) 8.
[42] Stephen Cretney, *Family Law in the Twentieth Century* (Oxford University Press, 2005) 251.
[43] Divorce Reform Act 1969, s 2.

that more women were exposed to the stigma of divorce. In the first two years after the enactment, the number of divorces jumped from 4,900 in 1937 to 8,200 in 1939.[44] However, the long-term impact of the statute is difficult to assess until after the end of the Second World War, at which time more than half of divorces started by women petitioners were based on the new grounds of desertion and cruelty,[45] showing the value of these alternative grounds for those women seeking divorce.

Further Reading

- AP Herbert, *Holy Deadlock* (Penguin Books, 1955).
- Henry Kha, 'The Spectacle of Divorce Law in Evelyn Waugh's *A Handful of Dust* and AP Herbert's *Holy Deadlock*' (2018) 30(2) *Law & Literature* 267.
- Sharon Redmayne, 'The Matrimonial Causes Act 1937: A Lesson in Art of Compromise' (1993) 13(2) *Oxford Journal of Legal Studies* 183.

[44] Stone, n 11, 435.
[45] ibid, 441.

30

R v Bourne (1938)

LESLEY HALL

R v Bourne (1938)[1] was a landmark case for defining grounds for abortion and therefore extending its legal availability to more women. The case under scrutiny – a termination performed on a girl of 14 who had been gang-raped – was chosen to arouse humanitarian sympathy, but the surgeon, Aleck Bourne, was determined to argue it on clinical grounds of physical and mental health. Summing up for the jury from the bench, Mr Justice Macnaghten stated:

> [I]f the doctor is of opinion on reasonable grounds, on adequate knowledge, that the probable consequences of the continuance of pregnancy would indeed make the woman a physical wreck or a mental wreck, then he operates, in that honest belief, 'for the purpose only of preserving the life of the mother.'

He continued that 'The unborn child must not be destroyed except for the purpose of preserving the yet more precious life of the mother.' The jury returned a Not Guilty verdict in under an hour.

I. Context

Abortion in England and Wales in the 1930s fell (as it still does) under section 58 of the Offences Against the Person Act (OAPA) 1861:

> [W]hosoever, with Intent to procure the Miscarriage of any Woman, whether she be or be not with Child, shall unlawfully administer to her or cause to be taken by her any Poison or other noxious Thing, or shall unlawfully use any Instrument or other Means whatsoever with the like Intent, shall be guilty of Felony.

Doctors had argued ever since that 'unlawfully' predicated 'lawful' conditions, that is undertaken by a registered medical professional, under which miscarriage might be procured. In 1929, the Infant Life (Preservation) Act, section 1 of which provided that

[1] *R v Bourne* [1938] 3 All ER 615.

> no person shall be found guilty of an offence under this section unless it is proved that the act which caused the death of the child was not done in good faith for the purpose only of preserving the life of the mother …

also seemed to suggest licit medical intervention. Textbooks of obstetrics, midwifery and forensic medicine strongly implied that abortion was 'legitimate treatment under certain circumstances',[2] and not criminal if 'performed by a registered medical practitioner and on absolutely justifiable grounds'.[3] Doctors were, however, exhorted as to the necessity of obtaining a second opinion in writing.[4]

Abortion was therefore, discreetly, available to better-off women able to consult élite private practitioners. This contrasted with the suffering created by self-induced and backstreet abortion among working women.[5] In 1934, the British Medical Association (BMA), representing less privileged echelons of the profession, set up a committee on the medico-legal aspects of abortion, publishing its report, after a good deal of controversy, in 1936. It concluded that while 'the law [was] in fact adaptable in practice', it was hardly fair to 'place upon the doctor the responsibility of interpreting public opinion'.[6]

Meanwhile, women were making the subject a topic of public discussion rather than internalist professional discourse. By 1930, the campaign to make birth control acceptable had achieved significant gains. A vanguard therefore advanced to campaigning to legalise abortion, basing their arguments on the ravages of self-induced and backstreet abortion.[7] On 3 November 1932, a meeting to discuss 'the present laws concerning abortion' was organised by the British Section of the World League for Sexual Reform.[8] In 1934, the annual conference of the Women's Cooperative Guild (a working-class organisation) voted by an overwhelming majority for a resolution in favour of legalising abortion and providing amnesty for convicted abortionists.[9] Similar resolutions were passed by the National Council of Women in 1935[10] and the National Council for Equal Citizenship in 1936.[11]

The subject was also given visibility in a flurry of novels (it had previously rarely, or evasively, been addressed in fiction): Jean Rhys's *Voyage in the Dark*

[2] *The Queen Charlotte's Text-Book of Obstetrics* (3rd edn, J & A Churchill, 1933) 484.

[3] Comyns Berkeley, JS Fairbairn and Clifford White (eds), *Midwifery by Ten Teachers under the Direction of Clifford White* (5th edn, Edward Arnold & Co, 1935) 693.

[4] *The Queen Charlotte's Text-Book of Obstetrics*, n 1.

[5] Alfred Swaine Taylor, *A Manual of Medical Jurisprudence* (J & A Churchill, 1879) 502–22.

[6] British Medical Association, *Report of Committee on Medical Aspects of Abortion* (BMA, 1936) paras 17–21, 9–11.

[7] Stephen Brooke, *Sexual Politics: Sexuality, Family Planning and the British Left from the 1880s to the Present Day* (Oxford University Press, 2011) 92–113.

[8] Ruby Lockie (Norman Haire's secretary) to Dora Russell, 20 October 1932 (Dora Russell papers, file 412 International Institute of Social History, Amsterdam [IISH]); 'World League for Sexual Reform' (1932) 11 *The New Generation* 137; FW Stella Browne, 'Sexual Reform' *The Week-end Review* (12 November 1932) (cutting in Dora Russell papers, file 408, IISH).

[9] FW Stella Browne, 'Cooperative Women Demand Legalization of Abortion' (1934) 13 *The New Generation* 78.

[10] FW Stella Browne, 'Light at Leicester' (November 1935) 14 *The New Generation* 124.

[11] FW Stella Browne, 'Abortion, Contraception and the NCEC' (1936) 3(4) *Plan: for world order and progress* 22.

and F Tennyson Jesse's *A Pin to See the Peepshow* in 1934; and a further flurry during 1935 and 1936, including Simon Blumenthal's proletarian novel *Jew Boy*, Naomi Mitchison's *We Have Been Warned*, Stevie Smith, *Novel on Yellow Paper*, Winifred Holtby, *South Riding*, Vera Brittain, *Honourable Estate*, Rosamond Lehmann, *The Weather in the Streets* and Aldous Huxley, *Eyeless in Gaza*. These covered a broad spectrum of predicaments and expedients.

Early in 1935, Dr Joan Malleson, a leading figure in the birth-control movement, organised a conference on the legalisation of abortion.[12] This resulted in the formation in 1936 of the Abortion Law Reform Association (ALRA) by a group of laywomen already active in this cause. They proposed repealing the existing law in favour of one 'freeing the medical profession from all legal restrictions except those required by medical or humanitarian considerations'.[13] An inaugural conference at Conway Hall, London[14] was followed by a campaign of lecturing to potentially sympathetic groups and coordinating letters to the press on the subject of abortion law reform.[15] In 1937, the Government set up an Inter-Departmental (Ministry of Health and the Home Office) Committee on Abortion chaired by the eminent lawyer, Norman Birkett KC. This heard extensive evidence from interested organisations and individuals.

II. The Landmark

In 1938, Malleson encountered a suitable test-case of the law. She made it known to leading gynaecological surgeon Aleck Bourne, who wanted to clarify 'great danger to health', even if there was 'no real danger to *life*', as constituting lawful grounds, and to establish the importance of mental as well as physical health.[16]

In June 1938 there was a widely-reported trial of three Troopers of the Royal Horse Guards for the gang-rape of a girl of 14. She became pregnant. Her 'respectable' working-class parents took her to Malleson. Before the case even went to trial, Malleson referred the young woman to Bourne, who examined her, with her parents present, in his private consulting room (not at the hospital, where medical students would be present). He obtained her father's written permission to operate and had the girl admitted to St Mary's Hospital for observation. Her reaction to a physically invasive examination for gonorrhoea confirmed to him that her outward calm concealed deep trauma. She was not infected – which would have contraindicated operation – and he undertook a curettage.

[12] 'Names of those invited to Dr Joan Malleson's Conference, 1935 …' ('ALRA pre-1949 material', SA/ALR/A.2/1, Abortion Law Reform Association Archives, Wellcome Library [ALRAA]). Janet Chance's chronology of abortion law reform in her scrapbook mentions '1935 Joan Malleson's meeting' but no further details (SA/ALR/B.1, ALRAA).

[13] 'Summary of discussion held at Ridgeway's, Jan 24th 1936' (ALRA Minute-book 1936–1952, SA/ALR/A.1/2/1, ALRAA).

[14] *Proceedings of a Conference on Abortion Law Reform*, 15 May 1936, 13–15 (Janet Chance's scrapbook, SA/ALR/B.1 and Dora Russell papers file 344 IISH).

[15] Minutes of executive committee meeting, 18 May 1936 (SA/ALR/A.1/2/1, ALRAA).

[16] Aleck Bourne, 'To the editor of *The Lancet*: Rex v Bourne' *The Lancet* (30 July 1938) 280.

Bourne rested his case firmly upon the clinical indications for termination. On the evening of the day he operated, Chief Inspector Bridger of the Metropolitan Police called at the hospital to warn Bourne that he would not countenance an operation on humanitarian grounds. Bourne responded that most of medicine was humanitarian, that he had already operated, and invited Bridger to arrest him. His case was that he had performed the abortion for therapeutic reasons: the physically deleterious effects on such a young woman of carrying a pregnancy to term, and the extreme mental trauma following her ordeal.[17]

The case went to the Central Criminal Court only a few weeks after the trial and conviction of the troopers there.[18] It immediately became front-page news.[19] Bourne and his defence counsel, Roland Oliver KC, defended his action on the grounds that the wording of the OAPA 1861, in invoking the term 'unlawful', implied lawful instances, and this was, implicitly, when the act was done 'by a skilled person, without any risk to the patient, for the purpose of saving her life'. Mr Justice Macnaghten concurred, and said that what was at stake was what was meant by 'preserving the life of the mother'. Macnaghten J's summing-up went on to contrast Bourne's idealism and charitable purpose with the profiteering illegal abortionists who normally came before the court. He observed that even lawyers and doctors were in some confusion about the law when it came to doctors operating in good faith to preserve the life of the mother. But in his view, 'preserving the life of the mother' was not just about life or death but whether continuing pregnancy would render her a physical or mental wreck. The 'precious life of the mother' was the priority. He confirmed that only members of the medical profession might properly perform such an operation.[20] The important point was the emphasis on the continuing quality of the woman's life and not just risk of death.

The jury (including two women) returned a Not Guilty verdict in under an hour: 'People stood up in their seats and a subdued murmur of approval ran through the court … instantly silenced by the police.'[21] At the BMA conference at Plymouth, 'delegates stood up in their places and cheered' at the news.[22]

[17] Photocopy of Bourne's deposition at the trial (GC/150/1, Bourne Abortion Trial papers, Wellcome Library).

[18] 'Three Troopers on Trial' *The Times* (28 June 1938) 11; 'Penal Servitude for Two Troopers: Crime Against A Girl' *The Times* (30 June 1938) 11.

[19] 'Summons after Operation: Challenge by Surgeon' *News Chronicle* (29 June 1938) 1; 'Surgeon Who Dared Goes to Trial. He Welcomes The Decision' *News Chronicle* (2 July 1938) 1; 'Famous Doctor: Police Action' *Daily Herald* (29 June 1938) 1; 'Surgeon's Trial: Attorney-General to Prosecute' *Daily Herald* (8 July 1938) 1; 'Surgeon's Acquittal May Start – New Move to Alter the Law of Abortion' *Birmingham Gazette* (20 July 1938) 1.

[20] 'Medico-Legal: Charge of Procuring Abortion: Rex v Bourne' (23 July 1938) *British Medical Journal* 199.

[21] 'Verdict which defines law for medical men' *The Journal* (20 July 1938) 7.

[22] 'Court Cheers for Surgeon's Acquittal' *Birmingham Gazette* (20 July 1939) 7.

III. What Happened Next

The Lancet, congratulating Bourne on his victory, suggested that, paradoxically, a less triumphant acquittal might have done more for a thorough examination of the state of the law.[23] This proved correct. The Birkett Committee finally reported in 1939. With reservations both individual and collective from members, and a dissenting Minority Report from Dorothy Thurtle of ALRA, no resolution on reforming the law was achieved.[24] Though obliged to cease operations during the war, in the 1950s ALRA lobbied Parliament for reform that would permit therapeutic abortion where pregnancy was the result of a sexual offence, for women with too many children and where the foetus showed 'abnormalities'.[25]

Private Members' Bills in 1954 and 1960 failed to progress in Parliament, but the *Bourne* judgment was nuanced by a couple of later cases, *R v Bergmann and Ferguson* in 1948 and *R v Newton and Stungo* in 1958,[26] which provided further clarification of the parameters within which a doctor might legally procure an abortion: a doctor's opinion as to the patient's state did not have to be correct, only made in good faith.[27] This went as far as most members of the medical profession wanted. Ample leeway was provided for psychiatric as well as physical indications for termination,[28] and these almost certainly came to predominate. Doctors who did not wish to have to deal with abortion did not have to do so.

By the late 1950s, abortions by qualified practitioners became much more widely affordable, provided women knew how to go about obtaining them and had the means to pay. Women who had made the rational decision to seek abortion were obliged to perform mental distress, or were coached to do so,[29] in order to obtain the psychiatrist's letter to authorise the surgeon to operate. A more covert grey area of GPs would perform abortions with somewhat less stringent legal safeguards.[30]

In practice, however, Macnaghten J's principle was heavily compromised. Backstreet operations of varying degrees of hygiene and competence and a racket in spurious 'female pills' continued.[31] Abortion provision had become – in the title of an ALRA publication authored by Alice Jenkins – a *Law for the Rich*.[32] For several

[23] Joan Ostry, née Bourne, 'Rex v Bourne 1938', 1988 (Papers relating to the Bourne case, Wellcome Library, GC/150).

[24] Ministry of Health, Home Office, *Report of the Inter-Departmental Committee on Abortion* (HMSO, 1939).

[25] Nicky Priaulx and Natalie L Jones, 'Abortion Act 1967' in Erika Rackley and Rosemary Auchmuty (eds), *Women's Legal Landmarks: Celebrating the History of Women and Law in the UK and Ireland* (Hart Publishing, 2019) 275.

[26] *R v Bergmann and Ferguson* (22 May 1948) *British Medical Journal* 1008; *R v Newton and Stungo* [1958] Crim LR 469.

[27] Paul Ferris, *The Nameless: Abortion in Britain Today* (rev edn, Penguin Books, 1967) 24–25.

[28] Barbara Brookes, *Abortion in England, 1900–1967* (Croom Helm, 1988) 142–44.

[29] Ferris, n 27, 78–79.

[30] ibid 3–8.

[31] ibid 29–58.

[32] Alice Jenkins, *Law for the Rich* (Victor Gollancz, 1960).

decades, safe abortion remained only haphazardly available via publicly-funded medical services. In the mid-1960s, Paul Ferris found that around 3,000–4,000 abortions were performed annually on the National Health Service (NHS), availability varying greatly by area. They were sometimes concealed as 'diagnostic D&C (dilation and curettage)' to protect any delicate sensibilities within the system.[33] But it is likely that possibly four or five times as many women per year were having private legal abortions in 'a comfortable industry' mainly situated in the West End of London.[34]

Perhaps due to this covert nature of abortion practice, there was no great agitation from doctors for further reform until the 1960s, when the teratogenic effects (causing malformations) of thalidomide and rubella introduced concerns not specifically covered under Macnaghten J's judgment.[35] In 1966, David Steel introduced a Medical Termination Bill that became, after amendment, the Abortion Act 1967. In requiring that two doctors must approve a termination, the Act preserved an established medical practice aimed at avoiding unpleasantness with the law and the General Medical Council and soothing ethical qualms.[36]

IV. Significance

Veteran campaigner Cicely Hamilton argued in the feminist periodical *Time and Tide* that the case had dramatically brought the issue before those who had not previously given it much, if any, thought.[37] The case, and the agitation generally of the 1930s, did reframe attitudes: the covert and euphemistic terms in which women wrote to Marie Stopes in the 1920s concerning unwanted pregnancy had become far more explicit and direct when women sought assistance from ALRA after the Second World War.[38] The topic increasingly figured as a motif in literature throughout the 1950s and 1960s,[39] and was aired in discussion programmes on radio and television.[40]

Macnaghten J's address to the jury had prioritised the 'yet more precious life of the mother'. While this had been a tacit understanding within the medical profession, it had never been explicitly stated as a judgment in law. Importantly also,

[33] Ferris, n 27, 96–106.

[34] ibid xiv.

[35] Brookes, n 28, 152. Thalidomide was a widely used drug licensed for use in the UK between 1958 and 1961, prescribed for the treatment of nausea in pregnant women. By 1960 it was apparent that it had caused thousands of severe birth defects.

[36] Lesley A Hall, Memorandum submitted to the House of Commons Science and Technology Select Committee inquiry: Scientific developments relating to the Abortion Act 1967, September 2007, para 1.4.11, para 2.2.7, History and Policy at www.historyandpolicy.org/docs/abortion_act_1967.pdf [accessed 13 December 2022].

[37] Cicely Hamilton, 'Aleck Bourne's Contribution to History' *Time and Tide* (23 July 1938) 1046–47.

[38] Emma L Jones, 'Attitudes to Abortion in the Era of Reform: Evidence from the Abortion Law Reform Association Correspondence' (2011) 20 *Women's History Review* 283.

[39] See further 'Literary Abortion', an archive of references in literary texts and texts about (mainly) literary women, to women procuring abortion, at www.lesleyahall.net/abortion.htm [accessed 23 January 2023].

[40] Brookes, n 28, 149.

emphasis was laid on the *quality* of the mother's life – not just a question of survival but whether continuing the pregnancy would render her a 'physical or mental wreck'. The principle was articulated overtly, foregrounding the interest of the woman.

While without doubt *Bourne* was symbolically important, its practical impact was more uneven. Although it made safe legal surgical abortion available to a wider section of the population, this was still largely contingent upon the woman's having the necessary information and the cash to access the private 'industry'. The issue was concealed by stigma and doctorly discretion, and a more searching examination of the question was, arguably, delayed by a situation over which the medical profession was complacent.

Following the 1967 Act, a constantly increasing number of abortions were performed under the NHS, but there were considerable challenges. Provision was subject to considerable regional variation between liberal and highly restrictive interpretations of the Act, leading to the setting up by ALRA members of the British Pregnancy Advisory Service to provide low-cost abortions in non-profit clinics.[41]

Attempts to amend the Act in a more restrictive direction began in 1969 and continued throughout the 1970s. Anti-abortion activism became more organised and pursued vigorous campaigns. As early as 1971, the Conservative Government set up a Committee of Enquiry into the Act (the Lane Committee), in the belief that this would recommend restriction. In fact it achieved consensus, approving the Act as humane and necessary, while recommending improved oversight of the private sector, where clinics had been profiteering from desperate foreign women.[42]

In 1970, the first Women's Liberation Movement Conference in the UK included 'Free contraception and abortion on demand' among its four demands.[43] However, in spite of the inception of a new militant organisation, the National Abortion Campaign, in 1975,[44] pro-abortion forces were pushed into a defensive position, having to protect existing gains against attempts to erode the Act and to ensure that abortion was actually accessible. Despite significant advances such as the abortion pill, laws made in very different eras continue to control abortion in the UK in the twenty-first century.

Further Reading

- Barbara Brookes, *Abortion in England, 1900–1967* (Croom Helm, 1988).
- Paul Ferris, *The Nameless: Abortion in Britain Today* (rev edn, Penguin Books, 1967).
- Keith Hindell and Madeleine Simms, *Abortion Law Reformed* (Peter Owen, 1971).

[41] Audrey Leathard, *The Fight for Family Planning* (Macmillan, 1980) 173–74.

[42] Stephen Brooke, *Sexual Politics: Sexuality, Family Planning, and the British Left from the 1880s to the Present Day* (Oxford University Press, 2011) 200–01.

[43] Sheila Rowbotham, *A Century of Women: The History of Women in Britain and the United States* (Viking, 1997) 401–02.

[44] Leathard, n 41, 208.

31

Inheritance (Family Provision) Act 1938

RICHARD HEDLUND

The Inheritance (Family Provision) Act 1938 ('the Inheritance Act') allowed surviving spouses and qualifying children to apply to court for a discretionary payment out of an estate where they had not been left enough in the deceased's will to ensure their proper maintenance. It introduced the family provision rule into English law, a rule that remains today in the Inheritance (Provision for Family and Dependants) Act 1975, which greatly broadened its scope. Although its proponents emphatically said it was not a 'women's Bill', the Inheritance Act had a particular impact on widows and their financial security, earning its place as a women's legal landmark.

I. Context

The Inheritance Act was the product of lengthy debates on inheritances and the gendered injustices that had previously been socially and legally permitted. As Rosemary Auchmuty explains in the landmark on the **Administration of Estates Act 1925**, until that year a woman's position on intestacy was precarious: the husband's land would go to the eldest son (or shared between the daughters, in the absence of sons) and his personal wealth would be divided between the surviving wife and the children. The Administration of Estates Act changed this to place the surviving spouse first in line to inherit. However, this improvement for women only applied on an intestacy and did not apply where the husband had written a will; here, testamentary freedom still applied.

At the start of the twentieth century, freedom of testation still applied: an adult could write a will and freely dispose of their property.[1] At the time, the norm was for the husband/father to own and control the family home and wealth. The duality of private ownership and testamentary freedom meant that the husband/father

[1] Wills Act 1837, ss 3, 7, 9 – trusts, entails, and so forth, of course placed practical limitations on testamentary freedom.

could use the threat of disinheritance as a means of coercive financial control over female family members (sons were expected to go out and ensure their own financial success).[2] These threats, whether carried out or not, caused 'very real hardships' to families.[3] Josiah Wedgwood, writing in 1939, found that few testators actually left anything outside the family, though that does not necessarily account for disinheritances within the family.[4] It is difficult, perhaps impossible, to say how many families had been affected by an unjust disinheritance, though it has been suggested that the number was 'substantial' and 'considerable'.[5] It was thought, however, that once surviving wives had obtained greater protections on intestacy, it was time to do something about 'the selfish and tyrannical father who holds the dread of disinheritance over wife and children'.[6]

The essence of the family provision rule is that qualifying family members, such as a surviving spouse or a child who has been disinherited, can apply to court for a financial award out of the deceased's estate. The award is at the court's discretion, and the judge will consider all the relevant facts to determine whether an award should be made. Other common law jurisdictions had already introduced such legislative protections. New Zealand was the first to pass such a statute in 1900, directly linked to the fact that women had gained suffrage seven years earlier and had been able to highlight this injustice in political discourse, and from 1906 in the Australian States, their women likewise enfranchised, introduced similar legislation.[7]

After British women gained the vote in 1918, similar discussions on inheritance law reform emerged in England and Wales, led by various feminist groups.[8] For example, the **Six Point Group**, founded by Lady Rhondda, posited better protections for widowed mothers as one of the eponymous six points, and worked to achieve fairness in inheritances.[9] Where the Six Point Group sought full equality, other feminist groups focused on the role of women within the family, seeking better protection for mothers and wives. One such group was the National Union of Societies for Equal Citizenship (NUSEC), led between 1919 and 1928 by Eleanor Rathbone.[10] Rathbone emphasised the primacy of the family as an institution and

[2] *Banks v Goodfellow* (1869–70) LR 5 QB 549, 564 (Cockburn CJ), noting that testamentary freedom acts as an 'incentive to industry in the acquisition of wealth' for men.

[3] HL Deb 16 May 1928, vol 71, col 38.

[4] Josiah Wedgwood, *The Economics of Inheritance* (Pelican, 1939) 110.

[5] *Report from the Joint Committee on the Wills and Intestacies (Family Maintenance) Bill*, 17 June 1931, 3; Eva Hubback, 'The Inheritance Bill' *The Times* (26 April 1934) 10.

[6] HC Deb 20 February 1931, vol 248, col 1673.

[7] See, for example, Testator's Family Maintenance Act 1900 (New Zealand), discussed in Rosalind Atherton, 'New Zealand's Testator's Family Maintenance Act of 1900 – The Stouts, The Women's Movement and Political Compromise' (1990) 7 *Otago Law Review* 202.

[8] Scottish succession law is quite different and beyond the scope of this chapter.

[9] Hilda Kean, 'Searching for the past in present defeat: the construction of historical and political identity in British feminism in the 1920s and 1930s' (1994) 3 *Women's History Review* 57, 62; Viscountess Rhondda, *This Was My World* (Macmillan, 1933) 299–300.

[10] Kean, n 9, 63; Lisa Regan, 'Introduction' in Lisa Regan (ed), *Winifred Holtby, "A Woman in Her Time": Critical Essays* (Cambridge Scholars Publishing, 2010) 6.

sought legal protections for women based on 'what women want', rather than asking for equal rights just 'because it is what men have got'.[11] Once Rathbone entered Parliament in 1929 (serving between 1929 and 1946 as an Independent MP), she became one of the main champions for introducing the family provision rule, though her most lasting legacy was the introduction of child maintenance payments to mothers.[12]

The Inheritance Act falls within the second category. Its purpose was not to ensure full equality (indeed, as shown below, the Inheritance Act was rather unequal in its application) but rather fairness and justice within the family, where the work of a wife and mother was legally recognised and protected. That could explain why the preceding Bills were described as not a 'Women's Bill' by Eva Hubback[13] and not a 'feminist Bill' by Mary Agnes Hamilton;[14] the family provision rule, they said, was a social reform aimed at promoting the idea of marriage as an equal partnership. This masked the underlying purpose, to ameliorate a situation where the gendered division of labour facilitated men's exploitation of their financial power. It may be that denying that the family provision rule was a feminist reform was a rhetorical reassurance to men that this was not designed to be a threat to their ownership of family property, thus overcoming any political reluctance to support women's causes – the failure of another unrelated Private Member's Bill in the early 1930s was partly blamed on the strong female backing behind it.[15]

The male parliamentarians who opposed reform to succession law instead suggested that campaigners should focus on changing social attitudes to marriage. This included 'equality feminist' supporters like Lord Buckmaster, a former (Liberal) Lord Chancellor,[16] whose view was that

> men and women should be socially and economically equal, free and independent … and that when a woman is left a widow society ought to be so organised that she should be just as able to protect herself as a man when his wife dies.[17]

He did concede that that reality was a far way off, but that should be the focus of reform, rather than interfering with testamentary freedom, which liberal men held dear.

[11] Eleanor Rathbone, 'The Old Feminism and the New' in Eleanor Rathbone (ed), *Milestones* (Liverpool, 1929) 29; Eleanor Rathbone, *The Disinherited Family: A Plea for the Endowment of the Family* (Edward Arnold & Co, 1924) ix.

[12] Enacted in the Family Allowances Act 1945: see Lucy Vickers, 'Family Allowances Act 1945' in Erika Rackley and Rosemary Auchmuty (eds), *Women's Legal Landmarks: Celebrating the History of Women and Law in the UK and Ireland* (Hart Publishing, 2019) 227.

[13] Suffragist, academic, feminist campaigner, principal of Morley College from 1927 and co-founder of the Townswomen's Guild in 1930.

[14] Labour MP for Blackburn 1929–31.

[15] Ann Taylor Allen, 'Feminism and Eugenics in Germany and Britain, 1900–1940: A Comparative Perspective' (2000) 23 *German Studies Review* 477, 498.

[16] He had acted for Miss Bebb in *Bebb v Law Society* [1914] 1 Ch 286.

[17] HL Deb 16 May 1928, vol 71, col 50.

II. The Landmark

The first parliamentary debate regarding the family provision rule was held in 1928. The motion was moved in the House of Lords by Viscount Astor, husband of **Nancy Astor MP**. Viscount Astor argued that testamentary freedom could lead to hardship and injustice. He gave as an example husbands who left the family wealth to their mistresses, thus excluding the archetypal 'loyal and dutiful' wife and relegating her to a life of penury.[18]

Given the centrality of private ownership in English legal culture, the objections from the male parliamentarians were understandably many. They argued that testators knew best about who should benefit from their estate, which was certainly a privilege no family patriarch would wish to lose, and that the right to dispose of assets through a will was an integral part of private ownership. Furthermore, it would be impossible for judges to determine if a disinheritance was unfair; indeed, it would be bizarre to ask a judge to poke around the deceased's private life on a purely moral quest to determine if a perfectly lawful will was nonetheless unjust. Finally, the adage that 'hard cases make bad law' was argued, though, as an editorial in the *Law Quarterly Review* responded, 'hard cases are often evidence that the law is bad'.[19]

The following year, an article in support of the family provision rule was published by Eva Hubback, a former suffragist and feminist campaigner who would go on to lead the National Council for Equal Citizenship, a successor group to NUSEC. Hubback insisted that many cases 'come to light' each year of wives not being provided for in their husband's will, and that this particularly affected those caught in the middle – that is, not wealthy enough to be protected by a marriage settlement but too well-off to qualify for a pension under the **Widows', Orphans' and Old Age Contributory Pensions Act 1925**.[20] Hubback noted that this precariousness was anomalous after the Administration of Estates Act 1925 reforms to intestacy.[21] She advanced two crucial arguments: first, that it was indefensible to allow a husband, who in his lifetime was bound to maintain his wife, to renege on that through disinheritance; second, that the threat of disinheritance was a 'very powerful weapon of intimidation' that husbands and fathers could wield against their families, and the family provision rule would soften that threat.[22]

In 1931, Rathbone introduced a Private Member's Bill into the House of Commons that would, in effect, have introduced a form of forced heirship into English law.[23] Fixed-entitlement provisions favouring the surviving spouse and/or children are common in civil law jurisdictions.[24] However, the Bill did not progress

[18] ibid cols 38–39; whilst English history is teeming with men with mistresses, it is harder to ascertain how commonly mistresses inherited through the man's will, and the proponents of the family provision rule could never provide firm statistics.

[19] Editor, 'Notes' (1928) 44 *Law Quarterly Review* 267, 283.

[20] Eva Hubback, 'Unjust Wills' (1929) 125 *Fortnightly Review* 541, 542.

[21] ibid 541.

[22] ibid 543.

[23] Wills and Intestacies (Family Maintenance) Bill 1931.

[24] Consider, for example, the Spanish Civil Code, Arts 763 and 807; French Civil Code, Arts 734 and 756; German Civil Code, Art 2303.

very far. The objections, from (male) Conservative MPs, had two prongs: the first was a principled objection to the interference in personal freedom; the second was that the Bill, as written, was deemed impractical and would cause considerable challenges when it came to administer any estate where there was a surviving spouse. The first objection might have come from a position of preserving the privileges of property ownership, but the latter objection does appear valid; the terms of the Bill would probably have caused far more problems than it could ever have solved.[25]

With public support for family provision, however, Rathbone pursued that goal, declaring that the family provision rule would help end the 'scandal of unjust wills, by which loyal and blameless wives or families are left destitute through the whim or cruel spite of those from whom they naturally expected help'.[26] A family provision Private Member's Bill was introduced in the 1933–34 parliamentary session, and had a second reading, but did not progress further. A final Bill was introduced twice in the 1937–38 parliamentary session, the first moved in January 1937 by the Labour MP Walter Windsor and the second moved in November 1937 by the Liberal MP Stanley Holmes. The final Bill received Royal Assent on 13 July 1938 and came into force one year later, finally, as the *Daily Mail* noted, bringing to an end 'dead men's malice'.[27]

Compared to the law today, the Inheritance Act took a restrictive approach to those who could claim. An application could only be made against a testate estate – that is, one where a will had been made. There were four classes of applicant. The first was a surviving husband or wife, though no application could be made if they received at least two-thirds of the income of the net estate in the will. The second was an unmarried daughter or a daughter who could not maintain herself due to a mental or physical disability. The third was a minor (that is, under 21) son. The fourth was an adult son who was unable to maintain himself due to a mental or physical disability. The list clearly reflected social values and expectations of the day, perpetuating the assumption that a healthy son, once of age, should provide for himself and that a father had financial responsibility for his daughter until she married, at which point she became the responsibility of her husband.

III. What Happened Next

There were two amendments to the Inheritance Act in the 1950s: the first extending the rule to intestate estates and the second permitting former, but not yet remarried, spouses to make an application.[28] In the 1970s, the Law Commission

[25] For more context, see Richard Hedlund, 'The End to Testamentary Freedom' (2021) 41(1) *Legal Studies* 55, 65.

[26] Eleanor Rathbone, 'When this Bill becomes law you can't disinherit your family' *Daily Mail* (10 May 1938) 10.

[27] 'MPs unite to frustrate unjust wills' *Daily Mail* (30 April 1938) 11.

[28] Intestates' Estates Act 1952 (extending the rule to intestacy) and the Matrimonial Causes (Property and Maintenance) Act 1958 (extending the rule to a former, and not remarried, spouse).

recommended a wider reform of the family provision rule.[29] This was accepted by Parliament, and the Inheritance Act was replaced by the Inheritance (Provision for Family and Dependants) Act 1975. One part of the reform was to align the rights of a surviving spouse with what they might expect through divorce. Another part was to allow *all* children, regardless of age or any other status, to make an application, and to include step-children and others being financially maintained by the deceased. This made the law gender-neutral. Since 1996, cohabitants, provided they had lived with the deceased for two years immediately before the deceased died, have been able to make an application.[30] These are important developments, accommodating societal changes in the make-up of the family unit and recognising the end of the traditional nuclear family.

Today, a disinherited wife or even female cohabitant is less likely to face financial ruin if she is left outside a will, either because she has her own income to support her or, whilst it is far from perfect, can fall back on the welfare system. Nonetheless, cases of disinherited wives facing penury still arise, and the family provision rule continues to provide the protections they need. For example, in *Kaur v Singh*, a 'wife who made a full and equal contribution to the marriage' was disinherited by her husband in favour of the sons, and (without opposition) was awarded half of her husband's estate.[31]

That said, many modern claims are not made by surviving spouses but rather by children unhappy about not inheriting, a recurring feature being that their parent's estate was left by will or on intestacy to a new partner.[32] Indeed, some cases involve the reverse, with a surviving partner claiming against the children of an earlier relationship when the children have inherited rather than the partner.[33] Given the rise in divorce, remarriage and so-called 'blended' families, such disputes are perhaps not surprising. Whilst the genesis of the family provision rule was to provide better protections for surviving wives, socio-economic changes over the past century means that the current role of the family provision rule may be more focused on resolving disputes within these blended families.

IV. Significance

At a time when few women owned their own homes or had their own financial independence, the Inheritance Act provided a welcomed safety-net for those who were unjustly disinherited. Had society remained static, that safety-net would undoubtedly have played a much greater role than perhaps it has done in practice.

[29] Law Commission, *Second Report on Family Property: Family Provision on Death* (1974) Law Com No 61.
[30] Law Reform (Succession) Act 1995, s 2.
[31] *Kaur v Estate of Karnail Singh* [2023] EWHC 304 (Fam) [29] (Peel J); also consider cases like *Woolridge v Woolridge* [2016] Fam Law 451.
[32] Consider *Ilott v The Blue Cross* [2017] UKSC 17, [2017] 2 WLR 979.
[33] Consider *Re Wynford Hodge* [2018] EWHC 688 (Ch).

Just a few weeks after the Inheritance Act came into force, however, Britain entered the Second World War. After the war, the welfare state was formed, and employment for women, including married women, gradually became the norm. More recently, (shared) home ownership has become more common. Financial inequality remains today, of course. A recent study showed that only 33 per cent of single mortgage-owners were women, but that there is an overall upward trend in women at all ages owning their homes.[34] There remain, however, women for whom family provision provides a necessary safeguard. Partners who cohabit without getting married, for example, have no right to inherit on intestacy and must rely on an Inheritance Act application.[35]

The debates on the Inheritance (Family Provision) Act highlighted the plight of unjustly disinherited wives and the evils of financial coercive control that a father and husband could hold over the family. They increased public awareness and shifted the public debate regarding acceptable expectations within the family, while also challenging the norm of male ownership of the family home and control over the family wealth. They formed part of a general discourse that linked to campaigns by feminist groups, such as that of the **Married Women's Association**, to turn marriage into an equal partnership, rather than one of male dominance and female subjugation.[36]

Further Reading

- Rosalind Croucher, 'How Free is Free? Testamentary Freedom and the Battle between "Family" and "Property"' (2012) 37 *Australian Journal of Legal Philosophy* 9.
- Richard Hedlund, 'The End to Testamentary Freedom' (2021) 41(1) *Legal Studies* 55.

[34] FT Advisor, How to understand trends in women's home ownership (8 September 2021) at www.ftadviser.com/ftadviser-focus/2021/09/08/how-to-understand-trends-in-women-s-home-ownership/ [accessed 12 May 2023]; Alex Bryson et al, *A Short History of the Gender Wage Gap in Britain* (IZA Institute of Labor Economics, IZA DP No 13289, May 2020) 3.

[35] Administration of Estates Act 1925, s 46(1)(i).

[36] Sharon Thompson, *Quiet Revolutionaries: The Married Women's Association and Family Law* (Hart Publishing, 2022) 4.

32

Formation of the Married Women's Association, 1938

SHARON THOMPSON

The Married Women's Association (MWA) was the first pressure group of the twentieth century to demand, as its core focus, legal and economic equality for spouses. Formed in 1938, the MWA emphasised the language of equal partnership in marriage and sought to reform the law so that spouses would acquire rights in their partners' property *during* marriage – an ambition that was never achieved yet influenced family law in subtler ways. In demanding what the MWA dubbed a 'new marriage law', the Association politicised the family sphere, arguing that legal and economic equality inside the home would enable women to be better equipped to also pursue equality in the public sphere. And by representing housewives in a legal setting, the MWA mounted the first significant challenge against the legal status of married women since the Married Women's Property Act (MWPA) 1882.[1]

I. Context

By 1928 the vote had been won,[2] but feminists of the day such as Hazel Huskins-Hallinan saw this as only 'the beginning' and 'a revolution unfinished'.[3] For once women had the vote, they could in theory use the ballot box to transform women's legal status on all fronts. Yet women's activism was fragmented in the 1930s; suffragettes were less likely to pursue the militant strategies they had relied upon previously because, once enfranchised, they did not wish to repudiate parliamentary methods.[4] Some former suffragettes *did* continue in their

[1] Andy Hayward, 'Married Women's Property Act 1882' in Erika Rackley and Rosemary Auchmuty (eds), *Women's Legal Landmarks: Celebrating the History of Women and Law in the UK and Ireland* (Hart Publishing, 2019) 73.

[2] Representation of the People (Equal Franchise) Act 1928.

[3] Hazel Huskins-Hallinan, 'A Revolution Unfinished' in H Huskins-Hallinan (ed), *In Her Own Right* (Harrap, 1968) 12.

[4] Brian Harrison, Prudent Revolutionaries: Portraits of British Feminists Between the Wars (Oxford University Press, 1987) 1.

campaigns, but an organised movement for women's rights was more difficult, as unemployment spread[5] and new, younger leaders with the popular appeal of the suffragettes did not emerge. However, in the aftermath of women's enfranchisement, the numerous legal disabilities they continued to experience were all the more stark. And for many women in this period, it seemed as if the root cause was often marriage.

Faced with the weight of social expectations, while isolated from the public sphere legally and politically, married women were exposed to deep discrimination. Even after the MWPA 1882 – which introduced separate property rights on marriage and enabled married women to own property independently of their husbands – married women continued to face the harmful effects of spousal unity. The notion that husband and wife became 'one flesh' continued to influence the law in spite of the blow to coverture dealt by the 1882 Act.[6] Legal judgments were not enforceable against married women in the same way as they were against men; and until 1935, women were not personally responsible for their own contracts and torts – their husbands were liable instead.[7] Women lost their British citizenship if they married a foreigner, often leaving them stateless and without a parliamentary vote.[8] The patriarchal idea of the husband as head of the household and possessor of his wife was reflected in every corner of property law affecting married women. As Lord Sumner asserted in 1925, the unity doctrine between husband and wife applied unless it was specifically excluded.[9] In addition, the harsh edges of separate property made things worse, as the law purported to treat women and men as economic equals when the reality for married women was very different.

Many of the lowest-paid jobs were traditionally women's jobs. Married women were often excluded from the workforce by the marriage bar.[10] Some women even married in secret to avoid losing their jobs.[11] Unequal pay was justified in part by the so-called 'family wage'; a larger pay packet that was paid to men with the expectation that they were the heads of a household. Yet their wives had no right to this wage, and often did not even know what their husbands earned.

Not only were married women legally pressed into a state of dependence on others by these legal restrictions; their economic rights within marriage were barely recognised in law. The marital home was normally purchased in the husband's name.

[5] See Daniel Benjamin and Levis Kochin, 'Searching for an Explanation of Unemployment in Interwar Britain' (1979) 87 *Journal of Political Economy* 441, 461–62.

[6] Stephen Cretney, *Family Law in the Twentieth Century* (Oxford University Press, 2003) 91.

[7] Law Reform (Married Women and Tortfeasors) Act 1935.

[8] This was reformed by the British Nationality Act 1948. See **'Formation of the Six Point Group, 1921'** for more information on this.

[9] *Edwards v Porter* [1925] AC 1.

[10] Helen Glew, *Gender, Rhetoric and Regulation: Women's Work in the Civil Service and the London County Council, 1900–55* (Manchester University Press, 2016) 16. See also **'*Short v Poole Corporation* (1926)'**.

[11] Helen McCarthy, Double Lives: A History of Working Motherhood (Bloomsbury, 2020) 151.

Even if a wife brought in money through taking lodgers into the home, or carefully managed the household budget so as to accumulate savings out of housekeeping money, this was ultimately deemed to be her husband's property.[12] And so the *reality* for most women in the 1920s and 1930s was financial dependence, because, after declining marriage rates in the Victorian and Edwardian periods, marriage had been reasserted as of such central importance that practically no other status for women was acceptable.[13] From 1934 to 1938, the marriage rate for women averaged around 47 per 1,000 unmarried women, compared with just 17.2 in 2019.[14] Against this context of dwindling women's rights campaigns and women's oppression in the home, new feminist ideas began to emerge. To some feminists in the 1930s, the experiences of housewives indicated an urgent need for reform. Dorothy Evans[15] – a leading figure of the **Six Point Group** (SPG) – was one such feminist, and founded an SPG sub-group for housewives, which sought to expose the ways in which the law had failed married women. This would become the MWA.

II. The Landmark

The MWA stemmed from the SPG, which since 1921 had been a pressure group seeking to work on six points that could be achieved by women with the vote at that time. By the 1930s, one of these barriers was the legal and economic oppression of the housewife, and SPG leader Dorothy Evans instigated a pressure group to address this issue.

Evans was a former militant suffragette with strongly held feminist views. She had been imprisoned a number of times, took part in hunger and thirst strikes, and suffered forcible feeding.[16] The connection between Evans and the MWA might appear unexpected at first, given that Evans was personally opposed to marriage and towards the end of her life was in a long-term relationship with fellow SPG member Sybil Morrison.[17] Nevertheless, Evans was convinced that feminists needed to focus on the legal position of married women to further the emancipation of *all* women. By the mid-1930s, SPG meetings had become increasingly turbulent[18] with members' anger triggered by the status of women and their lack of legal rights. And as their meeting records show, the rights of married women became an important point of discussion.[19]

[12] *Blackwell v Blackwell* [1943] 2 All ER 579.

[13] Rosemary Auchmuty, 'Law and the power of feminism: How marriage lost its power to oppress women' (2012) 20 *Feminist Legal Studies* 71, 72.

[14] Office for National Statistics, *Marriages in England and Wales: 2019* (19 May 2022).

[15] To be distinguished from the British trade unionist of the same name.

[16] Catherine Blackford, 'Evans, Dorothy (1888–1944)' *Oxford Dictionary of National Biography* (23 September 2004).

[17] Monica Whately, 'Dorothy Evans: The Story of a Militant' in Dorothy E Evans and Claire Madden (eds), *Dorothy Evans and the Six Point Group* (Six Point Group, 1945).

[18] Ruth Gorb, 'Wives' Unequal Battle' *Hampstead and Highgate Express* (11 July 1986).

[19] SPG Executive Minutes, 19 April 1937 (The Women's Library, LSE, 5SPG/A10/18).

In a report of an SPG meeting dated 19 April 1937, it was noted that the subcommittee on rights of the housewife had agreed the following:

> That a wife who manages the family home ought to have a legal claim on half her husband's income, collectible from the source of that income … where necessary. That both husband and wife should be jointly liable for the domestic expenses and that for this purpose any income earned or possessed by the wife should be regarded as part of the domestic fund.[20]

This early report laid the foundations of the MWA. It would mean pressing for a wife's work in the home to be recognised in financial terms, through rights over half of the income and joint control over expenses. In other words, the demand was recognition of women's work in the home. As the SPG was concerned with a broad range of matters for women outside marriage, it was decided that someone else was needed to chair the new SPG sub-group, and Evans decided that young, outgoing housewife Juanita Frances – who had recently become involved in feminist networks – was ideal for the role.

In the SPG minutes of 15 November 1937, it was noted that Frances would become 'Chairman' of its group for housewives.[21] She did not like being under the control of the SPG, partly because of a clash of personalities with SPG member Monica Whately, whose dominant influence over Frances' work caused friction[22] to the point that Frances decided to separate from the SPG only one month after its inception, at the beginning of 1938.[23] This move by Frances marked the beginning of the MWA as a separate autonomous organisation, with a distinctive ideology and a new plan to reform the law of marriage. Though Frances explained her decision as being due to tensions with Whately, historians considered her motivations to be pragmatic.[24] While Evans could see the importance of reforming structures that could improve the welfare of married women, many *other* prominent SPG members were much less enthusiastic about this cause. In an interview with historian Gillian Elinor, Frances recalled that before the MWA became independent, some SPG members made comments in meetings about 'women who were stupid enough to get married'.[25] And so the MWA would only be able to effectively develop and expand its work among married women if it maintained distance from the SPG.[26] The Association needed a membership that would not be hostile to marriage, seeking instead to reform its unequal structures through law.

[20] ibid.

[21] The Women's Library, LSE, 5SPG/A10/18.

[22] Michael Summerskill, interview with Juanita Frances (The Women's Library, LSE, SUMMERSKILL/1/46).

[23] Gillian Elinor,' An Outline of the Early Years of the MWA 1938–1950', October 1988 (The Women's Library, LSE, 5MWA/9/1).

[24] Catherine Blackford, 'Wives and Citizens and Watchdogs of Equality: Post-War British Feminists' in Jim Fyrth (ed), *Labour's Promised Land: Culture and Society in Labour Britain 1945–51* (Lawrence & Wishart, 1995) 60.

[25] Catherine Blackford, 'Ideas, Structures and Practices of Feminism 1939–64' (PhD thesis, University of East London, 1996) 88.

[26] Blackford, n 24, 60.

III. What Happened Next

With the aim of marriage-law reform, the MWA sought both to pressurise lawmakers and to awaken public opinion to the need for such reform. During the Second World War, when their membership numbers had peaked, the MWA used a range of strategies to mobilise and strengthen support at grass-roots level. It held public meetings, arranged debates and social activities, and cooperated with other organisations locally and nationally. It sent deputations to ministries and lobbied MPs. Luncheons were held at the House of Commons so that politicians and policymakers could participate in discussions about law reform. Over the years, the group's leadership included prominent political and legal figures, such as Dr Edith Summerskill MP and barrister Helena Normanton, as well as high-profile activists, such as Vera Brittain, Dora Russell and former suffragette Teresa Billington-Greig.

The MWA communicated directly with its members through its own feminist magazines. The 1940 *Journal of the MWA* evolved into *Wife and Citizen*, a magazine viewed by members as the 'organ of the Association'.[27] It gave the MWA an opportunity to circulate information about campaigns while promoting members' views, often publishing letters from deserted wives about their experiences of economic destitution because, in law, their husbands owned everything. Historians have regarded *Wife and Citizen* as 'an achievement against the odds', given the narrowly constrained focus on domestic life of other women's publications at this time.[28] It also helped the MWA to raise awareness of the need for legal reform, while garnering support for its 'new marriage law': the Equal Partnership Bill.

The Equal Partnership Bill was first drafted with the help of Dorothy Evans in 1939, and in its various iterations between the 1930s and the 1980s it broadly sought to provide married women with rights in property during marriage, followed by discretionary redistribution of assets on divorce. The MWA's campaigns for this Bill to be taken forward could be seen as the first significant challenge to married women's property rights since the MWPA 1882. Though this Bill was never passed, over the years the MWA did have some direct and indirect legislative success by pursuing piecemeal reform instead of its more comprehensive – and perhaps more unrealistic – ambition of a new marriage law. For instance, the Maintenance Orders Act 1958 gave women some recourse when their husbands refused to pay them maintenance, by enabling maintenance to be deducted from husbands' pay packets. This Act directly followed – and was inspired by – a failed Bill drafted by MWA members.[29] The MWA's pursuit of marital-property reform also triggered Edward Bishop MP's Matrimonial Property Bill in 1969, which was used to leverage an agreement to stall the passage of the Divorce Reform Act so that the

[27] *Wife and Citizen*, November 1948 (The Women's Library, LSE, 5MWA/8/2).
[28] Blackford, n 25, 101.
[29] Sharon Thompson, *Quiet Revolutionaries* (Hart Publishing, 2022) 167.

financial consequences of divorce could be addressed too.[30] Finally, the Married Women's Property Act 1964, which gave wives a one-half share in housekeeping savings, represented the first and only statute to allocate rights in property *during* marriage.[31] And it was a Private Member's Bill taken forward by the MWA's first President, Edith Summerskill. As the default in English law is still separate property ownership during marriage today, this 1964 Act continues to be an anomaly. It was a stepping-stone towards the MWA's ultimate ambition of equal sharing during marriage; a destination that was never reached.[32]

IV. Significance

The formation of the MWA is a landmark of women's legal history because it gave a platform to a demographic of women typically ignored in feminist history: middle-aged housewives. Equal-rights feminism has tended to dominate scholarship of this period, though the MWA was by no means the only group to have campaigned for reform to improve the lives of housewives and working-class women.[33] The Women's Cooperative Guild was concerned with the economic position of married women, and so advocated the extension of state welfare and an increase in family allowances (typically controlled by the male breadwinner), although this did little to alleviate married women's economic dependence upon their husbands. Other mainstream, mostly conservative groups, like the Women's Institute and the National Union of Townswomen's Guilds, campaigned for reform of social services, housing and education.[34]

However, the MWA went further than these other groups because, drawing on its roots in equality feminism, it understood that the married woman would need to be economically independent if she were to be equal. This could be achieved, members argued, through attaching economic value to women's work in the home. Its first slogan – 'Wages for Wives' – re-emerged as a key demand of the 1970s 'Wages for Housework' campaigns of the Women's Liberation Movement. Then, as Joyce Freeguard notes, this was considered 'new and revolutionary', even though it had been campaigned for by the MWA in the

[30] ibid 196; Rosemary Auchmuty, 'Feminism, Property and Divorce Law Reform in the 1960s' in Jo Miles, Daniel Monk and Rebecca Probert (eds), *Fifty Years of Divorce Law Reform Act 1969* (Hart Publishing, 2022) 75.

[31] See further Sharon Thompson, 'Married Women's Property Act 1964' in Rackley and Auchmuty (eds), n 1, 263.

[32] It is unclear when the MWA wound up, though archival records cease in 1989.

[33] Caitríona Beaumont, 'Citizens not feminists: the boundary negotiated between citizenship and feminism by mainstream women's organisations in England, 1928–39' (2000) 9 *Women's History Review* 411, 413.

[34] ibid 414.

early 1940s[35] and later by the group of defecting MWA members who formed the Council of Married Women.[36]

Moreover, though the MWA subsequently abandoned its 'Wage for Wives' policy, its new demands for joint ownership of property in marriage were radical too. During the Second World War, the Lord Chancellor's Office was forced to take notice of the MWA's campaign for married women to have a proprietary right to housekeeping savings because of its high-profile criticism of the National Savings Movement.[37] The MWA claimed that the Savings Movement encouraged housewives to use housekeeping money to buy savings certificates without ever making it clear that 'they are accumulating savings to which they have no legal right'.[38] And in raising awareness that the husband – not the wife – was the owner of housekeeping money, the MWA was actively discouraging housewives from investing in savings certificates that would help fund the war effort. As MWA member Anne Fraser wrote, 'many housewives now have a powerful incentive to spend every penny of the housekeeping money if not on household necessities, then on themselves'.[39] This campaign is an example of how the MWA could exert a subtle, intangible influence on the direction of law and policy reform. As MWA member and Labour MP Lena Jeger put it:

> It may be that the successful campaign is successful only when it coincides with the imperceptible tide. But are the imperceptible processes of themselves ever successful in the practical course of progress? Can they ever manage without the campaign? I think not.[40]

Though few major legislative reforms resulted directly from MWA campaigns, their activities accounted for a major shift in *perspective* about women's legal status in marriage. As the MWA observed in 1964, the language of partnership had slipped into the vocabulary, which they saw themselves as having contributed to: 'we have created by propaganda and agitation a public opinion that marriage is a partnership'.[41]

In most accounts of family law reform, the MWA's impact is ignored,[42] and its achievements tend to be viewed as 'piecemeal'.[43] This is because the minor legislative success of the MWA addressed only a tiny aspect of married women's grievances, and in hindsight, appeared neither radical nor controversial. But another perspective of MWA influence is possible. It could be said that *any* reform

[35] Joyce Freeguard, 'It's Time for Women of the 1950s to Stand Up and Be Counted' (PhD thesis, University of Sussex, 2004) 170.

[36] The 'Wages for Wives' and 'Wages for Housework' campaigns had some notable political differences, as summarised in Thompson, n 29, 83.

[37] Anon, 'Wives Seek War Savings Rule' *Daily Mail* (28 July 1943) 3.

[38] Letter from Anne Fraser to the National Savings Committee, 20 July 1943 (TNA, LC02/2777).

[39] ibid.

[40] Lena Jeger, 'Power in Our Hands' in Huskins-Hallinan (ed), n 3, 148.

[41] MWA Annual General Report, 10 June 1964 (The Women's Library, LSE, 5MWA/3/1).

[42] In the exceptional cases where the MWA is mentioned, it tends to be in footnotes: see, for example, Cretney, n 6.

[43] Thompson, n 29, 180.

threatening to interfere with men's private property rights is controversial. The MWA's campaign to enforce maintenance payments by attachment to earnings, for example, faced staunch opposition from trade unionists, for it threatened the sanctity of the pay cheque.

The MWA's reliance on Private Member's Bills also helps to explain why it faced more disappointment and setback than success in its efforts to have reform brought forward. But as was the case with feminist campaigners more generally, Private Members' Bills were MWA members' only option when their campaigns were ignored in government.

At a time when, as MWA vice president Teresa Billington-Greig put it, 'there was a certain attitude of opposition as between married and single women as to which remaining disabilities were most important',[44] by connecting equal pay outside the home with equal partnership inside it, the formation of the MWA was a turning point in the direction of the women's movement. Most significantly, it called attention to the need to value unpaid care and housework; an issue feminists continue to grapple with today.

Further Reading

- Catherine Blackford, 'Wives and Citizens and Watchdogs of Equality: Post-War British Feminists' in Jim Fyrth (ed), *Labour's Promised Land: Culture and Society in Labour Britain 1945–51* (Lawrence & Wishart, 1995) 60.
- Dale Spender, *There's Always Been a Women's Movement This Century* (Harper Collins, 1983).
- Sharon Thompson, *Quiet Revolutionaries: The Married Women's Association and Family Law* (Hart Publishing, 2022).

[44] Speech of Teresa Billington-Greig, MWA Newsletter, June 1958 (The Women's Library, LSE, 7TBG/2/J/08).

33

Infanticide Act 1938

KELLY-ANN COUZENS*

The Infanticide Act 1938 was one of two pieces of interwar legislation that established, and refined, the offence of infanticide within the criminal law in England and Wales. Under the Act, where a woman was found to have been responsible for the death of her child of less than 1 year of age, but at the time of the act the 'balance of her mind was disturbed by reason of her not having fully recovered from the effect of giving birth to the child or by reason of the effect of lactation', she could be found guilty of infanticide rather than capital murder, and be treated and punished as though she had been guilty of the lesser crime of manslaughter.[1]

I. Context

From the second quarter of the nineteenth century, expert medical testimony was deployed in child-murder cases to support the idea that some women acted violently against their offspring while suffering under a disturbed mental state following pregnancy, childbirth and breastfeeding.[2] For those who killed newborns shortly after birth, doctors could attribute such actions to a temporary insanity. When older children were murdered, a diagnosis of puerperal or lactational insanity could also be invoked. These labels were flexible and explained violent homicidal and suicidal behaviours that were out of character for mothers who were otherwise described as loving and kind.[3] Since violence against children challenged prevailing constructions of femininity and motherhood, situating maternal

* This research was funded by the Wellcome Trust [Grant number 221299/Z/20/Z].

[1] Infanticide Act 1938, ss 1–2.

[2] Hilary Marland, 'Getting Away With Murder? Puerperal Insanity, Infanticide and the Defence Plea' in Mark Jackson (ed), *Infanticide: Historical Perspectives on Child Murder and Concealment, 1500–2000* (Ashgate, 2002) 168.

[3] ibid 175.

violence as symptomatic of reproductive mental illness also helped explain away aberrant female behaviour, accommodating it within established social and gendered norms.[4]

Of course, there were other reasons why a woman might kill her infant. Prior to the watershed developments in women's reproductive rights in the second half of the twentieth century, a woman who found herself facing an unwanted pregnancy, or who was pregnant out of wedlock and unsupported by the child's father, faced a stark future.[5] Knowledge of and access to birth control were far from adequate, with women having limited control over their reproductive futures. Maternal mortality remained high, making childbirth a dangerous time for women. Abortion was a crime.[6] Limited access to childcare provision, poor financial support from the state and the social stigma associated with single motherhood,[7] all weighed against a woman's financial prospects and survival as a lone parent. For married women facing an unwanted pregnancy and struggling to raise other children against a backdrop of poverty and deprivation, financial dependence on their husbands compounded their helplessness. Alcohol and domestic abuse contributed to challenging home lives.

Jurors and judges were often keen to extend mercy toward mothers who killed in complex circumstances, by using whatever discretion they had available to them.[8] For jurors, this could include returning a verdict of insanity on limited supporting evidence or downgrading a capital charge of murder to the lesser offence of concealment of pregnancy in instances where a woman killed her newborn. For judges, imposing light tariffs on guilty women was an option, as was using their closing summary to direct juror decision-making. Judges might also use their sentencing remarks, which were widely reported in newspapers, to cast responsibility on the (frequently absent) reputed father of an illegitimate child who, having seduced and abandoned the woman and her infant, rarely faced punishment. Such discretion enabled justice to be more flexible and compassionate in practice than it was in principle. Although English and Welsh women convicted of the murder of their newly born infants were sentenced to death (just as any other defendant found guilty of murder), from the second half of the nineteenth century onwards they were never hanged.[9] Instead, the capital

[4] ibid 172.

[5] Anne-Marie Kilday, *A History of Infanticide in Britain, c 1600 to the Present* (Palgrave Macmillan, 2013) 151.

[6] See **'Ministry of Health Memorandum 153/MCW, 1930'**; **'*R v Bourne* (1938)'**.

[7] For a particularly good study of shame and infanticide, see Lynn Abrams, 'From Demon to Victim: The Infanticidal Mother in Shetland, 1699–1899' in Yvonne G Brown and Rona Ferguson (eds), *Twisted Sisters: Women, Crime & Deviance in Scotland Since 1400* (Tuckwell Press, 2002) 180.

[8] Tony Ward, 'The Sad Subject of Infanticide: Law, Medicine and Child Murder, 1860–1938' (1999) 8 *Social & Legal Studies* 163, 164–69.

[9] The Infanticide Act (Northern Ireland) was passed in May 1939. The Republic of Ireland passed its own legislation in 1949, modelled on the original 1938 Act. A good discussion of the Irish context can be found in Karen Brennan, '"Traditions of English Liberal Thought": A History of the Enactment of an Infanticide Law in Ireland' (2013) 50 *Irish Jurist* 100. Infanticide is not a distinct offence in Scotland, although culpable homicide (akin to manslaughter) and concealment of pregnancy have been allowed as alternatives to murder.

sentence was commuted.[10] Nevertheless, judges still observed the formality of the law and sentenced women to execution by donning the ceremonial black cap and pronouncing the ultimate sentence in court. This procedure, known as the 'black cap farce', was seen as unnecessarily cruel. Newspapers reported on the extreme emotional and physical responses of convicted women to the death sentence. In the case of Helen Allcorn, tried at the Old Bailey for the murder of her 2-year-old daughter by coal-gas poisoning in July 1936, it was reported that 'When she heard the jury's verdict Mrs Allcorn fainted and had to be supported by wardresses while the death sentence was passed.'[11]

Divergent political views among parliamentarians and policymakers, and concerns that significant change to the law on homicide might send a message that child murder was not as serious an offence as murder, led to repeated failures to reform the criminal law in the 1860s, 1870s and 1900s.[12] But the case of Edith Roberts, tried for the murder of her newly born daughter in June 1921, galvanised public opinion.[13] As a result of this case, some of the first female magistrates in Britain, such as Margaret Lloyd George, as well as Labour activists and feminists Marion Philips and Gertrude Tuckwell, actively campaigned the press and Home Office for infanticide law reform.

In early 1922, Labour MP Arthur Henderson introduced a Bill to reform the law on child murder into the House of Commons.[14] It was rejected by the Government who proceeded to draft its own legislation, and on 22 July the Infanticide Act 1922 was granted Royal Assent.[15] This established that a woman could be convicted of the new offence of infanticide if she was found to have caused 'the death of her newly-born child' while 'the balance of her mind was … disturbed' if she 'had not fully recovered from the effect of giving birth' to the child.[16] Women convicted for infanticide were to be 'dealt with and punished' as if they had committed manslaughter. The legislation had its first outing at Lincolnshire Assizes in October 1922, when Emma Temple was tried for the death of her newly born daughter. Following acceptance of her plea of infanticide, Mr Justice Lush sentenced Temple to four months' imprisonment and used his sentencing remarks to extol the new legislation as 'a fresh step in the improvement of criminal law' and 'a wise and humane piece of legislation' that made it unnecessary 'to put a girl on trial for murder'.[17]

[10] Nigel Walker, *Crime and Insanity in England: The Historical Perspective*, vol 1 (Edinburgh University Press, 1968) 128–29.

[11] 'Young Mother Not to Die' *Daily News* (22 July 1936) 7.

[12] Tony Ward, 'Legislating for Human Nature: Legal Responses to Infanticide, 1860–1938' in Jackson (ed), n 2, 257.

[13] Although sentenced to death, Roberts was later reprieved. For an insightful study on this case and the development of the 1922 Act, see Daniel JR Grey, 'Women's Policy Networks and the Infanticide Act 1922' (2010) 21 *Twentieth Century British History* 441.

[14] HC Deb 13 February 1922, vol 150, col 616.

[15] Ward, n 8, 170.

[16] Infanticide Act 1922, s 1.

[17] 'Most Wise New Act' *Daily Mirror* (31 October 1922) 2.

However, it was not long before the legislation came under fire. In the aftermath of the Temple case in November 1922, *The Vote* (journal of the Women's Freedom League) argued that the new legislation had not gone far enough in making fathers accountable for their part in infanticide cases.[18] Lack of clarity in the language of the legislation would also prove a stumbling block for police, coroners, lawyers and judges. In his charge to the grand jury in January 1925, Ernest Wild KC, Recorder at the Old Bailey, commented that the infanticide law

> was [a] beneficent but badly drafted Act. Under it the grand jury could do nothing where there was a charge of murder but bring in a bill for murder and leave the petty jury to find a verdict of infanticide.[19]

As a result, women were still being marked with the stigmatising label of 'murderess'.

The greatest issue with the 1922 Act, however, was how to define and interpret the phrase 'newly-born child'. The issue came to a head in the case of Mary O'Donoghue, convicted of the murder of her 35-day-old infant before Mr Justice Talbot at the Old Bailey in October 1927. Following consideration of the case at the Court of Appeal three weeks later, O'Donoghue's counsel argued that her deceased infant could be deemed 'newly-born' within the provisions of the 1922 legislation and that the jury should have been allowed to consider a verdict of infanticide. Lord Chief Justice Gordon Hewart upheld the original decision, stating that, 'with reference to a child of more than a calendar month of age … there was no evidence upon which … [Talbot J] could invite or permit a jury to find that that child was newly-born within the meaning of the statute'.[20]

The question of infanticide reform also provoked great discussion within medical circles. Dr Louise McIlroy took issue with the lack of clarity over the phrase in her address to the Medico-Legal Society in February 1928.[21] McIlroy argued that while the Act offered some protection to women who killed their babies immediately after childbirth, it continued to stigmatise mothers suffering from other forms of maternal mental illness who killed older children during the puerperium or while breastfeeding.[22] Her views were not without challenge. Reflective of British psychiatry's growing scepticism of a causal association between birth, lactation and insanity, Dr Hubert Bond challenged McIlroy's claim that women killed children while under the influence of distinct puerperal or lactational insanities.[23] Additionally, criminologist Dr Norwood East suggested that the current Act

[18] 'New Infanticide Act' *The Vote* (3 November 1922) 4.

[19] 'The Infanticide Act' *Gloucester Journal* (17 January 1925) 9.

[20] *R v O'Donoghue* (1927) 20 Cr App R 136.

[21] A Louise McIlroy, 'The Influence of Parturition Upon Insanity and Crime' (1927–1928) 22 *Transactions of the Medico-Legal Society* 53, 55–57. McIlroy was the first woman to be appointed professor of gynaecology and obstetrics at the Royal Free Hospital in London. She took a keen interest in matters pertaining to maternal health and reproduction, writing at length on the responsibilities of the medical profession in addressing these issues. See, for example, A Louise McIlroy, 'Some Factors In The Control of the Birth-Rate' (1921–1922) 15 *Transactions of the Medico-Legal Society* 137.

[22] McIlroy, 'The Influence of Parturition Upon Insanity and Crime', n 21, 57–61.

[23] ibid 63–65.

afforded far more sympathy to the plight of women than to that of men who also killed children in distressing circumstances. East reasoned that reform was unnecessary, for 'although the law was illogical in practice justice was done'.[24]

In January 1930, *The Vote* reported on the case of Kathleen Wise.[25] Wise, a 37-year-old pregnant mother of four illegitimate children, had been struggling to care for her family in the winter of 1930. The children's father had offered neither stability nor financial support throughout their relationship. Unable to gain admission to the local workhouse, she gassed her 9-month-old boy. Following her conviction for murder, Wise was sentenced to death. However, the empanelling of a jury of matrons confirmed her pregnancy and her sentence was later commuted.[26] In the aftermath of this case, former missionary and Labour MP Edith Picton-Turbevill introduced a Private Member's Bill to the House of Commons to abolish the death penalty for expectant women.[27] This was supported by feminists, including the National Union of Society's for Equal Citizenship.[28] Significantly, Picton-Turbevill was able to persuade the Prime Minister, Ramsay Macdonald, to accept her reform, on the ground that it would improve the standing of the Government amongst women's groups.[29] The Sentence of Death (Expectant Mothers) Act 1931 abolished the pronouncement of the death penalty on pregnant women, replacing this sentence with penal servitude for life.[30]

II. The Landmark

While pregnant women and mothers who killed their 'newly-born' children were now receiving more compassionate treatment under the law, the mid-1930s witnessed an increased focus on women who remained excluded from these provisions. In September 1935, the *Manchester Guardian* reported on Dr Edith Summerskill's campaign to have mothers who committed murder while suffering from puerperal insanity to be assessed by 'a committee of alienists and psychiatrists' and treated medically, rather than be subjected to the ordeal of committal and trial at police courts or assizes.[31] As an avowed socialist and feminist who took a keen interest in maternal health, birth control and welfare provision, Summerskill saw a direct causal link between maternal insanity and the economic struggles facing working families during the Depression, noting:

[24] ibid 72.

[25] 'A Distressing Case' *The Vote* (23 January 1931) 28.

[26] Kay Crosby, 'Abolishing Juries of Matrons' (2018) 39 *Oxford Journal of Legal Studies* 259.

[27] Edith Picton-Turbevill was one of 14 women MPs to sit in the House of Commons over the 1929–31 term.

[28] 'Sentence of Death (Expectant Mothers) Bill' *The Woman's Leader and The Common Cause* (20 March 1931) 7.

[29] Crosby, n 26, 277.

[30] Sentence of Death (Expectant Mothers) Bill, s 1.

[31] 'Infanticide and Unemployment' *Manchester Guardian* (2 September 1935) 10.

> I should not be surprised if there has been an increase in infanticide due to unemployment. The mothers, when their husbands are out of work, have such a time half-starved and worried by the extra addition to the family, and this all serves to aggravate their mental condition.[32]

The Howard League for Penal Reform and the National Council for the Abolition of the Death Penalty (NCADP) had also been working throughout 1935–36 to lobby sympathetic MPs in the House of Commons to amend the Infanticide Act.[33] Writing to its members in 1936, the NCADP was disturbed by the rise in the number of women sentenced to death for child murder: six in the previous year alone, in comparison to 10 in the entire decade 1924–34.[34] Irene Ward, Conservative MP for Wallsend and a party progressive who advocated for equal pay and welfare provision,[35] corresponded with the Home Office about an Infanticide Bill drafted under the recommendations of the NCADP.[36] The Bill would have extended the crime of infanticide to mothers who killed children up to the age of 8 while the balance of their mind was disturbed following childbirth, or from 'distress and despair arising from solicitude for her child or extreme poverty or other causes'.[37] Her proposal was rejected by the Home Secretary, Sir John Simon, as was a Bill introduced by John Jagger, Labour MP for Manchester Clayton, in November 1936.[38]

In the House of Lords, a separate campaign had been progressing under the authorship of Viscount Dawson of Penn. Dawson was a central figure within the medical elite of interwar Britain.[39] He had served as an adviser to successive governments on medical matters, been president of the Royal Society of Medicine, The British Medical Association and the Royal College of Surgeons, and was Royal Physician to the King. Dawson was also a eugenicist, who was deeply concerned with issues concerning the health and future of the British population. His interest in infanticide seems to have stemmed from his involvement as a defence witness in the trial of Brenda Hale in 1936. Hale was a 26-year-old Hertfordshire housewife who was discovered on 31 May 1936 in her home with self-inflicted wounds to her neck, alongside the body of her 3-week-old son.[40] She was subsequently prosecuted for murder and attempted suicide at the Old Bailey on 20 July 1936 before

[32] ibid.

[33] *11th Annual Report 1935–36*, Collections of the National Association for the Abolition of Capital Punishment, 7–8. MRC, University of Warwick.

[34] ibid 8.

[35] For a good discussion of Conservative women in the interwar years, including Irene Ward, see GE Maguire, *Conservative Women: A History of Women and the Conservative Party, 1874–1997* (Palgrave Macmillan, 1998) 96–113.

[36] 'Criminal: Infanticide Acts, 1922 and 1938', 1922–43 (TNA, HO 45/19230).

[37] 'Extract from 12 & 13 Geo 5 cap 18', 19 February 1936, ibid.

[38] HC Deb 24 November 1936, vol 318, cols 234–36. An undated Home Office Memorandum made it clear that Jagger's Bill would never be considered by the Government ('Memorandum' in 'Criminal: Infanticide Acts', n 36).

[39] Charles Webster, 'The Metamorphosis of Dawson of Penn' in Dorothy Porter and Roy Porter (eds), *Doctors, Politics and Society: Historical Essays* (Brill, 1993) 212.

[40] *DPP Case File: Brenda Hale*, 1936 (TNA, DPP 2/357).

Mr Justice Humphreys.[41] At trial, Dawson was called in support of the defence, who wanted Hale to be prosecuted under the terms of the 1922 Act. Dawson was asked to speak to Hale's mental state at the time of the offence and the meaning of the term 'newly-born' as defined by the medical profession. He argued that the phrase 'newly-born' should include any infant up to the age of 4 weeks at the time of its death. Despite this defence, Humphreys J held that he was bound by the Appeal Court's decision in *R v O'Donoghue*. Evidently unhappy with the limitations of the current law, the jury returned the verdict of 'Not guilty of murder but guilty of the act charged for which she was not responsible in law'. Hale was ordered to be detained at His Majesty's Pleasure.

Dawson introduced his Infanticide Bill into the House of Lords 18 months later, in December 1937. Significantly more conservative than the earlier reforms proposed by Summerskill, Ward and Jagger, it limited the offence of infanticide to mothers who killed their children, aged no more than 1 year, while the balance of their mind was disturbed following childbirth or lactation. While informed by established medical and lay thinking on maternal mental illness, the Bill was primarily a product of Dawson's own interest in family planning and racial fitness, and growing anxieties about population decline in the prelude to the Second World War. Although policy makers in the Home Office, Department of Public Prosecutions and Lord Chancellor's Office remained averse to reform, determining it to be 'a very silly Bill',[42] the appetite for legal change was strong in the British press and broadly popular among parliamentarians. Consequently, it was decided that it was 'not worthwhile for the Government to try to oppose the Bill'.[43] Accordingly, Dawson's Infanticide Bill passed into law, with minor amendments, on 23 June as the Infanticide Act 1938.

III. What Happened Next

The first beneficiary of the Infanticide Act 1938 was 29-year-old Jennie Margaret Dormer, who gassed her 10-week-old daughter in October 1938.[44] Dormer was depressed and had trouble feeding the infant. Her mental condition worsened amid the threat of hostilities with Germany. While incarcerated at Holloway Prison, Dormer's mental state improved, and at trial she pleaded guilty to infanticide. She was subsequently bound over for two years and released into the care of a friend. Thus, the first case tried under the provisions of the new Act received more attention as a symbol of public anxieties over the impeding global conflict than

[41] 'Unusual Verdict in Murder Trial' *Daily News* (22 July 1926) 7.

[42] 'Letter from Claud Schuster to Alexander Maxwell', 8 February 1938 in 'Infanticide', 1936–1938 (TNA, LCO 2/1329).

[43] Letter from Alexander Maxwell to Claud Schuster, 7 February 1938, ibid.

[44] 'Crisis Fears Made Mother Kill Baby' *Sunderland Daily Echo and Shipping Gazette* (17 November 1938) 13.

as a testament to legislative reform. Additionally, less than a month after the 1938 Act became law, medical, legal and public attention shifted to the issue of abortion, following the trial of eminent surgeon, Dr Aleck Bourne, at the Old Bailey in July 1938.[45] Nevertheless, the Act had a significant impact in the years that followed. Prosecutions for infanticide at Assize and Quarter Sessions increased from an annual average of 18 women between 1935 and 1939, to an annual average of 40 women between 1945 and 1949.[46]

Nonetheless, there have always been concerns about the Act's assumed link between motherhood and mental illness.[47] *The Butler Report* (1975) and the *Report of the Criminal Law Revision Committee* (1980) made conflicting recommendations about whether to retain it.[48] In 2006, the Law Commission concluded that 'the incidence of certain disorders is higher following childbirth. This temporal connection indicates that some women are more vulnerable to psychiatric disorder in the postpartum period.'[49] Therefore, despite the problems with the existing Act, the Law Commission conceded that it offered 'a practicable legal solution to a particular set of circumstances' and recommended keeping it without amendment.[50]

IV. Significance

The Infanticide Act 1938 created a distinct crime in which potentially adverse biological and psychological effects accompanying pregnancy and childbirth could be acknowledged and considered by courts in mitigation of the offence. While scholars, feminist critics and medical practitioners have raised concerns over the language and conceptual underpinnings of the legislation, '[t]he explanation for special treatment in law of childbearing mothers lies in the recognition that, for reasons that are still poorly understood, they are "at risk" of becoming mentally ill following … birth'.[51] Studies suggest that at least one in every 10 women will experience postnatal depression in the first year of their

[45] AB Austin, 'Surgeon Not Guilty' *Daily Herald* (20 July 1938) 1; **'*R v Bourne* (1938)'**.

[46] Extracted by the author from 'Table B', Home Office, *Criminal Statistics England and Wales 1950* (Cmd 8301, 1951) 6.

[47] See, for example, Susan SM Edwards, *Women on Trial: A Study of the Female Suspect, Defendant and Offender in the Criminal Law and Justice System* (Manchester University Press, 1984) 4–13, 79–100; Hilary Allen, *Justice Unbalanced: Gender, Psychiatry, and Judicial Decisions* (Open University Press, 1987) 27–28; R Kumar and Maureen Marks, 'Infanticide and the Law in England and Wales' in James Alexander Hamilton and Patricia Neel Harberger (eds), *Postpartum Psychiatric Illness: A Picture Puzzle* (University of Pennsylvania Press, 2016) 257, 269–70; Karen Brennan and Emma Milne, 'Criminalising Neonaticide: Reflections on Law and Practice in England and Wales' in Emma Milne et al (eds), *Women and the Criminal Justice System: Failing Victims and Offenders?* (Palgrave Macmillan, 2018) 106.

[48] Kumar and Marks, n 47, 265–69.

[49] Law Commission, *Murder, Manslaughter and Infanticide* (Law Com No 304, 2006) [8.25].

[50] ibid [8.3].

[51] Kumar and Marks, n 47, 257.

child's birth.[52] And although exceptionally rare, infants are still killed by their mothers.[53] Consequently, maintaining a space of protection and compassion for vulnerable mothers within the law can be viewed as a humane and necessary intervention today, and its creation a real landmark for women.

Further Reading

- Susan SM Edwards, *Women on Trial: A Study of the Female Suspect, Defendant and Offender in the Criminal Law and Justice System* (Manchester University Press, 1984).
- R Kumar and Maureen N Marks, 'Infanticide and the Law in England and Wales' in James Alexander Hamilton and Patricia Neel Harberger (eds), *Postpartum Psychiatric Illness: A Picture Puzzle* (University of Pennsylvania Press, 2016) 257.
- Tony Ward, 'Legislating for Human Nature: Legal Responses to Infanticide, 1860–1938' in Mark Jackson (ed), *Infanticide: Historical Perspectives on Child Murder and Concealment, 1550–2000* (Ashgate, 2002) 249.

[52] The NHS online advocates this more conservative figure. However, a 2021 metareview suggests postnatal depression may affect as many as 21.5% of women in the first year after birth in the UK. See Z Wang et al, 'Mapping Global Prevalence of Depression Among Postpartum Women' (2021) 11 *Translational Psychiatry* 1, 7. Postpartum psychosis is estimated to affect a much smaller proportion of women, approximately 1–2 women in every 1,000 births. See Susan Hatters Friedman and Renee Sorrentino, 'Commentary: Postpartum Psychosis, Infanticide, and Insanity – Implications for Forensic Psychiatry' (2012) 40 *Journal of the American Academy of Psychiatry and the Law Online* 326.

[53] One estimate suggests approximately 30–40 infants are the victim of homicide in England and Wales each year. In the case of neonates, recent research suggests an annual average of 7 newborn deaths. See Kumar & Marks n 47, 185–186; Brennan & Milne n 47, 97–98.

34

Bradford Third Equitable Benefit Building Society v Borders (1939)

ROSEMARY AUCHMUTY

Mrs Elsy Borders brought the first legal challenge to the unregulated collaboration between speculative house-builders and building societies that allowed the sale of thousands of homes of poor quality and defective workmanship to borrowers who had no redress. Her case led to the Building Societies Act 1939, which regulated some of the worst practices (though by no means all of them). It was the first of several struggles in the twentieth century to get mortgage lenders to take women's interests seriously.

I. Context

After the First World War, Prime Minister Lloyd George's promise of 'Homes Fit For Heroes' inaugurated two decades of frenetic house-building. Almost four million new dwellings were constructed in the years 1919–39, of which about a quarter were public housing and the rest for private sale.[1]

Before the war, almost everyone rented. The shift in government policy was largely facilitated by the building societies, which had been around for more than a century but were now flourishing, with an abundance of funds, and looking around for new investment opportunities in their traditional sphere of property development. They quickly grasped that the post-war housing shortage and large numbers of out-of-work builders offered a perfect opportunity to build houses, not for rental as in the past, but for people who could never have been able to afford to be owner-occupiers before. The building societies' decision to bridge the gap between supply and demand by providing mortgage finance brought home ownership within the reach of a whole new market.

Once the movement got going, every agency from government to popular magazines pushed the message that home ownership was everyone's most desired

[1] John Burnett, *A Social History of Housing 1815–1978* (Methuen, 1978) 246.

goal. In the words of the 'Building Society Supplement' in the *Daily Telegraph* of 29 May 1933:

> Clearly it encourages thrift, fosters the sense of security and self-dependence, and sensibly deepens citizens' consciousness of having a 'stake in the country', and the influence is surely one which, spreading from the individual to the community and linking up all classes, must contribute appreciably to national security.[2]

The propaganda focused on the family, the better to deliver the 'return to normality' message of the post-war years; but also, of course, to get women back into the home. During the war they had enjoyed unprecedented independence that, with the return of servicemen, must be curbed, and women must be made to feel they wanted no more than a peaceful domestic life in a home of their own:

> That was the image beloved of the time – men swopping [sic] flower cuttings, a housewife watching with respectful delight as the husband leaves with his golf-clubs on his back, whilst a happy child scooters up and down the new pavements as the sun casts long shadows from the lofty original parkland trees.[3]

For middle-class women, however, this new domestic existence was very different from that of pre-war days. Gone was the army of domestic servants, and few of the houses on the new estates made any provision for a maid's room. Housewives must thenceforth do their own housework, care for their own children, and cook and clean without live-in assistance. New working-class owners, of course, had never had such help. Thus the kitchens on these new estates were advertised as having 'every modern device' and being 'filled with all those conveniences so dear to the heart of the housewife'.[4] One firm employed Miss Helen Burke, 'home expert' of the *Sunday Pictorial*, to plug its properties: 'They're honest houses – well-planned, well-built – so labour-saving and so practical as to delight a housewife's heart.'[5]

By 1937, over 1,000 new houses were being completed *every day*. With more and more competition and an improving economy, prices fell. A home similar to one that would have cost just under £1,000 in 1920 had dropped to £400 by the beginning of the 1930s.[6] Interest rates fell too. The length of the mortgage was extended from 15 to 25 or even 30 years, thereby reducing monthly repayments by up to one-third.[7]

The final push to bring home ownership within the reach of ever more people came with the invention of the pooling agreement. Recognising that the size of the deposit (usually 25 per cent) remained too high for low earners, speculative

[2] Quoted in Noreen Branson and Margot Heinemann, *Britain in the Nineteen Thirties* (Panther, 1975) 206.

[3] Quoted in Dennis Edwards and Ron Pigram, *London's Underground Suburbs* (Baston Transport, 1986) 115.

[4] ibid 69.

[5] Quoted in Paul Oliver, Ian Davis and Ian Bentley, *Dunroamin: The suburban semi and its enemies* (Barrie and Jenkins, 1981) 101.

[6] Deirdre Beddoe, *Back to Home and Duty: Women between the wars 1918–1939* (Pandora, 1989) 95.

[7] Alan A Jackson, *Semi-Detached London: Suburban development, life and transport, 1900–1939* (George Allen & Unwin, 1973) 193–96.

builders and building societies came to an arrangement that the deposit would be reduced to, typically, 5 per cent, and the builders would provide building societies with funds to cover the difference between that and the amount of the loan. This 'pool' acted as collateral security on the property so that, in the event of borrower default, the building society could draw on it (as well as repossessing and selling the house) to recover its loan. This was a win–win arrangement for both parties: the building society could attract more borrowers with its attractive loans and the builder had an assured market for its houses, though its profit would be tied up until the mortgagor had repaid enough of the loan for it to be returned to the builder. Peter Craig estimated that over half of the building society loans granted in south-east England were made with a pooling agreement.[8]

II. The Landmark

In March 1934, Elsy and Jim Borders agreed to buy a semi-detached house on the newly-built Coney Hall Estate, Kingsway, West Wickham, Kent, on the outskirts of London. Though they visited the estate, they were unable to view the actual house as the roads were not yet made up. Mr Borders was a taxi-driver; no occupation is given for Mrs Borders. The original contract had been made out to Mr Borders, but he was unwilling to bind himself, so Mrs Borders took it on, with her husband as guarantor. The house was valued at £730, of which the Bradford Third Equitable Benefit Building Society provided £693 – 95 per cent of the valuation. The developer-sellers, Morrell's, were speculative builders who, in the words of the judge who heard the case, 'wanted to build houses and sell them as fast as they could'.[9] The large loan and low deposit granted to Mrs Borders were made possible because the building society had a pooling agreement with Morrell's.

The Borders had been encouraged to buy the house by the very positive tone of the builders' advertising literature, in particular the apparent endorsement of its quality by the building society: for example, 'the fact that a leading building society makes a more generous offer over a longer period than to any other estate in Great Britain speaks volumes for the construction of the houses'.[10] Advertisements emphasised the number of inspections made at each stage of construction and concluded 'This proves without a shadow of doubt, the amazing value of Morrell houses.'[11]

When Mr and Mrs Borders moved into their home, however, they discovered a catalogue of defects. Though these were not detailed in the case report, Peter Craig has summarised them from the transcript of the trial:

[8] Peter Craig, 'The house that Jerry built? Building Societies, the state and the politics of owner-occupation' (1986) 1 *Housing Studies* 87, 95–97.
[9] Quoted in Branson and Heinemann, n 2, 484.
[10] Jackson, n 7, 197.
[11] ibid, 198.

> The roof leaked and the house was damp throughout. The roof was unsound and tiles blew off in the wind. The stairs and the floors of the upper rooms shook. The interior woodwork and the window frames had warped; doors would not shut and windows would not open. The woodwork and the eaves were infested with vermin. The paintwork had begun to flake within a few months of having being completed and the front door had collapsed. The foundations were inadequate and the concrete was crumbling. The electrical wiring was defective and caused electric shocks if the walls were touched. Plaster disintegrated continuously in a shower of fine dust, the walls were cracking and the ceiling had buckled. The chimneys had not been properly rendered, allowing smoke to seep through.[12]

Faced with this barely habitable home, Mrs Borders refused to sign the mortgage deed or to pay any mortgage instalments until the defects were made good. She alleged in court that a new agreement was then drawn up containing this condition, which she did sign; and she started making repayments, though in arrears. The repairs were never made, and in June 1937, when her repayments were three months in arrears, the building society sued for possession.

Mrs Borders resisted, and the case came to the High Court in January 1938.[13] In 'what was perhaps the most crowded court the Chancery Division has seen in recent times',[14] Mrs Borders represented herself in court. The building society was represented by RF Roxburgh KC (later a distinguished judge) and a junior. In the Law Reports, Elsy Borders was simply described as 'a married woman, the wife of a London taxi-cab driver', but the press provided more detail:

> Youngish, wearing spectacles, and seemingly the very prototype of an ordinary suburban housewife, … she confronted the Building Society's team of barristers, solicitors and clerks headed by a King's Counsel, cross-examined the Society's witnesses in a manner which revealed a most remarkable grasp of the technical issues involved, … and some days later ended a six-hour speech by asking for an injunction to restrain the Society from using the assets of its members or conducting business until the defects in its houses had been remedied.[15]

The transcript reveals the truth of this description of her ability to identify the significant points. When she quizzed the secretary of the building society about its published claim that surveyors were required to report to the society about the quality of the construction, he was forced to admit 'Possibly before my time.' She asked how long he had been in post: '23 years.' 'We may say that that is before the time when jerry-building began to overrun the country,' was her acerbic response.[16]

As is so often the position with claims by women, the case ended up turning on a different issue altogether: whether the mortgage deed the building society produced in court, which contained no provisions for repair, was the one she had

[12] Craig, n 8, 97.
[13] *Bradford Third Equitable Benefit Building Society v Borders* [1939] 1 All ER 481.
[14] *Yorkshire Post and Leeds Intelligencer* (14 February 1939) 8.
[15] ibid.
[16] Evidence to High Court hearing, *Borders v Bradford Building Society*, Appeal Cases, series – 1941, B-C. Parliamentary Archives (HL/PO/JU/4/3/965).

signed. Mrs Borders contended that it was not her signature on the deed they showed.

She subsequently argued that the pooling agreement was *ultra vires* – beyond the powers of building societies under the provisions of the Building Societies Acts 1875 and 1895, which stated that their loans could only be secured on land – and, moreover, that it contravened the society's own regulations. Later still she counter-claimed for misrepresentation, stating that she had been induced to purchase the property on the basis of the extravagant endorsement as to quality given by the building society in the builder's sale publicity.

The three-page report of the case belies the length and complexity of the trial, which lasted for four days in January 1938 and another 13 days in October and November. Throughout that time, the building society industry remained on tenterhooks, recognising only too well that if the judge found in Mrs Borders' favour on the legality of pooling agreements, a large proportion of their security on loans already granted would be irrecoverable.

Public concern about pooling agreements had been growing for years. The perception was that they encouraged speculative builders to cut corners, leading to well-founded accusations of jerry-building. But if the Borders case was bad publicity for the builders, it was equally bad for the building societies because it suggested they were not taking enough care in their lending practices. The suspicion that all they really cared about was their ability to get their money back on default sullied their reputation as benevolent institutions investing responsibly for the benefit of their members.

The case was widely reported in the press. The fact that Mrs Borders was representing herself was an important factor in the publicity. She was characterised as 'the modern Portia', and much was made of this ordinary wife of an ordinary man standing alone against 'a wealthy society employing eminent counsel to pursue its claim … a forensic Goliath against a feminine David', as the *Yorkshire Post* picturesquely put it.[17] In point of fact, Mrs Borders was supported not only by the 1,500-strong Coney Hall and District Residents' Association, of which she and her husband were prominent members, but by the entire Federation of Tenants' and Residents' Associations in London, which had already organised a series of mortgage strikes in which 3,000 members withheld their repayments until the legality of builder's pools was settled and the defects remedied. A member of the Communist party, she also (rumour had it) had unofficial legal assistance from the left-wing Labour MP Sir Stafford Cripps.[18]

In March 1938, fearing an adverse outcome, the building societies appealed to the government for legislation that would retrospectively validate existing pooling agreements and legitimise future loans of this type. After some inaction – for there were more pressing concerns in 1938 – the government concluded that action was needed to restore confidence in the building societies and the building industry,

[17] *Yorkshire Post*, n 14.
[18] Craig, n 8, 98–100.

which had both become so important to the British economy. But they also recognised that, if there was too much interference, lending for home ownership would be compromised and they might have to find more money for public housing.

On 16 February 1939, Mr Justice Bennett handed down judgment in the *Borders* case. He held that the building society had not proved that the mortgage deed they produced in court had been signed by Mrs Borders; without an agreement, they could not take possession. This made consideration of her counter-claims unnecessary, but the judge, recognising that the building society was likely to appeal, did consider them. On the validity of pooling agreements, he held that they were outside the powers of the building society's directors but not against the law. On the misrepresentation claim, he held that the builders had indeed misrepresented the quality of their construction, but that the building society could not be held responsible for this. So Mrs Borders had no claim against the building society, but she could sue Morrell's – which would have a knock-on effect on the building society, which was bound by its pooling agreement with Morrell's. In any case, Morrell's had gone bankrupt.

III. What Happened Next

A week after the judgment, the Chancellor of the Exchequer, Sir John Simon, announced that the Government would introduce legislation. Simultaneously, Ellen Wilkinson, Labour MP for Jarrow, asked leave to introduce a Bill that would have required building societies to guarantee good workmanship and homes fit for habitation, and allow buyers to withhold mortgage repayments and take their case to the County Court if their home was not properly built. The Government persuaded her to withdraw her Bill while it drew up its own. But when the Building Societies Act 1939 appeared, most of the stringent provisions in earlier drafts had been watered down. The Act did not outlaw pooling agreements, but building societies were at least obliged to tell buyers if collateral security had been taken. A proposed requirement to disclose the property's real valuation was dropped, but building societies were put under a duty to ensure that they obtained the 'best price possible'. The outbreak of war saved the Government from having to make a proper investigation of lending practices. The war did, however, bring an end to the use of pooling agreements altogether.

Meanwhile, the building society appealed to the Court of Appeal.[19] This time Mrs Borders was represented by a KC and the court permitted her, because she had not had the benefit of legal representation in the High Court, to introduce a new counter-claim, that of fraud. On 29 January 1940, Lord Justice Clauson (in the 'unavoidable absence of the Master of the Rolls') gave the judgment of the Court, which upheld the lower court's finding that the lender's pooling agreements were *ultra vires* but not illegal, but disagreed on the misrepresentation issue, holding that

[19] *Bradford Third Equitable Benefit Building Society v Borders* [1940] Ch 202.

'Mrs Borders was induced by fraudulent misrepresentations, of which the plaintiffs had knowledge, to enter the contract' and was therefore entitled to damages for the reduced value of her property. Even if the plaintiffs had not had actual knowledge that the statements were false, they should have been more vigilant in checking. Sadly, however, when the building society appealed to the House of Lords in 1941[20] this ruling was overturned – fraud, the court said, required proof of *actual knowledge* that the statements relied on were false – and Mrs Borders lost her damages. This was probably a policy decision as the courts, like the Government, were conscious of the need not to interfere too much with the mortgage providers.

IV. Significance

There are three reasons why this case is significant for women. First, of course, it changed the law. While limited in scope, the Building Societies Act 1939 did challenge the oppressive link between the lenders and builders, and went some way towards restraining their careless dealings with a clientele powerless to obtain redress. Of this clientele, it was the women who spent so much time in the home and whose responsibility it was to keep it in good condition who suffered most.

The case is also significant in challenging ideas of female passivity in a period of strong ideological pressure on women to concern themselves only with domestic duties. Mrs Borders purchased the house in her name alone, rather than in her husband's or jointly. We do not know how unusual it was for a building society to be prepared to negotiate with a married woman, but perhaps building societies, so long as their security was safe, had become careless in their dealings with customers normally perceived to be poor-risk. That Mrs Borders represented herself in the High Court was an even rarer occurrence. But by fighting *this* battle, the battle for decent homes, she was able to represent both the housewives struggling to maintain substandard homes and the women claiming wider agency in property ownership and legal action. In none of the press reports I read was she ever criticised for what she was doing, indicating widespread public support and admiration.

Third, *Bradford Building Society v Borders* was the first of several legal confrontations between women and mortgagees across the twentieth century. The 1960s and 1970s saw the series of cases that culminated in *Williams & Glyn's Bank v Boland* (1981),[21] where the Court of Appeal and then the House of Lords ordered lenders to deal directly with the wives of legal owners or risk being caught by a possible overriding interest in the home. This forced a belated recognition on the part of lenders that women might have interests separate from their husbands'.[22]

[20] *Bradford Third Equitable Benefit Building Society v Borders* [1941] 2 All ER 205.
[21] *Williams & Glyn's Bank v Boland* [1981] AC 487.
[22] Rosemary Auchmuty, '*Williams & Glyn's Bank v Boland* (1981)' in Erika Rackley and Rosemary Auchmuty (eds), *Women's Legal Landmarks: Celebrating the History of Women and Law in the UK and Ireland* (Hart Publishing, 2019) 357.

The shift in conveyancing practice that followed, whereby homes were thenceforth usually put in the names of both husband and wife, produced the undue influence-in-mortgage cases that dominated the turn of the century, where once again lenders were forced by court decisions (in *Barclay's Bank v O'Brien* (1994)[23] and *Royal Bank of Scotland plc v Etridge (No 2)* (2002))[24] to take more care to ensure that mortgages were not obtained through pressure or misrepresentation by husbands on joint-owner wives.

As with these hundreds of cases, in which banks and building societies were claiming possession of family homes on mortgage default and the defendants were women, *Borders* exposed the way that the practices of the big lending institutions often operated unjustly against women. In all three instances the lenders resisted all the way up to the House of Lords, and in all three cases the solutions proffered by legislature or court went only a small way towards remedying the problem. The conflict between home as residence and home as financial asset remains a living issue in English property law, where the preference for creditors (enshrined in statute) hits women hardest because they are still the primary homemakers.

Further Reading

- Noreen Branson and Margot Heinemann, *Britain in the Nineteen Thirties* (Panther, 1975).
- Peter Craig, 'The house that Jerry built? Building Societies, the state and the politics of owner-occupation' (1986) 1 *Housing Studies* 87.
- Alan A Jackson, *Semi-Detached London: Suburban development, life and transport, 1900–1939* (George Allen & Unwin, 1973).

[23] *Barclay's Bank v O'Brien* [1994] 1 AC 180: Sarah Greer, '*Barclay's Bank v O'Brien* (1993)' in Rackley and Auchmuty (eds), n 22, 457; Rosemary Auchmuty, 'Men Behaving Badly: An analysis of undue influence cases' (2002) 11 *Social and Legal Studies* 257.

[24] *Royal Bank of Scotland plc v Etridge (No 2)* [2002] UKHL 44.

INDEX